Illinois
SCHOOL
LAW
SURVEY

Second Edition

David L. Franklin
Brian A. Braun

AUTHORS

DAVID L. FRANKLIN, Ph.D., is professor of educational administration and foundations at Illinois State University, in Normal, where he teaches courses in educational law and collective bargaining/labor relations, and is the editor of *Illinois School Law Quarterly*. He was formerly associate professor at Sangamon State University, in Springfield, 1972 to 1979, where he also taught courses in school law. He is the author of several books on school law and numerous articles, and has conducted legal research regarding the constitutionality of the Illinois system of public school finance for the Center for the Study of Educational Finance.

BRIAN A. BRAUN, J.D., of Champaign, is an attorney with the firm of Miller, Tracy, Braun & Wilson, Ltd. He was an attorney on the staff of the Illinois Association of School Boards, 1977 to 1983, and a language arts teacher in DuPage County, 1969 to 1977. He is a graduate of the University of Illinois College of Communications (1969) and the Depaul University College of Law (1974). He has lectured on school law and labor relations at a number of Illinois colleges and universities, and is a member of the Executive Board of the Council of School Attorneys of the National School Boards Association and a past chairman of the Illinois Council of School Attorneys of the Illinois Association of School Boards.

Illinois SCHOOL LAW SURVEY

Second Edition

ILLINOIS ASSOCIATION OF SCHOOL BOARDS

Headquarters
1209 South Fifth Street
Springfield, Illinois 62703

Regional Office
200 West 22nd Street, Suite 249
Lombard, Illinois 60148

May, 1992

ISBN: 1-880331-01-2

HOW TO USE
ILLINOIS SCHOOL LAW SURVEY

In addition to simply reading the text from front to back, the user of *Illinois School Law Survey* has two ways to locate information. The Table of Contents on pages viii through xii lists the broad topics covered in each chapter. In many cases, these topic headings will get the reader to the desired information.

However, the law regarding schools is not subject to neat packaging. Information on a particular legal question or topic can show up under any number of different headings. Moreover, broad topic headings often will not describe or suggest a particular question or narrow point of law. The user interested either in a narrow topic or in one with multiple facets should use the Quick Reference Index beginning on page 408. This alphabetical list of topics includes references too narrow to be listed in the Table of Contents and shows whether the topic is discussed at more than one place in the text.

New with this Second Edition is a table of court cases arranged in alphabetical order by name of plaintiff beginning on page 386. All court decisions cited in this book are listed in the table with a full legal reference. At the end of each case citation is listed the question(s) where the case is cited in the text.

The table of case law serves at least two purposes. The user who knows only a case name will be able to find a full citation and applicable questions and answers. Also, where an answer carries a case law citation, the reader can use the table to find other questions and answers related to the same case.

QUESTION NUMBERS

The number to the left of the colon in each question number reflects the chapter number, 1 through 26. Questions within each chapter are numbered to the right of each colon; that is, 1:10, 1:20, 1:25, 2:10, 2:15, and so on.

While questions are presented in numerical sequence, intervals between numbers are variable. Questions in the first edition were numbered at intervals of 10, leaving room for the insertion of new questions as needed in this second edition and in future editions.

CAUTIONARY NOTES

Illinois School Law Survey provides answers to general questions regarding statutes, case law, and administrative rules in force as of January 1, 1992. It is not intended to provide advice in the handling of specific situations. Rather, its purpose is to provide instruction in the basic principles of school law and to alert the reader to matters meriting further study or the assistance of legal counsel.

The reader is further reminded that the law is in a state of continual change through legislative enactments, court decisions, and the rulings of administrative bodies.

Finally, *Illinois School Law Survey* generally excludes laws that are unique to Chicago Public School District 299. The reader is referred to a companion publication, *Chicago School Law Survey,* for laws governing School District 299.

FOREWORD

We all face questions that arise about school law.

As parents or teachers, we may face knotty school law questions only occasionally; but there are large areas of the law that would be just nice to know if it weren't so difficult to find the information.

As school board members or administrators, however, just about anything we contemplate doing involves a law—usually a multitude of laws. Again, the continuous tide of questions would be tolerable if the answers weren't so difficult to find. Sometimes it seems to take another act of Congress just to find out whether there is, in fact, some law or laws involved—and if so, what is it?

These are just some of the needs that *Illinois School Law Survey* fills for people interested in, and involved with, the schools—answers to questions that come up in the every day conduct of school district affairs. The unusual question-and-answer format and the Quick Reference Index make it easy to quickly obtain the information we need.

In addition to serving the user who just wants to learn the answer to a particular question, *School Law Survey* guides the serious student who wants to know the full breadth of the law in a given subject area. The thorough documentation following each answer leads us directly to where the law is located. In this respect, *School Law Survey* is an indispensable guide to state statutes and applicable court decisions.

Both the education and legal communities were well-served by the first edition of *Illinois School Law Survey* and we believe this second edition is even bigger and better. Recognizing that even the greatest works of this sort are never finished, however, we invite all users to submit suggestions for improvements in future editions.

Wayne L. Sampson, Executive Director
Illinois Association of School Boards
May, 1992

CONTENTS

UNDERSTANDING LEGAL REFERENCES

All legal references in this book are cited in standard forms that employ numerous abbreviations. In order to retrieve legal source materials, therefore, the lay reader must (a) understand the abbreviations used in the legal citations and (b) know where to find the legal publications cited.

An explanation of all the abbreviations used in this book is provided on page xvi.

Citations involving statutes may be the easiest for the lay reader to locate. Law libraries and most attorneys and court houses will have current statutes available—the *United States Code* and the *Illinois Revised Statutes*. Numbering of chapters and sections are relatively easy to comprehend.

Administrative regulations may be the most difficult materials to locate. The *Illinois Administrative Code* is a relatively new publication and one not usually found in a law office or court house. Check a law library or consult the administrative agency that issued the regulation in question.

READING CASE CITATIONS

Publications that report court decisions are found in law libraries. In Illinois, law libraries are maintained by most universities and colleges and can be found in most county court houses. Small law libraries are maintained by many lawyers.

Court cases are cited by case name, which is printed in *italics*. Case citations following each case name reveal which court decided the case and in what year. Case citations also tell where to find the case cited. The format for each case citation is the same:

- The first number refers to the volume of the set of books in which the case can be found.
- The second reference is to the set of books in which the case can be found.
- The next reference is to the edition of that set of books;
- The final reference is to the page on which the case cited can be found in the volume and set.

For example, 23 Ill.App.3d 196 means the case referred to can be found in volume 23 of *Illinois Appellate Reports, Third Edition* on page 196.

Knowing the edition is important, because cases are reported chronologically. New editions of various reporters are issued randomly whenever the publishers think the volume numbers have gotten too high. Thus, when the publishers thought the volume numbers were getting too high in *Illinois Appellate Reports*, they simply went from volume 351 Ill.App. to volume 1 Ill.App.2d. Thus, knowing the volume and page number is not enough to find a case easily unless you know the edition number, too.

Cases are frequently reported in more than one set of books. Thus, the same case may be found in *Supreme Court Reporter*, in *United States Reports* and in *Lawyers' Edition*. Wherever possible we have given multiple citations for each case.

STATE COURTS

Cases which have been tried in the Illinois state court system are identifiable by their citations. There are three levels of courts in Illinois. The lowest is the circuit court, which is the trial level. Circuit court decisions are not generally reported, have very little precedential value, and are not referred to anywhere in this text.

A party may appeal an adverse circuit court decision to the appropriate Illinois appellate court as a matter of right. There are five geographically-determined Illinois appellate courts, which are designated by district numbers one through five. The First District Appellate Court hears Cook County appeals and the Second District Appellate Court covers Lake County and the northwestern part of the state. The Third and Fourth Districts hear north central and south central appeals, and the Fifth District hears cases originating in circuit courts located in the southern third of the state.

All Illinois appellate court citations are cited to one of the three editions of *Illinois Appellate Reports*—Ill.App. or Ill.App.2d or Ill. App.3d. Each appellate court citation also gives the reader information in a parenthetical notation about which appellate court decided the case cited and when it was decided. For example, (5th Dist. 1990) means the Fifth District Appellate court decided the case in 1990.

A party may ask the Illinois Supreme court to review an adverse appellate court decision. The Illinois Supreme Court may accept or reject most appeals at its pleasure. The reader can determine whether the Illinois Supreme Court has rendered a decision in a case, because all such cases are cited to *Illinois Reporter*. If a case has a citation to Ill. or Ill.2d, the reader will know the decision referred to was rendered by the Illinois Supreme Court.

FEDERAL COURTS

The federal court system is also three-tiered. Usually, in education law, lawsuits dealing with federal Constitutional questions are brought in federal court and questions which deal with state law are brought in state court.

The federal court system starts with a federal district court. There are three federal district courts in Illinois which are designated as the Northern District, Central District and Southern District. Federal District Court decisions are reported in a set of books called *Federal Supplement*. If the reader sees a citation to F. Supp., it means the case cited was decided by the lowest federal court, a federal district court.

A party may appeal an adverse federal district court decision to the appropriate federal circuit court of appeals as a matter of right. There are eleven federal circuit courts of appeals across the nation. All Illinois cases are heard by the Seventh Circuit Court of Appeals. All federal court of appeals cases are cited in this text to *Federal Reporter*. Therefore, if the reader sees a citation to F. or F.2d, this means the case cited was decided by a federal appeals court. Each court of appeals citation includes a parenthetical notation designating the court of appeals which rendered the decision and the year the decision was rendered. For example, (7th Cir. 1990) means the Seventh Circuit Court of Appeals decided the case in 1990.

A party may ask the United States Supreme Court to review an adverse decision rendered by a court of appeals. In most cases, the Supreme Court may review a decision or deny the right to review at its pleasure. All cases referred to in this text decided by the Supreme court are cited to *Supreme Court Reporter*. Therefore, if the reader sees a citation to S.Ct., this means the case was decided by the United States Supreme Court.

ABBREVIATIONS USED IN LEGAL CITATIONS

2d—second edition
ALR—*American Law Reporter*
aff'd.—affirmed
art.—article
c.—chapter
C.D.—Central District
C.F.R.—*Code of Federal Regulations*
    cert.—certiorari (the word is used in this text to describe a request to the United States Supreme Court to review an adverse court of appeals decision)
    cert. den.—certiorari denied (means the U.S. Supreme Court declined to review the case)
Cir.—circuit
C.J.S.—*Corpus Juris Secundum* (a legal encyclopedia)
Const.—Constitution
den.—denied
eff.—effective
et seq.—et sequentes (and the following)
F.Supp.—*Federal Supplement*
F.—*Federal Reporter*
IELRB—Illinois Educational Labor Relations Board
Ill.—*Illinois Reports*
Ill. Admin. Code—*Illinois Administrative Code*
Ill. App.—*Illinois Appellate Reports*
Ill. Dec.—*Illinois Decisions*
Ill. Rev. Stat.—*Illinois Revised Statutes*
L.Ed.—*Lawyers' Edition*
N.D.—Northern District
N.E.—*Northeastern Reporter*
P.A.—Public Act
par.—paragraph
PERI—*Public Employee Reporter for Illinois*
reh.—rehearing
rem.—remanded (returned to a lower court)
rev.—reversed
S.Ct.—*Supreme Court Reporter*
S.D.—Southern District
sec.—section
Slip op.—Slip opinion (not yet contained in law reporters)
sub nom.—sub nominee (in the name of)
U.S.—*United States Reports*
U.S.C.—*United States Code*
U.S.L.W.—*United States Law Week*

1: CONTROL OF ILLINOIS PUBLIC SCHOOLS

FEDERAL GOVERNMENT

1:10   Is education a state or federal function?

Early in the nineteenth century there was little state involvement in education. Later, education became almost entirely a function of state or local government. In the twentieth century, the state has assumed responsibility for the regulation of education. The Illinois State Constitution establishes a system of public schools, whereas the U.S. Constitution makes no mention of education. Ostensibly, therefore, education is a responsibility of the state.

Since the 1950s, however, the federal government has assumed a more aggressive role in the regulation of the schools by imposing requirements upon the states. Federal laws, such as the 1964 Civil Rights Act and its amendments and the Individuals with Disabilities Education Act, have greatly changed education in the last thirty years.

1:20   What federal agency is responsible for the administration of federal programs for public schools?

The U.S. Department of Education is the principal federal agency which regulates public schools.

20 U.S.C. 3411

STATE GOVERNMENT

1:30   Are public school districts governmental entities?

The Illinois Constitution provides:

"A fundamental goal of the People of the State is the educational development of all persons to the limits of their capacities.

"The State shall provide for an efficient system of high quality public educational institutions and services. Education in public schools through the secondary level shall be free. There may be such other free education as the General Assembly provides by law.

"The State has the primary responsibility for financing the system of public education."

Ill. Const. art. X, sec. 1

Board of Education of Community Consolidated School District 606, Tazewell County v. Board of Education of Community Unit District 124 of Mason and Tazewell Counties, 11 Ill.App.2d 408, 137 N.E.2d 721 (3rd Dist. 1956)

O'Connor v. Board of Education of School District No. 23, 645 F.2d 578 (7th Cir. 1981) cert. den. 102 S.Ct. 641, 454 U.S. 1084, 70 L.Ed.2d 619, on rem. 545 F.Supp. 376

1:40   Are all the laws which govern Illinois public schools found in The Illinois School Code?

The laws of Illinois are published in a six volume set titled Illinois Revised Statutes. The School Code is Chapter 122. There are many other chapters of the Illinois Revised Statutes which directly affect or regulate schools.

For example, Elections are administered by laws contained in Chapter 46. The Educational Labor Relations Act and other labor matters are found in Chapter 48, The Open Meetings Act is included in Chapter 102, Pensions are controlled by Chapter 108 1/2, and various laws relating to records are contained in Chapter 116.

There are many other chapters of Illinois Revised Statutes which are relevant to schools. Various state agencies have rules and regulations which are found in the Illinois Administrative Code. There are also numerous federal laws which apply to schools.

1:50   What is the difference between the terms "common schools," "free schools," and "public schools" ?

The terms "common schools," "free schools," and "public schools" are used interchangeably in the School Code.

Ill. Rev. Stat. c. 122, par. 1-3

SCHOOL DISTRICTS

1:60 What are "county school units"?

The territory in each county, exclusive of charter districts which are required to appoint their own school treasurers, constitute county school units. County school units of less than two million inhabitants are known as Class I county school units, and county school units of two million or more inhabitants are known as Class II county school units.

Ill. Rev. Stat. c. 122, par. 5-1

1:70 What types of school districts are there in Illinois?

The numerous school district designations in Illinois vary mostly in name and reflect, not important legal distinctions, but different statutory terminology in use at the time different school districts were organized. Many of the statutes under which Illinois school districts were first organized have since been repealed. Among the variations in district type that reflect important legal distinctions:

1) Unit districts, which were created under various designations, provide education for kindergarten through grade 12. Elementary districts (grades K-8) and high school districts (grades 9-12) create a dual structure.

2) Charter districts, originally created under charters granted by the state, typically are governed by special sections of the School Code. Schools in the City of Chicago, for example, are governed by article 34 of the School Code.

Ill. Rev. Stat. c. 122, par. 11A-1
Ill. Rev. Stat. c. 122, par. 11B-1
Ill. Rev. Stat. c. 122, par. 12-1
Ill. Rev. Stat. c. 122, par. 12-10
Ill. Rev. Stat. c. 122, par. 32-1.1
Ill. Rev. Stat. c. 122, par. 33-1
Ill. Rev. Stat. c. 122, par. 34-2

SCHOOL BOARDS

1:80   What is a school board?

The term "school board" refers to the governing body of any school district created under the authority of the School Code, including boards of school directors and boards of education. The majority of school boards are governed by Article 10 of the School Code. However, the boards of some larger school districts and some special charter districts are governed by Articles 32, 33 and 34 of the School Code.

Ill. Rev. Stat. c. 122, par. 10-1 et seq.
Ill. Rev. Stat. c. 122, par. 32-1 et seq.
Ill. Rev. Stat. c. 122, par. 33-1 et seq.
Ill. Rev. Stat. c. 122, par. 34-1 et seq.

1:90   Are school boards created by the state Constitution?

No, the Illinois Constitution does not refer to local school boards. They are creations of state statutes.

1:100 Do school districts or their governing bodies have inherent powers?

A school board is a creation of the state, and creations of the state are without inherent power. A school board may exercise only those powers which the legislature has specifically granted, or those powers which are reasonably implied from a specified power, to achieve the purposes which the legislature has assigned to them.

Goedde v. Community Unit School District No. 7, Macoupin County, 21 Ill.App.2d 79, 157 N.E.2d 266 (3rd Dist. 1959)

1:110 What kinds of school boards are there in Illinois?

The majority of school boards are governed by section 10-10 of the School Code, which requires each to have seven members elected for terms of four years. There are numerous exceptions allowed or required by law, however:

1) Section 10-3 provides for a three member board of school directors in school districts with fewer than 1,000 inhabitants, except that a consolidated district must have a board of seven directors;

2) Section 32-1.1 authorizes school boards of charter districts with 100,000 to one million inhabitants to expand from seven members to 11 members unless the district's original charter or other special law provides otherwise;

3) Article 34 provides for a 15-member school board appointed by the mayor in districts with more than 500,000 inhabitants;

4) Section 32-1.5 authorizes the voters of special charter districts to elect a school board of three, five or seven members;

5) Section 32-3.2 requires certain special charter districts in cities of more than 45,000 inhabitants to have 11 members appointed by the mayor.

6) Section 33-1 authorizes special charter districts in cities of 100,000 to 500,000 inhabitants to elect seven-member boards of education, with members serving five-year terms. The same boards are authorized by section 33-1a to adopt an alternative arrangement, subject to voter approval at a referendum, electing three board members at large and four members from school board districts that are substantially equal in population.

The school boards of special charter districts, which predate most of the laws creating school boards, operate under provisions of their own state charters unless they have chosen to adopt Article 10 of the School Code or have selected one of the other options available in Articles 32 or 33.

Ill. Rev. Stat. c. 122, par. 10-1
Ill. Rev. Stat. c. 122, par. 10-10
Ill. Rev. Stat. c. 122, par. 31-1.2
Ill. Rev. Stat. c. 122, par. 32-1 et seq.
Ill. Rev. Stat. c. 122, par. 33-1
Ill. Rev. Stat. c. 122, par. 34-3

1:120 May citizens claim that an improper type of school board exists in a given school district?

When a petition signed by 10 percent or 1,500 legal voters, whichever is less, is submitted to a regional superintendent of schools, the regional superintendent must take a special census of the school district to determine if the district has the proper type of school board, a board of school directors or a board of education. The expenses of this census are to be borne by the school district involved.

If the census shows that the proper type of board does not exist, then the regional superintendent is required to immediately notify the school district and to certify to the proper election authorities that an election shall be held at the next general election in order to select the appropriate and entirely new board of the type legally required for a given school district.

Ill. Rev. Stat. c. 122, par. 3-14.16

STATE BOARD OF EDUCATION

1:130 How was the State Board of Education created?

The State Board of Education was created by the Illinois Constitution, which provides in part:

"There is created a State Board of Education to be elected or selected on a regional basis. The number of members, their qualifications, terms of office and manner of election or selection shall be provided by law. The Board, except as limited by law, may establish goals, determine policies, provide for planning and evaluating education programs and recommend financing. The Board shall have such other duties and powers as provided by law.

"The State Board of Education shall appoint a chief state educational officer."

Ill. Const. art. X, sec. 2

1:140 How are members of the Illinois State Board of Education selected?

Members of the State Board of Education are appointed by the Governor with the advice and consent of the Senate. The State Board consists of 17 members appointed from a pattern of representation coterminous with the five Illinois appellate court judicial districts.

Eight appointees are selected from the First Judicial District, four of whom must be residents of Chicago and four of whom must be residents of Cook County outside the city limits of Chicago. Two appointees are selected from each of the four other judicial districts and one member is selected as a member-at-large.

At no time may more than nine members of the State Board be from one political party. Party membership is defined as having voted in the primary of the party in the last primary before appointment. Members of the State Board serve for six-year terms. No member may be appointed to more than two six-year terms.

Ill. Rev. Stat. c. 122, par. 1A-1 et seq.

1:150 What are the qualifications for membership on the State Board of Education?

The members of the State Board of Education must be citizens of the United States and residents of the State of Illinois and are selected on the basis of their knowledge of or interest and experience in problems of public education. No member of the State Board may be gainfully employed or administratively connected with any public school system or institution of higher learning, public or private, within Illinois nor shall they be members of a school board or board of school trustees of a public or nonpublic school, college, university, or technical institution within Illinois.

Ill. Rev. Stat. c. 122, par. 1A-2
Hoskins v. Walker, 57 Ill.2d 503, 315 N.E.2d 25 (1974)

1:160 Are State Board of Education members compensated?

State Board of Education members are reimbursed for all ordinary and necessary expenses incurred in performing their duties as members of the Board. They receive no other compensation. Expenses must be approved by the State Board and must be consistent with the laws, policies, and requirements of the State of Illinois regarding such expenditures. Any member may include in his claim for expenses $50 per day for meeting days.

Ill. Rev. Stat. c. 122, par. 1A-2

1:170 How is a vacancy on the State Board of Education created?

A vacancy on the State Board of Education is created when a member:

1) dies;

2) files a written resignation with the Governor;

3) is adjudicated to be a person under legal disability under the Probate Act or a person subject to involuntary admission under the Mental Health and Developmental Disabilities Code;

4) ceases to be a resident of the judicial district from which he or she was appointed;

5) is convicted of an infamous crime, or of any offense involving a violation of his or her legal duties;

6) fails to maintain the qualifications for membership required by law.

Ill. Rev. Stat. c. 91 1/2, par. 1-100 et seq.
Ill. Rev. Stat. c. 110 1/2, par. 1-1 et seq.
Ill. Rev. Stat. c. 122, par. 1A-2.1

1:180 How may a member of the Illinois State Board of Education be removed from office?

The Governor may remove a member of the State Board of Education for incompetence, neglect of duty, or malfeasance in office.

Ill. Const. art. V, sec. 10

1:190 What are the qualifications for the office of State Superintendent of Education?

The State Board of Education determines the qualifications of and appoints the State Superintendent of Education. The State Superintendent of Education serves at the pleasure of the State Board. No employment contract for a State Superintendent of Education may exceed three years. The State Superintendent cannot be a member of the State Board. The State Board establishes the compensation for the State Superintendent and establishes the duties, powers, and responsibilities of the office.

Ill. Rev. Stat. c. 122, par. 1A-4(B)

1:200 What are the duties and authorities of the State Superintendent of Education?

The State Superintendent of Education is the chief administrative officer of the State Board of Education. As such, he is responsible for the supervision and evaluation of all public schools, for enacting and enforcing rules governing the operation of public schools, and for carrying out the policies of the State Board of Education.

Ill. Rev. Stat. c. 122, par. 2-2 et seq.

1:210 What types of school district recognition does the State Board of Education grant?

There are three types of recognition status:

1) Full Recognition is granted to a school district or attendance center which meets the minimal standards required of public elementary and secondary schools and has submitted an annual application for recognition.

2) Probationary Recognition is given to a school district or attendance center which has not met minimal standards. Probationary Recognition is a warning the school must make certain improvements.

3) Non-recognition is given to a school district or attendance center which fails to submit an Annual Application for Recognition, fails to meet legal requirements, or fails to give evidence of meeting minimal standards. A school district which fails for any school year to maintain a recognized school shall not be eligible to file for such year any claim upon the common school fund or collect tuition from another school district.

School districts assigned Probationary Recognition or Non-recognition may request re-evaluation by the State Board of Education to substantiate corrections of the areas of noncompliance previously cited.

Ill. Rev. Stat. c. 122, par. 18-8
23 Ill. Admin. Code 1.50

REGIONAL GOVERNANCE

1:220 What is an educational service region?

An educational service region is a county or a group of counties administered for educational purposes by a regional superintendent of schools.

Ill. Rev. Stat. c. 122, par. 3A-1 et seq.

1:230 How are regional superintendents of schools selected?

Regional superintendents of schools are elected pursuant to general election laws by popular vote from all counties comprising the educational service region served.

Ill. Rev. Stat. c. 122, par. 3A-6

1:240 What is the difference between a county superintendent of schools, a regional superintendent of schools, and a regional superintendent?

These terms refer to the same elective office and are interchangeable.

Ill. Rev. Stat. c. 122, par. 3-01

1:250 What are the qualifications for regional superintendent of schools?

No one is eligible to file a petition of candidacy for the office of regional superintendent of schools at any primary or general election, or to enter into the duties of this office either by election or appointment, unless he possesses the following qualifications:

1) is of good character;
2) has a master's degree;
3) has earned at least 20 semester hours of credit in professional education at the graduate level;
4) holds a valid all-grade supervisory certificate, limited supervisory certificate, life supervisory certificate, or an administrative certificate with superintendent endorsement;

5) has had at least four years experience in teaching; and

6) was engaged for at least two years of the previous four years in full-time teaching or supervising in the common public schools or serving as a county or regional superintendent of schools for an educational service region in Illinois.

A candidate for office must file a statement of economic interests. If elected he must take an oath of office, post a bond of no less than $12,000, and may not practice any other profession during the term of office.

Ill. Rev. Stat. c. 122, par. 3-1 et seq.
Ill. Rev. Stat. c. 122, par. 3A-6
Ill. Rev. Stat. c. 127, par. 601-101

LOCAL-MUNICIPAL GOVERNMENT

1:260 May any other unit of local government regulate a school district?

The operation of public schools is a state function and not a function of local government. Local governmental entities may not regulate the operation of a school district.

Ill. Const. art. VII, sec. 1
Ill. Const. art. VII, sec. 10
Ill. Rev. Stat. c. 24, par. 10-4-1
Board of Education of Minooka Community High School District No. 111 Grundy, Kendall and Will Counties v. Carter, 119 Ill.App.3d 857, 458 N.E.2d 50, 75 Ill.Dec. 882, (3rd Dist. 1983)
Board of Education of School District No. 150 v. City of Peoria, 76 Ill.2d 469, 394 N.E.2d 399, 31 Ill.Dec. 197 (1979)
Board of Education of the City of Rockford v. Page, 33 Ill.2d 372, 211 N.E.2d 361 (1965)
Board of Education of School District 33 v. City of West Chicago, 55 Ill.App.2d 401, 205 N.E.2d 63 (2nd Dist. 1965)

1:270 May school districts enter into cooperative agreements with units of local government?

The Illinois Constitution allows intergovernmental cooperative agreements, providing in part:

"Units of local government and school districts may contract or otherwise associate among themselves, with the State, with other states and their units of local government and school districts, and with the United States to obtain or share services and to exercise, combine, or transfer any power or function, in any manner not prohibited by law or by ordinance. Units of local government and school districts may contract and otherwise associate with individuals, associations, and corporations in any manner not prohibited by law or by ordinance. Participating units of government may use their credit, revenues, and other resources to pay costs and to service debt related to inter-governmental activities.

"Officers and employees of units of local government and school districts may participate in intergovernmental activities authorized by their units of government without relinquishing their offices or positions.

"The State shall encourage intergovernmental cooperation and use its technical and financial resources to assist inter-governmental activities."

Ill. Const. art. VII, sec. 10(a) et seq.
Ill. Rev. Stat. c. 127, par. 741 et seq.
Village of Elmwood Park v. Forest Preserve District of Cook County, 21 Ill.App.3d 597, 316 N.E.2d 140 (1st Dist. 1974)

1:280 How is fire protection for school sites provided?

If the location of any public school building is not within any municipality or fire protection district, fire protection service is provided by the municipality or fire protection district which maintains the facility for fire fighting equipment which is closest to the school site. The school district must pay to the municipality or fire protection district the reasonable cost of such service.

Ill. Rev. Stat. c. 122, par. 16-10

STATE ACADEMIC STANDARDS

1:300 What factors are considered in the establishment of state recognition standards for student performance and school improvement?

The standards include, but are not necessarily limited to state assessment of student performance, local assessment results, student attendance rates, retention rates, expulsion rates and graduation rates.

Ill.Rev. Stat. c. 122, par. 2-3.25a

1:310 Does the State Board of Education have authority to collect school information from a school district to determine its level of recognition?

The State Board is authorized to collect information, data, test results, student performance and school improvement indicators with respect to school recognition standards, student performance and school improvement.

Ill.Rev. Stat. c. 122, par. 2-3.25b

1:320 What is the state academic watch list?

Schools that are not meeting standards of academic performance and improvement may be placed on a State Superintendent of Education academic watch list. An on-site visitation is held to determine whether extenuating circumstances exist as to why a school or schools should not be placed on the list.

Ill.Rev. Stat. c. 122, par. 2-3.25d

1:330 What is required of a school district which has a school or schools placed on the academic watch list?

A school district with a school or schools on the academic watch list must submit a revised school improvement plan listing the district's expectations for removing each school in the district from the watch list and for improving student performance in the school. The improvement plan must be developed in consultation with the staff of the affected school and must be approved by the board of education. The revised improvement plan must be submitted to the State Board of Education for approval and must have specific measurable outcomes for improving student performance so that performance equals or exceeds standards set for the school by the State Board.

Ill.Rev. Stat. c. 122, par. 2-3.25d

1:340 How soon may a school placed on the academic watch list get off the list?

A school or schools once placed on the academic watch list must remain on the list for at least one full school year. During the year, the school is evaluated and assessed by the State Board of Education as to whether it is meeting the outcomes identified in its school improvement plan.

Ill.Rev. Stat. c. 122, par. 2-3.25d

1:350 What happens if a school remains on the academic watch list after two years?

The State Superintendent of Education appoints a school improvement panel for such schools. The panel:

1) assists the school in the development and implementation of a revised school improvement plan;

2) makes progress reports and comments to the State Superintendent of Education; and

3) has authority to review and approve or disapprove all actions of the board of education that pertain to implementation of the revised school improvement plan.

Ill.Rev. Stat. c. 122, par. 2-3.25e

1:360 What may happen to a school district that fails to make reasonable efforts to implement an approved school improvement plan?

The school district may suffer loss of state funds by school district, attendance center, or program as the State Board of Education deems appropriate.

Ill. Rev. Stat. c. 122, par. 2-3.25f

1:370 What penalties may the State Board of Education impose on a school or school district that has been on the academic watch for more than four years?

School board members may be removed from office, and an independent authority may be appointed to operate the school or school district for purposes of improving pupil performance and school improvement or the State Board of Education may non-recognize the school or school district and reassign its students and administrative staff. If a school district is non-recognized in its entirety, it is automatically dissolved under a procedure established by law.

Ill.Rev. Stat. c. 122, par. 2-3.25f 2.
Ill.Rev. Stat. c. 122, par. 3-14.28

1:380 May the State Board of Education grant waivers from its administrative rules and regulations?

Waivers are limited to school improvement issues as defined by the State Board of Education and cannot conflict with statutory requirements. Waivers may not be granted from rules and regulations pertaining to special education or teacher certification. The request for waiver must be based on sound educational practice, must not endanger the health and safety of students or staff, must not compromise equal opportunity for learning and must have improved student performance as the primary goal.

Ill.Rev. Stat. c. 122, par. 2-3.25g

2: SCHOOL BOARDS

SCHOOL BOARD STRUCTURE

2:10 How is the membership of an Illinois school board structured?

Most Illinois school boards consist of seven members elected at large. School districts with less than 1,000 inhabitants are governed by three-member boards of school directors. Charter district boards also may have more or fewer than seven members, depending upon the section of the School Code that governs.

There also are exceptions to the at-large provision. The boards of many school districts must guarantee representation to unincorporated areas or ensure that congressional townships have proper representation. These requirements vary with type of district, when the district was created, and how resident population is distributed.

Ill. Rev. Stat. c. 122, par. 10-1
Ill. Rev. Stat. c. 122, par. 10-10
Ill. Rev. Stat. c. 122, par. 11A-8
Ill. Rev. Stat. c. 122, par. 11B-7
Ill. Rev. Stat. c. 122, par. 12-2

2:20 Are all school boards elected?

The Chicago School Board is nominated by a commission and appointed by the mayor with the consent of the city council. Special charter districts may have an appointed school board if such a procedure is set forth in the original charter and the charter has not been amended. Such is the case in Lake Forest District 67, although voters there have approved a measure to replace the appointed school board with an elected school board beginning in November, 1993. All other Illinois public school boards are elected.

Ill. Rev. Stat. c. 122, par. 9-1 et seq.
Ill. Rev. Stat. c. 122, par. 32-1.5 et seq.
Ill. Rev. Stat. c. 122, par. 34-3 et seq.
Latham v. Board of Education of Chicago, 31 Ill.2d 178, 201
N.E.2d 111 (1964)

**2:25   What are the territorial representation
           requirements that apply to Illinois school
           boards?**

The requirement for territorial representation applies to community unit districts and consolidated districts created prior to January 1, 1975, and to combined districts created prior to July 1, 1983.

Where such a district is smaller than two congressional townships or 72 square miles, but includes more than one congressional township or 36 square miles of unincorporated areas, not more than five members may be selected from incorporated areas.

Where such a district's territory is greater than two congressional townships or 72 square miles, not counting congressional townships of fewer than 100 inhabitants, not more than three board members may be selected from any one township unless:

• 75 to 90 percent of the population reside in one township, in which case four members must be selected from that township and three must be selected from the remaining townships, or

• more than 90 percent of the population reside in one township, in which case all board members may be selected from any one or more townships.

Territorial representation also applies to community high school districts as follows:

• if 15 to 30 percent of the district's taxable property is located in unincorporated territory, at least one board member must be selected from unincorporated territory;

• if 30 percent or more of the district's taxable property is located in unincorporated territory, at least two board members must be selected from unincorporated territory.

Ill. Rev. Stat. c. 122, par. 11A-8
Ill. Rev. Stat. c. 122, par. 11B-7
Ill. Rev. Stat. c. 122, par. 12-2

**2:30   May a school board be elected from
           representative districts rather than at-large?**

A school board may, by its own motion, or must if petitioned by the lesser of 2,500 or 5 percent of the voters registered in the district, submit to election the question of electing school board members by representative districts rather than at-large.

Ill. Rev. Stat. c. 122, par. 9-22

2:40   If the voters approve the election of school board members by representative districts, how are the representative districts formed?

The at-large school board must divide the school district into seven school board districts, each of which must be compact and contiguous and substantially equal in population to each other district. The terms of office of the board members incumbent at the time the proposition to elect from representative districts is adopted expire on the day of the next regular school election, at which time one member is elected from each school board district.

In districts which have four-year terms, those members first elected from representative districts must, by lot, determine three to serve for two years and four to serve for four years. Their successors serve four-year terms.

In school districts which have six-year school board terms, those members first elected from representative districts must, by lot, determine three to serve two-year terms, two to serve four-year terms, and two to serve six-year terms. Their successors serve six-year terms.

Ill. Rev. Stat. c. 122, par. 9-22

2:45   How are representative districts altered to reflect changes in population patterns?

The school board must reapportion the representative districts to reflect the results of each decennial census. The reapportionment plan must be approved by a majority of the board not less than 90 days before the last date for filing nominating petitions for the next board election in the year following the census. The school board also must, publicly by lot, divide the representative districts into two groups providing staggered terms. Board members from one group of districts will be elected for terms of four years, four years and two years, while those from the other group will be elected for terms of two years, four years and four years.

Ill. Rev. Stat. c. 122, par. 9-22

2:50   What is a school board member's term of office?

The term of office for a school board member is four years. A school board may, by resolution, submit to the voters the question of increasing the term of office to six years.

A school board member also may be appointed and/or elected to less than a full term to fill a vacancy on the board.

Ill. Rev. Stat. c. 122, par. 9-5
Ill. Rev. Stat. c. 122, par. 10-10

2:60   How many times may a school board member be elected?

There is no limit to the number of terms to which a school board member may be elected.

Ill. Rev. Stat. c. 122, par. 9-1

VACANCIES

2:70   What acts create a vacancy on a school board?

Elective offices become vacant within the meaning of the School Code, unless the context indicates otherwise, on the happening of any of the following events before the expiration of the term of the office:

1) death of the incumbent;

2) resignation in writing filed with the secretary or clerk of the board;

3) becoming a person under legal disability;

4) ceasing to be an inhabitant of the district from which the member was elected;

5) conviction of an infamous crime, or of any offense involving a violation of official oath;

6) removal from office;

7) the decision of a competent tribunal declaring the election void;

8) ceasing to be an inhabitant of a particular area from which the member was elected, if the residential requirements are violated.

Ill. Rev. Stat. c. 38, par. 124-1
Ill. Rev. Stat. c. 122, par. 10-10 et. seq.

Ill. Rev. Stat. c. 122, par. 11A-8
Ill. Rev. Stat. c. 122, par. 11B-7
Ill. Rev. Stat. c. 122, par. 12-2

2:80   If a school board member's conviction of an infamous crime is reversed, is the member's school board seat restored to him?

Any elected official of any school district convicted in any court of the State of Illinois or of the United States of an infamous crime is, upon conviction, ineligible to continue in office. If a final order reverses the conviction, eligibility to hold the office is restored, and the officer is reinstated for the duration of the term of office remaining.

Upon the conviction and ineligibility of any person, a successor is chosen to fill the vacancy. The successor holds office thereafter until a final order reversing the conviction is entered or the term expires, whichever occurs first.

Ill. Rev. Stat. c. 102, par. 120

2:85   Which public body has authority to determine whether or not a vacancy exists on a school board?

The school board has authority to determine whether or not the facts occasioning a vacancy exist.

Ill. Rev. Stat. c. 46, par. 25-3

2:90   How is a board of school directors vacancy filled?

When a vacancy occurs on a board of directors, the remaining directors must, within 30 days, fill the vacancy by appointment until the next regular school election. If they fail to do so, the regional superintendent must fill the vacancy by appointment within 30 days. If the regional superintendent fails to fill the vacancy, it is filled at the next regularly scheduled election.

Ill. Rev. Stat. c. 122, par. 10-4

2:100 How is a vacancy on a board of education filled?

Whenever a vacancy occurs on a board of education, the remaining members fill the vacancy by appointment until the next regular school election, at which election a successor is elected to serve the remainder of the unexpired term.

However, if the vacancy occurs with less than 28 months remaining in the term, or if the vacancy occurs less than 88 days before the next regularly scheduled election for the vacant office, then the person so appointed serves the remainder of the unexpired term, and no election to fill the vacancy is held.

Should a board of education fail to act within 45 days after the vacancy occurs, the regional superintendent must, within 30 days after the remaining members have failed to fill the vacancy, fill the vacancy by appointment.

Ill .Rev. Stat. c. 122, par. 10-10

2:110 What qualifications must a person have to be appointed to fill a school board vacancy?

To be appointed to fill a school board vacancy, a person must have the same qualifications as the person he was appointed to replace. On the date of appointment he must be at least 18 years of age, a resident of the state and the district for at least one year preceding appointment, a registered voter and not a school trustee or school treasurer.

The successor appointed to a board of education must have the same residential qualifications as his predecessor.

Ill. Rev. Stat. c. 122, par. 10-4
Ill. Rev. Stat. c. 122, par. 10-10
Ill. Rev. Stat. c. 122, par. 10-11
Ill. Rev. Stat. c. 122, par. 11A-8
Ill. Rev. Stat. c. 122, par. 11B-7
Ill. Rev. Stat. c. 122, par. 12-2

2:115 Where a school board's membership must include representation of particular congressional townships or unincorporated areas, must the person selected to fill a vacancy live in the same township or unincorporated area as the predecessor?

Any otherwise qualified person may be appointed or elected to fill a school board vacancy, regardless of where the predecessor board member resided, so long as the board's total membership complies with any residential requirements that apply to the district. A person filling a board vacancy need not live in the same congressional township or unincorporated area as the predecessor except where residence in the same area is necessary to maintain a minimum level of representation required by law or to avoid exceeding a maximum level in another geographic area.

The applicable law must be read carefully to ascertain the requirements in each instance. Where the law reads "no more than," it establishes a maximum number of members from that territory. The successor to a member elected from that territory need not live in the same territory, because the law establishes a maximum number, not a minimum. A new member may not be appointed or elected from that territory if the board's incumbent membership is already at the maximum.

Where the law reads "no less than," it establishes a minimum number of members from that territory. The successor to a member elected from that territory must be selected from the same territory in order to maintain the minimum representation required by law. On the other hand, if the board's incumbent membership already includes the minimum number from that territory, then the successor need not reside there, but could be selected from another part of the district.

Ill. Rev. Stat. c. 122, par. 10-10
Ill. Rev. Stat. c. 122, par. 10-11
Ill. Rev. Stat. c. 122, par. 11A-8
Ill. Rev. Stat. c. 122, par. 11B-7
Ill. Rev. Stat. c. 122, par. 12-2

SCHOOL BOARD POWERS AND DUTIES

2:130 Who holds the authority to establish rules and regulations in school districts?

School boards. Illinois law provides that school boards are to adopt and enforce all necessary rules for the management and government of the public schools of their district. The rules adopted by a school board are to be filed for public inspection in the administrative office of the district.

Ill. Rev. Stat. c. 122, par. 10-20.5

Board of Education of City of Chicago v. Chicago Teachers' Union, Local 1, 89 Ill. App.3d 861, 412 N.E.2d 587, 45 Ill.Dec. 236 (1st. Dist. 1980), rev. on other grounds 88 Ill.2d 63, 430 N.E.2d 1111 58 Ill.Dec. 860

Beck v. Board of Education of Harlem Consolidated School District No. 122, 27 Ill.App.3d 4, 325 N.E.2d 640 (2nd Dist. 1975) aff'd. 63 Ill.2d 10, 344 N.E.2d 440

2:135 What is the distinction between "school board powers" and the powers of a school board member?

A school board has powers and duties set forth in the law. A school board member acting as an individual has none of those powers and duties.

2:140 May a school board member acting alone exercise the powers granted to a school board?

A school board may act only at a legal meeting when a quorum is present and after a requisite number of "yea" votes is counted on a properly presented and seconded motion on an issue properly within the powers of the board.

Ill. Rev. Stat. c. 122, par. 10-12

Bunsen v. County Board of School Trustees of Lake County, 48 Ill.App.2d 291, 198 N.E.2d 735 (2nd Dist. 1964)

2:150 May a board member visit schools of the district to ensure their proper functioning?

A board of education is directed by law to "visit and inspect" schools and to see to their proper maintenance. Although boards lawfully delegate this duty to employees, it also is lawful for a board to include school visits as part of a properly convened meeting.

Unless so directed by official action of the board, however, the individual board member is free to visit and inspect schools only in accordance with board policies regulating public visitation. The individual board member may not assume powers or duties belonging to the full board, and has only the same rights and powers as other citizens when the board is not in session.

Ill. Rev. Stat. c. 122, par. 10-20.6
Ill. Rev. Stat. c. 122, par. 24-25

2:160 Where are the powers and duties of a school board enumerated in the law?

School board duties are enumerated in sections 10-20 et seq. and 10-21 et seq. of the School Code. Powers are enumerated in sections 10-22 et seq. and 10-23 et seq.

Ill. Rev. Stat. c. 122, par. 10-20 et seq.
Ill. Rev. Stat. c. 122, par. 10-21 et seq.
Ill. Rev. Stat. c. 122, par. 10-22 et seq.
Ill. Rev. Stat. c. 122, par. 10-23 et seq.

2:170 May a school board reverse a previously adopted official act?

In most cases a school board may revoke or rescind a previous action. Excepted are situations when the prior act has vested rights in third parties which would be prejudiced if the board's original action were reversed.

City of Kankakee v. Small, 317 Ill. 55, 147 N.E. 404 (1925)
Illinois ex rel. MacMahon v. Davis, 209 Ill.App. 117 (1st Dist. 1918), rev. 284 Ill. 439, 120 N.E. 326
Illinois v. Trustees of Schools, 42 Ill.App. 60 (2nd Dist. 1891)

2:180 Are the actions of a prior school board binding on a successor school board?

A school board is a continuing entity. While the individual membership of the board may change, the board itself is on-going. The lawful acts of a prior school board bind a successor school board unless the act of the prior board is reversible and the successor board votes to reverse.

City of Kankakee v. Small, 317 Ill. 55, 147 N.E. 404 (1925)

Illinois ex rel. MacMahon v. Davis, 209 Ill.App. 117 (1st Dist. 1918), rev. 284 Ill. 439, 120 N.E. 326

2:190 What happens if a local school board fails to forward reports required by law?

If the trustees of schools of any township in Class I or Class II county school units fail to prepare and forward, or cause to be prepared and forwarded, to the regional superintendent of schools reports required by the School Code, the regional superintendent is required by law to furnish such information or to employ a person to furnish such information as far as is practicable. Such a person shall have access to the books, records, and papers of the school district to enable him or her to prepare the reports required by law, and the school district is required to permit such person to examine their books, records, and papers at a time and place that may be desired for this purpose.

The regional superintendent is authorized by law to bill the district for such services in an amount to cover the cost of the preparation of the reports if an external person is employed to prepare them. For example, if a school district fails to submit the results of a local audit to the regional superintendent of schools on or before October 15 of each year, the regional superintendent of schools is empowered by law to cause the audit to be conducted in the school district. This is done by the regional superintendent employing an accountant who is licensed to practice accountancy in the State of Illinois to conduct the audit, and the regional superintendent will bill the district for this service or shall, with the personnel of the office, make such an audit to the regional superintendent's satisfaction and bill the district for that service.

Ill. Rev. Stat. c. 122, par. 3-7

Ill. Rev. Stat. c. 122, par. 3-15.1

2:200 Are school boards authorized to pay membership dues to professional organizations or associations?

A school board is authorized to pay both state and national association membership dues to school associations which benefit students.

A school board may also form, join and provide for the expenses of associations of Illinois school boards formed for the purpose of conducting county or regional school board institutes and otherwise disseminating and interchanging information regarding school board problems, duties and responsibilities.

There are statutory requirements which must be met by any such organization in order to qualify to receive financial support from school districts.

Ill. Rev. Stat. c. 122, par. 10-22.40
Ill. Rev. Stat. c. 122, par. 23-1 et seq.

2:210 May a school board appoint committees?

A school board may appoint committees to research and make recommendations to the board. A school board may not give up its non-delegable decision-making authority to a committee.

Thomas v. Board of Education of Community Unit School District of Pope County, 117 Ill.App.3d 374, 453 N.E.2d 150, 721 Ill.Dec. 845 (5th Dist. 1983)

Elder v. Board of Education of School District 127 1/2 of Cook County, 60 Ill.App.2d 56, 208 N.E.2d 423 (1st Dist. 1965)

Lindblad v. Board of Education of Normal School District, 221 Ill. 261, 77 N.E. 450 (1906)

3: SCHOOL BOARD MEMBERSHIP

QUALIFICATIONS

3:10   What are the qualfications for school board membership?

In order to qualify for school board membership, an individual must be, in each case as of the date of election: a United States citizen, a resident of the State of Illinois and of the school district for at least one year preceding election, at least 18 years of age, a registered voter, and neither a school trustee nor a school treasurer.

A school board member may not hold an incompatible office. Certain types of school districts have additional residency requirements.

Ill. Rev. Stat. c. 122, par. 10-1
Ill. Rev. Stat. c. 122, par. 10-3
Ill. Rev. Stat. c. 122, par. 11A-8
Ill. Rev. Stat. c. 122, par. 11B-7
Ill. Rev. Stat. c. 122, par. 12-2

3:20   What does residence mean in the context of qualification for school board membership?

Residence is physical presence in a particular place with intention to remain permanently.

Stein v. County Board of School Trustees of DuPage County, 40 Ill.2d 477, 240 N.E.2d 668 (1968)

INCOMPATIBILITY

3:30   What is meant by the term "incompatibility of offices"?

When two public offices are deemed incompatible under the law, it means that an individual may not hold those two offices simultaneously. A public official who accepts a second office that is incompatible constructively resigns or vacates the first office.

Ill. Const. art. IV, par. 2(e)
Ill. Const. art. VI, par. 13(b)
Ill. Rev. Stat. c. 122, par. 3-2
Ill. Rev. Stat. c. 122, par. 5-3
Ill. Rev. Stat. c. 122, par. 8-1
Illinois ex rel. Black v. Dukes, 108 Ill.App.3d 965, 439 N.E.2d 1305, 64 Ill.Dec. 497 (3rd Dist. 1982) vacated 96 Ill.2d 273, 449 N.E.2d 856, 70 Ill.Dec. 509 (1983)
Illinois ex rel. Myers v. Haas, 145 Ill.App. 283 (1st Dist. 1908)

3:40   What public offices are incompatible with school board membership?

The following offices are incompatible with school board membership by reason of the listed authority:

1) By reason of state Constitutional prohibition, certain elective offices in the judicial, executive or legislative branches of government are incompatible with membership on a school board. These incompatible offices include all classes of judges, such elected statewide officers as governor, attorney general and secretary of state, and members of the General Assembly. Other offices must be examined case by case.

2) By reason of statutory prohibitions, a school board member may not serve simultaneously as a school trustee, Cook County school treasurer, regional superintendent of schools, or member of the State Board of Education. A school board member elected to the board of a community college district may serve only the remainder of the unexpired school board term while serving on the community college board.

In addition, the Illinois Attorney General's office has at various times issued opinions that the following offices are incompatible with school board membership: alderman, board of review member, city council member, county board member, county zoning board of appeals member, town trustee, township assessor, township school trustee, township supervisor, and village president. Many other elective offices are incompatible with school board membership.

Ill. Const. art. IV, par. 2(e)
Ill. Const. art. VI, par. 13(b)
Ill. Rev. Stat. c. 122, par. 3-2

Ill. Rev. Stat. c. 122, par. 5-3
Ill. Rev. Stat. c. 122, par. 8-1
Ill. Rev. Stat. c. 122, par. 103-7
Illinois ex rel. Black v. Dukes, 108 Ill.App.3d 965, 439 N.E.2d
1305, 64 Ill.Dec. 497 (3rd Dist. 1982) vacated 96 Ill.2d 273, 449
N.E.2d 856, 70 Ill.Dec. 509 (1983)
Illinois ex rel. Myers v. Haas, 145 Ill.App. 283 (1st Dist. 1908)

COMPENSATION AND EXPENSES

3:50   May a school board compensate its members for services rendered?

No member of a school board may be compensated for services rendered except the secretary or clerk of the board, who may be paid an amount to a limit specified by statute.

Ill. Rev. Stat. c. 122, par. 10-10
Ill. Rev. Stat. c. 122, par. 10-22.32
Ill. Rev. Stat. c. 122, par. 22-1

3:60   May a school board member be advanced expenses to attend meetings?

A school board may advance its members the actual and necessary expenses incurred in attending the following meetings:

1) meetings sponsored by the State Board of Education or the Regional Superintendent of Schools;

2) meetings sponsored by the Illinois Association of School Boards; and

3) meetings sponsored by a national organization in the field of public school education.

Authorized expenses are those reasonably anticipated to be incurred on the days necessary for travel to and from, and for attendance at, such meetings. If moneys are so advanced, the member to whom money is advanced must submit an itemized verified expense voucher showing the amount of his actual expenditures, with receipts attached where possible. When moneys are advanced but not required for such actual reasonable expenses, the member must refund the excess amount.

The member may be reimbursed if the actual reasonable expenses exceed the amount advanced.

Ill. Rev. Stat. c. 122, par. 10-22.32
Ill. Rev. Stat. c. 122, par. 23-1

3:70   May a school board member receive reimbursement for actual expenses incurred by a non-member spouse who accompanies him to a school board function?

No.

Ill. Rev. Stat. c. 122, par. 10-22.32

3:80   May a school board member receive lost wages as a school board expense?

No.

Ill. Rev. Stat. c. 122, par. 10-22.32

DISCLOSURE OF ECONOMIC INTERESTS

3:90   Which school district personnel are required to file economic interest statements?

Each school board member must file annually an economic interest statement. Each school board employee (including a teacher) who is compensated for services at the rate of $35,000 per year or more is also required to file an economic interest statement each year.

In order to be placed on the ballot at a school board election, each candidate must have filed an economic interest statement with the county clerk and filed the county clerk's receipt with the school board secretary during the time period for filing nominating papers.

Anyone working for the school district as an independent contractor need not file an economic interest statement.

Ill. Rev. Stat. c. 122, par. 9-10

Ill. Rev. Stat. c. 127, par. 604A-101 (f)
Ill. Rev. Stat. c. 127, par. 604A-101 (i)
Ill. Rev. Stat. c. 127, par. 604A-105
Havens v. Miller, 102 Ill.App.3d 558, 429 N.E.2d 1292, 57 Ill.Dec. 929 (1st. Dist. 1981)

3:100 When must an economic interest statement be filed?

A person required to file an economic interest statement must do so upon initial appointment or employment and by May 1 of each year unless he has already filed a statement in that calendar year.

A candidate for elective office must file his economic interest statement not later than the end of the period during which he can file nominating papers if he has not already filed a statement in relation to the same unit of government within a year preceding such action.

Ill. Rev. Stat. c. 127, par. 604A-105
Miceli v. Lavelle, 114 Ill. App.3d 311, 448 N.E.2d 989 (1st. Dist. 1983)
Allen v. Love, 112 Ill.App.3d 338, 445 N.E.2d 514 (1st Dist. 1983)

3:110 What are the penalties for failure to file an economic interest statement?

Persons who fail to meet the May 1 filing deadline are subject to late filing penalties ranging from a late filing fee of $15 until May 15, to $100 per day from May 15 until May 31. Failure to file by May 31, or willful filing of a false or incomplete economic interest statement, is a class A misdemeanor and may cause forfeiture of office or employment. However, any filing within 30 days of actual notice of failure to file bars forfeiture of office or employment.

Ill. Rev. Stat. c. 127, par. 604A-101
Ill. Rev. Stat. c. 127, par. 604A-107
Miceli v. Lavelle, 114 Ill. App.3d 311, 448 N.E.2d 989 (1st. Dist. 1983)
Allen v. Love, 112 Ill.App.3d 338, 445 N.E.2d 514 (1st Dist. 1983)

3:120 Must a school board candidate disclose campaign contributions?

If a school board candidate accepts campaign contributions of any kind or makes campaign expenditures of any kind in an aggregate amount exceeding $1,000 during any 12 month period, he is subject to disclosure and filing requirements. The provisions of the applicable statutes include keeping a detailed account of every contribution in excess of $20, including the name and address of the person making the contribution and the date on which it was made.

Ill. Rev. Stat. c. 46, par. 9-1 et seq.

INTEREST IN CONTRACTS

3:130 What is the Corrupt Practices Act?

The Corrupt Practices Act provides in part:

"No person holding any office, either by election or appointment under the laws or constitution of this state, may be in any manner interested, either directly or indirectly, in his own name or in the name of any other person, association, trust or corporation, in any contract or the performance of any work in the making or letting of which such officer may be called upon to act or vote. No such officer may represent, either as agent or otherwise, any person, association, trust or corporation, with respect to any application or bid for any contract or work in regard to which such officer may be called upon to vote. Nor may any such officer take or receive, or offer to take or receive, either directly or indirectly, any money or other thing of value as a gift or bribe or means of influencing his vote or action in his official character. Any contract made and procured in violation hereof is void."

The Act contains exceptions similar in type to those contained in the School Code conflict of interest provisions applicable to school board members.

Ill. Rev. Stat. c. 102, par. 3
Ill. Rev. Stat. c. 122, par. 10-9
Brown v. Kirk, 33 Ill.App.3d 477, 342 N.E.2d 137, rev. on other grounds 64 Ill.2d 144, 355 N.E.2d 12 (1975)

3:140 What interest may a school board member have in a school contract?

A school board member is prohibited from having any interest directly or indirectly in any contract, work, or business of the school district or in the sale of any article to the school district. A school board member is prohibited from purchasing any school district property except a school board member may purchase a house constructed by the school district's vocational education students if the property is to be used as the board member's primary residence and if the sale is as otherwise provided for in the law.

These prohibitions are subject to certain limited exceptions. The exceptions permit certain small contracts to be let, and allow a limited business relationship with the school district if certain procedures are followed and the school board member owns less than a 7 1 / 2 percent interest in the company desiring to do business with the school district.

Ill. Rev. Stat. c. 122, par. 10-9
Ill. Rev. Stat. c. 122, par. 5-22

3:145 Is it a conflict of interest for an elected public school official to be employed as a substitute teacher in the same school district in which he is an elected official?

Yes. The conflict of interest statutes prevent an elected public school official from becoming interested in a contract let by his school district.

Ill. Rev. Stat. c. 122, par. 10-9
Ill. Rev. Stat. c. 38, par. 1005-8-1 et seq.

3:150 May a school board member avoid conflict of interest by abstaining on the vote to award a contract in which he is interested?

If the award of a contract would otherwise result in a conflict of interest, the conflict is not cured by a school board member's abstention on the vote or absence from the meeting when the vote is taken.

Ill. Rev. Stat. c. 122, sec 10-9

3:160   Is it a conflict of interest for a school board member to be married to a person employed by the district which the school board member serves?

This has been a controversial area of the law. It is probably not a conflict of interest if the employee was hired by the school district before the school board member was seated. A conflict of interest may result if the spouse of a school board member is hired during the school board member's term of office.

Ill. Rev. Stat. c. 102, par. 3

Ill. Rev. Stat. c. 122, sec 10-9

Ill. Rev. Stat. c. 127, par. 132.1-1

Hollister v. North, 50 Ill.App.3d 56, 365 N.E.2d 258, 8 Ill.Dec. 20 (4th Dist. 1977)

Illinois v. Simpkins, 45 Ill.App.3d 202, 359 N.E.2d 828, 3 Ill.Dec. 969 (5th Dist. 1977)

Shoresman v. Burgess, 412 F.Supp. 831 (N.D. Ill. 1976)

3:170   May a school board member or school employee have a financial interest in the books, apparatus, or furniture used in the district?

No state, county, township, or school officer or teacher may be interested in the sale, proceeds, or profits of any book, apparatus, or furniture used or to be used in any school with which such officer or teacher may be connected, except when the interest of the teacher is based upon authorship or development of instructional materials listed with the State Board of Education and adopted for use by a school board. Each teacher having an interest in instructional materials must file an annual statement so certifying with the secretary of the school board.

No employee or officer of a school district, special education joint agreement, office of a regional superintendent of schools or the State Board of Education may have a direct or indirect financial interest in any agreemnt between the entity of which the person is an employee or officer and any corporation, organization or other entity that collects or participates in the collection of payments from private health care benfit plans or federally funded health care programs.

Ill. Rev. Stat. c. 122, par. 14-7.04

Ill. Rev. Stat. c. 122, par. 22-5

RESIGNATIONS

3:180 When a school board member resigns, when is the resignation effective?

A school board member's resignation, once tendered, is final and is effective when filed with the school board secretary or clerk.

Ill. Rev. Stat. c. 122, par. 10-11

Cole v. McGillicuddy, 21 Ill.App.3d 645, 316 N.E.2d 109 (1st Dist. 1974)

Allen v. Powell, 42 Ill.2d 66, 244 N.E.2d 596 (1969)

3:185 When does the resignation of a public official take effect?

Although a resignation once tendered is effective on receipt and may not be thereafter withdrawn, a resignation specifying a future effective date does not take effect until the date specified therein. A vacancy does not exist in the office resigned until the future effective date contained in the resignation.

Ill. Rev. Stat. c. 122, par. 10-11

Cole v. McGillicuddy, 21 Ill.App.3d 645, 316 N.E.2d 109 (1st Dist. 1974)

Allen v. Powell, 42 Ill.2d 66, 244 N.E.2d 596 (1969)

REMOVAL AND FORFEITURE

3:190 May a regional superintendent of schools remove a school board member from office?

A regional superintendent of schools may remove a school board member from office for willful failure to perform official duties. A regional superintendent may not remove a school board member from office for any other cause.

Ill. Rev. Stat. c. 122, par. 3-15.5

Illinois ex rel. Kolker v. Blair, 8 Ill.App.3d 197, 289 N.E.2d 688 (5th Dist. 1972)

Illinois ex rel. Howard v. Harris, 164 Ill.App. 136 (3rd Dist. 1911)

3:193 May a school board member be removed from office for failure to attend meetings?

The regional superintendent of schools is empowered to remove a school board member from office for "willful failure to perform official duties." Regional superintendents have seldom exercised this power.

Ill. Rev. Stat. c. 122, par. 3-15.5

3:195 May voters remove a school board member from office by recall petition or election?

No.

Ill. Rev. Stat. c. 38, par. 33-3
Ill. Rev. Stat. c. 122, par. 3-15.5
Ill. Rev. Stat. c. 122, par. 10-10 et seq.
Ill. Rev. Stat. c. 127, par. 604A-107

3:200 Under what circumstances does a school board member forfeit office?

A school board member forfeits office if convicted of official misconduct. Official misconduct occurs when a board member, acting in his official capacity, intentionally or recklessly fails to perform any mandatory duty as required by law; knowingly performs an act he knows he is forbidden by law to perform; intends to obtain a personal advantage for himself or another by performing an act in excess of his lawful authority; or solicits or knowingly accepts for the performance of any act a fee or reward that he knows is not authorized by law.

A school board member also forfeits office when he willfully violates any of the laws governing a school district's working cash fund.

Ill. Rev. Stat. c. 38, par. 33-3
Ill. Rev. Stat. c. 122, par. 20-1 et seq.

3:210 May a school board member be subject to a fine for willfully violating any laws governing the operation of Illinois public school districts?

Under some conditions, fines against school board members may be assessed. For example, Illinois law provides that any member of a board of school directors or board of education of any school district, or any other person holding any office, trust, or employment under any school district, who willfully violates any of the provisions of the School Code governing a working cash fund shall be guilty of a business offense and fined not exceeding $10,000, and shall forfeit his right to his office, trust or employment and shall be removed therefrom.

Any member or other person is liable for any sum that may be unlawfully diverted from the working cash fund or otherwise used, to be recovered by a school district or by any taxpayer in the name and for the benefit of the school district in an appropriate civil action.

Ill. Rev. Stat. c. 122, par. 20-6
Ill. Rev. Stat. c. 122, par. 22-1 et seq.

4: SCHOOL ELECTION PROCEDURES

GENERAL ELECTION LAWS

4:10 What types of elections involve public school districts?

Elections conducted by public school districts include the election of school board members and various public policy propositions, such as to increase authorized property tax rates, issue bonds, consolidate districts, create single-member school board districts, or deactivate a high school. A school election also may involve an advisory question placed before the voters.

4:20 What laws govern the election of school board members?

School board elections are nonpartisan elections governed by the general election laws of the state. Provisions peculiar to school boards are found in the School Code.

Ill. Rev. Stat. c. 46, par. 1-1 et seq.
Ill. Rev. Stat. c. 122, par. 9-1 et seq.

4:30 When are school board members elected?

School board members are elected at the biennial nonpartisan election held on the first Tuesday after the first Monday in November in odd-numbered years. Special charter districts with 100,000 to 500,000 inhabitants elect school board members at the consolidated election held on the first Tuesday in April in odd-numbered years and at the general primary election on the third Tuesday in March in even-numbered years.

Ill. Rev. Stat. c. 46, par. 2A-1.1(c)
Ill. Rev. Stat. c. 46, par. 2A-1.2

4:40   What laws govern the holding of a school district referendum on a public policy issue, such as a proposition to increase tax rates, issue bonds or consolidate districts?

Article 28 of The Election Code represents the general election laws governing all public policy referenda. Article 9 of The School Code addresses some specific requirements of school district referenda.

However, school boards may place on the ballot only those public policy questions authorized by statute. Such authorization is found at several locations in the School Code, including Article 17 (increases in authorized tax rates), Article 19 (issuance of building bonds), and Article 20 (working cash fund bonds). Authority for elections on school district reorganization and consolidation are found in Articles 7, 7A, 11A, 11B and 11D.

To place a proposition on the ballot at a referendum, a school board must adopt a resolution citing the specific authorizing statute.

Ill. Rev. Stat. c. 46, par. 28-1 et seq.
Ill. Rev. Stat. c. 122, par. 9-1 et seq.

4:50   When may public policy issues be placed on the ballot?

A public policy referendum may be held only on any of the five scheduled election dates in each two-year election cycle. In even-numbered years, those dates are the third Tuesday in March (General Primary) and the first Tuesday after the first Monday in November (General Election).

In odd-numbered years, regular election dates are the last Tuesday in February (Consolidated Primary), the first Tuesday in April (Consolidated Election), and the first Tuesday after the first Monday in November (Non-partisan Election).

There are three exceptions to this schedule that may apply in different circumstances:

1) A proposition may not be placed on the ballot at any regular election where there is no contest for a public office on the ballot in at least one precinct within the school district.

2) A school board may petition the circuit court for an emergency election where the board believes it cannot reasonably wait until the next regular election date.

3) Not more than three propositions (other than propositions submitted by backdoor referendum) may be submitted to the voters of a school district at the same election.

Ill. Rev. Stat. c. 46, par. 2A-1.2(f)
Ill. Rev. Stat. c. 46, par. 2A-1.4
Ill. Rev. Stat. c. 46, par. 28-1

4:55   When must a school board submit a public policy advisory referendum to vote at a regularly scheduled election?

Whenever 10 percent or more of the registered voters of a school district submit a valid written petition regarding a question of public policy to a school board, the board must cause the question to be submitted to the voters.

Ill. Rev. Stat. c. 46, par. 28-6

ELECTION AUTHORITY

4:60   Who is in charge of conducting elections?

The Illinois State Board of Elections has general supervision over the administration of registration and election laws of the state.

Local elections are conducted by an election authority designated by statute. In most locales, the election authority is the county clerk. In a number of cities, a Municipal Board of Election Commissioners is the election authority. In DuPage County, a County Board of Election Commissioners is the election authority.

The election authority is responsible for voter registration, determining polling places, publishing notices, printing ballots, absentee voting, and other mechanics of running the election.

Ill. Rev. Stat. c. 46, par. 1-3
Ill. Rev. Stat. c. 46, par. 1A-1 et seq.

4:70 Does the school board have any duties related to the conduct of school elections?

The school board has no duties directly relating to the conduct of any election. However, certain duties and actions of the board relate to the election:

1) The board, by proper resolution, may place public policy propositions on the ballot at an election.

2) Members of the board make up an Electoral Board to hear and rule on objections to candidate nominating petitions and voter petitions.

3) The board must canvass the precinct returns and declare the results following each election of board members and school district referendum.

4) The school board secretary or clerk serves as the Local Election Official, assisted by designated representatives appointed by the board.

Ill. Rev. Stat. c. 46, par. 1-3
Ill. Rev. Stat. c. 46, par. 10-9
Ill. Rev. Stat. c. 46, par. 22-17
Ill. Rev. Stat. c. 122, par. 9-1.1
Ill. Rev. Stat. c. 122, par. 9-2(d)
Ill. Rev. Stat. c. 122, par. 9-10

4:80 What are the election duties of the school board secretary?

Duties of the school board secretary, in the capacity of local election official, are set out in Article 9 of the School Code and various sections of the Election Code. Those duties include:

1) Publish a legal notice of the time and place for filing nominating papers for the biennial school board election (an optional duty that is not required);

2) Receive and file the nominating papers of school board candidates;

3) Conduct a lottery to establish the order of names on the ballot in the event of simultaneous filings;

4) Provide each candidate with a notice of obligations under the Illinois Campaign Financing Act;

5) If any formal objections to a candidate's nominating papers are filed, forward the objections to the chairman of the local electoral board;

6) Receive voter petitions and school board resolutions calling for propositions to be placed on the ballot at a regular election;

7) Certify to the Election Authority the ballot to be used at the school board election, including the names of candidates in the manner and order they are to appear on the ballot;

8) Certify to the Election Authority any public policy propositions that are to appear on the ballot, including the wording of the proposition as taken from the school board resolution or voter petition;

9) Following the election, forward precinct results received from the Election Authority to the school board, which will canvass results.

Ill. Rev. Stat. c. 46, par. 10-1 et seq.
Ill. Rev. Stat. c. 46, par. 17-22
Ill. Rev. Stat. c. 122, par. 9-1 et seq.

ELECTION OF SCHOOL BOARD MEMBERS

4:90   What effect does consolidation of school districts have on the election of board members?

When a school district will cease to exist by consolidation, annexation or otherwise within six months after a regular school board election date, no election of school board members is held on that date and any board member whose term would otherwise terminate is continued until the old district ceases to exist.

Under certain circumstances relating to the consolidation, creation and/or combination of school districts, a new school board may be elected at the same election as the district's structural change is being voted on.

Ill. Rev. Stat. c. 122, par. 10-10
Ill. Rev. Stat. c. 122, par. 11A-3
Ill. Rev. Stat. c. 122, par. 11A-5
Ill. Rev. Stat. c. 122, par. 11A-8
Ill. Rev. Stat. c. 122, par. 11B-3
Ill. Rev. Stat. c. 122, par. 11B-6
Ill. Rev. Stat. c. 122, par. 11D-2
Ill. Rev. Stat. c. 122, par. 11D-6

4:100 Is the procedure for running for the school board in a newly organized school district's first election the same as when running for an existing school board?

The procedures are the same except that in a newly created district's first election, the regional superintendent of schools, rather than the school board secretary, performs all of the duties of the local election official.

Ill. Rev. Stat. c. 122, par. 9-10

CANDIDATE NOMINATIONS

4:110 How does a school board candidate acquire a place on the ballot?

To be placed on the ballot, a candidate must file a nominating petition and a statement of candidacy with the secretary of the school board or such other person as the school board may designate. The statement of candidacy must include a receipt showing that a statement of economic interests has been timely filed with the county clerk.

Ill. Rev. Stat. c. 122, par. 10-10
Ill. Rev. Stat. c. 127, par. 601-101 et seq.

4:120 When may a school board candidate circulate a nominating petition to gather signatures?

A school board candidate may circulate a petition no earlier than 90 days preceding the last day for the filing of the petition (161 days before the election).

Ill. Rev. Stat. c. 46, par. 10-4

4:130 During what time frame must a school board candidate file his nominating petition?

A candidate for school board must file his nominating petition and statement of candidacy no more than 78, nor less than 71 days before the date of election.

Ill. Rev. Stat. c. 46, par. 10-6(1)
Ill. Rev. Stat. c. 122, par. 9-10

4:140 With whom does a school board candidate file a nominating petition?

A school board candidate must file a nominating petition with the secretary of the school board or a person designated by the board to receive nominating petitions. The school board secretary must, within seven days of filing the nominating petition or on the last day for filing the petition, whichever is earlier, acknowledge to the petitioner in writing the secretary's acceptance of the nominating petition.

If the school board secretary is an incumbent school board member seeking re-election, a disinterested person must witness the filing of his petition.

Ill. Rev. Stat. c. 122, par. 9-10

4:150 What information is required on a petition of candidacy for school board?

A petition must include:

1) a statement of candidacy;

2) the name of the school district;

3) the name and place of residence of the candidate with specified street and number;

4) whether the candidate is seeking a full term or is seeking to fill a partial term caused by a board vacancy;

5) the date of the election;

6) the number of voter signatures required;

7) the notarized signature of the petition circulator;

8) a receipt from the county clerk showing the candidate has timely filed a statement of economic interests.

School board nominating petitions must be on sheets of uniform size, and must contain the circulator's affidavit and a statement of an individual's candidacy.

Ill. Rev. Stat. c. 46, par. 10-5

Ill. Rev. Stat. c. 122, par. 9-10

Klingelmueller v. Haas, 111 Ill.App.3d 88, 443 N.E.2d 782, 66 Ill.Dec. 856 (3rd Dist. 1982)

4:160 How many signatures are required on a school board candidate nominating petition?

Nominating petitions for board of education candidates must be signed by at least 50 registered voters who reside in the school district or 10 percent of the registered voters who reside in the school district, whichever is less. Nominating petitions for school directors must be signed by at least 25 registered voters who reside in the school district or 5 percent of the voters who reside in the school district, whichever is less.

Ill. Rev. Stat. c. 122, par. 9-10

4:170 Must a candidate for school board declare a political party affiliation?

School elections are nonpartisan. School board candidates are not required to declare political party affiliation.

Ill. Rev. Stat. c. 46, par. 2A-1.1(c)

4:180 May a school board candidate be required to sign a loyalty oath in order to file a nominating petition?

While a signed loyalty oath is required by the Election Code for filing a school board candidate's nominating petition, this requirement is unconstitutional and is, therefore, unenforceable. A school board candidate's nominating petition may not be refused for a candidate's failure or refusal to sign a loyalty oath.

Communist Party of Illinois v. Ogilvie, 357 F.Supp. 105 (N.D. Ill. 1972)

CANDIDATE WITHDRAWAL

4:190 May a school board candidate run for both a full term and a partial term created by a board vacancy?

No. A candidate for either a board of education or board of school directors who has filed nominating petitions for both a full term and a partial term at the same election must withdraw one petition or the other, in writing, within five business days following the last day for filing petitions.

Ill. Rev. Stat. c. 46, par. 10-7
Ill. Rev. Stat. c. 122, par. 9-10

4:200 How may a school board candidate withdraw his candidacy and have his name removed from the ballot?

A candidate may withdraw by filing a written request signed by the candidate and acknowledged before an officer qualified to take acknowledgement of deeds not later than the date for certification of candidates for the ballot. Filing is to bè made at the principal office of the school district.

Ill. Rev. Stat. c. 46, par. 10-7

OBJECTIONS TO NOMINATING PETITIONS

4:210 Who determines whether a candidate's nominating papers meet legal requirements?

The local election official who receives and files nominating papers makes an initial determination as to whether the papers are in apparent conformity with the law. The school board secretary shall receive and file only those petitions which include a statement of candidacy, the required number of voter signatures, the notarized signature of the petition circulator and a receipt from the county clerk showing that the candidate has filed a statement of economic interests on or before the last day file.

Ill. Rev. Stat. c. 122, par. 9-10

4:220 Is it possible to challenge a school board candidate's nominating petitions on the grounds that signatures are invalid or were improperly gathered or that other information contained in the petition is incorrect?

The local election official has no authority to question the accuracy or truthfulness of information contained in a nominating petition. However, candidate nominating petitions are open to public inspection and any legal voter of the district may file a written objection with the board secretary within five days after the last day for filing nominating petitions. The objector's petition must state fully the nature of the objection, the interest of the objector and the relief requested.

Ill. Rev. Stat. c. 46, par. 10-7
Ill. Rev. Stat. c. 46, par. 10-8

4:230 Who hears objections to school board candidate nominating petitions?

The Education Officers Electoral Board (EOEB) hears challenges to school board candidate nominating petitions. The EOEB is composed of the president of the school board (who is designated as chairperson), the school board secretary, and the school board member with the longest continuous service. The composition of the EOEB is altered to include the school board member with the second longest continuous service when one of the persons who would otherwise sit on the EOEB is the candidate whose nominating petition is being challenged.

Ill. Rev. Stat. c. 46, par. 10-9

4:240 What procedures are used by the Education Officers Electoral Board for hearing objections to nominating petitions?

When a school board secretary receives an objection to a nominating petition, the secretary must send a copy of the objection to the candidate. The original objection is sent to the chairperson of the Education Officers Electoral Board (EOEB) by registered mail, noting the day and hour the objector's petition was received.

The chairperson of the EOEB must call a meeting of the EOEB to hold a hearing on the objector's petition. The hearing must be held not less than three nor more than five days after the chairperson receives the secretary's notice of objection. A hearing notice must be sent to the objector and to the candidate(s) named in the objection by registered mail and the chairperson of the EOEB must cause the sheriff to serve the parties with notice.

Following a hearing to consider the objection, the EOEB must render a timely decision in writing. The decision of the Education Officers Electoral Board is subject to appeal to the circuit court within ten days of the EOEB's decision. If no court challenge is filed within the ten-day period, the EOEB must send a copy of its decision to the school board secretary by registered or certified mail.

Ill. Rev. Stat., c. 46, par. 10-8 et seq.

Schumann v. Kumarich, 102 Ill.App.3d 454, 430 N.E.2d 99, 58 Ill.Dec. 157 (1st Dist. 1981)

Gilbert v. Municipal Officers' Electoral Board of Deerfield, 97 Ill.App.3d 847, 423 N.E.2d 952, 53 Ill.Dec. 283 (2nd Dist. 1981)

Illinois ex rel. Talerico v. Lata, 96 Ill.App.2d 34, 238 N.E.2d 217 (1st Dist. 1968)

CERTIFICATION OF CANDIDATES

4:250 When does the board secretary certify school board candidates to the election authority?

The board secretary must certify candidates to the election authority not less than 61 days before the election, directing the election authority to place the names of candidates on the official ballot in the same manner as presented on the certification.

Ill. Rev. Stat. c. 46, par. 10-15

4:260 What determines the format of the school board election ballot?

Ballots for school board elections are prescribed in the School Code, which provides for differing formats that conform to differing residential restrictions on school board membership. Ballot formats include those for boards with members elected entirely at large, as well as for those with restrictions on the number of members that may be elected from less populous congressional townships and unincorporated areas.

Ill. Rev. Stat. c. 122, par. 9-12 et seq.
Ill. Rev. Stat. c. 122, par. 9-22
Ill. Rev. Stat. c. 122, par. 11A-8
Ill. Rev. Stat. c. 122, par. 11B-7
Ill. Rev. Stat. c. 122, par. 12-2

4:270 What determines the order of names on a school board election ballot?

Candidates' names appear on the ballot in the order filed with the school board secretary. The secretary must conduct a lottery to establish the order of candidates' names in the event of simultaneous filings, which includes only those petitions filed by persons standing in line at the normal opening hour of the office on the first day for filing and those petitions received in the first mail delivery of the day.

Where residency restrictions call for a ballot format that groups candidates by area of residence, the order in which petitions are filed or selected by lottery establishes the order in which candidates groupings appear on the ballot.

Ill. Rev. Stat. c. 122, par. 9-11.1 et seq.

4:275 Is the school board secretary required to use any particular lottery procedure in determining the order of candidates' names in the event of simultaneous filings?

By law the lottery must be conducted within nine days after the last day for filing nominating petitions and must be open to the public. The board secretary must give written notice to the candidates who filed simultaneously no later than seven days before the lottery. Notice of the lottery also must go to any citizen or organization entitled to have pollwatchers on the day of the election. A notice giving the time and place of the lottery must be posted at the entrance of the board secretary's office.

Although the School Code is silent on the matter of lottery procedure, the Election Code requires other election officials to use a lottery approved by the State Board of Elections. Board of

Election Rule 201.40 describes an approved lottery procedure which, summarized briefly, provides the following:

a) The names of all candidates who filed simultaneously for the same office shall be listed alphabetically and shall be numbered consecutively commencing with the number one, which is assigned to the candidate whose name is listed first on the alphabetic list. For example, if five candidates by the names of Downs, Brown, Edwards, Cook and Adams have filed simultaneously, they will be arranged alphabetically and assigned the numbers as follows: Adams, one; Brown, two; Cook, three; Downs, four; and Edwards, five.

b) All ties will be broken by a single drawing. A number is placed in a container representing each number assigned to each candidate as provided for above. For example, if there are five candidates involved in the lottery, the numbers one through five are placed in a container.

c) Numbers in the container are thoroughly shaken and mixed and then withdrawn one at a time. The candidate whose position on the alphabetical list corresponds to the first number drawn is certified ahead of the other candidates. The candidate whose position on the list corresponds to the second number drawn is certified second, and so on.

A separate but identical procedure is used in the event of simultaneous filings for a separate election to fill an unexpired term.

Ill. Rev. Stat. c. 46, par. 10-6.2
Ill. Rev. Stat. c. 122, par. 9-11.1
State Board of Elections Rule 201.40

4:280   Are write-in candidates permitted at a school board election?

Voters may write in and cast votes for persons not listed on the ballot. However, write-in votes shall not be counted unless the candidate has filed with the Election Authority a declaration of intent to run as a write-in candidate no later than 5:00 p.m. on the Friday immediately preceding the election.

If any candidate whose name appears on the ballot for the same office should die after the Friday deadline, the deadline for filing an intent to run as a write-in candidate is extended to 12:00 noon on Monday immediately preceding the election.

Ill. Rev. Stat. c. 46, par. 17-16.1
Ill. Rev. Stat. c. 46, par. 18-9.1

PUBLIC POLICY ELECTIONS

4:290 How does a school board get a public policy issue on the ballot?

A school board must pass a proper resolution at an official board meeting that a question be submitted to the voters in a referendum at a regularly scheduled election. The resolution must be adopted at least 65 days prior to the date of the regularly scheduled election. The resolution must state the regular election at which the referendum will be submitted to the voters.

The school board secretary is responsible for certifying the question to be submitted at the referendum to the county clerk at least 61 days before the election. This certification must include the form of the referendum question, the date the school board adopted the resolution, and a certified copy of the resolution passed by the school board.

Ill. Rev. Stat. c. 46, par. 28-1 et seq.

4:300 How many separate propositions may a school board have placed on the ballot at any one election?

Not more than three public policy questions other than back door referenda may be submitted to referendum at the same election.

Ill. Rev. Stat. c. 46, par. 28-1

4:310 How are voter-initiated petitions, including backdoor referenda and advisory referenda, placed on the ballot?

Except under certain conditions specified in statute, a voter-initiated petition must be filed with the school board secretary at least 78 days before the regularly scheduled election. The board secretary must certify the question to be placed on the

ballot to the county clerk at least 61 days prior to the regularly
scheduled election.

Ill. Rev. Stat. c. 46, par. 28-2
Ill. Rev. Stat. c. 46, par. 28-5
Ayers v. Martin, __ Ill.App.3d __, __ N.E.2d __, __ L.Ed. __, Docket
No. 4-91-0733 (4th Dist. December 30, 1991)

4:313 What information must be provided in the publication of a notice of a resolution which may be subject to backdoor referendum?

The publication of the resolution must include a notice of the
specific number of voters required to sign a petition requesting
that the public question be submitted to the voters, the time
within which the petition must be filed, and the date of the
prospective referendum.

Ill. Rev. Stat. c. 46, par. 28-2

4:315 Is it possible to challenge a voter-initiated petition on the grounds that signatures are invalid or were improperly gathered or that other information contained in the petition is incorrect?

The local election official has no authority to question the
accuracy or truthfulness of information contained in a voter-initiated petition.

The school board lacks standing to challenge the accuracy or
truthfulness of information contained in a voter-initiated petition. However, such petitions are open to public inspection and
any legal voter of the district may file a written objection with
the board secretary within five days after the last day for filing
voter-initiated petitions. The objector's petition must state fully
the nature of the objection, the interest of the objector and the
relief requested. Such objections frequently challenge whether
the petitions contain the required number of valid signatures by
identifying some signatures as forgeries, those of non-residents,
unregistered voters, or identify technical errors in the execution
of the petitions.

The objections are heard and ruled upon by the Education Officers Electoral Board in generally the same manner as objections to candidate nominating petitions.

Ill. Rev. Stat. c. 46, par. 10-8 et seq.
Ill. Rev. Stat. c. 46, par. 28-3

4:320 What is an emergency referendum?

An "emergency referendum" is a referendum conducted on other than a regularly scheduled election date. Whenever any public question is to be submitted pursuant to law, whether by action of the governing body of a school district, by petition, or by court order, the governing body of the school district whose powers or duties are directly affected by the result of the vote on the public question may petition the circuit court for an order declaring such proposition to be an emergency and fixing a date other than a regularly scheduled election date on which a special referendum election shall be held for the submission of the public question.

The petition shall set forth the public question and the action taken which requires the submission of the question, the next regularly scheduled election at which the proposition could otherwise be placed on the ballot, the estimated costs of conducting a separate special election, and the reasons why an emergency exists to justify such special election prior to the next ensuing regular election. The petition must be approved by a majority of the members of the school board.

The court shall conduct a hearing on the petition. Any resident of the area in which the referendum is to be conducted may oppose the petition. The court may approve the petition for an emergency referendum only upon a finding, supported by the evidence, that the referendum is necessitated by an imminent need for approval of additional authority in order to maintain the operations or facilities of the school district and that such need is due to circumstances beyond the control of the governing body.

Ill. Rev. Stat. c. 46, par. 2A-1.4

4:330 What information must be provided on the ballot and in a notice of election increasing a district's tax rate?

In addition to the notice requirements of the general election law, whenever a proposition to increase a school tax rate is submitted to be voted upon by the voters of any district, the notice of such election must include an estimate of the approximate amount of taxes extendible under the maximum rate then in force and an estimate of the approximate amount of taxes extendible under the proposed increased rate, such amounts being computed upon the last known full, fair cash value; provided that any error, miscalculation or inaccuracy in computing the amounts does not invalidate or affect the validity of any rate so increased.

The school board must make such estimate, and the secretary must certify such amount to the election authority as part of the certification of the proposition as required by the general election law. The estimate must appear on the ballot on which the proposition is printed but must not appear as a part of the proposition.

In addition, where the proposition is to authorize or increase a tax rate, the notice of election and the form of ballot must include:

1) the geographic or other common name of the school district by which that is commonly known and referred to, as well as the number of the district;

2) the maximum rate at which such tax may be levied if the proposition is approved;

3) the total dollar amount of the most recently approved annual budget of the district, what the total dollar amount of that budget would be if increased by the amount of additional tax which may be levied if the proposition is approved, and what the percentage increase in that annual budget would be if the total dollar amount were increased by that amount of additional tax; and

4) if the proposition is to increase the annual rate of an existing tax levied by the district, then the annual rate at which the tax is currently levied and the percentage of increase between the maximum rate at which such tax may be levied if the

proposition is approved and the annual rate at which such tax currently is levied.

Ill. Rev. Stat. c. 122, par. 9-11
Ill. Rev. Stat. c. 122, par. 17-3.4

ADVOCACY AND ELECTIONEERING

4:340 May a school board use school district funds to inform voters of its reason for seeking a tax rate increase, bond issue, or other public policy question?

The school board has an obligation to present voters with the facts so they might arrive at informed judgments. On the other hand, public funds belong to all the electorate—opponents as well as proponents—and cannot be used to represent just one side or to finance a campaign to influence the outcome of the referendum.

Public funds must not be used to urge any elector to vote for or against any candidate or proposition or be appropriated for political campaign purposes. This does not prohibit the use of public funds for dissemination of factual information relative to any proposition appearing on an election ballot.

Ill. Rev. Stat. c. 46, par. 101 et seq.
Citizens to Protect Public Funds v. Board of Education of Parsippany-Troy Hills, 13 N.J. 172 (1953)
Elsenau v. City of Chicago, 334 Ill. 78, 165 N.E. 129 (1929)

4:350 May a school board use district funds to disseminate printed information regarding a public policy question on the ballot?

Yes, so long as the printed information presents the facts, both pro and con, and does not urge voters to vote for or against the issue.

Ill. Rev. Stat. c. 46, par. 101 et seq.
Citizens to Protect Public Funds v. Board of Education of Parsippany-Troy Hills, 13 N.J. 172 (1953)
Elsenau v. City of Chicago, 334 Ill. 78, 165 N.E. 129 (1929)

4:360 May supporters of a school board referendum urge voters to support the ballot proposition?

Yes, provided that:

1) no public funds are used by supporters of such an effort;

2) any individual or organization which accepts or expends $1,000 or more in supporting or opposing a school referendum organizes as a "Local Political Committee" under the Election Code;

3) the school board and school employees, in their official capacities, treat proponents and opponents with an equal hand.

Ill. Rev. Stat. c. 46, par. 9-1 et seq.

Ill. Rev. Stat. c. 46, par. 101 et seq.

Citizens to Protect Public Funds v. Board of Education of Parsippany-Troy Hills, 13 N.J. 172 (1953)

Elsenau v. City of Chicago, 334 Ill. 78, 165 N.E. 129 (1929)

4:370 What is required of a local political committee?

Such a committee must file a statement of organization and must report contributions and expenditures. Forms are obtained from and filed with the County Clerk. Obligations are set forth in Manual of Instructions, Illinois Campaign Financing Act, issued by the State Board of Elections.

Ill. Rev. Stat. c. 46, par. 9-1 et seq.

4:380 What legal requirements apply to the literature of a political committee?

The Election Code requires that any person or group that publishes and distributes literature related to a referendum must be clearly identified on that literature. The state supreme court has found this requirement a violation of constitutional free speech rights.

Because a school board may not use public funds to pay for political literature, of course, a board is not covered by statutes governing publication of political literature. However, any literature issued by the board should be clearly identified as to source and purpose. To avoid allegations of illegality, it is in the school district's interests if it is made clear that the political literature of a citizens committee was not financed with public funds.

Ill. Rev. Stat. c. 46, par. 29-14
Illinois v. White, 116 Ill.2d 171, 506 N.E.2d 1284, 107 Ill.Dec. 229 (1987)

4:385 May a candidate for public office distribute anonymous campaign literature?

Campaign literature need not contain the name and address of the person who published and distributed it.
Illinois v. White, 116 Ill.2d 171, 506 N.E.2d 1284, 107 Ill.Dec. 229 (1987)

4:390 May a local political committee of citizens assign pollwatchers to polling places on election day?

Yes, each organization of proponents and opponents of a ballot proposition which has registered with the Election Authority at least 40 days before the election is entitled to have one pollwatcher per precinct. Each pollwatcher must be registered to vote from a residence in the county where the proposition is being voted on and must have obtained necessary credentials from the Election Authority. Credentials shall be available for distribution at least two weeks before the election.

Ill. Rev. Stat. c. 46, par. 17-23

DETERMINING ELECTION RESULTS

4:400 How does a school board canvass election votes?

The county clerk must send the school board secretary an original sealed tally sheet and certificate of result for each school district voting precinct. The school board secretary must, within 24 hours, give these documents to the school board which, acting as a whole, functions as a canvassing board. The school board must canvass the returns within seven days of the election. The school board thereafter transmits a signed copy or original duplicate of its canvass to the county clerk and to the Illinois State Board of Elections.

Ill. Rev. Stat. c. 46, par. 17-22
Ill. Rev. Stat. c. 46, par. 22-17 et seq.

4:405 Where candidates for the school board must be grouped into residential areas, may the canvassing school board select winners in a manner that ensures all seats are filled?

No. With just one exception, the canvassing school board must seat candidates in order from the highest vote getter on the ballot to the lowest vote getter. Where seating a high vote getter would exceed the maximum number of board members who may be elected from a particular geographic area, the board must skip that candidate and go to the next highest vote getter. This sequence of seating winners should be followed, for example, even where an unexpired term on the ballot combines with residential groupings and the order of vote totals to force the board to leave a seat unfilled. Such an unfilled seat must then be filled by appointment until the next school board election.

4:410 What steps must be taken by a successful write-in candidate and by the canvassing school board prior to seating a winning write-in candidate?

Election statutes are silent with respect to the seating of successful write-in candidates in a school board election. However:

1) Every school board member must have a statement of economic interests on file with the county clerk. Therefore, as soon as possible after the canvass, a successful write-in candidate should file a statement of economic interests with the county clerk.

2) Statutes governing the seating of successful write-in candidates at primary and consolidated elections call for the filing of a statement of candidacy. Because a canvassing school board has no practical means of determining whether the write-in candidate meets legal qualifications, the board might reasonably require that a statement of candidacy and a receipt from the county clerk for the economic interests statement be filed with the secretary before seating a successful write-in candidate. The

statement of candidacy provides a notarized affirmation that legal qualifications are met.

Ill. Rev. Stat. c. 46, par. 7-60 et seq.
Ill. Rev. Stat. c. 127, par. 604A-101 et seq.

4:415 What steps must be taken to determine the winner in the event of a tie vote among two or more school board candidates?

The canvassing board has the duty of breaking the tie in order to declare a winner. However, the law is unclear as to how such ties are to be broken. Presumably any lottery method would be acceptable if it is a fair and impartial method of random selection. The lottery prescribed by the State Board of Elections for determining ballot order of names in the event of simultaneous filings would be such a method.

Ill. Rev. Stat. c. 46, par. 10-6.2
Ill. Rev. Stat. c. 46, par. 22-17 et seq.
Ill. Rev. Stat. c. 122, par. 9-11.1
State Board of Elections Rule 201.40

4:420 On what bases are school board elections invalidated?

The mandatory requirements of the election laws must be met or an election will be set aside. Whether a provision of election law is mandatory or not is subject to the following analysis:

1) Does the statutory scheme expressly or impliedly provide that the failure to follow the provision will render an election void?

2) Does the failure interfere with the result of the election?

3) Was any person legally eligible to vote not permitted to vote?

4) Was any person voting not a resident of the territory sought to be organized?

5) Were the polling places chosen for any improper motive?

6) Was there fraud in, or resulting from, the selection of the polling places?

Jones v. Municipal Officers Electoral Board, 122 Ill.App.3d 926, 446 N.E.2d 173, 61 Ill.Dec. 684 (1st Dist. 1983).

Madden v. Schumann, 105 Ill.App.3d 900, 435 N.E.2d 173, 61 Ill.Dec. 684 (1st Dist. 1982)

Schumann v. Kumarich, 102 Ill.App.3d 454, 430 N.E.2d 99, 58 Ill.Dec. 157 (1st Dist. 1981)

Havens v. Miller, 102 Ill.App.3d 558, 429 N.E.2d 1292, 57 Ill.Dec. 929 (1st Dist. 1981)

Goble v. Board of Education of Iuka Community Consolidated School District No. 7, Marion County, 83 Ill.App.3d 284, 404 N.E.2d 343, 38 Ill.Dec. 919 (5th Dist. 1980)

Menssen v. Eureka Unit District No. 140, 70 Ill.App.3d 9, 388 N.E.2d 273, 26 Ill.Dec. 649 (4th Dist. 1979)

Gibson v. Kankakee School District No. 111, 34 Ill.App.3d 948, 341 N.E.2d 447 (3rd Dist. 1975)

Gann v. Harrisburg Community Unit School District, 73 Ill.App.2d 103, 218 N.E.2d 833 (5th Dist. 1966)

VOTING

4:500 Who is eligible to vote in elections of school board members and on public policy issues placed on the ballot by a school board?

To vote in a school board election or public policy referendum presented by a school board, an individual must be registered to vote from a residence within the boundaries of the school district.

In school board elections where board membership is at-large, the voter may vote for as many seats as are up for election. The same is true where the number of board members elected from particular townships or incorporated areas is regulated by law. In the latter case, a voter may vote for more candidates than may be lawfully elected from a particular geographic area.

In a school district where board members are elected from board member districts, the school district is divided into seven voting districts of substantially equal population. Voters living within each voting district elect one school board member from among candidates running from residences within that voting district.

Ill. Rev. Stat. c. 46, par. 6-27
Ill. Rev. Stat. c. 122, par. 9-12 et seq.
Ill. Rev. Stat. c. 122, par. 9-22
Ill. Rev. Stat. c. 122, par. 11A-8
Ill. Rev. Stat. c. 122, par. 11B-7
Ill. Rev. Stat. c. 122, par. 12-2

5: SCHOOL BOARD OFFICERS

ELECTED OFFICERS

5:10   What officers must a school board elect?

The School Code requires boards of school directors to elect a president and a clerk. Boards of education must elect a president, vice president and a secretary. The secretary need not be a member of the school board, but all other board officers must be members.

No other officers are required by the School Code, but additional offices may be created by vote of the school board.

Ill. Rev. Stat. c. 122, par. 10-5
Ill. Rev. Stat. c. 122, par. 10-13 et seq.

5:20   May school board officers be elected by secret ballot?

The Open Meetings Act requires the election of school board officers by open vote at a public meeting. The voting may not be done by use of any form of secret ballot.

Ill. Rev. Stat. c. 102, par. 41
Illinois ex rel. Hopf v. Barger, 30 Ill.App.3d 525, 332 N.E.2d 649 (2nd Dist. 1975)

5:30   For how long are school board officers elected?

Officers of boards of education serve two-year terms unless the school board adopts a resolution and policy fixing the term at one year. Illinois law does not specify a term of office for officers of boards of directors. In such districts, officers' terms may be fixed by board resolution.

Ill. Rev. Stat. c. 122, par. 10-5
Ill. Rev. Stat. c. 122, par. 10-13 et seq.

5:40   Who serves as the president of the school board in the absence of the elected president?

The vice-president of the school board performs the duties of the president if there is a vacancy in the office or in the president's absence or inability to act.

Ill. Rev. Stat. c. 122, par. 10-13 et seq.

5:50   May school board officers be paid for their services?

Only the secretary of a board of education may be compensated. Other officers of the board may not be paid for their services.

Ill. Rev. Stat. c. 122, par. 10-14

5:60   Are there limitations on compensation of the board secretary?

The secretary of the board of education, whether a member of the board of education or not, may be paid. The rate of pay must be set by the board of education before the secretary is elected.

If the secretary is a member of the board, the rate of pay may not exceed the statutory limit set forth in the School Code. There is no statutory limit on the compensation for a secretary who is not a member of the board.

Ill. Rev. Stat. c. 122, par. 10-14

5:70   Who serves as board secretary or clerk in the absence of the elected secretary or clerk?

If a clerk or secretary is absent from a board meeting or refuses to perform the duties of the office, a secretary or clerk pro tempore must be appointed by the remaining board members.

Ill. Rev. Stat. c. 122, par. 10-14

5:75   May a school board officer be removed from office for failure to attend meetings?

No. However, the statutes which provide for the election of school board officers also allow the appointment of pro tempore officers in the absence, inability to act, or incapacity of the elected officer.

Ill. Rev. Stat. c. 122, par. 10-13 et seq.

TREASURERS

5:80   What is a school treasurer?

The school treasurer is the only lawful custodian of school funds, is responsible for all receipts, disbursements and investments of school funds, and pays orders issued by the school board.

Ill. Rev. Stat. c. 122, par. 8-1 et seq.

5:90   How is a school treasurer elected or appointed?

In Class I county school units (all counties other than Cook), each school board either:

1) elects one of its members to serve as treasurer without salary for a period of one year, or

2) appoints a non-member as treasurer and fixes compensation. The appointed treasurer (non-member of the board) serves at the pleasure of the board.

In Class II county school units (Cook County), the trustees of schools appoint a township treasurer unless the Class II county school unit is no longer subject to the the jurisdiction and authority of the trustees of schools as may occur in a number of different ways pursuant to a complicated statutory scheme.

Ill. Rev. Stat. c. 122, par. 5-1
Ill. Rev. Stat. c. 122, par. 8-1 et seq.

5:100   May the county treasurer be designated the treasurer of a school district?

Yes.

Ill. Const. art. VII, sec. 4(e)

5:110   How is a vacancy in the office of school treasurer filled?

In Class I county school units and Class II county school units no longer within the jurisdiction of the trustees of schools and township treasurer, when a vacancy occurs in the office of school treasurer by death, resignation, or removal from office, the school board appoints a new treasurer.

In Class II county school units still within the jurisdiction of the trustees of schools, the trustees of schools elect a treasurer to fill the unexpired term.

Ill. Rev. Stat. c. 122, par. 8-1

5:120   How is the school treasurer paid?

In Class I county school units, a school board may elect one of its members as school treasurer to serve without compensation or appoint a non-member and fix compensation.

In Class II county school units no longer within the jurisdiction of the trustees of schools and township treasurer, the person appointed treasurer by the school board must be a resident of the school district and not a member of the school board or superintendent of schools. The school board fixes compensation.

In Class II county school units still within the jurisdiction of the trustees of schools, the school treasurer cannot be a trustee or school board member and is compensated.

Compensation for a school treasurer must be fixed prior to the appointment of the treasurer and may not be decreased during the treasurer's term of office.

Ill. Rev. Stat. c. 122, par. 5-1
Ill. Rev. Stat. c. 122, par. 8-1
Ill. Rev. Stat. c. 122, par. 8-3

5:130   Who is responsible for checking a school treasurer's books?

The regional superintendent of schools is required to examine all books, accounts, and vouchers of every school treasurer in the region at least once each year. If any irregularities are found, the regional superintendent is required to report the irregularities at once in writing to the trustees of Class II county school units or to the respective school boards of those school districts which form a part of a Class II county school unit but which are not subject to the jurisdiction of the trustees of schools of any township in which any such district is located or to the respective school boards of districts in Class I county school units. The trustees or the school board is required to take immediate action as the case demands.

The regional superintendent is also required to examine all notes, bonds, mortgages, and other evidence of indebtedness which the township or school treasurer holds officially, and if any of the papers are found not to be in proper order or the securities are insufficient, the regional superintendent is required to report the problem in writing to the board of trustees.

Ill. Rev. Stat. c. 122, par. 3-14.11 et seq.

5:140 When may a school treasurer be removed from office?

In Class I county school units (all counties except Cook) and in Class II county school units (Cook County) which are no longer subject to the jurisdiction of the trustees of schools and township treasurer, an appointed school treasurer serves at the pleasure of the school board and may be removed by the board at any time for cause. The School Code does not provide a method to remove an elected school treasurer from office during the treasurer's one-year term.

In Class II county school units still within the jurisdiction of the trustees of schools, the trustees of schools may remove a school treasurer from office for cause.

Ill. Rev. Stat. c. 122, par. 8-1
Hertel v. Boismenue, 229 Ill. 474, 82 N.E. 298 (1907)

6: SCHOOL BOARD MEETINGS

PUBLIC MEETINGS

6:10 What is a meeting under Illinois law?

The Open Meetings Act defines a meeting as any gathering of a majority of a quorum of the members of a public body held for the purposes of discussing public business.

The definition of "public body" includes committees and subcommittees of the school board, as well as the school board itself.

The provisions of the Open Meetings Act do not apply to collective bargaining negotiations or grievance arbitrations.

Ill. Rev. Stat. c. 48, par. 1718

Ill. Rev. Stat. c. 102, par. 41.02

Nabhani v. Coglianese, 552 F.Supp. 657 (N.D. Ill. 1983)

Illinois ex rel. Difanis v. Barr, 83 Ill.2d 191, 414 N.E.2d 731, 46 Ill.Dec. 678 (4th Dist. 1980)

Illinois ex rel. Cooper v. Carlson, 28 Ill.App.3d 569, 328 N.E.2d 675 (2nd Dist. 1975)

6:15 Must a school board comply with the Open Meetings Act?

School boards are governed by the notice and conduct of meeting provisions of the Open Meetings Act.

Ill. Rev. Stat. c. 102, par. 41 et seq.

Ill. Rev. Stat. c. 122, par. 10-6

Ill. Rev. Stat. c. 122, par. 10-16

6:20 Are school board meetings open to the public?

A school board meeting must be open to the public unless:

1) the purpose of the meeting is collective bargaining negotiations or grievance arbitration; or

2) the school board excludes the public by voting to convene in closed session for one or any combination of the permissible reasons for closed session.

Ill. Rev. Stat. c. 48, par. 1718

Ill. Rev. Stat. c. 102, par. 42 et seq.

Gosnell v. Hogan, 179 Ill.App.3d 161, 534 N.E.2d 434, 128 Ill.Dec. 252 (5th Dist. 1989), appeal den. 126 Ill.2d 558, 541 N.E.2d 1106, 133 Ill.Dec. 668

6:30 May school boards or school board members hold unofficial meetings to discuss school business?

No. It is public policy in Illinois that public business is to be conducted in public, and both the actions and deliberations of public bodies are to be conducted in public. The conduct of school business is limited to official meetings of the school board.

A discussion of school business by a majority of a quorum—three members of a seven-member school board—would be a violation of the Open Meeting Act.

Ill. Rev. Stat. c. 102, par. 41 et seq.

Ill. Rev. Stat. c. 122, par. 10-6

Ill. Rev. Stat. c. 122, par. 10-16

Illinois News Broadcasters Association v. City of Springfield, 22 Ill.App.3d 226, 317 N.E.2d 288 (4th Dist. 1974)

6:35 Does the Open Meetings Act apply to school board committee meetings?

The Open Meetings Act applies to all school board committees. Committees composed of faculty or administration are not school board committees and, therefore, are not subject to the Open Meetings Act.

Ill. Rev. Stat. c. 48, par. 1718

Ill. Rev. Stat. c. 102, par. 41.02

Illinois ex rel. Difanis v. Barr, 83 Ill.2d 191, 414 N.E.2d 731, 46 Ill.Dec. 678 (1980)

Rockford Newspapers, Inc. v. Northern Illinois Council on Alcoholism and Drug Dependence, 64 Ill.App.3d 94, 380 N.E.2d 1192, 21 Ill.Dec. 16 (2nd Dist. 1978)

Pope v. Parkinson, 48 Ill.App.3d 797, 363 N.E.2d 438, 6 Ill.Dec. 756 (4th Dist. 1977)

6:40   Are school staff meetings subject to the Open Meetings Act?

Staff meetings involving teachers, administrators or other employees are not subject to the Open Meetings Act even when such meetings are held to prepare presentations for the school board.

Illinois ex rel. Cooper v. Carlson, 28 Ill.App.3d 569, 328 N.E.2d 675 (2nd Dist. 1975)

6:50   May citizens make audio or video tape recordings of school board meetings?

Citizens may tape, film, or use other means of recording the activities at open school board meetings. School boards may prescribe reasonable rules to govern the making of such recordings.

Ill. Rev. Stat. c. 102, par. 42-05

6:60   What is the penalty for violation of the Open Meetings Act?

Any person, including the state's attorney of the county in which the school district is located, may bring a civil action in circuit court alleging a violation of the Open Meetings Act. Circuit courts are authorized to award attorney fees and costs to a successful complainant. The court may provide such other relief as it may deem appropriate. The school board may be ordered to open a future meeting or meetings to the public or to make available to the public all or parts of the minutes of the improperly closed session.

The court has the power to declare null and void any final action taken at an illegal meeting, and may enjoin the school board from future violations of the Open Meetings Act.

Ill. Rev. Stat. c. 102, par. 43

Bromberek School District No. 65 v. Sanders, 174 Ill.App.3d 301, 508 N.E.2d 1336, 124 Ill.Dec. 228 (1st Dist. 1988) appeal den. 124 Ill.2d 553, 535 N.E.2d 912, 124 Ill.Dec. 147

6:70   Are individuals subject to criminal charges for Open Meetings Act violations?

Violation of the Open Meetings Act by an individual is a Class C misdemeanor, punishable by a fine of up to $500 and/or 30 days in jail.

Ill. Rev. Stat. c. 102, par. 43

CALLING MEETINGS

6:80   When must a newly-constituted board of education first meet?

Within seven days after each election of members, a school board must organize by electing its officers and fixing a time and place for regular meetings.

Ill. Rev. Stat. c. 122, par. 10-16

6:90   When may a school board hold meetings?

Meetings of school boards must be public and held at times and places convenient to the public.

A school board may hold regular meetings at such times as it designates in the annual notice of its regular meetings. Special meetings may be called by the president or any three members of a board of education or any two members of a board of school directors.

Public notice of all meetings must be given and no official business may be transacted except when a quorum of members is present at a regular or a special meeting.

For a three-member board of directors, two members constitute a quorum. For a seven-member board, a quorum consists of four members.

Meetings subject to the Open Meetings Act may not be held on legal holidays except when a regular meeting date falls on a legal holiday.

Ill. Rev. Stat. c. 102, par. 42-01 et seq.
Ill. Rev. Stat. c. 122, par. 10-16

6:100 How must a school board give notice of its regular meetings?

A school board is required to give notice of all regular meetings of the board. At the beginning of each calendar or fiscal year, the school board must give public notice of the schedule of all its regular meetings for the year. The schedule must state the times, dates, and places of the meetings and must be posted at the principal office of the district, or, if there is no such office, at the building in which the meeting is to be held.

Ill. Rev. Stat. c. 102, par. 42.02 et seq.
Ill. Rev. Stat. c. 122, par. 10-16
Argo High School Council of Local 571, I.F.T., A.F.T.,
A.F.L.-C.I.O. v. Argo Community High School District 217, 163
Ill.App.3d 578, 516 N.E.2d 834, 114 Ill.Dec. 679 (1st Dist. 1987)

6:110 How does a school board change its schedule of regular meeting dates?

A school board may change the dates of its regularly scheduled meetings by giving 10 days notice in a manner set forth by statute.

Ill. Rev. Stat. c. 102, par. 42.02
Ill. Rev. Stat. c. 102, par. 42.03
Argo High School Council of Local 571, I.F.T., A.F.T.,
A.F.L.-C.I.O. v. Argo Community High School District 217, 163
Ill.App.3d 578, 516 N.E.2d 834, 114 Ill.Dec. 679 (1st Dist. 1987)

6:120 How does a school board call a special meeting?

Special meetings may be called by the president or by any three members of a board of education or any two members of a board of school directors.

Board members must be given notice of special meetings in writing, stating the time, place, and purpose of the meeting. The notice may be served by mail 48 hours before the meeting or by personal service 24 hours before the meeting.

Public notice at least 24 hours in advance of special meetings is required. Notice also must be given to any news medium that has provided necessary information in the same manner as is given to members of the board.

Special meeting notices must include an agenda.

Ill. Rev. Stat. c. 102, par. 42.02

Ill. Rev. Stat. c. 122, par. 10-6

Ill. Rev. Stat. c. 122, par. 10-16

Gosnell v. Hogan, 179 Ill.App.3d 161, 534 N.E.2d 434, 128 Ill.Dec. 252 (5th Dist. 1989), appeal den. 126 Ill.2d 558, 541 N.E.2d 1106, 133 Ill.Dec. 668

Argo High School Council of Local 571, I.F.T., A.F.T., A.F.L.-C.I.O. v. Argo Community High School District 217, 163 Ill.App.3d 578, 516 N.E.2d 834, 114 Ill.Dec. 679 (1st Dist. 1987)

6:130 May a school board adjourn a meeting to another meeting?

A meeting may be adjourned to another meeting as many times as the school board deems necessary so long as the school board complies with the provisions of the Open Meetings Act with respect to each reconvened meeting.

Public notice, including an agenda, must be given for each reconvened meeting unless the original meeting was open to the public and is to be reconvened within 24 hours. Public notice also is not required where an announcement of the time and place of the reconvened meeting was made at the original public meeting and there is no change in the agenda.

Ill. Rev. Stat. c. 102, par. 41 et seq.

NOTICE OF MEETINGS

6:140 How must public notice of school board meetings be given?

Public notice must be given by posting a copy of the notice at the principal office of the school board or, if no such office exists, at the building in which the meeting is to be held. The board must supply copies of the notice of its regular meetings, and of the notice of any special, emergency, rescheduled, or reconvened meeting, to any news medium which has filed an annual request for notice. Any such news medium must also be given the same notice of all special, emergency, rescheduled, or reconvened meetings in the same manner as is given to members of the school board provided such news medium has given the school board an address or telephone number within the territorial jurisdiction of the school board at which such notice may be given.

Public notice must include an agenda in the case of a special, rescheduled, or reconvened meeting.

Ill. Rev. Stat. c. 102, par. 42.02

6:150 May a school board hold an unscheduled emergency meeting without notice?

Yes. In a bona fide emergency, notice requirements may be waived. However, notice must be given as soon as practicable prior to such meeting to any news media that have filed annual requests for meeting notices.

Ill. Rev. Stat. c. 102, par. 42.02

6:160 What must a school board include in its meeting agenda?

The contents of a school board meeting agenda is at the discretion of the board. The Open Meetings Act requires only that an agenda be included with the public notice of special meetings, rescheduled regular meetings, and reconvened meetings for which public notice is required.

Ill. Rev. Stat. c. 102, par. 42.02

6:165 May a school board conduct business not listed on its agenda at a special, rescheduled or reconvened meeting?

At a special meeting or a rescheduled or reconvened meeting that requires an agenda, the school board may transact only the business that is germane to items listed on the agenda. Action taken on any item not identified on the agenda may be held invalid by a court.

Ill. Rev. Stat. c. 102, par. 42.02

CLOSED MEETINGS

6:170   When may a school board hold a closed meeting?

The Open Meetings Act requires all meetings of school boards to be open meetings. Meetings or portions of regular or special board meetings may be closed to the public only under the exceptions provided for in the Act. They are:

1) collective bargaining negotiations and grievance arbitrations which are exempt from the provisions of the Open Meetings Act;

2) collective negotiating matters between the school district and its employees;

3) when the acquisition (purchase or lease) of real property is considered or when the selling price of real estate is being considered;

4) to discuss litigation against, affecting, or on behalf of the school board that is filed or pending before a court or administrative tribunal, or meetings to discuss litigation which is probable or imminent. In the latter instance, a statement of the basis for the finding must be recorded into the minutes of the closed meeting;

5) to consider information regarding appointment, employment, or dismissal of an officer or employee or to hear testimony on a complaint against an officer or employee to determine its validity;

6) when the Illinois Constitution provides for a closed meeting;

7) meetings required to be closed under federal regulation;

8) to hear student discipline cases;

9) to discuss matters relating to individual students in special education programs;

10) meetings of an advisory committee appointed to provide the school board with professional consultation on matters germane to its field of competence may be closed to consider matters of professional ethics or performance;

11) meetings with representatives of a school board association organized under Article 23 of the School Code for the purpose of discussing the board's self-evaluation, practices and procedures, or professional ethics;

12) to consider the appointment of a member to fill a vacancy on the school board;

13) to establish reserves or settle claims pursuant to the Local Governmental and Governmental Employees Tort Immunity Act, if holding an open meeting would prejudice the disposition of a claim or potential claim;

14) to review or discuss claims, loss or risk management information, records, data, advice or communications from or with respect to any insurer of the school board, risk management association or self insurance pool;

15) to respond to actual danger to the safety of students, staff, and school premises, including discussion of emergency security procedures and the use of personnel and equipment to respond to such danger. The motion to close the meeting must describe the actual danger.

Ill. Rev. Stat. c. 48, par. 1718
Ill. Rev. Stat. c. 102, par. 42

6:180   What final actions of a school board may be taken in closed session?

None. All final actions of a school board must be taken in open session.

Ill. Rev. Stat. c. 102, par. 42

6:190   May a school board poll it members or take a straw vote in closed session?

A school board may poll its members in closed session so long as the final vote is taken in open session.

Jewell v. Board of Education DuQuoin Community Unit Schools, 19 Ill.App.3d 1091, 312 N.E.2d 659 (5th Dist. 1974)

6:200   What procedure is required to enter closed session?

A school board must, by roll call vote in open session, pass a motion to go into closed session. The motion to close must include a legally sufficient reason for the closed session and must be entered in board minutes. Only those topics specified in the vote to close may be deliberated during the closed session.

Ill. Rev. Stat. c. 102, par. 42a

6:210 If a school board meeting is to consist entirely of a closed session, must a board give notice?

Yes. Such a meeting presumably would be either a special meeting or a reconvened meeting stemming from a formal vote of the board at an earlier public meeting. Notice requirements for special or reconvened meetings would apply.

A public vote to go into closed session is required at the opening of the special or reconvened meeting or during the original adjourned meeting.

Ill. Rev. Stat. c. 102, par. 42.02

6:220 With respect to the term "employment," what may a school board discuss in closed session?

A school board may meet in closed session to consider information regarding the employment of individual employees. The term "employment" probably includes renewal or continuance of employment of an individual as well as questions related to initial hiring.

The term "employment" probably does not include matters of policy or matters involving classifications of employees. Such matters that relate to collective bargaining may fall under the collective bargaining exception.

Even when discussion of employment may be held in closed session, final action must be taken in open session.

Ill. Rev. Stat. c. 102, par. 42
Illinois v. Board of Education of District 170 of Lee and Ogle Counties, 40 Ill.App.3d 819, 353 N.E.2d 147 (2nd Dist. 1976)

6:225 May a school board insist that complaints against employees be heard only in closed session?

Yes. A school board may vote to meet in open or, on a permissible subject, in closed session. A permissible subject for a closed meeting is for the school board to hear testimony on complaints lodged against employees. With respect to any alleged right to criticize an employee in public at a school board meeting, the School Code allows a school board to establish reasonable rules governing public comment at its meetings.

Ill. Rev. Stat. c. 102, par. 42
Ill. Rev. Stat. c. 122, par. 10-16
Stachura v. Truszkowski, 763 F.2d 211 (6th Cir. 1985)

6:226   What effects are there to public disclosure of the causes for an employee's dismissal?

Public employees have constitutionally protected liberty interests in personal reputation, integrity and the right to have access to future employment opportunities. When a school board seeks to dismiss an employee for causes which may impugn his reputation or character, and makes the stigmatizing charges public, the employee must be provided a hearing at which he has the opportunity to refute the charges.

Hayes v. Phoenix Talent School District, 893 F.2d 235 (9th Cir. 1990)

Brandt v. Board of Co-op Educational Services, Third Supervisory District, Suffolk County, New York, 820 F.2d 41, appeal after remand 845 F.2d 416 (2nd Cir. 1988)

Bishop v. Wood, 96 S.Ct. 2074, 426 U.S. 341, 48 L.Ed.2d 864 (1976)

Board of Regents of State Colleges v. Roth, 92 S.Ct. 2701, 408 U.S. 564, 33 L.Ed.2d 548 (1972)

CONDUCTING MEETINGS

6:230   What rules of procedure must a school board follow with respect to the conduct of school board meetings?

School boards are not required to follow any particular rules of procedure in the conduct of their meetings. The School Code authorizes school boards to adopt rules and regulations for the management and governance of the schools. Rules adopted by a school board must be made available for public inspection in the administrative office of the school district.

Ill. Rev. Stat. c. 122, par. 10-20.5

6:233 Must a school board's rules of procedure be in writing?

In order to have any legal effect, rules must be in writing and available for public inspection. Moreover, written rules of procedure increase the likelihood that all members of the public body will understand and abide by them and decrease the opportunity for misunderstanding and legal challenges to board actions.

Ill. Rev. Stat. c. 122, par. 10-20.5

6:235 Must a school board abide by any rules of procedure that it has adopted?

A public body may formally change its own rules or may temporarily suspend them. Decisions regarding rules and whether they are changed or suspended are made by majority vote of the public body. Rules which are required by law (for example, the minimum number of votes required to discharge a teacher) may not be changed.

6:240 Must a school board allow time for public comment at a school board meeting?

At each public meeting of the school board, employees and members of the public must be afforded time, subject to reasonable constraints, to comment or ask questions of the board.

Ill. Rev. Stat. c. 122, par. 10-6
Ill. Rev. Stat. c. 122, par. 10-16

6:250 What is a quorum of a school board?

For a seven-member board, a quorum is four and a majority of a quorum is three. For a three-member board, two members is a quorum and two members is also a majority of a quorum.

Ill. Rev. Stat., c. 122, par. 10-6
Ill. Rev. Stat., c. 122, par. 10-12

6:260 May a school board adjourn a meeting when a quorum is not present?

If a quorum is not present at a special or regularly scheduled meeting, those members present, by a majority vote, may adjourn the meeting to a specific time and place, provided the date to which the adjournment is taken is prior to the date of the next regularly scheduled board meeting.

Ill. Rev. Stat. c. 102, par. 42.02

6:270 May school board officers vote on motions?

Any school board member, including the president, vice president, secretary or clerk (provided they are members of the board), may make motions, second motions, participate in debate, and vote.

On any motion requiring a record of the voting, the vote of the president and each other officer should be recorded as yes, no, abstain, or absent.

Ill. Rev. Stat. c. 122, par. 10-7

6:280 How many members of a school board must vote for a measure in order for it to carry?

A quorum of the school board must be present to have an official meeting and to conduct business. No vote, except a vote to adjourn, has any weight and effect without a quorum present.

Unless otherwise provided by law, a motion is decided by a majority of the votes cast. Notable exceptions are:

1) a motion to dismiss a teacher requires an affirmative vote by a majority of the entire school board (four of seven members);

2) the sale of school real estate or improvements thereon must be approved by at least two-thirds of the school board (five of seven members), as must a lease agreement for a term longer than 10 years.

A tie vote defeats the motion.

Ill. Rev. Stat. c. 122, par. 5-22
Ill. Rev. Stat. c. 122, par. 10-12
Ill. Rev. Stat. c. 122, par. 10-22.11
Ill. Rev. Stat. c. 122, par. 10-22.12
Ill. Rev. Stat. c. 122, par. 24-12

6:290 How is a vote of present or abstain counted?

If a quorum is present, a motion that requires only a simple majority is carried by a majority of those voting yea or nay. A vote of present or abstain is recorded as such and is not counted with either side.

Thus, if six members abstain, one vote carries or defeats the motion (unless it is a motion requiring a majority of the full board or other super majority in order to carry).

Prosser v. Village of Fox Lake, 91 Ill.2d 389, 438 N.E.2d 134, 63 Ill.Dec. 396 (1982)

6:295 May a member of a public body cast a vote by proxy?

The Open Meetings Act requires that public business be conducted openly. A proxy vote is in conflict with the legislative purpose of the Act.

Ill. Rev. Stat. c. 102, par. 41 et seq.
Ill. Rev. Stat. c. 122, par. 10-12

MINUTES

6:300 How should minutes be recorded?

The secretary or clerk must keep a record of the official acts of the school board in a punctual, orderly, and reliable manner. The minutes must be signed by the president and the secretary or clerk of the board.

The minutes, whether of open or closed session, must minimally include the date, time, and place of the meeting; list board members present or absent; and give a general description of all matters proposed or discussed. The minutes must record all motions, identify the board members making the motion and the second, and show the result of the voting.

On matters requiring a roll call vote, the yeas and nays must be recorded.

Ill. Rev. Stat. c. 102, par. 42.06
Ill. Rev. Stat. c. 122, par. 10-7
Ill. Rev. Stat. c. 122, par. 10-14
Davis-El v. O'Leary, 626 F.Supp. 1037 (N.D. Ill. 1986)

6:305 Must a public body give official approval to the minutes of its meetings?

No law specifically requires a public body to approve the minutes of its meetings. For all practical purposes, minutes are official as soon as the secretary types them into a readable form. In fact, the secretary's handwritten notes or tape recordings may be considered official for some purposes if that is all that is available or if a court orders an investigation of what actually happened at a meeting.

However, Illinois law recognizes that the approval process gives the public body an opportunity to correct any errors that the secretary might have made in recording what happened at the meeting. The Open Meetings Act provides that "the minutes of meetings open to the public shall be available for public inspection within 7 days of the approval of such minutes by the public body."

The School Code requires that a school district maintain a mailing list of persons requesting to be included thereon and mail them certain documents, including, "within 10 days of each board meeting, a copy of the approved meeting minutes."

Ill. Rev. Stat. c. 102, par. 42.06(b)
Ill. Rev. Stat. c. 122, par. 10-21.6

6:307 Must the minutes be read aloud at a public meeting before the public body approves them?

No. An acceptable and more common practice is to provide each member of the public body with a copy of the minutes for review and to adopt a motion to "approve the minutes as written and distributed."

6:310 May a school board amend its minutes after official approval?

A school board may amend its minutes or other official record after approval in order to make the minutes or record conform to the facts. This may be done at any time by formal board action.

However, alteration of the minutes will not suffice to change the outcome of a vote or otherwise reverse or alter a previous act. Rather, a legally sufficient vote of the school board reversing the previous act or vote is required.

Menssen v. Eureka Unit School District 140, 70 Ill.App.3d 9, 388 N.E.2d 273, 26 Ill.Dec. 649 (1979)

6:315 Must a public body make the minutes of its public meetings available for public inspection and copying?

Yes. The Open Meetings Act provides "the minutes of meetings open to the public shall be available for public inspection within 7 days of the approval of such minutes by the public body."

The School Code requires a school district maintain a mailing list of persons requesting to be included thereon and mail them certain documents, including, "within 10 days of each board meeting, a copy of the approved meeting minutes." A subscription fee approximating actual costs may be charged.

The Freedom of Information Act provides that public records, including the minutes of public meetings, must be made available to the public for copying as well as inspection.

Ill. Rev. Stat. c. 102, par. 42.06(b)
Ill. Rev. Stat. c. 116, par. 203(a)
Ill. Rev. Stat. c. 122, par. 10-21.6

6:320 Must a school board keep minutes of its closed sessions?

A school board must keep minutes of each closed session. Closed session minutes may be kept confidential, but the board must review its closed session minutes at least every six months to determine if there is a continuing need for confidentiality as to all or any part of those minutes.

Ill. Rev. Stat. c. 102, par. 42.06
Ill. Rev. Stat. c. 122, par. 10-7

6:330 Can a board of education be required to release the minutes of a closed session?

Courts have authority to examine closed session minutes in camera (privately) in deciding litigable issues. Courts also have authority to require school board members to testify about what occurred in closed session, and may order the release to the public of closed session minutes.

Ill. Rev. Stat. c. 102, par. 43(b) et seq.

Ill. Rev. Stat. c. 116, par. 211(d),(f)

Illinois Educational Labor Relations Board v. Homer Community Consolidated School District No. 208, 160 Ill.App.3d 730, 514 N.E.2d 465, 112 Ill.Dec. 802, aff'd. 132 Ill.2d 29, 547 N.E.2d 182, 138 Ill.Dec. 213 (1989)

7: SCHOOL DISTRICT RECORDS

APPLICABLE STATUTES

7:10 Which statutes govern access to school district records?

School district records which were prepared or received prior to July 1, 1984, are governed by the Local Records Act; reports and records prepared or received on or after July 1, 1984, are governed by the Freedom of Information Act.

Student records are regulated by the Illinois Student Records Act and the federal Family Educational Rights and Privacy Act.

The records of school employees are regulated by the state Personnel Records Review Act.

Ill. Rev. Stat. c. 48, par. 2002 et seq.
Ill. Rev. Stat. c. 116, par. 43.115
Ill. Rev. Stat. c. 116, par. 201 et seq.
Ill. Rev. Stat. c. 122, par. 50-1 et seq.
20 U.S.C. 1232g
Spinelli v. Immanual Evangelical Lutheran Congregation, Inc., 144 Ill.App.3d 325, 494 N.E.2d 196, 98 Ill.Dec. 269 (2nd Dist. 1986), aff'd. in part, rev. in part 118 Ill.2d 389, 515 N.E.2d 1222, 113 Ill.Dec. 915

7:20 Which school district records covered by the Local Records Act are available for public access and inspection?

The Local Records Act requires the maintenance of certain school district financial records and allows public access and inspection of those records. The Local Records Act applies to records prepared or received by a school district before July 1, 1984.

Ill. Rev. Stat. c. 116, par. 43.103a

7:30   For how long must a school board keep state aid records?

A school board must keep records to substantiate its state aid claims for at least three years.

Ill. Rev. Stat. c. 122, par. 10-20.1

PERSONNEL RECORDS

7:40   Do school district employees have a right to inspect their school district personnel records?

School employees may have the right to access their personnel records if a collective bargaining agreement so provides or pursuant to the Illinois Personnel Records Review Act.

The Act applies to school districts having five or more employees. Under the Act, an employee may inspect most personnel documents dated July 1, 1984 or later which have been or are intended to be used for employment, promotion, transfer, additional compensation, discharge, or discipline.

Ill. Rev. Stat. c. 48, par. 2000 et seq.
Spinelli v. Immanual Evangelical Lutheran Congregation, Inc., 144 Ill.App.3d 325, 494 N.E.2d 196, 98 Ill.Dec. 269 (2nd Dist. 1986), aff'd. in part, rev. in part 118 Ill.2d 389, 515 N.E.2d 1222, 113 Ill.Dec. 915

7:50   What procedures govern the inspection of personnel records?

The procedures governing the inspection of employee records may be covered in a local employee collective bargaining agreement. Rules regarding inspection of personnel records are subject to bargaining when a recognized bargaining unit is involved.

In other cases, the procedures which may be used are contained in the Personnel Records Review Act.

Ill. Rev. Stat. c. 48, par. 2000 et seq.

7:60   What parts of an employee's personnel record may a school board withhold from inspection?

Provided an applicable collective bargaining agreement does not provide to the contrary, a school board may withhold from inspection and copying:

1) letters of reference;

2) any portion of a test document, except that the employee may see a cumulative total test score for either a section or the entire test document;

3) materials which are used by the school board for management planning including, but not limited to, judgments, external peer review, documents, or recommendations concerning future salary increases and other wage treatments, school board bonus plans, promotion and job assignments, or other comments or ratings used for a school board's planning purposes;

4) information of a personal nature about a person other than the employee if disclosure of the information would constitute a "clearly unwarranted invasion of the other person's privacy;"

5) any records relevant to any pending claim between the school board and the employee which might be discovered in a legal proceeding;

6) investigatory or security records maintained by the school board to investigate criminal conduct by an employee or other activity by the employee which could reasonably be expected to harm school property, operations, or business, or could by the employee's activity cause the school board financial liability unless and until the school board takes adverse personnel action based on information in that record.

Ill. Rev. Stat. c. 48, par. 2007
Ill. Rev. Stat. c. 48, par. 2010

7:70   May an employee copy the contents of his personnel file?

An employee may obtain copies of non-confidential information contained in his personnel file. A school board may charge a copying fee not to exceed the cost of duplication.

Ill. Rev. Stat. c. 48, par. 2003

7:80   Are employee personnel records subject to public access and inspection?

Employee personnel records are exempt from the requirements of laws granting public access to and inspection of school district records. The exemption is permissive, however, and may be waived.

Ill. Rev. Stat. c. 116, par. 207

7:90   May a school board make employee disciplinary records public over the employee's objections?

A school board may not divulge a disciplinary report, letter of reprimand, or other disciplinary action to a third party other than the employee's labor organization or the employee's representative unless advance written notice is provided to the employee by first class mail to the employee's last known address.

However, advance written notice to the employee is not required under any of these conditions:

1) the employee has specifically waived the requirement of written notice as part of a written and signed employment application;

2) the disclosure is ordered in a legal proceeding or arbitration;

3) the information is requested by a government agency as a result of a claim by an employee or in connection with a criminal investigation by a governmental agency.

Ill. Rev. Stat. c. 48, par. 2007(l)

7:100   Are school boards restricted in what information may be collected and inserted in employee personnel records?

An employer may not gather or keep records of employee associations, political activities, publications, communications, or nonemployment activities unless the employee submits the information in writing or authorizes the employer in writing to keep or gather the information. These prohibitions do not apply to activities which occur on the employer's premises or during working hours which interfere with the performance of the employee's duties or the duties of other employees or activities, regardless of when and where occurring, which constitute criminal conduct or may reasonably be expected to harm the employer's property, operations, or business, or could, by the employee's action, cause the employer financial liability. The employer must purge from an employee's file records relating to a Department of Children and Family Services investigation which results in an unfounded report.

Ill. Rev. Stat. c. 48, par. 2009
Ill. Rev. Stat. c. 48, par. 2013

7:120 What is meant by the prohibition against keeping records as to employee associations?

A school board is prohibited from keeping records of employee activities or associations when these activities or associations are not related to the employee's job. The prohibition is intended to prevent the accumulation and retention of information as to non-job related employee politics, religion, affiliation and belief.

Ill. Rev. Stat. c. 48, par. 2009

7:130 Under what circumstances must a school board delete disciplinary information from an employee personnel file?

Disciplinary reports, letters of reprimand, or other disciplinary records which are more than four years old must be deleted from a personnel file when the contents of the personnel file are provided to third parties except in conjunction with a legal proceeding or arbitration.

Ill. Rev. Stat. c. 48, par. 2008

7:140 May an employee remove material from his personnel file?

Except in the case of Department of Children and Family Service investigations which have been returned unfounded, An employee does not have a statutory right to remove material from his employer-maintained personnel file.

Ill. Rev. Stat. c. 48, par. 2006
Ill. Rev. Stat. c. 48, par. 2013

7:150 What are the employee's rights if the employee disagrees with information contained in his personnel file?

In the event an employee disagrees with some portion of the contents of his personnel file, the employee may submit a written statement and the employer is required to attach the statement to the disputed portion of the file.

Ill. Rev. Stat. c. 48, par. 2006

STUDENT RECORDS

7:160 What is the purpose of the Student Records Act?

The purpose of the Student Records Act is to establish a degree of privacy and confidentiality with regard to student records. It gives parents and students limited access to student records, to inspect and copy the contents of the records, and the right to challenge material contained in them. The Act restricts who may have access to student records and what may be disclosed from them.

Ill. Rev. Stat. c. 122, par. 50-1 et seq.

7:170 What are student records within the meaning of the Student Records Act?

A student record is any writing or other recorded information created on or after January 1, 1975 concerning a student and by which a student may be individually identified, maintained by a school or at its direction or by an employee of a school, regardless of how or where the information is stored. The Student Records Act applies to the records of current students and students previously enrolled.

Records maintained by a school employee for his personal use are not covered by the Act if those records are destroyed no later than the student's graduation or permanent withdrawal from school.

Ill. Rev. Stat. c. 122, par. 50-1 et seq.

7:180 What is a student records custodian?

Each public school must designate an official records custodian who is responsible for the maintenance, care, and security of all student records regardless of whether or not the records are in his personal custody or control. The custodian must take all reasonable measures to prevent unauthorized access to, or dissemination of, student records. School boards must take reasonable measures to assure persons affected by the Student Records Act are informed of their rights and obligations.

Ill. Rev. Stat. c. 122, par. 50-3 et seq.

Human Rights Authority of the State of Illinois Guardianship and Advocacy Commission by Aune v. Miller, 124 Ill.App.3d 701, 464 N.E.2d 833, 79 Ill.Dec. 929 (3rd Dist. 1984)

7:190 Does federal law govern student records?

The federal Family Educational Rights and Privacy Act regulates student records. Its provisions are similar to those of the Illinois Student Records Act.

20 U.S.C. par. 1232

7:200 Who has the right to access, inspect and copy student records?

Parents and any person designated a representative by a parent have rights of access, inspection, and copying with regard to both permanent and temporary student records. Students have a right to access, inspect, and copy their permanent records and may be permitted access to their temporary records. The following categories of persons are also permitted access:

1) employees or officials of the school district or the State Board of Education who have a current educational or administrative interest in the student;

2) the records custodian of another school in which the student has enrolled or will enroll;

3) any person for research, statistical reporting or planning purposes, provided no student or parent can be identified from the records;

4) persons designated by court order; or

5) persons required by state or federal law.

Ill. Rev. Stat. c. 122, par. 50-5 et seq.

23 Ill. Admin. Code 375.20

7:210 When do parental rights to access student records end?

All rights and privileges held by the parent with respect to accessing student records become exclusively those of the student on the student's eighteenth birthday, when the student is legally emancipated, upon graduation from high school, marriage, or entry into military service.

Ill. Rev. Stat. c. 122, par. 50-2(g)

7:220 When a parent, representative or student requests to inspect and copy student records, how promptly must the records be produced?

Access must be granted within a reasonable time, but in no case later than 15 school days after the date of receipt of the request by the official records custodian.

Ill. Rev. Stat. c. 122, par. 50-5(c)

7:230 What student records may be withheld from parental or student access?

A parent or student may be denied access to confidential letters and statements of recommendation furnished in connection with applications for employment or admission to a post-secondary educational institution, or the receipt of an honor or honorary recognition, provided that the letters and statements are not used for purposes other than those for which they were specifically intended and were either:

1) placed in a school student record prior to January 1, 1975; or

2) the student waives access after being advised of the right to obtain the names of persons making the confidential recommendations.

Communications otherwise protected by law as privileged or confidential, including but not limited to information communicated in confidence to a physician, psychologist, or other psychotherapist, or information which is communicated by a student or parent in confidence to school personnel may also be withheld.

Ill. Rev. Stat. c. 122, par. 50-5(e)

John K v. Board of Education for School District No. 65, Cook County, 152 Ill.App.3d 543, 504 N.E.2d 797, 105 Ill.Dec. 512 (1st Dist. 1987) appeal den. 115 Ill.2d 542, 511 N.E.2d 429, 110 Ill.Dec. 457

7:240 May a student's school records or report card be withheld from the student or parent as a disciplinary measure?

No.

Ill. Rev. Stat. c. 122, par. 50-8

7:250 What must be contained in a parent and student notification of student records rights?

School districts must notify students and parents of their rights to inspection and copying under the Student Records Act. The notification must contain the following information:

1) the types of information contained in the permanent and temporary records of students;

2) the right to inspect and copy permanent and temporary records;

3) the cost of copying such records;

4) the right to control access and release of student records;

5) the right to request a copy of information released;

6) the rights and procedures for challenging the contents of student records;

7) the persons, agencies, or organizations having access to student records without parental consent;

8) the right to copy student records or information contained in a student record which is proposed to be destroyed or deleted and the school's schedule for reviewing and destroying such information;

9) the categories of information the school has designated as "directory information" and the right of parents to prohibit the release of such information;

10) a statement informing the parents that no person may condition the granting or withholding of any right, privilege, or

benefits or make as a condition of employment, credit, or in-surance the securing by any individual of information from a student's temporary record which such individual may obtain through the exercise of any right secured under the Act or these regulations;

11) the right of parents to inspect and challenge the informa-tion contained in a student record forwarded to another school district; and

12) the student record policies of the school district which are not included in the Act.

Ill. Rev. Stat. c. 122, par. 50-3
23 Ill. Admin. Code 375.30

7:260 What are student permanent records?

Student permanent record means the "minimum personal information necessary to a school in the education of the student and contained in a school student record". A permanent record must include the student's name, birth date, address, grades and grade level, parents' names and addresses, attendance records, gender, place of birth, class rank, graduation date, scores on college entrance examinations, accident reports, health records, and the records pertaining to any release of permanent record information.

Honors and awards received, information about participation in school-sponsored activities or athletics, or offices held in school-sponsored organizations may be included in the student's permanent record. No other information may be included in a student's permanent record.

Ill. Rev. Stat. c. 122, par. 50-2(e)
23 Ill. Admin. Code 375.10

7:270 What are student temporary records?

Student temporary record means all information contained in a school student record but not contained in the student permanent record. A temporary record may include family background information; intelligence test scores; aptitude test scores; reports of psychological evaluations including informa-tion on intelligence, personality and academic information ob-tained through test administration, observation or interview;

elementary and secondary achievement level test results; participation in extra curricular activities including any offices held in school sponsored activities; honors and awards received; teacher anecdotal records; disciplinary information; special education files including the report of the multi-disciplinary staffing on which placement was based and all records relating to special education placement, hearings and appeals; and other information of clear relevance to the education of the student.

Ill. Rev. Stat. c. 122, par. 50-2(f)

Ill. Rev. Stat. c. 122, par. 50-4(c), (d)

23 Ill. Admin. Code 375.10

John K v. Board of Education for School District No. 65, Cook County, 152 Ill.App.3d 543, 504 N.E.2d 797, 105 Ill.Dec. 512 (1st Dist. 1987) appeal den. 115 Ill.2d 542, 511 N.E.2d 429, 110 Ill.Dec. 457

7:280 For how long must a school preserve a student's permanent record?

A student's permanent record must be maintained by a school for a minimum of 60 years after the student has transferred, graduated or otherwise permanently withdrawn from school.

Ill. Rev. Stat. c. 122, par. 50-4(e)

7:290 For what period may a school retain a student's temporary record?

A student's temporary record may be maintained for its period of usefulness to the student and the school, but in no case longer than five years after the student has transferred, graduated or otherwise withdrawn from school.

Ill. Rev. Stat. c. 122, par. 50-4(f)

7:300 What directory information contained in student records may be made public by a school district?

A school district may publish directory information such as student names; addresses; gender; grade level; birth date; birthplace; parents' names and addresses; academic awards; degrees and honors; information in relation to school-sponsored activities, organizations, and athletics; major field of study; period of attendance in school; and other identifying information and similar publications so long as such publications comply with the regulations of the State Board of Education.

This information may be released to the general public, unless a parent requests that the information not be released. Each school is required to provide notice of which information it considers to be directory. Non-directory information may not be disclosed without prior written consent of the parent or student.

Ill. Rev. Stat. c. 122, par. 50-6(e)
23 Ill. Admin. Code 375.80

7:310 What notice must be given to parents before a school releases student records to another school district?

No information from student records may be released to another school unless otherwise permitted by the Student Records Act or unless the parents receive prior written notice of the nature and substance of the information proposed to be released. Also, prior to the release of school records, the parents must be given an opportunity to inspect and copy the records and challenge their contents.

Ill. Rev. Stat. c. 122, par. 50-5(b)
23 Ill. Admin. Code 375.70

7:320 Does the Illinois Freedom of Information Act provide public access to student records?

The Freedom of Information Act provides that information prohibited from disclosure by state or federal law is exempt from access under the Act. Therefore, access to student records is not possible under the Act.

Ill. Rev. Stat. c. 116, par. 207
Ill. Rev. Stat. c. 122, par. 50-6
Bowie v. Evanston Community Consolidated School District No. 65, 165 Ill.App.3d 101, 522 N.E.2d 669, 119 Ill.Dec. 7 (1st Dist. 1988) appeal allowed 122 Ill.2d 570, 530 N.E.2d 239, 125 Ill.Dec. 211

7:330 Must a school maintain a record of the information which is released from a student record?

A record of any information released from a student record must be made and kept as a part of the student record. The record of release must be maintained for the life of the student record and is available only to the parent, student, and the official records custodian. Each record of release must include:

1) the nature and substance of the information released;

2) the name and signature of the official records custodian releasing the information;

3) the name of the person requesting the information, the capacity in which the request has been made, and the purpose of the request;

4) the date of the release; and

5) a copy of consent to the release.

Except for parents and students, no person to whom information is released, and no person designated a representative by a parent, may permit any other person to have access to information without a prior consent of the parent.

Ill. Rev. Stat. c. 122, par. 50-6(c), (d)

7:340 May a school district restrict parental access to student psychological reports or do parents have a right to review raw material?

Parents may review any material contained in student records, including material upon which further conclusions are drawn and any raw psychological data. The school or the parent may elect to have present at the time of review a qualified professional to assist in the interpretation of raw data.

Ill. Rev. Stat. c. 122, par. 50-5 (a), (b)

John K v. Board of Education for School District No. 65, Cook County, 152 Ill.App.3d 543, 504 N.E.2d 797, 105 Ill.Dec. 512 (1st Dist. 1987) appeal den. 115 Ill.2d 542, 511 N.E.2d 429, 110 Ill.Dec. 457

7:350 May parents challenge the contents of a student's records?

Parents may challenge the accuracy, relevance, or propriety of any entry in a student record except academic grades. There are hearing procedures by which disputed information may be removed from a student record as a result of parental challenge.

Parents may insert in their child's school student record a statement of reasonable length setting forth their position on any disputed information contained in the record. The school must include a copy of this statement in any subsequent dissemination of the information in dispute.

Ill. Rev. Stat. c. 122, par. 50-7

7:360 What are the hearing procedures for student record challenges?

Each school board must establish administrative procedures for parents to challenge the content of student records. The procedural aspects of the policy must include at minimum:

1) A method by which a challenge may be initiated by a request for hearing. The request must be submitted in writing to the school record custodian and must contain notice of the specific entry or entries to be challenged and the basis of the challenge.

2) Upon receipt of a challenge, an initial informal conference must be held within 15 days. If the conference does not resolve the challenge, the following procedures are utilized.

3) A hearing officer must be appointed by the school. The hearing officer may not be an employee assigned to the attendance center where the student is enrolled.

4) A formal hearing must be conducted within 15 days after the informal conference, unless the parties mutually agree to an extension. A verbatim record of the hearing must be kept. The conduct of the hearing must include the right to present evidence and to call witnesses, the right to cross-examine witnesses, the right to counsel, and the right to a written statement of decision and the reasons therefor.

5) The decision of the hearing officer must be rendered no later than ten school days after the conclusion of the hearing. A copy of the decision must be transmitted to the parents or student and the school. Any decision must be based solely upon

the information presented at the hearing. The hearing officer may require the challenged contents in the school record be maintained, removed, changed, clarified, or added to.

6) The results of the hearing may be appealed to the appropriate regional superintendent of schools within 20 days after the decision is transmitted. If a parent appeals, the school must be notified by the parent within 10 school days of the appeal, and the school must forward all documents regarding the hearing to the regional superintendent.

7) The regional superintendent must render a decision within 20 school days of receipt of the hearing record.

8) Either party may appeal the decision of the regional superintendent to the circuit court of the county in which the school is located.

Ill. Rev. Stat., c. 122, par. 50-7
23 Ill. Admin. Code 375.90

7:370 What are a school board's duties with respect to maintenance of the records of students not enrolled in school on or after the enactment of the Student Records Act (March 24, 1976)?

Schools are not required to separate permanent and temporary records, or to destroy records according to any statutorily established schedule for students not enrolled in school on or after the effective date of the Student Records Act (March 24, 1976).

However, the parents of a student not enrolled in school on or after March 24, 1976, may request a school board to comply with the Student Records Act with respect their child's records, and the school board must honor this request.

Ill. Rev. Stat. c. 122, par. 50-4(i)

7:380 How often must a school district review the contents of student records?

Each school district is required to review student records periodically as necessary, but not less than once every four years or upon a student's change in attendance center, whichever occurs first.

The purpose of review is to verify entries and eliminate or correct out-of-date, misleading, inaccurate, unnecessary, or irrelevant information.

Ill. Rev. Stat. c. 122, par. 50-4(g)
23 Ill. Admin. Code 375.40 b)

7:390 What is the penalty for violation of the Student Records Act?

Any person who is aggrieved by any violation of the Student Records Act may seek injunctive relief. Any person who is injured by a willful or negligent violation of the Act may sue for damages. Costs and attorneys fees are available to a successful plaintiff in either cause.

The State Board of Education or designated state's attorneys also may seek injunctive relief to secure compliance with the Act.

Willful failure to comply with any provision of the Act is a petty offense, except that willful or malicious falsification of student records is a Class A misdemeanor.

Absent proof of malice, no cause of action or claim for relief, civil or criminal, is possible against any school, employee, or official of a school, or person acting at the direction of a school for any statement made or judgment expressed in any entry to a school student record of a type which does not violate the Act or the regulations issued by the State Board of Education.

Ill. Rev. Stat. c. 122, par. 50-9

John K v. Board of Education for School District No. 65, Cook County, 152 Ill.App.3d 543, 504 N.E.2d 797, 105 Ill.Dec. 512 (1st Dist. 1987) appeal den. 115 Ill.2d 542, 511 N.E.2d 429, 110 Ill.Dec. 457

FREEDOM OF INFORMATION ACT

7:400 What are records within the meaning of the Freedom of Information Act?

The Freedom of Information Act defines public records broadly. It includes all records, reports, forms, writings, letters, memoranda, books, papers, maps, photographs, microfilms, cards, tapes, recordings, electronic data processing records, recorded information and all other documentary materials regardless of physical form or characteristics. It includes, but is not limited to:

1) administrative manuals, procedural rules, and instructions to staff, except those covered by a statutory exemption;

2) final opinions and orders made in the adjudication of cases, except adjudication of student or employee grievance or disciplinary cases;

3) substantive rules;

4) statements and interpretations of policy which have been adopted;

5) final planning policies, recommendations, and decisions;

6) factual reports, inspection reports, and studies;

7) all information in any account, voucher, or contract dealing with the receipt or expenditure of public or other funds;

8) the names, salaries, titles, and dates of employment of all employees and officers;

9) materials containing opinions concerning the rights of the state, the public, a subdivision of state or a local government, or of any private persons;

10) the name of every official and final records of voting in all proceedings of the school board;

11) applications for any contract, permit, grant, or agreement, except where covered by a statutory exemption;

12) each report, document, study, or publication prepared by independent consultants or other independent contractors for the school board;

13) all other information required by law to be made available for public inspection or copying; and

14) information relating to any grant or contract made by or between the school board and another public body or private organization.

Ill. Rev. Stat. c. 116, par. 202(c)

Kenyon v. Garrels, 184 Ill.App.3d 28, 540 N.E.2d 11, 132 Ill.Dec. 595 (4th Dist. 1989)

7:410 Who has the right to inspect and copy school board records under the Freedom of Information Act?

Any person may access, inspect, or copy school board public records. A person is any "individual, corporation, partnership, firm, organization, or association, acting individually or as a group."

Ill. Rev. Stat. c. 116, par. 202(b)

7:420 May a school board limit public access to school board records to residents of the school district?

No. Access to public records may not be limited based on residency or any other criterion.

Ill. Rev. Stat. c. 116, par. 202

7:430 What must be contained in Freedom of Information Act notice to the public?

A school board must prominently display at each of its administrative or regional offices, make available for inspection and copying, and send through the mail if requested to do so, the following:

1) A brief description of the school district, including but not be limited to, a short summary of its purpose, a block diagram giving its functional subdivisions, the total amount of its operating budget, the number and location of all of its separate offices, the approximate number of full and part-time employees, and the identification and membership of any board, commission, committee, or council which operates in an advisory capacity relative to the operation of the school board, or which exercises control over its policies or procedures, or to which it is required to report; and

2) A brief description of the methods whereby the public may request information and public records, a directory designating by titles and addresses those employees to whom requests for public records should be directed, and any fees allowable under the Act.

Ill. Rev. Stat. c. 116, par. 204

7:435 Must a school board maintain a list of records it maintains?

A school board must maintain and make available for inspection and copying a reasonably current list of all types or categories of records under its control which were prepared or received after July 1, 1984. The list must be reasonably detailed in order to aid persons in obtaining access to the public records. A school board must also furnish upon request a description of the manner in which public records stored by means of electronic data processing may be obtained in a form comprehensible to persons lacking knowledge of computer language or printout format.

Ill. Rev. Stat. c. 116, par. 205

7:440 May a school board adopt rules regulating the time and place at which citizens may have access to public records?

A school board may promulgate rules regulating the times and places where publicly accessible records will be made available, the person from whom the records may be obtained, and rules or regulations pertaining to both the availability of district records and the procedures to access the records.

Ill. Rev. Stat. c. 116, par. 203(g)

7:450 What records are exempt from public access and inspection under the Freedom of Information Act?

The Freedom of Information Act exempts numerous records from public access and copying. Some of the most common categories of records which are exempt are:

1) All records if compliance with the request would be unduly burdensome, the request cannot be narrowed, and the burden on the school board to comply would outweigh the public interest in the information requested.

2) Records which are in immediate use by persons exercising official duties which require the use of the records.

3) Information prohibited from disclosure by federal or state law or by rules or regulations adopted pursuant thereto.

4) Information which, if disclosed, would constitute a clearly unwarranted invasion of personal privacy, unless such disclosure is consented to in writing by the individual subjects of the information. The disclosure of information that bears on the public duties of public employees and officials shall not be considered an invasion of personal privacy. Material exempted under this section includes:

a) files and personal information maintained with respect to clients, patients, residents, students or other individuals receiving social, medical, educational, vocational, financial, supervisory or custodial care or services directly or indirectly from federal agencies or school boards;

b) personnel files and personal information maintained with respect to employees, appointees or elected officials of a school board or applicants for such positions;

c) files and personal information maintained with respect to any applicant, registrant or licensee by any public body cooperating with or engaged in professional or occupational registration, licensure or discipline;

d) information required of any taxpayer in connection with the assessment or collection of any tax unless disclosure is otherwise required by state statute; and

e) information revealing the identity of persons who file complaints with or provide information to administrative, investigative, law enforcement or penal agencies.

5) Preliminary drafts, notes, recommendations, memoranda and other records in which opinions are expressed, or policies or actions are formulated, except that a specific record or relevant portion thereof shall not be exempt when the record is publicly cited and identified by the president of the school board.

6) Minutes of closed sessions of school board meetings which are closed to the public as provided in the Open Meetings Act, until such time as the board makes such minutes available to the public.

7) Test questions, scoring keys and other examination data used to administer an academic examination or determine the qualifications of an applicant for a license or employment.

8) Library circulation and order records identifying library users with specific materials.

9) Information received by a primary or secondary school, college or university under its procedures for the evaluation of faculty members by their academic peers.

10) Information concerning any school board's adjudication of student or employee grievances or disciplinary cases, except for the final outcome of such cases.

11) Course materials or research materials used by faculty members

12) Investigatory records compiled for state or local administrative law enforcement purposes or for internal matters of a school board under certain conditions.

13) Proposals and bids for any contract, grant, or agreement, including information which, if it were disclosed, would frustrate procurement or give an advantage to any person proposing to enter into a contract or agreement with the board, until an award or final selection is made and information prepared by or for the board in preparation of a bid solicitation until an award or final selection is made.

14) Valuable formulae, designs, drawings and research data obtained or produced by any school board when disclosure could reasonably be expected to produce private gain or public loss.

15) Architects' and engineers' plans for buildings.

16) Communications between the school board and an attorney or auditor representing the board that would not be subject to discovery in litigation, and materials prepared or compiled by or for a board in anticipation of a criminal, civil, or administrative proceeding upon the request of any attorney advising the board, and materials prepared or compiled with respect to internal audits of school boards.

17) Administrative or technical information associated with automated data processing operations, including, but not limited to, software, operating protocols, computer program abstracts, file layouts, source listings, object modules, load modules, user guides, documentation pertaining to all logical physical design of computerized systems, employee manuals, and any other information that, if disclosed, would jeopardize the security of the system or data contained therein or the security of materials exempt under the Act.

18) Documents or materials relating to collective negotiating matters between school boards and their employees or repre-

sentatives, except that any final contract or agreement is subject to inspection and copying.

19) Drafts, notes, recommendations, and memoranda pertaining to the financing and marketing transactions of the board and the records of ownership, registration, transfer, and exchange of municipal debt obligations, and of persons to whom payment with respect to such obligations is made.

20) The records, documents, and information relating to real estate purchase negotiations until those negotiations have been completed or otherwise terminated; with regard to a parcel involved in a pending or actually and reasonably contemplated eminent domain proceeding under Article VII of the Code of Civil Procedure, records, documents, and information relating to that parcel shall be exempt, except as may be allowed under discovery rules adopted by the Illinois Supreme Court; the records, documents, and information relating to a real estate sale shall be exempt until a sale is consummated.

21) Any and all proprietary information and records related to the operation of an intergovernmental risk management association or self-insurance pool or jointly self-administered health and accident cooperative or pool.

22) Information related solely to the internal personnel rules and practices of a school board.

There are numerous other categories of information which are exempted from disclosure under the Act.

Ill. Rev. Stat. c. 116, par. 43.103a
Ill. Rev. Stat. c. 116, par. 201
Ill. Rev. Stat. c. 116, par. 203(f)
Ill. Rev. Stat. c. 116, par. 207
Ill. Rev. Stat. c. 122, par. 50-1 et seq.

Bowie v. Evanston Community Consolidated School District No. 65, 165 Ill.App.3d 101, 522 N.E.2d 669, 119 Ill.Dec. 7 (1st Dist. 1988) appeal allowed 122 Ill.2d 570, 530 N.E.2d 239, 125 Ill.Dec. 211

Illinois Educational Labor Relations Board v Homer Community Consolidated School District No. 208, 160 Ill.App.3d 730, 514 N.E.2d 465, 112 Ill.Dec. 802 (4th Dist. 1987) appeal allowed 118 Ill.2d 542, 520 N.E.2d 385, 117 Ill.Dec. 224

7:460 What is disclosed if a requested record includes both disclosable and exempt material?

When any public record that is exempt from disclosure under the Freedom of Information Act contains any material that is not exempt, the school board must separate the exempt material from the non-exempt material and make the non-exempt available for inspection and copying.

Ill. Rev. Stat. c. 116, par. 208
Hamer v. Lentz, 132 Ill.2d 49, 547 N.E.2d 191, 138 Ill.Dec. 222 (1989)

7:470 Must a school board comply with a request to make public the names and salaries of its employees?

The names and salaries of school board employees are public record and available for public inspection.

Ill. Rev. Stat. c. 116, par. 202(c)
Illinois ex rel. Recktenwald v. Janura, 59 Ill.App.3d 143, 376 N.E.2d 22, 17 Ill.Dec. 129 (1st Dist. 1978)
Stein v. Howlett, 52 Ill.2d 570, 289 N.E.2d 409 (1972)

7:480 How quickly must a school board respond to a Freedom of Information Act request?

A school board must either comply with the request or deny the request for public records within seven working days after the request has been received. A request may be either fully or partially fulfilled or denied.

If a school board fails to respond to a written request within seven working days after it is received, the request is deemed denied.

Ill. Rev. Stat. c. 116, par. 203(c)

7:490 May a school board extend the time to respond to a Freedom of Information Act request beyond seven days?

A school board may extend the time limit to respond to a request to access or copy school records for not more than an additional seven working days for any of the following reasons:

1) The requested records are stored in whole or in part at other locations than the office having charge of the requested records.

2) The request requires the collection of a substantial number of specified records.

3) The request is couched in categorical terms and requires an extensive search for the records responsive to it.

4) The requested records have not been located in the course of routine search and additional efforts are being made to locate them.

5) The requested records require examination and evaluation by personnel having the necessary competence and discretion to determine if they are exempt from disclosure or should be revealed only with appropriate deletions.

6) The request for records cannot be complied with by the school board within the time limits prescribed without unduly burdening or interfering with the operation of the school.

7) There is a need for consultation, which shall be conducted with all practicable speed, with another public body or among two or more components of a public body having a substantial interest in the determination or in the subject matter of the request.

When additional time is required for any of the above reasons, the school board must notify the person making the request by letter within the seven-day time limit fixed for responding to the request of the reasons for the delay and the date by which the records will be made available or that a denial will be forthcoming.

Ill. Rev. Stat. c. 116, par. 203(d) et seq.

7:500 What appeal is available to the public following denial of a request to inspect and copy public records?

Any person denied access to inspect and copy any school district record may appeal the denial by sending a written notice of appeal to the school board president or superintendent of schools. Upon receipt of the appeal, the public record must be reviewed to determine whether the record is open to inspection and copying. The person who has requested the appeal must be notified of the determination within seven working days after the appeal has been received.

Ill. Rev. Stat. c. 116, par. 202(e)
Ill. Rev. Stat. c. 116, par. 210

7:510 What are the procedural requirements necessary to deny a request to inspect and copy records?

A school board may refuse a request to inspect and copy records when an exemption is provided in the law or when responding would be unduly burdensome. When a request is denied, the school board must notify the person making the request in writing of the decision to deny, the reasons for the denial, and the name and title or position of each person responsible for the denial.

The notice also must inform the person of his right to appeal to the president of the school board, and each notice of denial must inform the person of his right to seek judicial review in a circuit court of proper jurisdiction.

When a request for school district records is denied on the grounds the records are exempt under the Freedom of Information Act, the notice of denial from the school board must specify the exemption claimed.

Copies of each denial issued by a school board must be retained in a single, central office file which is open to the public. The file must be indexed according to the type of exemption and, to the extent feasible, according to the type of records which have been requested.

Ill. Rev. Stat. c. 116, par. 209

7:520 Is any further appeal available to an individual denied access to public records following appeal to the school board president?

Any person who has been denied access to inspect or copy public records and who has exhausted administrative remedies may file suit in the circuit court of the county where the school district is located.

Ill. Rev. Stat. c. 116, par. 211

7:530 Does the Freedom of Information Act require a school board to create or maintain any specific records?

The Act does not require a school board to create or maintain any record not otherwise required by law, rule or regulation, or maintained at the discretion of the school board.

Ill. Rev. Stat. c. 116, par. 201

8: CHANGING SCHOOL DISTRICT BOUNDARIES AND TERRITORY

DISTRICT CONSOLIDATION

8:10 May two or more entire elementary districts or two or more entire high school districts combine to form a new district?

Yes. Any contiguous territory having an equalized assessed valuation of at least $5,000,000 and a population of not less than 1,500 and not more than 500,000 may be formed into a combined school district. A petition calling for the combination of districts must be filed by the school boards of each district affected or by 10 percent of the legal voters residing in each district affected. The petition must be filed with the regional superintendent of the region in which the greater portion of the equalized assessed valuation of the territory described in the petition is located. The petition must be approved by the regional superintendent after hearing on the petiton and by the State Superintendent of Education and the proposal placed on the ballot at an election in the affected territory. The proposed combination of districts must be approved by a majority of voters casting ballots in the election.

Ill. Rev. Stat. c. 122, par. 11B-2 et seq.

8:20 May new community consolidated or community high school districts be formed?

All statutory references to the creation of community consolidated school districts were removed from the School Code by the General Assembly. It is possible for two or more contiguous unit school districts; or one or more unit school districts and one or more high school districts, all of which are contiguous, to dissolve and form a single new high school district and one or more new elementary districts. It is not possible under other circumstances to form a new high school district. A single unit school district may not, for example, divide into high school and elementary districts. Almost all the existing community consolidated and township high school districts were formed before statutory restrictions limiting the formation of such districts were enacted.

Ill. Rev. Stat. c. 122, par. 7A-1 et seq.
Ill. Rev. Stat. c. 122, par. 10-21.5
Ill. Rev. Stat. c. 122, par. 11D-1 et seq.
Ill. Rev. Stat. c. 122, par. 12-1
Board of Education of Hamilton County Community Unit School District No. 10, Hamilton County v. Regional Board of School Trustees of Jefferson and Hamilton Counties, 121 Ill.App.3d 848, 460 N.E.2d 100, 77 Ill.Dec. 241 (5th Dist. 1984)

8:30   What kind of school district may be newly created under current law?

Any type of school district except a community consolidated district may be newly created, although some types of school districts may be newly created only under very limited circumstances.

Ill. Rev. Stat. c. 122, par. 7-1 et seq.
Ill. Rev. Stat. c. 122, par. 7A-1 et seq.
Ill. Rev. Stat. c. 122, par. 11A-1 et seq.
Ill. Rev. Stat. c. 122, par. 11B-1 et seq.
Ill. Rev. Stat. c. 122, par. 11D-1 et seq.

8:33   What is a unit school district?

A unit school district is one that offers education for all children in grades kindergarten through 12 who live within the territory of the district.

8:36   What is a dual district?

A dual district is an area served by two separate school districts, one an elementary district providing education through grade 8 and the second a high school district providing education from grades 9 through 12. Boundaries of the elementary district and high school district may be coterminous but often are not. One high school district may cover all or some of the same geographic area as two or more elementary districts.

Or an elementary district may serve portions of the same area served by two or more high school districts.

8:40 How is a community unit district created?

Creation of a community unit school district begins with the filing of a petition with the regional superintendent of schools and concludes with approval of the voters and election of a new school board. The petition may be filed by the boards of education of each of the school distiricts wholly or partially included in the territory described in the petition, or the petition may be filed by a specified number of voters residing in the affected school districts. The petition must be approved by the regional superintendent and State Superintendent of Education.

At the election, the proposition must be approved by a majority of the votes cast in each of the affected school districts. (The proposition loses if it is defeated by a majority of the votes cast in any one of the affected school districts, even if it receives a majority of the votes in all of the districts combined.)

The School Code sets forth specific requirements for: (a) the territory to be included in the proposed unit district; (b) signatures required on the petition; (c) the filing of the petition; (d) hearing procedures; (e) the referendum on the proposal, and (f) the election of a new school board.

Ill. Rev. Stat., c. 122, par. 11A-3

Adsit v. Sanders, 157 Ill.App.3d 416, 510 N.E.2d 547, 109 Ill.Dec. 679, appeal dismissed 117 Ill.2d 541, 517 N.E.2d 1083, 115 Ill.Dec. 397 (4th Dist. 1987)

8:50 Who may vote in an election to organize a community unit school district?

Only those residents in the territory described in the petition for organizing a community unit school district may vote in such an election. The proposition must be approved by a majority of the votes cast in each of the affected school districts, not merely by a majority of the votes cast in the total combined territory.

Ill. Rev. Stat. c. 122, par. 11A-8

8:60 What assistance does the State Board of Education provide to a school district considering consolidation?

The State Board of Education Department of School District Organization assists school districts in studying school district organizational problems. It provides consultation to school districts considering consolidation.

Ill. Rev. Stat. c. 122, par. 2-3.35

8:70 How does school district reorganization affect state aid?

The State provides financial incentives to encourage school district consolidation. For fixed specified periods of time after a consolidation, the State may provide additional supplementary state aid to newly consolidated districts. The supplementary state aid wholly or partially offsets the costs incurred by a district in acquiring another district's deficits and differences in financial structure and partially offsets the costs associated with merging the teacher salary schedules of combining school districts.

Ill. Rev. Stat. c. 122, par. 18-8 et seq.
Ill. Rev. Stat. c. 122, par. 18-8.2
Ill. Rev. Stat. c. 122, par. 18-8.3

BOUNDARY CHANGES

8:80 How may school district boundaries be changed?

School district boundaries may be changed by detachment, annexation, division, dissolution, or any combination thereof. The regional board(s) of school trustees is authorized to change the boundaries when petitioned under certain circumstances: (1) by the boards of each of the districts affected; (2) by a majority of the registered voters in each district affected by the boundary change; (3) by two-thirds of the registered voters in any territory proposed to be detached from one or more districts; (4) by 2/3 of the registered voters in each of one or more districts proposed to be annexed to another district, or 5) if there are no legal voters residing in the territory to be detached, by all of the owners of record.

The regional board of trustees must detach and annex any elementary or high school district territory constituting no more than 10 percent of the detaching district's equalized assessed property value when petitioned to do so by two-thirds of the registered voters of the detaching territory and where granting the petition makes the boundaries of the annexing district coterminous with its dual district counterpart (elementary or high school).

Ill. Rev. Stat. c. 122, par. 7-1
Ill. Rev. Stat. c. 122, par. 7-2
Ill. Rev. Stat. c. 122, par. 7-2b

8:90 May a school district be entirely dissolved?

Yes. Upon petition by a majority of the legal voters residing in the district proposed to be dissolved, or by a petition filed by the board of education of the school district seeking dissolution, the regional board of school trustees may dissolve a school district and annex its territory to another district or districts.

Ill. Rev. Stat. c. 122, par. 7-2a

8:100 What is detachment and annexation?

Detachment is the removal of a portion of the territory of a school district. Annexation is the addition of territory to a school district. Detachment and annexation, therefore, is the removal of territory from one school district and the addition of it to the territory of another school district.

Ill. Rev. Stat. c. 122, par. 7-1 et seq.

8:105 Do provisions for dissolution, detachment and annexation apply to all school districts in Illinois?

Yes. However, statutory procedures for detachment and annexation involving a special charter district differ somewhat from the procedures applicable for other districts. Procedures that apply to special charter districts are addressed beginning with question 8:300.

NON-CHARTER DISTRICT
DETACHMENT AND ANNEXATION

8:110 May territory be detached and annexed to a school district if the resulting district is not compact and contiguous?

School district boundaries resulting from detachment and annexation must be compact and contiguous, although a school district may have "highly irregular" boundaries and still be compact and contiguous if children residing therein can reasonably avail themselves of school. In general, corridors are compact and contiguous; islands are not.

Illinois on rel. of Community Unit School District No. 1, Macon County v. Decatur School District No. 61, 45 Ill.App.2d 33, 194 N.E.2d 659 (3rd Dist. 1963)

Streator Township High School District No. 40 v. County Board of School Trustees of Livingston County 14 Ill.App.2d 251, 144 N.E.2d 531 (2nd Dist. 1957)

Illinois ex rel. Warren v. Drummet, 415 Ill. 411, 114 N.E.2d 364 (1953)

Illinois ex rel. McLain v. Gardner, 408 Ill. 228, 96 N.E.2d 551 (1951)

Illinois v. Deatherage, 401 Ill. 25, 81 N.E.2d 581 (1948)

Illinois ex rel. Bartlett v. Vass, 325 Ill. 64 (1927)

8:120 What is the effective date of change for the change of boundaries of a school district?

In case a petition is filed for the creation of or the change in boundaries of or for an election to vote on the proposition of creating any school district after August 1, and the change is granted or the election carries, and no appeal is taken, the change is effective after the time for appeal has run for the purpose of all elections; however, the change does not affect the administration of the schools until July 1 following the date the petition is granted or upon which the election is held and the school boards of the districts as they existed prior to the change exercise the same power and authority over their own territory until that date; however, the new districts can organize and elect officers within the time prescribed by the general election law.

In the event that the granting of a petition has become final, the change in boundaries becomes effective immediately. However, if the granting of the petition becomes final between September 1 and June 30 of any year, the administration of and attendance at the schools is not affected until the following July 1, when the change in boundaries becomes effective for all purposes. After the granting of a petition has become final, the date when the change is effective for purposes of administration and attendance may be accelerated or postponed by stipulation of each of the school boards of each district affected and approved by the regional board of school trustees.

Ill. Rev. Stat. c. 122, par. 7-9

8:130   When do school board members' terms of office expire after the annexation of the school district from which they were elected?

Upon the close of the current school year during which any school district is annexed to another school district, the terms of office of the school board members of the annexed school district are terminated and the school board of the annexing district performs all of the duties and has all of the powers of the school board of the annexed district.

Ill. Rev. Stat. c. 122, par. 7-12

8:140   What happens to the assets and liabilities of an annexed district?

The annexing district as it is constituted on and after the time of annexation usually receives all the assets and assumes all the obligations and liabilities, including the bonded indebtedness, of the original annexing district and of the district annexed. In certain dissolutions and under certain conditions in the case of a detachment-annexation, the bonded indebtedness does not become the obligation of the annexing district but remains the obligation of the taxable property that was situated within the boundaries of the district at the time of the issuance of each bond issue.

When two or more school districts receive territory from a dissolved school district, the regional board of school trustees has authority to divide the assets and liabilities of the dissolved school district. As a practical matter, however, the division of assets and liabilities of the dissolved district is generally resolved by intergovernmental agreement between the annexing districts. The intergovernmental agreement is usually ratified by the regional board of school trustees.

Ill. Rev. Stat. c. 122, par. 7-11
Ill. Rev. Stat. c. 122, par. 7-12
Ill. Rev. Stat. c. 122, par. 7-14
Board of Education of Community Unit School District No. 325, Peoria County v. Board of Education of Special Charter School District No. 150, Peoria County, 2 Ill.App.3d 643, 276 N.E.2d 732 (3rd Dist. 1971)

8:145 Are state financial incentives provided to offset the cost to an annexing district of absorbing non-certificated personnel?

No state incentives are provided to offset the costs of absorbing non-certificated personnel. The lack of incentives can be an important disincentive when there are large differences between the salaries and benefits paid to non-certificated employees in the two districts affected.

Ill. Rev. Stat. c. 122, par. 18-8

DETACHMENT AND ANNEXATION PETITIONS

8:150 How frequently may a petition for detachment be submitted?

Any territory involved in a boundary change proceeding that is not approved may not be involved in another boundary change proceeding for at least one full year after final determination of the first proceeding.

Ill. Rev. Stat. c. 122, par. 7-8
Board of Education of Community Unit School District No. 300, Kane, Cook, McHenry and Lake Counties v. County Board of School Trustees of Kane County, 60 Ill.App.3d 415, 376 N.E.2d 1054, 17 Ill.Dec. 725 (2nd Dist. 1978)
Hall Township High School District No. 502 Bureau County v. School Trustees of Bureau County, 80 Ill.App.2d 475, 225 N.E.2d 228 (3rd Dist. 1967)
Board of Education of Consolidated School District No. 138 of Winnebago County v. County Board of School Trustees of Winnebago County 37, Ill.App.2d 166, 185 N.E.2d 374 (2nd Dist. 1962)

8:160 May a detachment petition be filed when a school district affected by the petition has a bond referendum pending?

No. When notice of a bond issue election has been published, no petition affecting the boundaries of the school district may be filed pending defeat of the bond issue proposal, issuance of the bonds, a board resolution abandoning its plan to issue bonds, or the elapse of 75 days following the election, whichever comes first. This prohibition applies only to the first such election called in any calendar year, and the period of the prohibition may be affected if the district is involved in a legal boundary dispute at the time the election notice is published.

Ill. Rev. Stat. c. 122, par. 7-3

8:170 May a petitioner remove his name from an annexation or detachment petition?

A petitioner may have his name removed from a detachment or annexation petition at any time prior to final determination by the regional board of school trustees.

Konald v. Board of Education of Community Unit School District No. 220, 114 Ill.App.3d 512, 448 N.E.2d 555, 69 Ill.Dec. 837 (2nd Dist. 1983)

Board of Education of Avoca School District No. 37, Cook County, v. Regional Board of School Trustees of Cook County, 82 Ill.App.3d 1067, 403 N.E.2d 578, 38 Ill.Dec. 347 (1st Dist. 1980)

Board of Education of Metropolis Community High School District No. 20, Massac County v. County Board of School Trustees, Massac County, 34 Ill.App.3d 901, 341 N.E.2d 10 (5th Dist. 1976)

REGIONAL BOARD OF SCHOOL TRUSTEES

8:180 With what body is a detachment or annexation petition filed?

A detachment or annexation petition is filed with the appropriate regional board(s) of school trustees.

Ill. Rev. Stat. c. 122, par. 7-1 et seq.
Ill. Rev. Stat. c. 122, par. 7-2a

8:190   When a petition seeks to detach territory in two educational service regions, is approval of both regional boards of school trustees necessary?

Yes. A joint hearing is held, but approval of both regional boards is required.

Ill. Rev. Stat. c. 122, par. 7-6 et seq.
Carver v. Bond/Fayette/Effingham Regional Board of School Trustees, __ Ill.2d __, __ N.E. __, __ L.Ed. __, Docket No. 71022 (Slip op. January 30, 1992)

8:200   What happens following the filing of a detachment and annexation petition?

The secretary of the regional board of school trustees sends the petition to the school board of each school district involved. Notice is published in a local newspaper pursuant to statutory requirements, and a hearing before the regional board of school trustees is held between 10 and 15 days after the publication of the notice.

Ill. Rev. Stat. c. 122, par. 7-6
Board of Education of Rockford School District No. 205 Winnebago and Boone Counties v Hearing Board of Counties of Boone and Winnebago, 152 Ill.App.3d 936, 505 N.E.2d 32, 105 Ill.Dec. 906 (2nd Dist. 1987) appeal den. 115 Ill.2d 535, 511 N.E.2d 425, 110 Ill.Dec 453
Phillips v. Special Hearing Board of Boone and Winnebago Counties, 154 Ill.App.3d 799, 504 N.E.2d 1251, 105 Ill.Dec. 733, appeal den. 115 Ill.2d 550, 511 N.E.2d 436, 110 Ill.Dec. 464 (2nd Dist. 1986)
Board of Education of Niles Township High School District 219, Cook County v. Regional Board of School Trustees of Cook County, 127 Ill.App.3d 210, 468 N.E.2d 1247, 82 Ill.Dec. 467 (1st Dist. 1984)

8:210   Who bears the burden of proof in a detachment or annexation proceeding?

The petitioners bear the burden of proof in a detachment or annexation proceeding.

Rhinehart v. Board of Education of Bloomington School District No. 87, McLean County, 132 Ill.App.2d 1078, 271 N.E.2d 104 (4th Dist. 1971)

8:220 What factors must regional boards consider in ruling on detachment petitions?

The regional board of school trustees must consider the ability of the districts affected to meet statutory standards of recogniton, and whether the detaching district will be able to remain financially healthy after annexation. It must also consider what is best for the pupils in the entire area, as well as for the school districts affected by the petition. The overall benefit to the annexing district and detachment area must clearly outweigh the detriment to the losing district and surrounding community as a whole. There must not be serious harm done to the financial or educational resources of either district.

Ill. Rev. Stat. c. 122, par. 7-2.6

Carver v. Bond/Fayette/Effingham Regional Board of Schoot Trustees, __ Ill.2d __, __ N.E. __, __ L.Ed. __, Docket No. 71022 (Slip op. January 30, 1992)

Board of Education of Golf School District No. 67 v. Regional Board of School Trustees of Cook County, 89 Ill.2d 392, 433 N.E.2d 240, 60 Ill.Dec. 443 (1982)

Board of Education of Pearl City Community Unit School District No. 200 v. Regional Board of School Trustees of Stephenson County, 98 Ill.App.3d 599, 424 N.E.2d 808, 54 Ill.Dec. 58 (2nd Dist. 1981)

Board of Education of Jonesboro Community Consolidated School District v. Regional Board of School Trustees of Union County, 86 Ill.App.3d 230, 407 N.E.2d 1084, 41 Ill.Dec. 586 (5th Dist. 1980)

Richmond v. County Board of School Trustees of Whiteside County, 93 Ill.App.2d 142, 235 N.E.2d 657 (3rd Dist. 1968)

Sesser Community Unit District No. 196, Franklin County v. County Board of School Trustees of Franklin County, 74 Ill.App.2d 152, 219 N.E.2d 364 (5th Dist. 1966)

Board of Education of Community Unit School District No. 323, Winnebago and Stephenson Counties v. County Board of School Trustees of Winnebago and Stephenson Counties, 19 Ill.App.2d 196, 153 N.E.2d 378 (2nd Dist. 1958)

Oakdale Community Consolidiated School District No. 1 v. County Board of School Trustees, 12 Ill.2d 190, 145 N.E. 736 (1957)

Illinois v. Deatherage, 401 Ill. 25, 81 N.E.2d 581 (1948)

8:230 May a regional board of school trustees amend a detachment or annexation petition?

No. In ruling on a detachment or annexation petition, a regional board of school trustees may allow or deny a petition but cannot modify it.

Board of Education of Wellington Community Unit School District No. 7 of Iroquois County v. County Board of School Trustees of Vermillion County, 13 Ill.App.2d 561, 142 N.E.2d 742 (3rd Dist. 1957)

Trico Community Unit School District No. 176 v. County. Board of School Trustees, 8 Ill.App.2d 494, 131 N.E.2d 829 (5th Dist. 1956)

Oakdale Community Consolidated School District No. 1, v. County Board of School Trustees of Randolph County, 12 Ill.App.2d 260, 139 N.E.2d 795 (4th Dist. 1956)

8:240 May a detachment petition be granted solely based on expanded educational opportunities for a student?

When there are no countervailing factors, and when the best interests of the children involved are served by the detachment. the courts usually apply the "whole child" and "community of interest" tests.

The "whole child" test considers whether or not there will be increased participation in school activities by the students and their families and how the educational, social and extracurricular needs of the student can best be satisfied. The "community of interest" test considers whether the detachment area is identified with the school district and community to which annexation is sought.

Carver v. Bond/Fayette/Effingham Regional Board of School Trustees, __ Ill.2d __, __ N.E. __, __ L.Ed. __, Docket No. 71022 (Slip op. January 30, 1992)

Fixmer v. Regional Board of School Trustees of Kane County, 146 Ill.App.3d 660, 497 N.E.2d 152, 100 Ill.Dec. 272 (2nd Dist. 1986)

City National Bank of Kankakee v. Schott, 113 Ill.App.3d 388, 447 N.E.2d 478, 69 Ill.Dec. 261 (3rd Dist. 1983)

Granfield v. Regional Board of School Trustees of Bureau County, 108 Ill.App.3d 703, 438 N.E.2d 497, 64 Ill.Dec. 246 (3rd Dist. 1982)

Board of Education of Golf School District No. 67 v. Regional Board of School Trustees of Cook County, 89 Ill.2d 392, 433 N.E.2d 240, 60 Ill.Dec. 443 (1982)

Board of Education of Community High School District No. 154, McHenry County v. Regional Board of School Trustees of McHenry County, 84 Ill.App.3d 501, 405 N.E.2d 495 (2nd Dist. 1980)

Burnidge v. County Board of School Trustees of Kane County, 25 Ill.App.2d 503, 167 N.E.2d 21 (3rd Dist. 1960)

8:250 What is the benefit-detriment analysis?

The benefit-detriment analysis is used to determine whether the benefit derived from the annexation of the affected territory will outweigh the detriment to the losing district, the territory, and the community as a whole.

Carver v. Bond/Fayette/Effingham Regional Board of School Trustees, __ Ill.2d __, __ N.E. __, __ L.Ed. __, Docket No. 71022 (Slip op. January 30, 1992)

Burnidge v. County Board of School Trustees of Kane County, 25 Ill.App.2d 503, 167 N.E.2d 21 (3rd Dist. 1960)

Illinois v. Deatherage, 401 Ill. 25, 81 N.E.2d 581 (1948)

8:260 May the regional board of school trustees consider parental preference and convenience in deciding a petition for detachment and annexation?

While they may be treated as one factor in ruling on the detachment petition, parental preference and convenience alone are usually insufficient to support a detachment and annexation petition.

Carver v. Bond/Fayette/Effingham Regional Board of School Trustees, __ Ill.2d __, __ N.E. __, __ L.Ed. __, Docket No. 71022 (January 30, 1992)

Eble v. Hamilton, 52 Ill.App.3d 550, 367 N.E.2d 788 (3rd Dist. 1977)

Ottawa Township High School District No. 140 of LaSalle County v. County Board of School Trustees, 106 Ill.App.2d 439, 246 N.E.2d 138 (3rd Dist. 1969)

Burgner v. County Board of School Trustees of Peoria County, 60 Ill.App.2d 267, 208 N.E.2d 54 (3rd Dist. 1965)

Trico Community Unit School District No. 176 v. County. Board of School Trustees, 8 Ill.App.2d 494, 131 N.E.2d 829 (4th Dist. 1956)

8:270 What considerations apply to detachment and annexation petitions involving territory where no students reside?

In detachment and annexation hearings concerning property which is either uninhabited and /or in which no students reside, it is the duty of the regional board of school trustees to determine whether the annexation would be beneficial to the educational welfare of any pupils who might later reside in that area. Educational welfare is to be determined by considering whether or not the territory involved is part of an integral or main activity of the community served by the receiving school district, the residential potential of the tract of land involved, and the distance students would travel along and across any heavily traveled roads in order to attend school.

Pontiac Township High School District No. 90 v. Regional Board of School Trustees for Livingston County, 183 Ill.App.3d 885, 539 N.E.2d 885, 132 Ill.Dec. 322 (4th Dist. 1989)

City National Bank of Kankakee v. Schott, 113 Ill.App.3d 388, 447 N.E.2d 478, 69 Ill.Dec. 261 (3rd Dist. 1983)

Rhinehart v. Board of Education of Bloomington School District No. 87, McLean County, 132 Ill.App.2d 1078, 271 N.E.2d 104 (4th Dist. 1971)

Board of Education of Springfield School District No. 186 v. Scott, 105 Ill.App.2d 192, 244 N.E.2d 821 (4th Dist. 1969)

8:280 Who may appeal an annexation, detachment or dissolution decision of a regional board of school trustees?

Any resident or any petitioner who enters an appearance at the hearing may file a complaint for judicial review within 35 days of service of the decision by registerd mail in detachment-annexation cases ands within 10 days of service of the decision by registered mail in dissolution-annexation cases.

Ill. Rev. Stat. c. 122, par. 7-7

Ill. Rev. Stat. c. 122, par. 7-11

8:290 What happens if an annexation, detachment or dissolution decision of a regional board of school trustees is appealed?

If a decision of a regional board of school trustees is appealed, the complaint for judicial review operates as a stay of enforcement, and there is no enforcement of the decision until there is final disposition of the review. This means the entire matter of the dissolution, detachment or annexation is in limbo until all appeals have been exhausted.

Ill. Rev. Stat. c. 122, par. 7-7
Ill. Rev. Stat. c. 122, par. 7-11

8:295 What happens if the regional board of school trustees fails to act on a detachment, annexation, division or dissolution petition?

If within nine months after a petition is submitted under section 7-1 of the School Code the regional board of school trustees fails to approve or deny the petition, the school boards or registered voters of the districts affected that submitted the petition (or the committee of ten) may submit a copy of the petition directly to the State Superintendent of Education for approval or denial.

Ill. Rev. Stat. c. 122, par. 7-6 (l)

CHARTER DISTRICT
DETACHMENT AND ANNEXATION

8:300 How is a petition for annexation to or detachment of territory from a charter district filed?

A request for annexation or detachment of territory may be initiated by any district affected by the filing of a petition signed by the school board and by a petition signed by 25 percent or 1,000 of the legal voters of the district, whichever is less, or by a petition signed by 50 percent of the legal voters residing in any territory requesting to be annexed or detached, or if there are no legal voters residing within the territory proposed to be detached or annexed, the petition may be signed by 50 percent of the owners of real estate of record.

Ill. Rev. Stat. c. 24, par. 1-1 et seq.

Ill. Rev. Stat. c. 122, par. 7-2.3 et seq.

Schreiber v. County Board of School Trustees of Peoria County, 31 Ill.2d 121, 198 N.E.2d 848 (1964)

Illinois ex rel. Community Unit School District No. 1, Macon and DeWitt Counties v. Decatur School District No. 61, 45 Ill.App.2d 33, 194 N.E.2d 659 (4th Dist. 1964)

8:310 With what body is a charter district detachment or annexation petition filed?

A detachment or annexation petition is filed with the governing body of the special charter district. A certified copy of the petition must be sent to each district affected and to the board of school trustees of the counties in which the territory to be detached is located.

Ill. Rev. Stat. c. 24, par. 1-1 et. seq.

Ill. Rev. Stat. c. 122, par. 7-2.4

8:320 What happens following the filing of a charter district detachment and annexation petition?

If no objection is filed with the regional board of school trustees or the governing body of the special charter district within 30 days after notice of the petition has been given to affected districts, the detachment/annexation takes effect subject however to stay rules in the event of appeal and other statutory time lines. If an objection is filed, the regional board of school trustees and the school district must appoint a hearing board. The regional board of school trustees appoints two members and the school board appoints two members. These four members meet and appoint three more members who reside outside the area to be detached or annexed.

Ill. Rev. Stat. c. 122, par. 7-2.5 et seq.

Ill. Rev. Stat. c. 122, par. 7-9

Board of Education of Rockford School District No. 205 Winnebago and Boone Counties v. Hearing Board of Counties of Boone and Winnebago, 152 Ill.App.3d 936, 505 N.E.2d 32, 105 Ill.Dec. 906, appeal den. 115 Ill.2d 535, 511 N.E.2d 425, 110 Ill.Dec 453 (2nd Dist. 1987)

*Board of Education of Rockford School District No. 205
Winnebago and Boone Counties v Regional Board of School Trustees
of Boone and Winnebago Counties,* 135 Ill.App.3d 486, 481 N.E.2d
1266, 90 Ill.Dec. 355 (2nd Dist. 1985)

*Board of Education of Niles Township High School District 219,
Cook County v. Regional Board of School Trustees of Cook County,*
127 Ill.App.3d 210, 468 N.E.2d 1247, 82 Ill.Dec. 467 (1st Dist. 1984)

8:330 What factors must the hearing board consider in ruling on petitions?

The hearing board must consider: (a) the school needs and
conditions of the territory in the area within and adjacent to the
area to be attached or detached and the ability of the districts
affected to meet the standards of recognition as prescribed by
the State Board of Education, (b) the division of funds and assets
which will result from any change of boundaries, (c) the will of
the people of the area affected, and (d) the best interests of the
schools of the area and the educational welfare of the pupils.

Ill. Rev. Stat. c. 122, par. 7-2.6

First National Bank of Elgin v. West Aurora School District 129,
200 Ill.App.3d 210, 558 N.E.2d 686, 146 Ill.Dec. 723 (2nd Dist. 1990)

*Desmond v. Regional Board of School Trustees, Malta Community
Unit School District No. 433,* 183 Ill.App.3d 316, 538 N.E.2d 1350,
131 Ill.Dec. 794 (2nd Dist. 1989), appeal den. 127 Ill.2d 614, 545
N.E.2d 108, 136 Ill.Dec. 584

*Phillips v. Special Hearing Board of Boone and Winnebago
Counties,* 154 Ill.App.3d 799, 504 N.E.2d 1251, 105 Ill.Dec. 733,
appeal den. 115 Ill.2d 550, 511 N.E.2d 436, 110 Ill.Dec. 464 (2nd
Dist. 1986)

City National Bank of Kankakee v. Shott, 113 Ill.App.3d 388, 447
N.E.2d 478, 69 Ill. Dec. 261 (4th Dist. 1983)

Wirth v. Green, 96 Ill.App.3d 89, 420 N.E.2d 1200, 51 Ill.Dec. 642
(3rd Dist. 1981)

*Board of Education of Springfield School District No. 186,
Sangamon County v. Scott,* 105 Ill.App.2d 192, 244 N.E.2d 821 (4th
Dist. 1969)

*Board of Education of City of Bloomington, McLean County v.
County Board of School Trustees of McLean County,* 77 Ill.App.2d
368, 222 N.E.2d 343 (4th Dist. 1966)

*Horth v. Board of Education of School District No. 205,
Winnebago County,* 42 Ill.App.2d 65, 191 N.E.2d 601 (2nd Dist. 1963)

8:340 What is the effective date of change for the creation or change of boundaries of a charter school district?

When a petition is filed for the change in boundaries of a charter school district, the commencement of any action for judicial review acts as a stay of enforcement, and no further proceedings may be had until final disposition of the review. A petition for rehearing operates as a stay until the hearing board enters its final order on the petition for rehearing. In the event the granting if a petition becomes final, either through failure to seek administrative review, or by final decision of a court on review, the change in boundaries becomes effective immediately. If, however, the granting of a petition becomes final between September 1 and June 30 of any year, there is no change in administration or attendance of the schools affected until the following July 1 unless all the affected school boards and the regional board of school trustees agree otherwise.

Ill. Rev. Stat. c. 122, par. 7-2.6
Ill. Rev. Stat. c. 122, par. 7-2.7
Ill. Rev. Stat. c. 122, par. 7-9

9: CONTROL AND USE OF SCHOOL PROPERTY

ACQUISITION AND OWNERSHIP

9:10 What was the original source of school property in Illinois?

The Northwest Ordinance in 1787 set aside the sixteenth section (640 acres) in every congressional township for the maintenance of public schools. This land was used for school sites or, more often, for rental or sale with proceeds used to support the schools. Common school land today is defined as "the sixteenth section in every township and the sections and parts of sections granted in place of all or part of the sixteenth section."

1 U.S. Land Laws 852
Ill. Rev. Stat. c. 122, par. 15-1

9:20 Who holds title to public school property?

Public school property is actually state property, but title is held by boards of school trustees—township school trustees or the regional board of school trustees in Class II counties (Cook) and county school trustees in Class I counties (all others). Trustees hold title to the property for the use and benefit of the school district.

Title to public school property in Chicago is held by the city.

Ill. Rev. Stat. c. 122, par. 5-1
Ill. Rev. Stat. c. 122, par. 5-21
Ill. Rev. Stat. c. 122, par. 34-20

9:30 May a school board hold title to real property?

A school board may hold title to real or personal property acquired from a direct grant, gift, donation or legacy to the board. A school board also may hold title to property acquired for educational or vocational training of pupils.

Ill. Rev. Stat. c. 122, par. 5-21
Ill. Rev. Stat. c. 122, par. 10-23.3
Ill. Rev. Stat. c. 122, par. 16-1

9:40   How may a school board acquire property?

A school board may acquire school property by purchase or lease; condemnation; grant, gift, donation, devise, or bequest, or by receipt of a beneficial interest from a trust.

Ill. Rev. Stat. c. 24, par. 11-78-1 et seq.
Ill. Rev. Stat. c. 30, par. 156 et seq.
Ill. Rev. Stat. c. 122, par. 10-22.35A
Ill. Rev. Stat. c. 122, par. 10-23.6

9:50   May a school board exercise power of eminent domain?

In appropriate circumstances, a school district may benefit from acquisition of private property by eminent domain. The Illinois Constitution provides in pertinent part:

"Private property shall not be taken or damaged for public use without just compensation as provided by law. Such compensation shall be determined by a jury as provided by law."

Ill. Const., art. I, sec. 15

Scheller v. Trustees of Schools, Township 41 North, 67 Ill.App.3d 857, 384 N.E.2d 971, 24 Ill.Dec. 104 (2nd Dist. 1978)

County Board of School Trustees of DuPage County v. Boram, 26 Ill.2d 167, 186 N.E.2d 275 (1962)

9:60   How is the price determined when property is acquired by eminent domain?

The courts establish the price to be paid when the governmental unit and the property owner cannot agree upon a price. Fair market value is the price standard applied. Fair market value is established by competent evidence.

Ill. Rev. Stat. c. 122, par. 16-6

Chicago in Trust for Schools v. Albert J. Schorsch Realty Co., 6 Ill.App.3d 1074, 287 N.E.2d 93 (1st Dist. 1972)

Board of Junior College District 515 v. Wagner, 3 Ill.App.3d 1006, 279 N.E.2d 754 (1st Dist. 1971)

9:70 May a school board acquire property which is not contiguous to school grounds for use as a playground or athletic field?

Property acquired by a school board for use as playgrounds, recreational fields, or athletic fields need not be contiguous to any school grounds.

Ill. Rev. Stat. c. 122, par. 16-7

9:80 May a school board purchase land located outside the boundaries of its school district?

Under certain conditions, a school district may have statutory authority to purchase land outside the boundaries of its school district. Such authority is frequently required to accommodate the school building requirements of joint agreements and cooperative education arrangements.

Ill. Rev. Stat. c. 122, par. 10-22.31b
Ill. Rev. Stat. c. 122, par. 10-23.6
Ill. Rev. Stat. c. 122, par. 22-16

9:90 May a municipality transfer real estate to a school district?

A municipality may transfer real estate to a school district. The corporate authority of municipalities includes the power to transfer all of the rights, title, and interest held by it to a school district.

Ill. Rev. Stat. c. 30, par. 157

9:100 May a school district require a land developer to set aside property for school purposes?

A school district has no direct means to require a developer to set aside land. A municipality may require a developer to set aside land and/or money for school purposes by passing an ordinance to that effect.

Ill. Rev. Stat. c. 24, par. 11-12-4
Ill. Rev. Stat. c. 34, par. 5-1041.1

Krughoff v. Naperville, 68 Ill.2d 352, 369 N.E.2d 892, 12 Ill.Dec. 185, (1977)

Board of Education School District No. 68 DuPage County v. Surety Developers, Inc., 24 Ill.App.3d 638, 321 N.E.2d 99 (2nd Dist. 1974)

Board of Education Community Consolidated School District No. 59, Cook County v. E.A. Herzog Construction Co., 29 Ill.App.2d 138, 172 N.E.2d 645 (1st Dist. 1961)

DISPOSING OF SCHOOL PROPERTY

9:110 Who has power to decide that a school site is unnecessary, unsuitable, or inconvenient for a school building?

A school board may decide when a site or building has become unnecessary, unsuitable, or inconvenient for use as a school. By resolution adopted by at least two-thirds of its membership, a school board may elect to sell, enter into a contract for deed or convey a site under a seller-will-finance agreement.

Ill. Rev. Stat. c. 122, par. 5-22

9:120 Under what conditions may a school board deactivate its high school and send its students to another school district?

There is a statutory process whereby a school district may deactivate its high school and send its high school students to another school district. The process requires voter approval and is subject to numerous statutory limitations and conditions.

Ill. Rev. Stat. c. 122, par. 10-22.2b

9:130 May one school district sell school land to another school district?

If a school board decides a schoolhouse site, with or without a building, is of no further use to the district and agrees on a price with the school board of another school district within or next to the boundaries of the site, it may, after complying with statutory procedures, transfer the use of the site to the purchasing district.

Ill. Rev. Stat. c. 122, par. 16-3

9:140 How may a school board offer real estate for public sale?

School real estate may be sold by auction or sealed bid, with or without a minimum selling price. If the school board specifies a minimum selling price and the price is not met, or no bids are received, a real estate broker may be employed pursuant to statutory terms. If at any time the school board lowers the minimum selling price, a new auction or sealed bid procedure must follow. The school board may increase the minimum selling price without repeating the public sale procedures.

Ill. Rev. Stat. c. 122, par. 5-22

9:145 Must a school district selling property notify a buyer of hazardous materials in school buildings and on school grounds?

In most cases, a school district selling real property must disclose to the buyer the presence of hazardous materials on the property. A disclosure statement is required by law to identify the existence of asbestos or certain underground storage tanks, for example.

Ill. Rev. Stat. c. 30, par. 901 et seq.
42 U.S.C.A. 11022

9:150 May the citizens of a school district initiate the sale of school land?

Citizens may petition a school board to sell school buildings and grounds to another school district or other municipality. The petition must be signed by at least 10 percent of the voters of the district. Upon receipt of the petition, the school board must adopt a resolution for the sale, fix the price, and order the school board secretary to certify the proposition to the election authorities for submission to the voters.

Ill. Rev. Stat. c. 122, par. 5-24
Ill. Rev. Stat. c. 122, par. 15-7

9:160 If a school board decides to close a school building and sell the property, may the land be sold separately from the building?

Title to any building erected on school grounds may be disposed of separately from the site upon which it is located.

Miner v. Yantis, 410 Ill. 401, 102 N.E.2d 524 (1952)

9:165 How may the school board take payment for real estate?

The school board may take cash, may enter into a contract for deed, mortgage, or may sell on the basis of another seller-financed basis as determined by the school board.

Ill. Rev. Stat. c. 122, par. 5-22

9:170 May a school board exchange school property for other property?

By a two-thirds majority vote of its members, a school board may exchange a school site or a site with a building on it for another site. To do so, the school board must file a Certificate of Findings and Declarations with the Recorder of Deeds and comply with other statutory procedures.

Ill. Rev. Stat. c. 122, par. 5-23

9:180 How may a school board use the proceeds from the sale of school property?

A school board must use the proceeds from the sale of school sites, buildings, or other real estate first to pay the principal and interest on any outstanding bonds on the property being sold. After all such bonds have been retired, the proceeds from the sale may be used for any authorized purpose and may be deposited into any district fund.

Ill. Rev. Stat. c. 122, par. 5-22

9:190 May a school board lease school property to a third party?

A school board may lease school property to another school district, municipality, not-for-profit school organization, suitable lessee for educational purposes, another governmental body, or for any other purpose which serves the interests of the community. The permissible terms of the initial lease vary according to the type of lessee.

A referendum is required for leasing to a private not-for-profit school organization for use in the care of the trainable and educable mentally handicapped or for the education of the gifted.

A lease for a permissible term in excess of ten years or the modification of a lease whose unexpired term is in excess of ten years requires a vote of two-thirds of the full membership of the school board.

Ill. Rev. Stat. c. 122, par. 10-22.11 et seq.

SCHOOL BUILDINGS

9:200 May a school board construct school buildings?

A school board is authorized to build or purchase schools or office facilities upon voter approval at a referendum. A board also may issue bonds to finance construction upon voter approval.

Ill. Rev. Stat. c. 122, par. 10-22.36
Ill. Rev. Stat. c. 122, par. 19-1 et seq.

9:210 May a school board accumulate operating funds for the purpose of constructing a school building?

A building intended for permanent use as school property may be constructed only after voter approval at a referendum. Voter approval is also required for the accumulation of funds in the operations and maintenance fund.

Ill. Rev. Stat. c. 122, par. 10-22.36
Ill. Rev. Stat. c. 122, par. 17-5.1

9:215 Must a school district make its facilties handicapped accessible?

New building construction and alterations which affect the usability of the facility or a part of it must be handicapped accessible if first occupancy is after January 26, 1993. There is no requirement that existing facilities be altered to be handicapped accessible unless a student's individualized education program, an accomodation for a handicapped employee, or some other specific accomodation so requires.

42 U.S.C.S. 12201 et seq.

9:220 Is a school board authorized to build an athletic stadium or arena for spectator sports?

A school board may issue revenue bonds to build an athletic stadium or arena and has wide authority to operate, control and manage it. Funds to retire the bonds are acquired through charges and fees for the use of the facility.

Ill. Rev. Stat. c. 122, par. 19a-1 et seq.

9:230 Does the State offer financial assistance to public school districts in the construction of school facilities?

For school districts which qualify and when monies are appropriated by the legislature for this purpose, the State offers assistance in the building of school facilities. The Capital Development Board distributes and administers assistance funds.

Ill. Rev. Stat. c. 122, par. 35-1 et seq.
Ill. Rev. Stat. c. 122, par. 1201 et seq.
Ill. Rev. Stat. c. 127, par. 753 et seq.

9:240 What is the Illinois Capital Development Board?

The Illinois Capital Development Board is a state agency which administers distribution of funds for school sites, buildings and equipment subject to statutory limitations. The State Board of Education establishes eligibility standards and priorities and notifies the Capital Development Board of approved construction projects.

Ill. Rev. Stat. c. 122, par. 1201 et seq.

Ill. Rev. Stat. c. 127, par. 783 et seq.

9:250 How does a school district get a Capital Development Board grant?

A school district may apply to the State Board of Education for a school construction project grant. A school district must establish eligibility for such a grant by submitting a District Facility Plan, subject to review and approval by the State Board of Education.

Ill. Rev. Stat. c. 127, par. 783.4

9:260 How does the Capital Development Board prioritize the building needs of school districts?

The Capital Development Board considers the current average daily attendance in the district and its attendance areas and the probable average daily attendance for the succeeding five years in the light of the growth trend of the district, the effect of slum clearance and large-scale housing projects, the pattern of attendance between private and public schools and plans for the curtailment or additions to private school facilities in the area, and any other factors bearing upon the probable continuing building needs of the district. It also determines the number of available classrooms which meet the minimum requirements specified by the State Board of Education. It proceeds on the assumption that each district needs one classroom for every 32 pupils in average daily attendance in grades K-6, one classroom for each 28 students in average daily attendance in grades 7-9, and one classroom for every 25 students in average daily attendance in grades 10-12.

Ill. Rev. Stat. c. 122, par. 35-6 et seq.

9:270   What qualifications must a school district meet in order to receive assistance from the Capital Development Board?

No school district is entitled to have a building acquired or constructed by the Capital Development Board (CDB) unless:

1) The CDB determines the district will require, in addition to its present classrooms and those for which funds have been provided by the district, classrooms for at least 110 pupils in average daily attendance in grades 9-12 and 200 pupils in average daily attendance in grades K-12 at the beginning of the ensuing fall school term and the need for such additional classrooms will continue through five ensuing school years.

2) The district has either reduced its bonding power to less than $5,000 or will have done so in complying with the provisions of this requirement.

3) The school board has been authorized to levy a special tax sufficient in amount to provide the rent for the facilities to be so provided, but the CDB may approve an application for the construction of a classroom in a district contingent upon compliance with this provision within 60 days after such approval.

Ill. Rev. Stat. c. 122, par. 35-7

9:280   May the Capital Development Board lease facilities to school districts?

The Capital Development Board may lease facilities to school districts.

Ill. Rev. Stat. c. 122, par. 22-17
Ill. Rev. Stat. c. 122, par. 35-5(c)
Ill. Rev. Stat. c. 122, par. 35-5(i)

9:290   If a school district is to build a facility with Capital Development Board assistance, who has control over site selection?

The Capital Development Board may reject any site selected by a school board if the site does not meet minimum engineering and construction standards.

Ill. Rev. Stat. c. 127, par. 780.16

9:300 Must a school district pay "prevailing wages" to workers on a construction contract?

Laborers, workers, and mechanics employed by or on behalf of a school district, its contractors, or subcontractors to perform construction work other than maintenance work must be paid not less than the hourly wage generally prevailing for similar work in the area. The school district must ascertain the prevailing rate of wages on a per-hour basis or ask the Department of Labor to ascertain the rate. The school district must specify in its resolution and call for bids that the prevailing hourly rate will be paid for each worker, and must stipulate in the contract that all workers must be paid no less than such prevailing rate. The school district must require contractors to include in their bonds provisions to guarantee the payment of prevailing wage rates.

Ill. Rev. Stat. c. 48, par. 39s-1 et seq.

Illinois ex rel. Bernardi Roofing Systems, Inc., 101 Ill.2d 424, 463 N.E.2d 123, 78 Ill.Dec. 945 (1984)

Beaver Glass and Mirror Co. v. Board of Education of Rockford School District No. 205, 59 Ill.App.3d 880, 36 N.E.2d 377, 17 Ill.Dec. 378 (2nd Dist. 1978)

City of Monmouth v. Payes, 39 Ill.App.2d 32, 188 N.E.2d 48 (2nd Dist. 1963)

Bradley v. Casey, 415 Ill. 576, 114 N.E.2d 681 (1953)

9:310 Is school district property subject to a mechanic's lien?

School district real estate is not subject to a mechanic's lien. Subcontractors may acquire a mechanic's lien on the money, bonds, or warrants due or which may become due.

Ill. Rev. Stat. c. 82, par. 23

Board of Education of School District No. 108, Tazewell Co. for Use of A.Y. McDonald Manufacturing Company v. Collum, 77 Ill.App.2d 479, 222 N.E.2d 804 (3rd Dist. 1966)

Spaulding Lumber Company v. Brown, 171 Ill. 487, 49 N.E. 725 (1898)

SAFETY

9:320 Is school district property subject to any laws regarding safety?

School building construction and maintenance are subject to State Board of Education regulations contained in the Illinois Life-Safety Code. Schools also are subject to the occupational safety standards of the Illinois Department of Labor. Other safety standards applicable to schools include various environmental requirements, such as asbestos abatement and safe drinking water, traffic safety, and the common law "duty of care" owed to students while on school premises.

9:330 What is the Life-Safety Code?

The Life-Safety Code is the common name used to identify State Board of Education regulations governing school building construction and safety specifications.

Ill. Rev. Stat. c. 122, par. 2-3.12
23 Ill. Admin. Code 175
23 Ill. Admin. Code 185
Board of Education of City of Rockford v. Page, 33 Ill.2d 372, 211 N.E. 2d 361 (1965)
Board of Education of School District No. 33, DuPage County v. City of West Chicago, 55 Ill.App.2d 401, 205 N.E.2d 63 (2nd Dist 1965)

9:340 Who is responsible for school inspections under the Life-Safety Code?

The regional superintendent of schools is charged with the responsibility to inspect the plans and specifications for the heating, ventilating, lighting, seating, water supply, toilets, and fire safety of all the public school rooms and buildings within his region to ensure compliance with the Life-Safety Code. If the regional superintendent of schools does not approve or deny plans submitted to him within 30 days, the school board may submit the plans or specifications directly to the state superintendent of schools for approval or denial.

Ill. Rev. Stat. c. 122, par. 3-14.20 et seq.

9:345 What agencies have authority to inspect school cafeterias for health and safety?

The county health department has such authority. The regional superintendent does not have exclusive authority to conduct inspections for sanitation or health control.

Macon County v. Board of Education of Decatur School District No. 61, 165 Ill. App.3d 1, 518 N.E.2d 653, 116 Ill.Dec. 31 (4th Dist. 1987) app. den. 119 Ill.2d 558, 517 N.E.2d 1246, 119 Ill.Dec. 387

9:350 Can a regional superintendent of schools condemn a school building?

If a regional superintendent of schools believes a school building to be unsafe, he may request the Department of Public Health, the State Fire Marshal, or the supervising architect to inspect public school buildings and temporary school facilities which appear to him to be unsafe, unsanitary, or unfit for occupancy. These officials must inspect, and if, in their opinion, the buildings or temporary facilities are unsafe, unsanitary, or unfit for occupancy, they must state in writing in what particular they are deficient. When he receives the statement, the regional superintendent must condemn the building or temporary facility and notify the school board in writing stating the reasons for the condemnation.

Ill. Rev. Stat. c. 122, par. 3-14.22

9:360 Which standards control fire prevention and safety for public school buildings, those of the State Fire Marshal or the Illinois State Board of Education?

The State Board of Education Life-Safety Code applies. The State Fire Marshal's Grey Book does not apply.

Board of Education of Minooka Community High School District No. 111 Grundy, Kendall and Will Counties v. Carter, 119 Ill.App.3d 857, 458 N.E.2d 50, 75 Ill.Dec. 882, (3rd Dist. 1983)

9:365 Are sprinkler systems required in schools?

Sprinkler systems are required in all new public school buildings, building additions, and remodeling projects involving 50 percent or more of a school building.

Ill. Rev. Stat. c. 85, par. 2208.15
Ill. Rev. Stat. c. 122, par. 22-23

9:370 What is the Illinois Health and Safety Act?

The Health and Safety Act requires employers, including school districts, to provide employees with a safe workplace. It is administered by the Illinois Department of Labor, which has enacted rules implementing the statute. Employers are required, among other things, to: (a) post notices of employee rights under the act, including the right to file complaints with the Department of Labor; (b) submit to IDOL inspections and provide access to requested information and records, and (c) keep records of injuries arising in the workplace.

Ill. Rev. Stat. c. 48, par. 137.1 et seq.

9:380 Is a school board required to provide crossing guards for students walking to and from school?

A school board may employ persons to direct traffic on school grounds, or on or along streets and highways within a radius of one mile from school grounds. If a board elects to hire crossing guards, the cost may be shared with any unit of local government.

Ill. Rev. Stat. c. 122, par. 10-22.28a

9:390 May a school board establish a school safety patrol?

A school board may establish a school safety patrol. Student participation requires written parental consent.

Ill. Rev. Stat. c. 122, par. 10-22.28

9:400 May a school district install traffic signals at crossings where students walk to and from school?

A school board may acquire, install, operate, and maintain traffic signals outside city, village or incorporated town limits and within a one-mile radius of school grounds, subject to certain statutory limitations.

Ill. Rev. Stat. c. 122, par. 10-22.28a

9:410 What is the purpose of the Asbestos Abatement Act?

The purpose of the Illinois Asbestos Abatement Act is to provide for the identification, containment, or removal of those asbestos materials that constitute a significant health hazard to students, school personnel, parents, or visitors in the public elementary and secondary schools of the State of Illinois.

Ill. Rev. Stat. c. 122, par. 1401 et seq.

USE OF SCHOOL FACILITIES

9:420 May a school district hold a child's parents financially responsible for damage the child does to school property?

A civil suit under common law may be instituted. Recovery is also possible pursuant to the Parental Responsibility Act, under which a school district may hold a minor's parents responsible for actual damages or for the willful or malicious acts of a minor, to a maximum of $1000, for injury to persons or school property. A minor in this context is any unemancipated person who is over 11 but not yet 19 years of age and who lives with his parents or legal guardian.

Ill. Rev. Stat. c. 70, par. 53 et seq.

9:430 May a school board allow an outside organization to use school facilities during non-school hours?

A school board may permit use of school facilities by outside organizations during non-school hours. Statutory authority exists for use for religious meetings, Sunday schools, evening schools, literary societies, and for such other meetings as the school board deems proper.

Ill. Rev. Stat. c. 122, par. 10-22.10

Resnick v. East Brunswick Township Board of Education, 77 N.J. 88, 389 A.2d 944 (1978)

Board of Education of the City of Chicago v. Crilly, 312 Ill.App. 177, 37 N.E.2d 873 (1941)

9:440   May or must a school board charge fees to outside organizations for the use of school facilities?

A school board may establish fees for the use of school facilities, but is not required to do so. However, any fees not applied equally to all organizations must be structured by some reasonable classification, such as with lower fees or no fees for school-related groups (e.g., PTA, band boosters) or non-for-profit groups. Fees structured to discriminate against groups espousing unpopular views, for example, may be subject to challenge on constitutional grounds.

Ill. Rev. Stat. c. 122, par. 10-22.10

9:450   Must school boards permit student religious groups to use school property when not in use by the district for other school purposes?

The federal Equal Access Act provides that student religious organizations must be given the same access to high school facilities as any other student organization unless the school board limits access to those organizations that are curriculum related.

Equal Access Act 20 U.S.C. 4071

Board of Education of Westside Community Schools v. Mergens, 110 S.Ct. 2365, __ U.S. __, 110 L.Ed.2d 191 (1990)

Garnett v. Benton School District, 865 F.2d 1211 (9th Cir. 1989)

Widmar v. Vincent, 102 S.Ct. 269, 454 U.S. 263, 70 L.Ed.2d 440 (1981)

9:460 May teachers hold prayer meetings with students in school facilities before or after school?

No.

May v. Evansville-Vanderburg School Corporation, 787 F.2d 1005 (7th Cir. 1986)

10: THE EDUCATIONAL PROGRAM

CURRICULAR AUTHORITY

10:10 What authority does a school board have to establish curriculum?

The School Code mandates certain courses of study for all pupils in Illinois public schools. School boards may set requirements in excess of those mandated by the State.

Ill. Rev. Stat. c. 122, par. 10-20.8
Ill. Rev. Stat. c. 122, par. 27-1 et seq.
Illinois ex rel. McKeever v. Board of Education of Drummer Township High School, 176 Ill.App. 491 (3rd Dist. 1913)

10:20 Who has authority to determine appropriate class size?

Except with respect to special education, and unless a collective bargaining agreement provides otherwise, the school board has authority to determine appropriate class size. Class size is, however, a manadatory subject of bargaining, and a school board decision affecting class size may trigger a demand to bargain from affected employee bargaining units.

Board of Education Decatur District No. 61 v. Illinois Educational Labor Relations Board, 180 Ill.App.3d 770, 536 N.E.2d 743, 129 Ill.Dec. 693 (4th Dist. 1989)

10:30 Who establishes requirements for high school graduation?

The school board has the authority to establish the requirements for high school graduation. However, by law, those requirements must include the following core curriculum:

1) three years of language arts (two units in a three-year high school);

2) two years of mathematics, one of which may be related to computer technology;

3) one year of science;

4) two years of social studies, at least one of which must be American history or a combination of history of the United States and American government, and;

5) one year chosen from music, art, foreign language, or vocational education.

State law also requires the student to acquire 16 units in grades 9-12 (for four-year high schools) and 12 units in grades 10-12 (for three-year high schools). Students also must receive instruction in the principles of representative government and other specified related subjects.

Students who seek admission to any Illinois public community college, college, or university beginning in 1993 must have completed four years of English; three years each of social studies, mathematics, and science; and two years of music, art, or a foreign language.

Ill. Rev. Stat. c. 122, par. 27-1 et seq.
Ill. Rev. Stat. c. 122, par. 27-22
23 Ill. Admin. Code 1.440

10:40 May a school board grant academic credit on the basis of a proficiency exam?

A school board may, by policy, determine to allow or prohibit proficiency credit. Note, however, the School Code requires students to "successfully complete" those courses required for high school graduation and probably does not contemplate exemption by proficiency examination except where expressly allowed.

Ill. Rev. Stat. c. 122, par. 27-22
23 Ill. Admin. Code 1.460

10:50 May a student, by demonstrating proficiency, become exempt from state-required instructional programs?

Only the state's consumer education requirement permits exemption based on proficiency. The State Board of Education each year provides high schools a uniform Consumer Education Proficiency Test. The test is administered to students who elect to take it, and those that make a passing score are exempt from the consumer education course requirement. No student can take the test more than once in any school year.

Ill. Rev. Stat. c. 122, par. 27-12.1

10:60   May a student be permitted to receive credit by demonstrating proficiency in behind-the-wheel driver education?

A school district may adopt a policy to permit proficiency examinations for the practice driving part of driver's education after three hours of behind the wheel instruction.

School districts are required by law to offer driver education to high school students but students are not required by law to take the course.

Ill. Rev. Stat. c. 122, par. 27-24.3
Acorn Auto Driving School, Inc. v. Leyden High School District No. 212, 27 Ill.2d 93, 187 N.E.2d 722 (1963)

10:70   May a school board award academic credit for foreign language proficiency?

A school board may award credit to high school students who have studied a foreign language in an approved ethnic school or may grant one year of high school foreign language credit to any student who has graduated from elementary school and who can demonstrate proficiency in a foreign language. Foreign language includes American Sign Language.

Ill. Rev. Stat. c. 122, par. 2-3.44 et seq.
Ill. Rev. Stat. c. 122, par. 10-22.43 et seq.

10:80   By whom are high school equivalency tests administered?

The regional superintendent of schools must make a high school equivalency testing program available to qualified individuals residing within the region.

Ill. Rev. Stat. c. 122, par. 3-15.12

10:90 May a school board make sex education a required course offering?

A school board may not require a pupil to take or participate in a sex education class if the pupil's parent or guardian submits a written objection to the school district. A student may not be disciplined by reason of the parental objection.

Ill. Rev. Stat. c. 122, par. 27-9.1 et seq.

Bergstrand v. Rock Island Board of Education, School District No. 41, 161 Ill.App.3d 180, 514 N.E.2d 256, 112 Ill.Dec. 790 (3rd Dist. 1987)

10:100 May a school board require its students to receive instruction on disease?

A student is not required to take or participate in instruction on disease if the student's parent or guardian submits written objections on constitutional grounds. A student may not be disciplined by reason of the parental objection.

Ill. Rev. Stat. c. 122, par. 27-11

10:105 Who is a gifted student?

Gifted and talented children means children whose mental development is accelerated beyond the average, or who have demonstrated a specific aptitude or talent and can profit from specially planned educational services to the extent they need them. The term includes children with exceptional ability in academic subjects, high level thought processes, divergent thinking, creativity, and the arts.

Ill. Rev. Stat. c. 122, par. 14A-1 et seq.

10:106 Must boards of education provide special programming for gifted or talented children similar to that of the individualized educational program provided for handicapped children?

A school district must make available a program for gifted and talented children. A school district may voluntarily create such a program or enter into joint agreements for the creation of specific programs. Such programs are under the supervision of the state Board of Education and may be administered by the local district, regional superintendent, community college, college, or university and may include area service centers, experimental projects, institutes, special summer programs, and similar program offerings.

The laws governing the operation of gifted or talented programs do not require school districts to provide individualized educational programs for children enrolled in them.

Ill. Rev. Stat. c. 122, par. 14A-1 et seq.

Board of Education of City of Peoria School District No. 150 v. Sanders, 150 Ill.App.3d 755, 502 N.E.2d 730, 104 Ill.Dec. 233, app. den. 115 Ill.2d 536, 508 N.E.2d 208, 108 Ill.Dec. 47, cert. den. 108 S.Ct. 290, __ U.S. __ , 98 L.Ed.2d 250

10:110 May a school district include religious instruction in its curriculum?

A school district may include instruction in comparative religions and may educate students about religion in general, but may not sponsor or advocate the teaching of a particular religion or group of religions (such as Christianity, Judaism, or Islam), religious practice, or religious belief.

School District of Abington Township v. Schempp, 83 S.Ct. 1560, 374 US 203, 10 L.Ed.2d 844 (1963)

10:120 Under what conditions may a child be excused from the daily physical education requirement?

A child may be excused from physical education when an appropriate excuse is submitted by a doctor, parent or guardian. A school board may excuse pupils in grades 11 or 12 who request to be excused if the student is an ongoing participant in interscholastic athletics. A student in grades 11 or 12 also may be excused from physical education in order to enroll in a class which if not taken would prevent the student from graduating or result in the student's being denied admission to the institution of higher learning of the student's choice.

Ill. Rev. Stat. c. 122, par. 27-6

10:130 May a school district offer a summer school program?

A school board may operate a summer school program. Tuition may be charged in an amount not to exceed the per capita cost of the program. A school board may give regular school credit for satisfactory completion of summer school courses which are approved for credit by the State Board of Education. A statutory funding formula provides limited funds to support summer school programs.

Ill. Rev. Stat. c. 122, par. 10-22.33a
Ill. Rev. Stat. c. 122, par. 18-4.3

10:140 When is a school district required to provide transitional bilingual education?

Every school age child of limited English speaking ability must be provided a program in transitional bilingual education (or, under certain circumstances, a transitional instructional program in his own language) for a period of three years or until the child learns sufficient English language skills to allow him to perform successfully in classes taught in English, whichever occurs first.

Ill. Rev. Stat. c. 122, par. 14B-1 et seq.
Castenada v. Pickard, 648 F.2d 989 (5th Cir. 1981)
Teresa P. v. Berkeley Unified School District, 724 F. Supp. 698 (N.D. Cal. 1989)

10:150 How are school district work experience programs limited by child labor laws?

Child labor laws regulate the work which may be performed by minors. Generally, minors below age 14 are subject to stringent regulation and are, in most cases, prohibited from employment. The employment of minors between the ages of 14 and 16 is permitted in limited circumstances. The child labor laws state at what age minors may be employed in specific occupations, how many hours a day they may work, and cover many other work related subjects.

Ill. Rev. Stat. c. 48, par. 31.1 et seq.

10:160 May a school board establish a full-day kindergarten?

A school board may provide a full-day or half-day kindergarten. However, if a full-day program is offered, a half-day program must also be offered as an alternative for parents.

Ill. Rev. Stat. c. 122, par. 10-22.18
Ill. Rev. Stat. c. 122, par. 10-22.19a
Morgan v. Board of Education of Trico Community Unit School District 176, 22 Ill.App.3d 241, 317 N.E.2d 393 (5th Dist. 1974)

10:170 May a school board establish a before or after school day care center?

There is statutory authorization for the establishment of before or after school programs for grades K-6. The school district may charge parents of participating students a fee not to exceed the cost of the program. The program may include time for homework, physical exercise, afternoon nutritional snacks, and educational offerings which are in addition to those offered during the regular school day.

The schedule of these programs may follow the work calendar of the local community rather than the regular school calendar. Programs must be coordinated by teachers or persons who meet the requirements for supervising day care centers.

Ill. Rev. Stat. c. 122, par. 10-22.18b

10:180 If a school board chooses to establish a before or after school day care center, must it provide transportation for the students?

The parents or guardians of the participating students are responsible for the transportation of the students to and from a before or after school day care center operated by a school district.

Ill. Rev. Stat. c. 122, par. 10-22.18b

10:190 May a school board offer adult education classes?

A school board may establish classes for the instruction of persons 21 years of age and over and of persons less than 21 and

not otherwise in attendance in public school. A statutory funding formula provides limited funds to support such programs. If
a school board establishes an adult education program, it must
provide transportation and child care. A school board may
establish a tuition charge for persons enrolled who are not
subject to state reimbursement not to exceed the per capita cost
of the classes.

Ill. Rev. Stat. c. 122, par. 10-22.20

10:200 May a school district operate a nursery school?

School districts maintaining grades 1-8 or 1-12 may establish
nursery schools for the instruction of children between the ages
of 2 and 6 years if sufficient funds obtained from sources other
than local district taxes are available to pay the costs of the
nursery school.

Ill. Rev. Stat. c. 122, par. 10-23.2

10:210 May school boards enter into joint agreements with other school districts or agencies to provide educational programs?

Two or more educational agencies, including school districts,
may establish an educational joint agreement or cooperative by
agreeing in writing to work together to provide some educational
program. Common examples are vocational and special education cooperatives. In some cases, a new joint agreement school
district results from the cooperative effort, and in some cases an
existing school district becomes the administrative district for
the resulting cooperative and, as a result, no new entity is
formed. Some cooperative agreements require voter approval.

School districts with small high schools also may agree to
jointly operate a cooperative attendance center.

Ill. Rev. Stat. c. 122, par. 10-22.22c
Ill. Rev. Stat. c. 122, par. 10-22.31 et seq.

10:220 May a school district and a park district operate a joint recreational program?

Park districts have authority to develop, operate, finance, and participate in joint recreational programs with school districts and to enter into joint agreements.

Ill. Rev. Stat. c. 105, par. 8-18
Ill. Rev. Stat. c. 105, par. 9.1-5 et seq.

THE SCHOOL YEAR AND DAY

10:230 What is the minimum number of days in a school year?

Each school board is required by law to annually prepare a calendar for the school term which specifies both the opening and closing dates of the term. The calendar must provide a minimum term of at least 185 days which generally includes five emergency days and four teacher institute days in order to ensure 176 days of actual pupil attendance. Any teachers' institute day not used for an institute or used as a parental institute increases the minimum term of 176 pupil attendance days by the number of unused teacher institute days.

The adoption of a school calendar may have collective bargaining implications with respect to recognized bargaining units.

Ill. Rev. Stat. c. 122, par. 10-19
Ill. Rev. Stat. c. 122, par. 10-22.18d
Ill. Rev. Stat. c. 122, par. 24-1
Board of Education Arbor Park School District No. 145, Cook County v. Ballweber, 105 Ill.App.3d 412, 434 N.E.2d 448, 61 Ill.Dec. 295 aff'd. 96 Ill.2d 520, 451 N.E.2d 858, 71 Ill.Dec. 704 (1982)
Miller v. School District No. 189 East St. Louis, 26 Ill.App.3d 172, 325 N.E.2d 43 (5th Dist. 1975)

10:240 What is an "institute day"?

An "institute day" is any educational gathering, demonstration of methods of instruction, or visitation of schools or other institutions or facilities held or approved by the regional superintendent. Teacher "institutes" may include inservice training workshops or equivalent professional education experiences.

Under circumstances provided for in the law, a school district may have up to two parental institute days in any given year instead of teacher institute days.

Ill. Rev. Stat. c. 122, par. 3-11
Ill. Rev. Stat. c. 122, par. 10-22.18d
Miller v. School District No. 189, East St. Louis, 26 Ill.App.3d 172, 325 N.E.2d 43 (5th Dist. 1975)

10:245 What is a parental institute day?

A school district may use up to two teacher institute days to conduct parental institutes for the parents and guardians of students. Parental institute days require the consent of the district's inservice advisory committee or, if the district does not have an in-service advisory committee, parental institute days must be approved by the district's teachers.

Parental institute days may be held during that period of the day which is not part of the regular school day and may be held on Saturday. A school district may establish reasonable fees, not to exceed the cost of holding the parental institute but must waive the fee for parents or guardians who cannot afford the fee.

Ill. Rev. Stat. c. 122, par. 10-22.18d

10:250 When may institute days be used?

A regional superintendent of schools may arrange for or conduct district, regional or county institutes or equivalent professional educational experiences not more than four days annually. Of those four days, two days may be used as a teacher's workshop when approved by the regional superintendent, up to two days may be used for conducting parent-teacher conferences or up to two days may be used as parental institute days under conditions specified in the law. A school district may use one of its institute days on the last day of the school term. Institute days may be held on consecutive or separate days at the option of the regional superintendent of schools.

Ill. Rev. Stat. c. 122, par. 3-11
Ill. Rev. Stat. c. 122, par. 10-22.18d

10:260 Are there days on which school employees cannot be required to work?

A school board may not require teachers to teach on Saturdays or legal school holidays. Noncertificated school employees who are necessary because of an emergency or who are required for the continued operation of the schools may be required to work on school holidays. No deduction may be made from the time or compensation of a school employee on account of any legal or special holiday. Treatment of holidays may have collective bargaining implications with respect to recognized bargaining units.

Ill. Rev. Stat. c. 122, par. 24-2

District 300 Education Association v. Board of Education of Dundee Community Unit School District No. 300 of Kane County et al, 31 Ill.App.3d 550, 334 N.E.2d 165 (2nd Dist. 1975)

10:270 What is the minimum school day?

A school day must consist of no less than five clock hours under the direct supervision of teachers in order to meet State Board of Education standards and to qualify as a full day of school in calculating state aid entitlements. Some exceptions are authorized.

Ill. Rev. Stat. c. 122, par. 18-8

10:280 What are the exceptions to the minimum five clock hour school day?

There are five exceptions:

1) Four clock hours may be counted as a day of attendance for first-graders.

2) Two clock hours may be counted as a half-day of attendance for kindergartners.

3) One clock hour may count as a half-day of attendance for handicapped children below the age of six who cannot attend a two-hour session because of handicap or immaturity.

4) Days of attendance may be less than five clock hours on the opening and closing days of the school term, and upon the second or third day of the school term if the first and second days are used as institutes or teachers' workshops. Four clock hours may be counted as a day of attendance upon certification by the

regional superintendent and approval of the State Superintendent of Education.

5) A session of three or more clock hours up to a maximum of five half-days per school year may be counted as a full day of attendance when the remainder of the day is used for an in-service training program for teachers. Two full days may be used for parent-teacher conferences. Any full day used reduces the number of allowable half-days by two. In either instance, the programs must have the prior approval of the State Board of Education's Public School Approval Section.

23 Ill. Admin. Code 1.420

TESTING AND REPORTING

10:290 May a school district require minimum competency testing?

Minimum competency testing is standardized testing to measure the acquisition of skills at or beyond a certain defined minimum standard. The use of minimum competency testing is within the discretionary authority of a school board.

Ill. Rev. Stat. c. 122, par. 2-3.42
Ill. Rev. Stat. c. 122, par. 10-20.25
Ill. Rev. Stat. c. 122, par. 14-6.01

10:300 What student proficiency assessments are required by law?

School districts must assess the proficiency of all pupils except those receiving special educational services in the third, sixth, eighth, and eleventh grades. The State Board of Education prescribes the assessment procedures to be used; ensures that test items necessary for statewide reporting are included; and provides model assessment procedures from which school districts may select.

Ill. Rev. Stat. c. 122, par. 2-3.64

10:310 What must a school board report publicly with respect to the performance of the district's schools and students?

Each school district must submit to parents, taxpayers of the district, the Governor, the General Assembly, and the State Board of Education a school report card assessing the performance of its schools and students. The report card must describe the performance of students by school attendance center and must describe the district's use of financial resources. This report card must be presented at a regular school board meeting, must be made available to a newspaper of general circulation serving the district, and must be sent home to parents. The report card must include indicators of parental involvement in each attendance center.

The report card form is prepared by the State Board of Education and is disseminated prior to October 31 in each school year.

Ill. Rev. Stat. c. 122, par. 10-17a

GRADES AND GRADING

10:320 Who has final authority to determine whether a student is promoted or retained at grade level?

Except in the case of a student who has been found to be in need of special education, a school board has general authority to determine retention and promotion. Such decisions must be made uniformly, based on objective, nondiscriminatory criteria, and consistent with teacher evaluation of student progress.

Ill. Rev. Stat. c. 122, par. 10-20.9a

Morgan v. Board of Education of Trico Community Unit School District 176, 22 Ill.App.3d 241, 317 N.E.2d 393 (5th Dist. 1974)

10:330 May a school district adopt a policy permitting student grade reduction for disciplinary infractions?

This area of school law is unsettled. Some courts have allowed policies which tie grade reductions to disciplinary infractions, and some have not. Whether or not any such policy is permissible will depend upon the terms of the policy and the facts relating to its implementation.

Hamer v. Board of Education of Township High School District 113, 66 Ill.App.3d 7, 383 N.E.2d 231, 22 Ill.Dec. 755 (2nd Dist. 1978)

Knight v. Board of Education of Tri-Point Community Unit School District 6J, 38 Ill.App.3d 603, 348 N.E.2d 299 (4th Dist. 1976)

10:340 Can a non-custodial parent require a school district to report student progress?

In the absence of a court order to the contrary, upon the request of either parent of a pupil whose parents are divorced, a school board must mail all correspondence and reports which are furnished to one parent to the other parent.

Ill. Rev. Stat. c. 122, par. 10-21.8

EDUCATIONAL MATERIALS

10:350 What statutory authority is given a school board with respect to the adoption of textbooks?

A school board has statutory authority to adopt such printed instructional materials as are needed in the schools. A record of the adoption of texts and other print materials must be filed with the regional superintendent of schools.

Ill. Rev. Stat. c. 122, par. 28-6

10:360 Do citizens have a right to inspect instructional materials?

Any member of the public may inspect all text and instructional material used in the public schools. The term instructional material includes both printed and nonprint materials that are used in the educational process.

Ill. Rev. Stat. c. 122, par. 28-19.1 et seq.

10:370 May a school board charge a rental fee for textbooks?

A school board may purchase textbooks and rent them or resell them to students.

Ill. Rev. Stat. c. 122, par. 10-22.25

Ill. Rev. Stat. c. 122, par. 28.8

Hamer v. Board of Education, School District No. 109, Lake County, 9 Ill.App.3d 663, 292 N.E.2d 569 (2d Dist. 1977)

10:380 Under what circumstances must a school district provide free textbooks to all its students?

Whenever petitioned by five percent or more of the voters, a school board must submit to the voters at a general election the question of whether to furnish free school textbooks.

Ill. Rev. Stat. c. 122, par. 28-14 et seq.

10:390 Must a school board provide textbooks at no charge to children whose parents are unable to pay for them?

A school board must provide at no charge textbooks for children whose parents are unable to afford them.

Ill. Rev. Stat. c. 122, par. 10-20.13

Ill. Rev. Stat. c. 122, par. 28-19.2

Latham v. Board of Education of City of Chicago, 31 Ill.2d 178, 201 N.E.2d 111 (1964)

11: STUDENTS AND PARENTS

COMPULSORY ATTENDANCE

11:10 What are the ages of compulsory school attendance in Illinois?

A child must attend school from his seventh birthday until his 16th birthday.

Ill. Rev. Stat. c. 122, par. 13-3
Ill. Rev. Stat. c. 122, par. 26-1
Chicago Board of Education v. Terrile, 47 Ill.App.3d 75, 361 N.E.2d 778, 5 Ill.Dec. 455 (1st Dist. 1977)
Scoma v. Chicago Board of Education, 391 F.Supp. 452 (N.D. Ill. 1974)

11:20 What is the minimum age for kindergarten attendance?

Any child who will be five on or before September 1 of any school year may attend school at the beginning of the school term. Based on an assessment of a child's readiness, a school district may permit a child to enter at a younger age.

Ill. Rev. Stat. c. 122, par. 10-20.12
Morrison by Morrison v. Chicago Board of Education, 188 Ill.App.3d 588, 544 N.E.2d 1099, 136 Ill.Dec. 324 (1st Dist. 1989)
Morgan v. Board of Education of Trico Community Unit School District No. 176, 22 Ill.App.3d 241, 317 N.E.2d 393 (5th Dist. 1974)

11:30 Do compulsory attendance laws require that children attend kindergarten?

Kindergarten attendance is optional. Compulsory attendance laws do not require children to attend kindergarten.

Ill. Rev. Stat. c. 122, par. 26-1
Morgan v. Board of Education of Trico Community Unit School District No. 176, 22 Ill.App.3d 241, 317 N.E.2d 393 (5th Dist. 1974)

**11:40   Under what circumstances is a child of
compulsory school age exempt from compulsory
attendance?**

A child is exempt from public school attendance under the
following circumstances:

1) if the child attends a private or parochial school where
instruction is in the English language;

2) if the child is physically or mentally unable to attend school
or is excused for temporary absence for cause by the principal
or teacher of the school which the child attends;

3) if the child is necessarily and lawfully employed consistent
with child labor laws, the child may be excused from school by
the regional superintendent of schools or the superintendent of
the public school which the child should be attending, and upon
approval in either instance of the child's school board;

4) if the child is over 12 and under 14 years of age the child
must be excused to attend confirmation classes;

5) a child must be excused if the tenets of his religion prohibit
secular activity on a particular day or days or at a particular
time of day.

Ill. Rev. Stat. c. 122, par. 26-1

Illinois v. Berger, 109 Ill.App.3d 1054, 441 N.E.2d 915, 65 Ill.Dec.
600 (2nd Dist. 1982)

Morton v. Board of Education of City of Chicago, 69 Ill.App.2d 38,
216 N.E.2d 305 (1st Dist. 1966)

Illinois ex rel. Latimer v. Board of Education of City of Chicago,
394 Ill. 228, 68 N.E.2d 305 (1946)

TRUANCY

11:50   What is a truant?

A truant is a child subject to compulsory school attendance
who is absent from school without valid cause for a school day
or any portion of a school day.

Ill. Rev. Stat. c. 37, par. 803-1

Ill. Rev. Stat. c. 122, par. 26-2a

Illinois v. R.G., 131 Ill.2d 328, 546 N.E.2d 533, 137 Ill.Dec. 588
(1989)

In Interest of Burr, 119 Ill.App.2d 134, 255 N.E.2d 57 (4th Dist.
1969)

11:60 What duty does a school district have to notify parents of student absence?

If a child in grades K-8 is absent from school, and there is no record the absence is for a valid cause and there is no notification the absence has been authorized, the school must, within two hours after the first class in which the child is enrolled, make a reasonable effort to telephone and notify the parent, legal guardian, or other person having legal custody of the child of the child's absence from school.

Ill. Rev. Stat. c. 122, par. 26-3b

11:70 What is the penalty for encouraging truancy?

Any person who has custody or control of a child subject to compulsory attendance who knowingly or willfully permits the child to persist in truancy, if convicted, is guilty of a Class C misdemeanor and may be subject to up to 30 days imprisonment and/or a fine of up to $500. Any person who willfully induces or attempts to induce any child to be absent from school or who knowingly employs or harbors any child who is unlawfully absent from school for three consecutive school days, if convicted, is guilty of a Class C misdemeanor.

In any such proceeding against parents or guardians the school district must demonstrate it has attempted to counsel the student and the person(s) having custody and control of the student and has provided support services, alternative programs and other school resources in an effort to correct the truant behavior.

Ill. Rev. Stat. c. 122, par. 26-8 et seq.

11:80 Who has jurisdiction to act with respect to truant minors?

Under given circumstances a school district, the school district truant officer, the regional superintendent of schools, the state's attorney and/or the Illinois Department of Children and Family Services may have jurisdiction.

Ill. Rev. Stat. c. 23, par. 2051 et seq.
Ill. Rev. Stat. c. 37, par. 803-1 et seq.
Ill. Rev. Stat. c. 122, par. 26-2a et seq.

11:90   What is a chronic or habitual truant?

A chronic or habitual truant is a child subject to compulsory attendance laws who is absent without valid cause from school for ten percent or more of the previous 180 regular attendance days.

Ill. Rev. Stat. c. 122, par. 26-2a

11:100 What restrictions are placed on a school district in dealing with a chronic or habitual truant?

Compulsory attendance laws provide a school district may take no punitive action against a chronic or habitual truant for truancy until the district has made available to the student all support services and other school resources in order to correct the chronic or habitually truant behavior.

Ill. Rev. Stat. c. 122, par. 26-12

11:110 How are truant officers appointed?

Truant officers are appointed in one of two ways. A school board may appoint a truant officer and fix and pay his salary from school district funds. The regional superintendent of schools is required to appoint a truant officer for those districts which fail to appoint. The person appointed by the regional superintendent of schools must post a bond upon appointment, receives such compensation as may be fixed by the county board, and is paid by the county. The county truant officer appointment must be approved by a circuit judge.

Ill. Rev. Stat. c. 122, par. 3-13
Ill. Rev. Stat. c. 122, par. 26-5
Burris v. Board of Education, 221 Ill.App. 397 (4th Dist. 1920)

RIGHT TO ATTEND SCHOOL

11:120 Who is authorized to establish school attendance boundaries?

A school district with two or more attendance centers at the same grade level may establish attendance boundaries for each attendance center. A school board may not cause students to be segregated between two or more elementary schools on the basis of such factors as race, color, creed, national origin, sex, religion or other constitutionally-impermissible factor. In the absence of such factors, the establishment of school attendance zones is a discretionary power of a school board and neither students nor their parents may require the school board to assign them to any particular attendance center.

Ill. Rev. Stat. c. 122, par. 10-21.3

Tometz v. Board of Education Waukegan City School District No. 61, 39 Ill.2d 593, 237 N.E.2d 498 (1968)

11:130 What constitutional principle underlies school desegregation?

School segregation by race deprives minority students of equal protection which is guaranteed by the Fourteenth Amendment to the Constitution of the United States.

Brown v. Board of Education of Topeka, Shawnee County, Kansas, 74 S.Ct. 686, 347 U.S. 483, 98 L.Ed. 873, 38 ALR2d 1180, supp. 75 S.Ct. 753, 349 U.S. 294, 99 L.Ed. 1083 (1954)

11:14 What is the role of the Illinois State Board of Education in preventing school segregation?

When the State Board of Education receives a complaint signed by at least 50 residents of a school district or 10 percent of the residents of a district, whichever is less, charging either students have been segregated on the basis of race, nationality, or religion, or school employees or applicants for employment have been discriminated against on the same basis, the State Board must notify the district of the complaint and, within 30 days, set a hearing on the charges. If, after hearing, it is determined the charges are valid, the State Board must send its findings to the Illinois Attorney General for prosecution.

Ill. Rev. Stat. c. 122, par. 18-12

Aurora East School District No. 131 v. Cronin, 92 Ill.2d 305, 442 N.E.2d 511, 66 Ill.Dec.85 (1982)

11:150 What is Title IX?

Title IX is a federal statute which prohibits discrimination on the basis of sex. Title IX provides in part:

"No person in the United States shall, on the basis of sex, be excluded from participation in, be denied the benefits of, or be subjected to discrimination under any education program or activity receiving Federal financial assistance."

20 U.S.C. par. 1681

11:160 May a student be excluded from school because she is pregnant?

A school board may not exclude a student because of pregnancy. A school district is required to provide home instruction, correspondence courses or other courses of instruction for students who are unable to attend school because of pregnancy and for up to three months following the birth of a child or miscarriage.

Ill. Rev. Stat. c. 122, par. 10-22.6a
Ill. Rev. Stat. c. 122, par. 26-1

11:170 May a school district discipline a student because she is pregnant out of wedlock?

No.

20 U.S.C. 1681
Wort v. Vierling, 778 F.2d 1233 (7th Cir. 1985)

STUDENT RESIDENCY AND TUITION

11:180 Is a child living in a school district necessarily entitled to tuition free enrollment in the schools of the district where he lives?

A child is entitled to tuition free enrollment in the school district wherein he resides. Residency, in this context, has a specific meaning in the law. A child is presumed to be a resident of the school district wherein his parents reside. After a divorce, a child is presumed to reside with the custodial parent. A school district has a duty to charge tuition to nonresident pupils.

Ill. Rev. Stat. c. 122, par. 10-22.5

Ill. Rev. Stat. c. 122, par. 10-20.12a

Martinez Morales v. Bynum, 103 S.Ct. 1838, 461 U.S. 321, 75 L.Ed.2d 879 (1983)

Kraut v. Rachford, 51 Ill.App.3d 206, 366 N.E.2d 497, 9 Ill.Dec. 240 (1st Dist. 1977)

Turner v. Board of Education North Chicago Community High School District 123, 54 Ill.2d 68, 294 N.E.2d 264 (1973)

11:190 May a school district waive tuition for a nonresident student?

In most cases, a school district need not admit a nonresident pupil and may require the student to attend school in the school district in which he resides. However, if the school district elects to admit a nonresident pupil, it has a duty to charge tuition and may not waive tuition charges except in circumstances authorized by statute.

Ill. Rev. Stat. c. 122, par. 10-22.5

Ill. Rev. Stat. c. 122, par. 10-20.12a

11:200 For purposes of school attendance, what is residence?

Residence is physical presence with an intention to remain on a permanent basis.

Connelly v. Gibbs, 112 Ill.App.3d 257, 445 N.E.2d 477, 68 Ill.Dec. 29 (1st Dist. 1983)

11:210 Can residence of a child for school purposes be established by the temporary transfer of custody of the child to a relative?

The facts surrounding any temporary transfer of custody will determine whether or not residency has been established. The mere creation of a guardianship, transfer of custody, or change of address is not sufficient to establish residence for school attendance purposes.

Kraut v. Rachford, 51 Ill.App.3d 206, 366 N.E.2d 497, 9 Ill.Dec. 240 (1st Dist. 1977)

Turner v. Board of Education North Chicago Community High School District 123, 54 Ill.2d 68, 294 N.E.2d 264 (1973)

11:220 Which school district must pay for a child's special education costs if the child is placed in an out-of-district residential facility?

A child in need of special education who is properly placed in a residential facility is presumed to be a resident of the school district in which his parents reside. Unless a contrary residence is proven (usually by showing that the parents no longer have custody and control of the child) the school district in which the parents reside is responsible for the costs of the residential placement.

William C. v. Board of Education, City of Chicago, 71 Ill.App.3d 793, 390 N.E.2d 479, 28 Ill.Dec. 312 (1st Dist. 1979)

School District No. 153, Cook County v. School District 154 1/2, Cook County, 54 Ill.App.3d 587, 370 N.E.2d 22, 12 Ill.Dec. 399 (1st Dist. 1977)

11:221 Which school district must pay for a child's educational costs if the child is in a residential program to correct alcohol or drug dependency?

Except in the case of special education students, and unless otherwise agreed by the parties involved and unless educational services are not otherwise provided for, if an Illinois student under the age of 21 is enrolled in a residential program designed to correct alcohol or other drug dependency, the child's education is provided by the school district in which the residential facility is located and paid for by the school district in which the child resides.

Ill. Rev. Stat. c. 122, par. 10-20.12a

11:230 What is the amount of tuition for a nonresident pupil?

A school board has a duty to charge nonresident pupils tuition in an amount not to exceed 110 percent of the per capita cost of maintaining the schools of the district for the preceding school year. Per capita costs are computed by dividing the total cost of conducting and maintaining the schools of the district by the average daily attendance, including tuition pupils.

Ill. Rev. Stat. c. 122, par. 10-20.12a

HEALTH EXAMINATION AND IMMUNIZATIONS

11:240 At what grade levels are students required to show proof of health examination and immunization?

Proof of health examination and proof of immunization against preventable communicable disease are required upon entry to kindergarten or the first grade level a school offers, prior to entrance into nursery school, upon entering fifth and ninth grades, and upon first entry into any school. Additional examinations, including dental and vision examinations, may be required when deemed necessary by school authorities.

Ill. Rev. Stat. c. 122, par. 27-8.1

11:250 May a school board exclude a student for failure to show proof of immunization?

If a child does not present proof of health examination and immunizations by October 15 of a year in which such proof is required, the school board is required to suspend the child from school. There are limited statutory medical and/or Constitutional circumstances under which the October 15 deadline may be extended for a particular child.

Ill. Rev. Stat. c. 122, 27-8.1

11:255 May a child be exempted from immunizations or health examinations for religious reasons?

Children whose parents or guardians object to health examinations or immunizations on religious grounds may be exempted from examinations or immunizations on presentation to the local school authority a signed statement of objection.

Ill. Rev. Stat. c. 122, par. 27-8.1 (8)

STUDENT FEES

11:260 May a school district charge student fees?

No fees may be charged which would have the effect of abridging a student's right to a free appropriate public education. Reasonable fees may be charged for services and activities which are tangential to the educational program; however, a school board must waive fees for those unable to pay. Book and towel rental fees have been held permissible. Tuition fees are not permissible.

Ill. Rev. Stat. c. 122, par. 10-20.13
Ill. Rev. Stat. c. 122, par. 10-22.25
Hamer v. Board of Education, School District No. 109, Lake County, 9 Ill.App.3d 663, 292 N.E.2d 569 (2d Dist. 1977)
Polzin v. Rand, McNally & Co., 250 Ill. 561, 95 N.E. 623 (1911)

11:270 May a school district charge a fee for driver education?

A school district may charge up to $50 for district residents between the ages of 15 and 21 years who take part in the driver education course. However, the fee must be waived for any such resident who is unable to pay, regardless of whether the individual is in school or out of school.

When space permits, the district also may provide driver education for residents above age 55 who have never been licensed to drive and may charge a fee not to exceed actual costs.

Ill. Rev. Stat. c. 122, par. 27-23

STUDENT INSURANCE

11:280 Must a school board provide health insurance for student athletes?

A school board may provide accident and health insurance on a group or individual basis, or through nonprofit hospital service corporations or medical service plan corporations, or both, for its pupils who are injured while participating in any athletic activity under the jurisdiction of or sponsored or controlled by the district. The cost of the insurance, when paid from the funds of the district, must, to the extent there is sufficient money to do so, be paid from money derived from athletic activities. To the extent that money derived from athletic activities is insufficient, the cost may be paid from the educational fund.

Ill. Rev. Stat. c. 122, par. 22-15

Frederich v. Board of Education of Community Unit School District No. 304, 59 Ill.App.3d 49, 375 N.E.2d 141, 16 Ill.Dec. 510 (2nd Dist. 1978)

EMANCIPATED STUDENTS

11:290 What is an emancipated minor?

An emancipated minor is a person 16 to 18 years old who has demonstrated the ability and capacity to manage his own affairs and to live wholly or partially independent of his parents or guardians. Such an individual may petition a circuit court for a declaration of complete or partial emancipation. Marriage emancipates a minor for most purposes in the law.

Ill. Rev. Stat. c. 40, par. 2202 et seq.

Kowalski v. Liska, 78 Ill.App.3d 64, 397 N.E.2d 39, 33 Ill.Dec. 706 (1st Dist. 1979)

11:300 May an emancipated minor establish residence in a school district other than that in which his parents reside?

An emancipated minor may establish his own residence.

Ill. Rev. Stat. c. 40, par. 2202 et seq.

CHILD ABUSE AND NEGLECT

11:310 What is an "abused" child?

An "abused child" is a child whose parent or immediate family member, or any person responsible for the child's welfare, or any individual residing in the same home as the child, or a paramour of the child's parent does any of the following:

1) inflicts, causes to be inflicted, or allows to be inflicted upon such child physical injury, by other than accidental means, which causes death, disfigurement, impairment of physical or emotional health, or loss or impairment of any bodily function;

2) creates substantial risk of physical injury to such child by other than accidental means which would be likely to cause death, disfigurement, impairment of physical or emotional health, or loss or impairment of any bodily function;

3) commits or allows to be committed any sex offense against such child, and extending the Criminal Code definitions of sex offenses to include children under 18 years of age;

4) commits or allows to be committed an act or acts or torture upon such child; or

5) inflicts excessive corporal punishment.

Ill. Rev. Stat. c. 23, par. 2053

11:320 What is a "neglected" child?

A "neglected child" is any child whose parent or other person responsible for the child's welfare withholds or denies nourishment or medically indicated treatment, including food or care denied solely on the basis of present or anticipated mental or physical impairment as determined by a physician acting alone or in consultation with other physicians or otherwise does not provide the proper or necessary support, education as required by law, or medical or other remedial care recognized under state law as necessary for a child's well-being, or other care necessary for his well-being, including adequate food, clothing, and shelter; or who is abandoned by his parents or other person responsible for the child's welfare.

Ill. Rev. Stat. c. 23, par. 2053

11:330 Are school personnel responsible for reporting suspected cases of child abuse or neglect?

All school personnel are required to report any suspected child abuse or neglect directly to the Illinois Department of Children and Family Services (DCFS) by telephoning a toll-free number to a DCFS central register.

Any person required by law to report child abuse and neglect who willfully fails to report is guilty of a Class A misdemeanor.

Ill. Rev. Stat. c. 23, par. 2053
Ill. Rev. Stat. c. 23, par. 2054.02
Ill. Rev. Stat. c. 23, par. 2057

11:340 What information must be included in a report of child abuse or neglect?

All reports from educational employees required by law to report cases of child abuse or neglect must include, when known, the name and address of the child and his parents or other persons having his custody, the child's age, the nature of the child's condition including any evidence of previous injuries or disabilities, and any other information which the person reporting believes might be helpful in establishing the cause of such abuse or neglect and the identity of the person believed to have caused the abuse or neglect.

Ill. Rev. Stat. c. 23, par. 2057

11:350 What action may be taken against a school employee who files a report of child abuse or neglect that turns out to be false?

School personnel are granted broad immunities against civil and criminal claims when they file a report of suspected child abuse or neglect in good faith, even if the report proves groundless. Such immunities are not available, however, to the individual who knowingly files a false report.

Ill. Rev. Stat. c. 23, par. 2054
Ill. Rev. Stat. c. 23, par. 2059

STUDENT TRANSPORTATION

11:360 For which students must a school board provide free transportation to and from school?

All school districts except charter districts must provide free transportation for students residing one and one half miles or more from any school to which they are assigned for attendance unless adequate public transportation is available. A school board is also required to provide free transportation to certain classes of students (such as handicapped special education students and parochial school students) regardless of the distance these students live from school.

Ill. Rev. Stat. c. 122, par. 29-3

11:370 For purposes of requiring a school board to bus students to and from school, how is the one and a half mile minimum distance measured?

The one and one half mile minimum distance is measured from the exit of the property where the student resides to the point where pupils are normally unloaded at the school attended. The distance is measured by determining the shortest distance on normally travelled roads or streets.

Ill. Rev. Stat. c. 122, par. 29-3

11:380 When must a school board provide free transportation for students living less than one and one half miles from school?

A school board must provide free transportation for students living less than one and one half miles from school when conditions are such that walking constitutes a serious hazard to the safety of the pupil due to vehicular traffic. Transportation need not be provided if adequate public transportation is available. The initial determination of what constitutes a serious hazard is made by the school board with review by the Illinois Department of Transportation (IDOT) in consultation with the State Superintendent of Education. IDOT's decision may be appealed to circuit court under the provisions of the Administrative Review Act.

Ill. Rev. Stat. c. 110, par. 3-101 et seq.

Ill. Rev. Stat. c. 122, par. 29-3

11:390 Is a school district required to provide transportation to and from summer school classes?

A school district is not required to provide summer school transportation except for special education students. If the school district chooses to provide transportation, it may charge participating students a transportation fee not to exceed cost.

Ill. Rev. Stat. c. 122, par. 29-3.2a

12: STUDENT DISCIPLINE

DISCIPLINARY AUTHORITY

12:10 Who is responsible for maintaining student discipline in the public schools?

Teachers and other certificated employees have a statutory duty to maintain discipline in school, on school grounds, at extra-curricular events, and with respect to all school programs. Each school board must establish a policy on student discipline.

Ill. Rev. Stat. c. 122, par. 24-24

Prest by Prest v. Sparta Community Unit School District No. 140, 157 Ill.App.3d 569, 510 N.E.2d 595, 109 Ill.Dec. 727 (5th Dist. 1987)

12:20 What is "in loco parentis"?

"In loco parentis" means in place of parent. The phrase is used in education to describe the relationship of certificated school officials to students. While certain school officials have in loco parentis authority by statute, the power of school officials to exercise control over students is not so broad as that of a parent.

The doctrine of in loco parentis protects certain school district employees from liability for employment related acts of ordinary negligence. Such employees may create liability for the school district resulting from certain employment related acts which constitute willful and wanton misconduct.

Ill. Rev. Stat. c. 122, par. 24-24

Ausmus by Ausmus v. Board of Education of City of Chicago, 155 Ill.App.3d 705, 508 N.E.2d 298, 108 Ill.Dec. 137 (1st Dist. 1987)

Montag v. Board of Education, School District No. 40, Rock Island County, 112 Ill.App.3d 1039, 446 N.E.2d 299, 68 Ill.Dec. 565 (3rd Dist. 1983)

Illinois v. Davis, 88 Ill.App.3d 728, 410 N.E.2d 673, 43 Ill.Dec. 673 (2nd Dist. 1980)

Thomas v. Chicago Board of Education, 60 Ill.App.3d 729, 377 N.E.2d 355, rev. on other grounds 77 Ill.2d 178, 395 N.E.2d 538, 32 Ill.Dec. 308 (1978)

Kobylanski v. Chicago Board of Education, 63 Ill.2d 165, 347 N.E.2d 705 (1976)

12:30 May a school district extend its disciplinary control of students to instances of misbehavior which occur off school grounds?

A school district's authority to regulate student conduct on or off school grounds is limited to that conduct which relates to the administration of the school's educational process.

Klein v. Smith, 635 F.Supp. 1440 (Me. 1986)

Board of Education of Rogers, Arkansas v. McCluskey, 102 S.Ct. 3469, on remand 688 F.2d 596, reh. den. 103 S.Ct. 16 (1982)

McNaughton v. Circleville Board of Education, 46 Ohio Misc. 12, 345 N.E.2d 649 (1974)

12:40 May a school board establish rules of conduct governing spectators at extracurricular activities?

A school board may make and enforce reasonable rules of conduct and sportsmanship for all athletic and extracurricular school events. Any person who violates the rules, whether adult or student, may be denied admission to school events for not more than one year, provided a written 10-day notice of the violation is given and a hearing held on the violation by the school board.

The administration of any school may sign a complaint as agent of the school against any person committing any offense at a school event.

Ill. Rev. Stat. c. 122, par. 24-24

12:45 May students be disciplined by assignment of Saturday detentions?

A school district may assign students to serve Saturday detentions. However, teachers may not be required to teach on Saturdays. Provided the school district has complied with its bargaining obligations, it may seek teacher volunteers to supervise a Saturday detention class.

Ill. Rev. Stat. c. 122, par. 24-2

12:46 Must a school district provide transportation for students required to attend after-school detention?

If the student is required to attend the detention, the school district must provide advance notice to the parents and transportation. The common method of avoiding the requirement is to offer a punishment alternative to the student and his parents.

Ill. Rev. Stat. c. 122, par. 29-3
Ill. Rev. Stat. c. 122, par. 29-3.1

12:50 May a school board or school administration establish a student dress code?

Courts have, with regularity, recognized a student's right to freedom of expression with respect to manner of dress and length of hair. While there is not absolute uniformity of judicial interpretation, extreme caution with respect the adoption of student dress codes or hair length regulations is advisable. To safely regulate, a school board must demonstrate disruption of the orderly process of a school function or endangerment to health or safety. While voluntary dress codes are permitted by statute, mandatory dress codes are still constitutionally suspect.

Ill. Rev. Stat. c. 122, par. 10-22.25b
Olesen v. Board of Education of School District 228, 676 F.Supp. 820 (N.D. Ill. 1987)
Harper v. Edgewood Board of Education, 655 F.Supp. 1353 (S.D. Ohio 1987)
Copeland v. Hawkins, 352 F.Supp. 1022 (E.D. Ill. 1973)
Arnold v. Carpenter, 459 F.2d 939 (7th Cir. 1972).
Laine v. Dittman, 125 Ill.App.2d 136, 259 N.E.2d 824 (2nd Dist. 1970)
Breen v. Kahl, 419 F.2d 1034 (7th Cir. 1969)

12:60 What input on student discipline policies must a school board allow members of the public?

Every school board is required to establish a parent-teacher advisory committee on student discipline. Schools are required to provide parents with a copy of the student discipline policy within fifteen days of the start of school each year or within fifteen days after a student who transfers into the district starts classes and must inform students of the contents of the student discipline policy.

Ill. Rev. Stat. c. 122, par. 10-20.14
23 Ill.Admin.Code 1.280 c) et seq.

PARENT AND STUDENT PROTECTIONS

12:70   What is due process?

There are two types of due process, substantive and procedural. Both relate to the fairness of rules regulating conduct. Substantive due process requires rules be reasonably defined, fairly administered and related to a valid purpose. Procedural due process refers to the procedures employed to guarantee substantive due process.

Cleveland Board of Education v. Loudermill, 105 S.Ct. 1487, 470 U.S. 532, 84 L.Ed.2d 494 (1985) on rem. 763 F.2d 202
Goss v. Lopez, 95 S.Ct. 729, 419 U.S. 565, 42 L.Ed.2d 725 (1975)
Wood v. Strickland, 95 S.Ct. 992, 420 U.S. 308, 43 L.Ed.2d 214, reh. den. 95 S.Ct. 1589, 42 U.S. 921, 43 L.Ed.2d 790 (1975)

12:80   In what instances is a student entitled to a hearing before discipline can be invoked by school authorities?

Some form of hearing is required in each instance when, as a result of the discipline, the student will be deprived of access to educational services.

Ill. Rev. Stat. c. 122, par. 10-22.6
Goss v. Lopez, 95 S.Ct. 729, 419 U.S. 565, 42 L.Ed.2d 725 (1975)
Wood v. Strickland, 95 S.Ct. 992, 420 U.S. 308, 43 L.Ed.2d 214, reh. den. 95 S.Ct. 1589, 42 U.S. 921, 43 L.Ed.2d 790 (1975)
Linwood v. Board of Education of Peoria School District 150, 463 F.2d 763 (7th Cir. 1972)

12:100 Are communications between a student and an administrator or guidance counselor considered privileged?

There is no privilege with respect to communications between school officials and students. School officials, including guidance counselors, may be required to testify as to the content of conversations they have with students.

Cook County Federal Savings and Loan Association v. Griffin, 73 Ill.App.3d 210, 391 N.E.2d 473, 29 Ill.Dec.210 (1st Dist. 1979)

12:110 May a parent bring a suit for damages against a drug dealer who sells drugs to the parent's child?

The Parental Right of Recovery Act provides any person who (1) sells or transfers an illegal drug to a minor, or (2) supplies to a seller or to any other person an illegal drug which is ultimately sold or transferred to a minor under circumstances where it is reasonably foreseeable the drug may eventually be sold or transferred to a minor is liable to the parent or legal guardian of the minor to whom such illegal drug is sold or transferred for any damages proximately caused by the sale or transfer. The parent or legal guardian may recover actual damages suffered by the parent or legal guardian resulting from the sale or transfer of the illegal drug to the minor, including pain and suffering. A parent or legal guardian who is awarded damages under the Act may be entitled to punitive damages and/or attorney fees.

Ill. Rev. Stat. c. 70, par. 603

STUDENT SPEECH

12:120 Does the First Amendment protect student political expression?

The First Amendment protects student speech. A school board may not regulate a student's individual political expression unless it can show the expression is obscene or that without regulation there would be material and substantial disorder or invasion of the rights of others.

Tinker v. Des Moines Independent School District, 89 S.Ct. 733, 393 U.S. 503, 21 L.Ed.2d 731 (1969)

12:130 May school officials regulate student publications?

School officials may regulate the contents of school sponsored student expression under certain limited circumstances. In instances when the expression is not in the context of a public forum and a valid educational purpose for regulation exists, reasonable regulation of school sponsored speech is permissible. These principles would most often apply to publications produced in class as part of the curriculum or to publications sponsored by the school for particular educational purposes.

Regulation of student personal expression is not subject to the same limitations, and is broadly protected by the First Amendment. Thus, publications not sponsored by the school are not subject to regulation by the school, other than through reasonable rules regulating distribution on school premises.

Hazelwood v. Kuhlmeier, 108 S.Ct. 562, 484 U.S. 260, 98 L.Ed.2d 592, on rem. 840 F.2d 596 (1988)

Scoville v. Board of Education of Joliet Township High School District 204, 425 F.2d 10 (7th Cir. 1972)

Fujishama v. Board of Education, 460 F.2d 1355 (7th Cir. 1972)

12:140 May a school board adopt rules regulating the distribution of student publications?

A school board may establish reasonable regulations setting forth the time, manner, and place at which distribution of student written material may occur.

Fujishama v. Board of Education, 460 F.2d 1355 (7th Cir. 1972)

PROHIBITED BEHAVIORS

12:150 Are there criminal penalties for the unlawful use of weapons on school grounds?

There are criminal penalties ranging from Class A misdemeanor to Class 2 felony for unlawful use of weapons on school grounds. The statutory definition of what constitutes a weapon is broad.

Ill. Rev. Stat. c. 38, par. 24-1

12:160 What is the penalty for unlawful sale or delivery of firearms on school property?

Any person 18 years of age or older who sells, gives, or delivers any firearm to any person under 18 years of age in any school or on the real property comprising any school commits a Class 3 felony.

Ill. Rev. Stat. c. 38, par. 24-3.3

12:165 May a student possess an electronic paging device or a cellular telephone in school?

Electronic paging devices and cellular telephones are prohibited in the schools unless the use or possession of such a device has first been expressly authorized by the building principal and the school board.

Ill. Rev. Stat. c. 122, par. 10-20.28
Ill. Rev. Stat. c. 122, par. 10-21.10

12:170 Are fraternities, sororities or secret organizations permitted in public schools?

A school board must suspend or expel any pupil who is a member or who becomes, promises to become a member, or who becomes pledged to become a member or who solicits any other person to promise to join or be pledged to become a member of any public school fraternity or sorority or secret society.

Ill. Rev. Stat. c. 122, par. 31-3 et seq.

12:180 Are there criminal penalties for using threats to recruit students into street gangs?

A person who expressly or impliedly threatens to do bodily harm or does bodily harm to an individual or to that individual's family or uses any other criminally unlawful means to solicit or cause any person to join any organization or association, regardless of the nature of such organization or association, is guilty of a Class 3 felony. The matter becomes a Class 2 felony when a person older than 18 years threatens a person younger than 18 years.

Ill. Rev. Stat. c. 38, par. 12-6.1 et seq.

In Interest of V.W., 112 Ill.App.3d 587, 445 N.E.2d 445, 67 Ill.Dec. 965 (1st. Dist. 1983)

CORPORAL PUNISHMENT

12:190 Does state law authorize the use of corporal punishment in Illinois schools?

The School Code permits teachers to use reasonable force "to maintain safety for the other students." This authority is limited to actions by teachers which are defensive in nature and does not address corporal punishment or other acts of aggression or physical punishment of students by school personnel.

The School Code is silent with respect to corporal punishment. Therefore, the school board may regulate the use of corporal punishment or may prohibit it altogether.

Ill. Rev. Stat. c. 122, par. 24-24

Carter v. State Board of Education, 90 Ill.App.3d 1042, 414 N.E.2d 153, 46 Ill.Dec. 431 (1st Dist. 1980)

12:195 May a parent prevent a school district from administering corporal punishment to his child?

The State Board of Education has promulgated the following rule:

"If corporal punishment is to be used by school districts as a penalty for misbehavior, the district shall notify parents upon initial enrollment of the student that they may submit a written request that corporal punishment not be administered to their child or children."

23 Ill.Admin.Code 1.280 b)

12:200 Under what conditions may a teacher use corporal punishment as a disciplinary measure?

If permitted by school board policy, rules, and regulations, and provided the parent of the child does not have a written objection to corporal punishment on file with the school, a teacher may use corporal punishment as a means of maintaining discipline. A child is entitled to due process before corporal punishment may be administered and the corporal punishment itself must be reasonable. There may be liability for damages if corporal punishment is improperly administered. It is possible that individuals who have improperly administered corporal punishment may be charged criminally.

23 Ill.Admin.Code 1.280 b)

Thrasher v. General Casualty Co. of Wisconsin, 732 F.Supp. 966 (W.D. Wisc. 1990)

Metzger by and through Metzger v. Osbeck, 841 F.2d 518 (3rd Cir. 1988)

Wisconsin v. Pea Ridge School District, 855 F.2d 560 (8th Cir. 1988)

Hall v. Tawney, 621 F.2d 607 (4th Cir. 1980)

Ingraham v. Wright, 97 S.Ct. 1401, 430 U.S. 651, 51 L.Ed.2d 711 (1977)

Baker v. Owen, 395 F.Supp. 294, aff'd. 423 U.S. 907 (1975)

Illinois v. Ball, 58 Ill.2d 36, 317 N.E.2d 54 (1974)

City of Macomb v. Gould, 104 Ill.App.2d 361, 244 N.E.2d 634 (3rd Dist. 1969)

12:210 Is corporal punishment cruel and unusual, and thereby violative of a student's constitutional rights?

No.

Ingraham v. Wright, 97 S.Ct. 1401, 430 U.S. 651, 51 L.Ed.2d 711 (1977)

12:220 Must a due process hearing be held before a school official administers corporal punishment?

No hearing is necessary, but some due process must be provided the student. Before the administration of corporal punishment, a student must have been informed his misbehavior would result in corporal punishment. A student must be given an opportunity, in a neutral environment, to explain his version of the events giving rise to the discipline. A second official must be informed before the administration of corporal punishment and in the student's presence of the reason for the corporal punishment, and must be present at the time corporal punishment is administered. An official who has administered corporal punishment must provide the child's parent, upon request, a written explanation of the reasons for the discipline and the name of the second official who was present when the corporal punishment was administered.

Baker v. Owen, 395 F.Supp. 294, aff'd. 423 U.S. 907 (1975)

STUDENT SEARCHES

12:230 What is permissible in conducting student searches?

The Fourth Amendment's prohibition of unreasonable searches and seizures applies to searches conducted by public school officials. The balance between a student's legitimate expectations of privacy and a school's legitimate need to maintain an appropriate environment for learning requires some easing of the restrictions to which searches by public authorities are ordinarily subject.

School officials need not obtain a warrant before searching a student. A search is justified at its inception when there are reasonable grounds for suspecting the search of a particular child will turn up evidence the student has violated or is violating either the law or the rules of the school.

A search is permissible in its scope when the measures adopted are reasonably related to the objectives of the search and not excessively intrusive in light of the age and sex of the student and the nature of the infraction.

Howlett by and through Howlett v. Rose, 110 S.Ct. 2430, __ U.S. __, 110 L.Ed.2d 332 (1990)

New Jersey v. T.L.O., 105 S.Ct. 733, 469 U.S. 325, 83 L.Ed.2d 720 (1985)

12:240 May school officials search school lockers used by students?

If school officials inform students school lockers are school district property made available to students for their convenience, and if school officials warn students before a search that lockers may be subject to search, lockers may be searched provided school officials have reasonable cause. The nature of locker use and locker construction create evidentiary problems which make it difficult to discipline students solely on the basis of the fruits of a locker search.

Chicago Firefighters Local 2 v. Chicago, 717 F.Supp. 134 (N.D. Ill. 1989)

O'Connor v. Ortega, 107 S.Ct. 1492, 480 U.S. 709, 94 L.Ed.2d 714 (1987)

New Jersey v. T.L.O., 105 S.Ct. 733, 469 U.S. 325, 83 L.Ed.2d 720 (1985)

Picha v. Wieglos, 410 F.Supp. 1214 (N.D.Ill. 1976)

POLICE SEARCHES AND ARRESTS

12:250 What standard applies to student searches when law enforcement officers are involved?

When school officials involve police officers in searches of students conducted in schools, the search standard increases in many cases from "reasonable suspicion" to "probable cause." A search warrant may be required under certain circumstances when police officials are involved with school officials in the conduct of a search.

Skinner v. Railway Labor Executives' Association, 109 S.Ct. 1402, 489 U.S. 602, 103 L.Ed.2d 639 (1989)

Treasury Employees' Union v. Van Raab, 109 S.Ct. 1384, ___ U.S. ___, 103 L.Ed.2d 685 (1989)

New Jersey v. T.L.O., 105 S.Ct. 733, 469 U.S. 325, 83 L.Ed.2d 720 (1985)

Picha v. Wieglos, 410 F.Supp. 1214 (N.D.Ill. 1976)

12:260 Are police dog searches of school grounds legal?

Police dogs may not be used to conduct generalized searches of students or places where students have a reasonable expectation of privacy. Police dogs may be used to conduct searches of public places on school grounds, including school parking lots. Whether or not additional cause or a warrant may be necessary before a more intrusive search is conducted after a police dog alerts is a matter which depends on the facts surrounding the particular search.

Horton v. Goose Creek, 690 F.2d 470 reh. den. 693 F.2d 524 (5th Cir. 1982) cert. den. 103 S.Ct. 3536, 363 U.S. 1207, 77 L.Ed.2d 1387

Zamora v. Pomeroy, 639 F.2d 662 (10th Cir. 1981)

Doe v. Renfrow, 475 F.Supp. 1012, aff'd in part, rem. in part, 631 F.2d 582 (7th Cir. 1979) cert. den. 101 S.Ct. 3015, 451 U.S. 1022, 69 L.Ed.2d 395

Camara v. Municipal Court of City and County of San Francisco, 87 S.Ct. 1727, 387 U.S. 523, 18 L.Ed.2d 930 (1967)

12:270 Under what circumstances may law enforcement authorities enter school buildings?

Law enforcement authorities may enter school buildings when they have reason to believe a crime has been committed, when they possess a warrant, or when they have been invited into the school by school officials. A school district may regulate by policy access to students by law enforcement authorities who do not possess warrants.

42 U.S.C. 1983

New Jersey v. T.L.O., 105 S.Ct. 733, 469 U.S. 325, 83 L.Ed.2d 720 (1985)

Doe v. Renfrow, 631 F.2d 91 (7th Cir. 1980)

Picha v. Wieglos, 410 F.Supp. 1214 (N.D.Ill. 1976)

12:280 Must a school district allow police officials to question or arrest students during the school day?

A police officer must be permitted to arrest a student on school property during the school day when the officer possesses a warrant or when the officer is in hot pursuit of a suspect. A school district may regulate by policy warrantless police interrogations.

Doe v. Renfrow, 631 F.2d 91 (7th Cir. 1980)

Picha v. Wieglos, 410 F.Supp. 1214 (N.D.Ill. 1976)

12:290 What notice does a school district receive if one of its students is involved in juvenile proceedings?

All courts and law enforcement agencies of the state and its political subdivisions must report to the principal of any public school whenever an enrolled child is detained for proceedings under the Juvenile Court Act or for any criminal offense or any violation of a municipal or county ordinance.

The information derived from this report must be kept separate from and must not become a part of the official school record of the child and is not a public record. Such information must be used solely by the principal, counselors, and teachers of the school to aid in the rehabilitation of the child.

Ill. Rev. Stat. c. 122, par. 22-20

SUSPENSION AND EXPULSION

12:300 What is a student disciplinary suspension?

A student disciplinary suspension is a temporary removal from school or from riding a school bus for a maximum of ten days per suspension. Except under some circumstances involving some students classified as in need of special education, a suspension is permitted for gross disobedience or misconduct. A suspension from riding a school bus may exceed ten days for safety reasons.

Ill. Rev. Stat. c. 122, par. 10-22.6
Goss v. Lopez, 95 S.Ct. 729, 419 U.S. 565, 42 L.Ed.2d 725 (1975)
Linwood v. Board of Education of Peoria School District 150, 463 F.2d 763 (7th Cir. 1972)

12:310 Which school officials may suspend a student from school?

A school board may authorize the superintendent, principal, assistant principal, or dean of students to suspend a student for gross disobedience or misconduct if the student has been provided the requisite due process and proper notice has been given.

Ill. Rev. Stat. c. 122, par. 10-22.6

12:320 What procedures must be followed to notify a student's parents of his suspension from school?

Any suspension must be immediately reported to the parents or guardian of a student along with a full statement of the reasons for the suspension and a notice of right to a review, a copy of which must be given to the school board.

Upon request of the parents or guardian, the school board or a hearing officer appointed by it must review the action of the suspending school official. At the review, the parents or guardian of the student may appear and discuss the suspension with the school board or its hearing officer.

If a hearing officer is appointed by the board, he must report to the board a written summary of the evidence heard at the meeting. After its hearing, or upon receipt of the written report of its hearing officer, the board may take such action as it finds appropriate.

Ill. Rev. Stat. c. 122, par. 10-22.6

12:330 What due process is required with respect to a student suspension from school?

A student must be provided with the following due process in connection with any suspension from school:

1) oral or written notice of the charges and evidence supporting the charges;

2) if the charges are denied, a student must be given an opportunity to explain his version of the events to the suspending school official;

3) the suspension (except from riding a bus for safety reasons) may not exceed ten days;

4) to have his parents or guardian immediately receive a report of the suspension along with a full statement of the reasons for it and a notice of right to review;

5) if a hearing is requested, the parents or guardian may appear and may discuss the suspension with the board or its hearing officer;

6) any decision rendered must be based upon the evidence; and

7) with respect to any suspension invoked, the student has a

right to be informed of its beginning and ending dates.

The rules regulating the suspension of a student identified as in need of special education are different, and disposition will depend upon the facts presented in each case.

Ill. Rev. Stat. c. 122, par. 10-22.6

Carey v. Piphus, 97 S.Ct. 1642, 435 U.S. 247, 52 L.Ed.2d 355 (1978)

Goss v. Lopez, 95 S.Ct. 729, 419 U.S. 565, 42 L.Ed.2d 725 (1975)

12:340 What is a student disciplinary expulsion?

A student disciplinary expulsion is the removal of a student from school for a period of time ranging from in excess of ten days to the balance of a school term for gross disobedience or misconduct.

Ill. Rev. Stat. c. 122, par. 10-22.6

Robinson v. Oak Park and River Forest High School, Board of Education District 200, 213 Ill.App.3d 77, 571 N.E.2d 931, 156 Ill.Dec. 951 (1st Dist. 1991)

Betts v. Board of Education of City of Chicago, 466 F.2d 629 (7th Cir. 1972)

12:350 What school officials have authority to expel a student from school?

Only a school board may expel a student. Its authority to expel may not be delegated. A school board may consider recommendations from the administration and may appoint a hearing officer to conduct an expulsion hearing, but must retain authority to render the final decision.

Ill. Rev. Stat. c. 122, par. 10-22.6

12:360 May a school board expel a student for an indefinite period?

A student, other than a student identified as in need of special education, may be expelled for a period of time not exceeding the end of the school term.

Linwood v. Board of Education of Peoria School District 150, 463 F.2d 763 (7th Cir. 1972)

12:370 What procedures must a school board follow in expelling a student from school?

When a student is accused of gross disobedience or misconduct sufficiently severe to warrant expulsion, the expulsion may not take place until after the parents have been requested to appear at a meeting of the school board, or with a hearing officer appointed by it, to discuss the student's behavior. Notice of hearing must be made by registered or certified mail and must state the time, place, and purpose of the meeting. The school board or a hearing officer appointed by it must state the reasons for the expulsion and the date on which the expulsion is to become effective.

If a hearing officer is appointed by the board, he must report to the board a written summary of the evidence heard at the meeting and the board may take such action thereon as it finds appropriate. The rules regulating the expulsion of students identified as in need of special education are different than the above.

Ill. Rev. Stat. c. 122, par. 10-22.6

Robinson v. Oak Park and River Forest High School, Board of Education District 200, 213 Ill.App.3d 77, 571 N.E.2d 931, 156 Ill.Dec. 951 (1st Dist. 1991)

Linwood v. Board of Education of Peoria School District 150, 463 F.2d 763 (7th Cir. 1972)

Betts v. Board of Education of City of Chicago, 466 F.2d 629 (7th Cir. 1972)

Whitfield v. Simpson, 312 F.Supp. 889 (N.D.Ill. 1970)

12:380 What due process is required with respect to a student expulsion from school?

A student must be provided with the following due process with respect to any expulsion from school:

1) The expulsion shall take place only after a student's parents or guardian have been requested to appear at a meeting of the school board, or with a hearing officer appointed by it, to discuss the student's behavior. A student may be suspended from school pending this meeting but must be provided the due process required to support a suspension;

2) A notice of hearing must be sent to the parents or guardian by registered or certified mail stating the time place and purpose of the hearing;

3) The school board or its appointed hearing officer must provide a full statement of the reasons for the proposed expulsion at the hearing and must provide notice of the date on which the proposed expulsion is to become effective;

4) The student is entitled to counsel at the student's expense;

5) Adequate time must be given to prepare a defense;

6) The student must be given an opportunity to call and examine witnesses, to cross-examine opposing witnesses, and to introduce evidence;

7) The decision to expel or not to expel must be made by the school board and must be based upon the evidence presented.

Ill. Rev. Stat. c. 122, 10-22.6

Carey v. Piphus, 97 S.Ct. 1642, 435 U.S. 247, 52 L.Ed.2d 355 (1978)

Wood v. Strickland, 95 S.Ct. 992, 420 U.S. 308, 43 L.Ed.2d 214 reh. den. 95 S.Ct. 1589, 42 U.S. 921, 43 L.Ed.2d 790 (1975)

Linwood v. Board of Education of Peoria School District 150, 463 F.2d 763 (7th Cir. 1972)

13: HANDICAPPED STUDENTS AND SPECIAL EDUCATION

SPECIAL EDUCATION DEFINED

13:10 What is "special education"?

"Special education" is instruction provided at no cost to parents or guardians specifically designed to provide the handicapped child with a "free appropriate public education." Special education may include the provision of non-educational services necessary to support education.

20 U.S.C. par. 1401(16)
Ill. Rev. Stat. c. 122, par. 14-8.02
Irving Independent School District v. Tatro, 104 S.Ct. 3371, 468 U.S. 883, 82 L.Ed.2d 664, on remand 741 F.2d 82 (1984)

13:20 What are the elements of a "free appropriate public education?"

A free appropriate public education for handicapped students includes special education and related services which (1) are provided at public expense, under public supervision and direction, and without charge; (2) meet the standards of the State Board of Education and federal rules and regulations; (3) include preschool, elementary, or secondary school education; and (4) are provided in conformity with the individualized education program as required by state and federal law.

20 U.S.C. par. 1401(18)
34 C.F.R. 300.4
34 C.F.R. 300.340 et seq.

13:30   Must school buildings and/or programs be accessible to handicapped persons?

The Rehabilitation Act requires program accessibility for handicapped persons. It mandates:

1) All new facilities must be constructed so as to be readily accessible and usable by handicapped persons.

2) Although every existing facility need not be totally physically accessible, programs must be accessible.

3) While flexibility is allowed in choosing methods which make programs in existing facilities accessible, structural changes in facilities must be undertaken if no other means of assuring program accessibility is available.

The Americans with Disabilities Act also contains requirements which apply to schools.

29 U.S.C. 701 et seq.
42 U.S.C. 12101 et seq.
45 C.F.R. par. 84.21 et seq.
71 Ill. Admin. Code 400.110 et seq.
71 Ill. Admin. Code 400.1830

13:40   What is an individualized education program (IEP)?

The term individualized education program (IEP) means a written statement for each handicapped child developed in any meeting by a representative of the local educational agency or an intermediate educational unit who shall be qualified to provide, or supervise the provision of, specially designed instruction to meet the unique needs of handicapped children, the teacher, the parents or guardian of the child, and whenever appropriate, such child. The IEP statement must include:

1) a statement of the present levels of educational performance of the child,

2) a statement of annual goals, including short-term instructional objectives,

3) a statement of the specific educational services to be provided to the child and the extent to which the child will be able to participate in regular educational programs,

4) the projected date for initiation and anticipated duration of services, and

5) appropriate objective criteria and evaluation procedures and schedules for determining, on at least an annual basis, whether instructional objectives are being achieved.

An IEP commits the school district to its terms.

20 U.S.C. 1401(a)(19)
Ill. Rev. Stat. c. 122, par. 14-8.02
23 Ill. Admin. Code 226.560

13:50 What is "mainstreaming?"

"Mainstreaming" is educational jargon for the principle of "least restrictive environment." Mainstreaming is the placement of handicapped children, to the maximum extent appropriate, with children who are not handicapped. Placement in special classes, separate schools, or other removal of handicapped children from the regular educational environment may occur only when the nature or the severity of the handicap is such that education in a regular class with the use of supplementary aids and services cannot be achieved.

34 C.F.R. 300.550
Ill. Rev. Stat. c. 122, par. 14-8.02
23 Ill. Admin. Code 226.5
23 Ill. Admin. Code 226.125
Evans v. District No. 17 of Douglas County, 841 F.2d 824 (8th Cir. 1988)
Martin v. School Board of Prince Georges County, 3 Va.App.197, 348 S.E.2d 857 (1986)
Community High School District No. 155 v. Denzby Veronico, 124 Ill.App.3d 129, 463 N.E.2d 998, 79 Ill.Dec. 444 (2nd Dist. 1984)

ELIGIBILITY FOR SPECIAL EDUCATION

13:60 What is the special education meaning of "handicapped"?

A "handicapped" student is any child between the ages of 3 and 21 who is mentally retarded, hard of hearing, deaf, speech impaired, visually handicapped, seriously emotionally disturbed, orthopedically impaired, other health impaired, deaf-blind, multihandicapped, or who has specific learning disabilities and who, because of these impairments, needs special education and related services.

34 C.F.R. 300.5
Ill. Rev. Stat. c. 122, par. 14-1.02

13:70 For which children must a public school district provide special education?

Every public school district must provide special education facilities and programs to all children between the ages of three and 21 who are residents of the school district who are found to require special education services. Under most circumstances a school district is responsible for the delivery of special education to children residing in the district who are enrolled in nonpublic schools or are wards of the state, children who are living in orphanages, foster homes, children's homes, and state housing units located within the district.

20 U.S.C. 1412
Ill. Rev. Stat. c. 122, par. 14-7.03
Nickerson v. Thompson, 504 F.2d 813 (7th Cir. 1974)

13:71 What is meant by "children with disabilities" as defined by The Individuals with Disabilities Education Act?

"Children with disabilities" is defined as children with mental retardation; hearing impairments, including deafness, speech or language impairments; visual impairments, including blindness; serious emotional disturbance; orthopedic impairments; autism; traumatic brain injury; other health impairments or specific learning disabilities and who by reason thereof need special education and related services.

20 U.S.C. 1401 (a)(1)(A)(i) et seq.

13:72 What is meant by "children with disabilities" for children aged 3-5 as defined by The Individuals with Disabilities Education Act?

"Children with disabilities" for children aged 3-5 includes children with developmental delays as defined by the State and as measured by appropriate diagnostic instruments and procedures in one or more of the following areas: physical development, cognitive development, communication development, social or emotional development, or adaptive development and who by reason thereof need special education and related services.

20 U.S.C. 1401 (a)(1)(B)(i) et seq.

13:80 How is a child's eligibility for special education programs and services determined?

A free appropriate public education must be available to all handicapped children. Children are eligible for special education if a determination of eligibility results from a case study reviewed by professional personnel in a multidisciplinary staff conference and after recommendation of qualified specialists.

20 U.S.C. 1400 et seq.

Ill. Rev. Stat. c. 122, par. 14-8.02

Max M. v. Illinois State Board of Education, 585 F.Supp. 317, on reconsideration 629 F.Supp. 1504 (N.D. Ill 1984)

Max M. v. Thompson, 585 F.Supp. 317, on reconsideration 592 F.Supp. 1437 (N.D. Ill. 1984)

13:90 Who are "children with specific learning disabilities?"

"Children with specific learning disabilities" means children between the ages of 3 and 21 years who have a disorder in one or more of the basic psychological processes involved in understanding or in using language, spoken or written, which may manifest itself in imperfect ability to listen, think, speak, read, write, spell, or do mathematical calculations. Such disorders include conditions such as perceptual handicaps, brain injury, minimal brain dysfunction, dyslexia, and developmental aphasia.

The term does not include children who have learning problems that are primarily the result of visual, hearing or motor handicaps, of mental retardation, emotional disturbance or environmental disadvantage.

Ill. Rev. Stat. c. 122, par. 14-1.03a

13:100 Do children with Acquired Immune Deficiency Syndrome (AIDS) qualify for special education?

The Individuals with Disabilities Education Act applies to AIDS victims only if their physical condition is such that it adversely affects their educational performance.

34 C.F.R. 104.35
Robertson by Robertson v. Granite City Community Unit School District No. 9, 684 F.Supp. 1002 (S.D. Ill. 1988)
Doe by Doe v. Belleville Public School District No. 118, 672 F.Supp. 342 (S.D. Ill. 1987)

13:110 Are public schools required to provide special education services to eligible students who reside in the school district but who attend nonpublic schools?

A school board is required to accept for part-time attendance eligible handicapped children who reside in the school district but are enrolled in nonpublic schools. Transportation for students in part-time attendance must be provided only if required in the child's individualized educational program on the basis of the child's handicapping condition or as the location of the special education program may require.

34 C.F.R. 300.452
Ill. Rev. Stat. c. 122, par. 14-6.01

SPECIAL PROGRAMS AND SERVICES

13:120 What special education facilities and services must school districts provide for qualified handicapped students?

Special educational facilities and services include special schools; special classes; special housing, including residential facilities; special instruction; special reader service; braillists and typists for visually handicapped children; sign language interpreters; transportation; maintenance; instructional material; physical and or occupational therapy; professional consultant services; medical services only for diagnostic and evaluation purposes provided by a physician licensed to practice medicine in all its branches to determine a child's need for special education and related services; psychological services; school social worker services; special administrative services; salaries of all required special personnel; and other special educational services, including special equipment for use in the classroom required by the child because of his disability if such services or special equipment are approved by the State Super-intendent of Education and the child is eligible under the regulations of the State Board of Education.

20 U.S.C. 1421 et seq.
Ill. Rev. Stat. c. 122, par. 14-1.08

13:130 Must each school district maintain special education facilities?

Each school district must establish and maintain such special educational facilities as may be needed for handicapped children who are residents of the school district. School districts need not provide special education facilities independently, however. School districts are empowered to enter into joint agreements as a means for providing such required facilities.

Ill. Rev. Stat. c. 122, par. 14-4.01

13:140 What are "related services" in the context of special education?

"Related services" means transportation and such developmental, corrective, and other supportive services (including speech pathology and audiology, psychological services, physical and occupational therapy, recreation, and medical services for diagnostic and evaluation purposes only) as may be required to assist a handicapped child to benefit from special education and includes the early identification and assessment of handicapping conditions in children.

20 U.S.C. par. 1401(a)(17)
34 C.F.R. 300.13

13:150 Under what circumstances must a school district provide a handicapped child with medical services?

A school district is not required to provide special education students with medical services except for purposes of diagnosis or evaluation. Medically related services which could be provided by a nurse or a trained layperson which are necessary to permit a student to benefit from special education must be provided.

Ill. Rev Stat. c. 122, par. 10-22.21b

Bevin H. by Michael H. v. Wright, 666 F.Supp. 71 (W.D.Pa. 1987)

Irving Independent School District v. Tatro, 104 S.Ct. 3371, 468 U.S. 883, 82 L.Ed.2d 664, on remand 741 F.2d 82 (1984)

Max M. v. Illinois State Board of Education, 585 F.Supp. 317, on reconsideration 629 F.Supp. 1504 (N.D. Ill 1984)

Max M. v. Thompson, 585 F.Supp. 317, on reconsideration 592 F.Supp. 1437 (N.D. Ill. 1984)

Darlene L. v. Illinois State Board of Education, 568 F.Supp. 1340 (N.D. Ill. 1983)

T.G. on Behalf of D.G. v. Board of Education of Piscataway, New Jersey, 576 F.Supp. 420 (D.C. N.J. 1983), aff'd., 738 F.2d 420, cert. denied 105 S.Ct. 592, 469 U.S. 1086, 83 L.Ed.2d 701

13:155 Must a school district make all its busses handicapped accessible?

A school district need not retrofit busses which were in service prior to the effective date of the Americans with Disabilities Act (ADA) unless a student's individualized education program requires the change; but vehicles put in service after the effective date of the ADA must be handicapped accessible. There are very limited exceptions to this rule in the ADA.

42 U.S.C.S. 12142 et seq.

13:160 Must a school district provide an interpreter for a deaf student?

If the child's individual educational plan (IEP) requires an interpreter, an interpreter must be provided at school district expense.

23 Ill. Admin. Code 226.250 4)

Board of Education of Hendrick Hudson Central School District, Board of Education Westchester County v. Rowley, 102 S.Ct. 3034, 458 U.S. 176, 73 L.Ed.2d 690 (1982)

13:170 What special training is required of persons employed to work in special education programs?

No person may be employed to teach any class or program in special education who does not hold a valid teaching certificate as provided by law and unless he has had special training as the State Board of Education may require. All other professional personnel employed in any class, service, or program authorized by law must hold the certificate and shall have received such training as the State Board of Education may require. A school board may employ necessary workers to assist properly certified teachers with the special education facilities, but such workers must have training prescribed by the State Board of Education.

Ill. Rev. Stat. c. 122, par. 14-9.01

13:180 What are the special education class size limits?

The principle determinants of the number of students served in each special education instructional program is the age of the students, the nature and severity of their exceptional characteristics, and the degree of intervention necessary.

All exceptions to the program size limitations require the written approval of the State Board of Education prior to the implementation of the program.

Specific limitations are as follows:

1) Early childhood instructional programs must have a maximum ratio of one qualified teacher to five students in attendance at any one time; total enrollment shall be limited according to the needs of the students for individualized programming.

2) Instructional programs which primarily serve children whose exceptional characteristics are either profound in degree or multiple in nature shall have a maximum enrollment of five students.

3) Instructional programs which primarily serve children whose principle exceptional characteristics are severe visual, auditory, physical, speech or language impairments, or behavioral disorders shall have a maximum enrollment of eight students.

4) Instructional programs which primarily serve children whose principle exceptional characteristics are learning disabilities or severe mental impairment; programs which are primarily diagnostic or developmental; or programs which serve children with differing exceptional characteristics shall have a maximum enrollment of 10 students.

5) Instructional programs which primarily serve children whose principal exceptional characteristics are moderate visual or auditory impairment shall have a maximum enrollment of 12 students.

6) Instructional programs which primarily serve children whose principal exceptional characteristics are educational handicaps or mild/moderate mental impairment shall have a maximum enrollment of 12 students at the primary level and 15 students at the intermediate, junior high, and secondary levels.

A school district may increase the enrollment in a special education instructional program by a maximum of two additional students to meet unique circumstances which occur during the school year. Such additions may be made only when the educational needs of all students who would be enrolled in the expanded program can be adequately and appropriately met, or the school district may increase the enrollment in a special education instructional program by a maximum of five additional students when the program is provided with a full-time, noncertified assistant.

23 Ill. Admin. Code 226.225

EVALUATION AND PLACEMENT

13:190 What is the definition of "evaluation" in the context of special education?

Evaluation means procedures used in accordance with federal and state regulations to determine whether a child is handicapped and the nature and extent of the special education and related services the child needs. The term means procedures used selectively with an individual child and does not include basic tests administered to or procedures used with all children in a school grade or class.

> 34 C.F.R. 300.500
> 34 C.F.R. 300.530 et seq.

13:200 Who may refer a child for a special education evaluation?

A child may be referred for a special education evaluation by school district personnel, the parents of the child, community service agencies, persons having primary care and custody of the child, other professional persons having knowledge of the child's problems, the child, or the State Board of Education.

> 23 Ill. Admin. Code 226.515 b)

13:210 How often must a special education student be reevaluated?

Special education students must be reevaluated at least once every three years or more frequently if conditions warrant. Reevaluation must be considered upon parental request. The educational status and continued special education placement of each child must be reviewed at least annually in a conference attended by those professionals working with the student, the parents, the child when appropriate, the special education director or designee who is qualified to supervise the provision of special education, and others at the discretion of the parent or school district.

> 23 Ill. Admin. Code 226.578

13:215 Does a special education student's individualized education program (IEP) necessarily follow him from elementary school to high school?

When a special education student reaches 14 1 / 2 years old, the elementary district in which the student resides must notify the high school district in which the student resides of the student's special education eligibility, program and evaluation data. The high school district may accept the current placement or may elect to conduct its own evaluation and multidisciplinary conference and formulate its own IEP.

Ill. Rev. Stat. c. 122, par. 14-6.01

13:216 What happens to a special education student's individualized education program (IEP) when the student and his family change their residence from one school district to another?

When a parent presents a copy of the student's then current IEP to the new school, the student must be placed in a special education program in accordance with that described in the student's IEP.

Ill. Rev. Stat. c. 122, par. 50-8.1

3:220 When is a special education student eligible for placement in a residential facility?

When a residential placement for educational purposes is considered, the necessity for such placement must be individually based upon evidence the student's needs are so profound or unusual that his educational needs cannot be met in a less restrictive placement. The evidence from recent diagnostic assessments and other pertinent information must indicate that, while the student can benefit from instructional services, he is so severely handicapped his educational needs cannot be met in a less restrictive environment.

If there is evidence of a condition which presents a danger to the physical well-being of the student or to other students, the evidence must be considered a factor in making a residential placement.

23 Ill. Admin. Code 226.420
Vander Malle v. Ambach, 667 F.Supp. 1015 (S.D. N.Y. 1987)
Cochran v. District of Columbia, 660 F.Supp. 314, (D.D.C. 1987)
Christopher T. by Brogna v. San Francisco Unified School District, 553 F.Supp. 1107 (D.C.Cal. 1982)

RIGHTS OF CHILDREN AND PARENTS

13:230 What notice must a school board publish concerning the education of handicapped children residing in the district?

A school board must publish a public notice regarding the right of all handicapped children to a free appropriate public education. The notice must be published in a school district newsletter of general circulation or in the newsletter of another governmental entity of general circulation in the district or, if neither is available in the district, in a newspaper of general circulation in the district.

The notice must identify the location and phone number of the office or agent of the school district to whom inquiries should be directed regarding the identification, assessment, and placement of such children. A school board must provide, upon request, written materials and other information that indicates the specific policies, procedures, rules, and regulations regarding the identification, evaluation, or educational placement of handicapped children. Such information shall include all rights and entitlements of such children and of the opportunity to present complaints with respect to any matter relating to educational placement of the student, or the provision of a free appropriate public education, and to have an impartial due process hearing on the complaint. The notice must inform the parents or guardian in the parents' or guardian's native language, unless it is clearly not feasible to do so, of their rights and all procedures available. The notice shall also inform the parents or guardian of the availability upon request of a list of free or low-cost legal and other relevant services available locally to assist parents or guardians in exercising their entitlements under the School Code.

Ill. Rev. Stat. c. 122, par. 14-6.01

13:240 Must a school district obtain parental consent before conducting a special education evaluation of a student?

A school district must obtain written parental consent to evaluate a student for special education. If consent is not given by the parent or guardian, a school district may request a due process hearing to determine if the evaluation should be conducted.

Ill. Rev. Stat. c. 122, par. 14-8.0
23 Ill. Admin. Code 226.525
23 Ill. Admin. Code 226.530

13:250 If the school district has obtained a proper parental consent for a special education evaluation, must the school district obtain another parental consent for any reevaluation?

Yes.

23 Ill. Admin. Code 226.525

13:260 May parents challenge the conclusions and recommendations of a multi-disciplinary staff conference?

Yes. At the conclusion of the multidisciplinary staff conference, the parent or guardian of the child must be given a copy of the multidisciplinary conference summary report and recommendations, which includes options considered, and must be informed of their right to obtain an independent educational evaluation if they disagree with the findings. If the school district's evaluation is shown to be inappropriate, the school district must reimburse the parent for the cost of the independent evaluation.

The State Board of Education supplies school districts with a list of suggested independent evaluators and must make the list available to parents at their request. A school district must make the list available to parents at the time they are informed of their right to obtain an independent educational evaluation. However, a school district may initiate an impartial due process hearing within five days of any written parent or guardian request for an independent educational evaluation to show that its evaluation is appropriate. If the final decision is the evaluation is appropriate, the parent retains the right to an independent educational evaluation, but not at public expense.

An independent educational evaluation at public expense must be completed within 30 days of a parent or guardian's written request unless the school district initiates an impartial due process hearing or the parent or guardian or school district offers reasonable grounds to show that the 30-day time period should be extended. If the due process hearing decision indicates the parent or guardian is entitled to an independent educational evaluation, it must be completed within 30 days of the decision unless the parent or guardian or the school district offers reasonable grounds to show the 30 day period should be extended.

If a parent disagrees with the summary report or recommendations of the multidisciplinary conference or the findings of any educational evaluation which results therefrom, the school district cannot proceed with a placement based upon the evaluation and the child must remain in his regular classroom setting or other current placement.

Ill. Rev. Stat. c. 122, par. 14-8.02

13:270 What right of review exists if the parents and the school district fail to agree on an appropriate special education placement for a particular child?

If there is disagreement between the parent or guardian and the school about the appropriate placement of a handicapped student, either the parent or guardian or the school district may seek a due process hearing before an impartial hearing officer. The decision of the hearing officer may be appealed by either party.

Ill. Rev. Stat. c. 122, par. 14-8.02

13:275 Is parental hostility to a school district's proposed educational placement an appropriate factor to consider when analyzing the placement's expected educational benefits?

Yes. Although hostility is a fact question which may be rebutted with evidence to the contrary at hearing.

Board of Education of Community Consolidated School District 21 v. Brozer, __ F.2d __ (7th Cir. 1991)

13:280 Is a school district required to permit parental involvement in formulating and implementing an individualized educational program (IEP)?

Parents must be given, on an ongoing basis, reasonable opportunity for comment on and input into their child's educational program.

23 Ill. Admin. Code 226.562

Muth v. Central Bucks School District, 839 F.2d 113 (3rd Cir. 1988), cert. denied 109 S.Ct. 103, cert. granted 109 S.Ct. 52, rev. sub nom. on other grounds *Dellmuth v. Muth,* 109 S.Ct. 2397, 491 U.S. 223, 105 L.Ed.2d 181 (1989), on remand sub nom. *Muth v. Central Bucks School District,* 884 F.2d 1384

13:290 Do the course requirements for receiving a high school diploma apply to special education or handicapped students whose education is governed by an individualized education program?

No.

Ill. Rev. Stat. c. 122, par. 27-22

13:300 May a handicapped student be retained in grade level or prevented from graduating for failure to pass a minimal competency test?

No handicapped student may be denied promotion, graduation or a general diploma on the basis of failing a minimal competency test when the failure can be directly related to the student's handicapping condition.

Ill. Rev. Stat. c. 122, par. 14-6.01

13:310 What special provisions exist for special education students affected by a teachers strike?

If a strike by educational employees results in the closing of schools, and the district is party to a joint agreement for special education, any resident students who are enrolled in special education programs of the joint agreement district must be permitted to attend special education programs in any other district which is a party to the same joint agreement and whose schools are not closed as a result of the strike.

Ill. Rev. Stat. c. 122, par. 10-22.31

FINANCIAL OBLIGATIONS

13:320 If a school district accepts a properly placed non-resident handicapped child, which school district bears the cost of the child's education?

If a school district accepts a non-resident handicapped child for admission into any of its special education programs pursuant to the child's individualized educational plan (IEP), the school district in which the child resides bears the cost of educational services provided the child.

Doe v. Sanders, 189 Ill.App.3d 572, 545 N.E.2d 454, 136 Ill.Dec. 930 (1st Dist. 1989)

William C. v. Board of Education of the City of Chicago, 71 Ill.App.3d 793, 390 N.E.2d 479, 28 Ill.Dec. 312 (1st Dist. 1979)

13:330 May a school district pass on to parents any portion of the tuition charge for a handicapped student who is appropriately placed in a nonpublic school?

The education of handicapped children is the responsibility of the school district and no part of the tuition charged by a nonpublic facility may be passed on to the parents of the handicapped child if the child is appropriately placed in the nonpublic facility.

Elliot v. Board of Education of the City of Chicago, 64 Ill.App.3d 229, 380 N.E.2d 1137, 20 Ill.Dec. 928 (1st Dist. 1978)

13:340 What is the effect of unilateral residential placement of special education students by their parents?

If a handicapped child has available a free appropriate public education and the parents choose to place the child in a private school or facility, the school board is not required to pay for the child's education at the private school or facility. Disagreements between a parent and a school regarding the availability of a program appropriate for the child and the question of financial responsibility are subject to due process procedures.

20 U.S.C. 1412(2)(B)
20 U.S.C. 1415
34 C.F.R. 300.403
Burlington School Committee of the Town of Burlington, Massachusetts v. Department of Education of Massachusetts, 105 S.Ct 1996, 471 U.S. 359, 85 L.Ed.2d 385 (1985)

13:350 Are there circumstances under which a school district may be held liable for the costs associated with the parent of a handicapped child removing the child from a public school program and unilaterally placing the child in a private facility?

A school district may be liable for the costs of such a placement if the child's physical health would be endangered if an alternative placement were not made or if the school district has acted in bad faith by failing to comply with statutory provisions for resolving the dispute over the child's educational placement.

Anderson v. Thompson, 658 F.2d 1205 (7th Cir. 1981)

DISCIPLINE OF HANDICAPPED STUDENTS

13:360 May a school district suspend a special education student for disciplinary reasons?

The suspension from school of a special education student for disciplinary reasons for a cumulative period not to exceed ten days in any school year is permissible.

20 U.S.C. 1415(e)(3)
23 Ill. Admin. Code 226.605
Board of Education City of Peoria v. Illinois State Board of Education, 531 F.Supp. 148 (C.D. Ill. 1982)

13:370 May a school district expel a special education student from school?

Unlike a short term disciplinary suspension, an expulsion is a change in placement. If the behavior giving rise to the expulsion is found to be related to the child's handicapping condition, expulsion may not be invoked. The law is unsettled as to whether a special education student may be expelled from school when the behavior giving rise to the discipline is not related to the child's handicapping condition.

In either case, a formal special education staffing must be held prior to any disciplinary hearing to determine the relatedness of the student's alleged misbehavior to his handicap. A school district may seek injunctive relief to bar a dangerous student from school pending disposition of change in placement proceedings.

Ill. Rev. Stat. c. 122, par. 14-8.01

Honig v. Doe, 108 S.Ct. 592, 98 L.Ed.2d 686 (1988)

SPECIAL EDUCATION HEARINGS

13:380 Under what circumstances may the parent or legal guardian of a handicapped child demand a due process hearing?

A hearing may be requested by the child, the parents, other persons having primary care and custody of the child, or the school district regarding, but not limited to, the following:

1) objection to signing consent for proposed case study evaluation or initial placement;

2) failure of the local school district to provide a case study evaluation that has been requested by the parents, other persons having primary care and custody of the child, the child, or the Illinois State Board of Education;

3) failure of a local school district to consider evaluations completed by qualified professional personnel outside the school district;

4) objection to a proposed special education placement, either an initial placement, a continuation of a previous placement, or a major change in the placement;

5) termination of a special education placement;

6) failure of the local school district to provide a special education placement consistent with the finding of the case study evaluation and the recommendations of the multidisciplinary conference;

7) failure of the local school district to provide the least restrictive special education placement appropriate to the child's needs;

8) provision of special education instructional or resource programs, or related services in an amount insufficient to meet the child's needs;

9) a suspension totaling individually or in aggregate ten or more school days in a given school year of a child who is either (a) in a special education instructional or resource program or who receives special education related services, or (b) who is eligible for such programs or services but is not receiving them;

10) reasonable belief by the parents, other persons having primary care and custody of the child, or the child, that the child's suspension or expulsion resulted from behavior or a condition symptomatic of an exceptional characteristic as defined by statute;

11) recommendation for the graduation of an exceptional child;

12) failure of the local school district to comply with any of these rules and/or the School Code;

13) failure of the local school district to provide an exceptional child with a free appropriate public education.

Ill. Rev. Stat. c. 122, par. 14-8.02
23 Ill. Admin. Code 226.605

13:390 What change in placement is possible for a handicapped child from the time a local level due process hearing is requested until all appeals have been exhausted?

During the pendency of any special education proceeding, unless the school district and the parents or guardian otherwise agree, the student must remain in his then current educational placement, or if applying for initial admission to the school district, must, with the consent of the parents or guardian, be placed in the school district program until all such proceedings have been completed.

20 U.S.C. 1415(e)(3)
Ill. Rev. Stat., c. 122, par. 14-8.02(k)
Honig v. Doe, 108 S.Ct. 592, 484 U.S. 305, 98 L.Ed.2d 686 (1988)
Walker v. Cronin, 107 Ill.App.3d 1053, 438 N.E.2d 582, 63 Ill.Dec. 651 (1st Dist. 1982)

13:400 Do parents of handicapped students have a right to counsel at special education due process hearings?

Parents and guardians of handicapped students have the right to be represented by counsel at their own expense. After certain findings, the school district may be required to reimburse the parents and guardians of handicapped students for their attorney fees.

McSomebodies v. Burlingame Elementary School, 897 F.2d 974 (9th Cir. 1989)

Moore v. District of Columbia, 886 F.2d 335 (D.C. Cir. 1989)

Mitten by and through Mitten v. Muscogee County School District, 877 F.2d 932 (11th Cir. 1989) cert. den. 110 S.Ct. 1117, ___ U.S. ___, ___ L.Ed.2d ___

Duane M. v. Orleans Parish School Board, 861 F.2d 115 (5th Cir. 1988)

Eggers v. Bullit County School District, 854 F.2d 892 (6th Cir. 1988)

Daniel B. v. Wisconsin Dept. of Public Instruction, 581 F.Supp. 585 (D.C. Wisc.), 776 F.2d 1051 (7th Cir. 1984), cert. den. 106 S.Ct. 1462, 475 U.S. 1083, 89 L.Ed.2d 719 (1984)

New York Gaslight Club, Inc. v. Carey, 100 S.Ct. 204, 444 U.S. 897, 62 L.Ed.2d 132 (1980)

SPECIAL EDUCATION FACILITIES

13:410 May a school board use its special education tax levy to construct buildings?

Yes. By proper resolution, the school board may accumulate funds in the special education fund for up to eight years for building purposes.

Ill. Rev. Stat. c. 122, par. 17-2.2a

13:420 What may school districts do with special education facilities no longer needed for special education purposes?

If it is no longer feasible or economical to utilize classroom facilities constructed with revenues raised and accumulated by the tax for special education building purposes, the district may use such facilities for regular school purposes with the approval of the regional superintendent of schools and the State Superintendent of Education. The district must make comparable facilities available for special education purposes at another attendance center which is in a more practical location due to the proximity of the students served.

By unanimous consent of participating school districts, a cooperative special education district may exercise the same discretion.

Ill. Rev. Stat. c. 122, par. 17-2.2a

14: RELIGION AND THE PUBLIC SCHOOLS

CONSTITUTIONAL PRINCIPLES

14:10 What constitutional principle underlies all legal questions regarding separation of church and state?

The First Amendment to the United States Constitution provides in part:

"Congress shall make no law respecting the establishment of religion, or prohibiting the free exercise thereof."

The first part is known as the "establishment" clause and the second part is known as the "free exercise" clause. It is balancing the establishment clause against the free exercise clause that makes the analysis of religious freedom questions difficult. Often a situation which seems clearly consistent with the establishment clause is not so clearly consistent with the free exercise clause, and vice versa.

14:20 What test do the courts apply to determine whether a government action is constitutional under the establishment clause?

The government action must have a secular purpose, its primary effect must neither advance nor inhibit religion, and the action must not cause excessive government entanglement with religion.

Lemon v. Kurtzman, 91 S.Ct. 2105, 403 U.S. 602, 29 L.Ed.2d 745, reh. den. 92 S.Ct. 24, 404 U.S. 876, 30 L.Ed.2d 123, on remand 348 F.Supp. 300, aff'd. 93 S.Ct. 1463, 411 U.S. 192, 36 L.Ed.2d 151 (1971)

14:30   May the state compel students to attend public schools?

The free exercise clause of the First Amendment has been read by the courts to prevent the state from compelling public school attendance. The state may require all students, public and parochial, to receive a minimum number of hours of instruction from qualified teachers in a prescribed secular curriculum.

Ill. Rev. Stat. c. 122, par. 26-1 et seq.

Wisconsin v. Yoder, 92 S.Ct. 1526, 406 U.S. 205, 32 L.Ed.2d 15 (1972)

Board of Education of Central School District No. 1 v. Allen, 88 S.Ct. 1923, 392 U.S. 236, 20 L.Ed.2d 1060 (1968)

Pierce v. Society of Sisters of the Holy Names of Jesus and Mary, 45 S.Ct. 571, 268 U.S. 510, 69 L.Ed 1070 (1925)

Meyer v. State of Nebraska, 43 S.Ct. 625, 262 U.S. 390, 67 L.Ed. 1042 (1923)

14:40   May a school district release students during the school day for religious instruction?

A school district must allow any child over 12 and under 14 years of age release time to attend confirmation classes. Whether release time is permissible for other kinds of religious instruction depends upon the underlying facts. The more the facts suggest public school endorsement of, or entanglement with, religion, the less likely the courts will approve any particular practice. Release time for religious classes held within the public schools or the expenditure of public funds for religious education are, in most cases, prohibited.

Ill. Rev. Stat. c. 122, par. 26-1

Zorach v. Clauson, 92 S.Ct. 679, 343 U.S. 306, 96 L.Ed. 954 (1952)

Illinois ex rel. McCollum v. Board of Education of School District No. 71, Champaign County, Illinois, 68 S.Ct. 461, 333 U.S. 203, 92 L.Ed. 649 (1948)

Illinois ex rel. Latimer v. Board of Education of the City of Chicago, 394 Ill. 228, 68 N.E.2d 305 (1946)

SYMBOLIC ACTS

14:50 Is a moment of silence for voluntary student prayer permissible?

The recitation of any state composed or endorsed prayer in school is constitutionally prohibited. This is true even if students are not required to participate in the prayer, and even if the prayer is facially neutral as to religious denomination. Moment of silence statutes have been invalidated by the courts as serving no secular purpose.

Illinois has a moment of silence statute, known as the Silent Reflection Act, but its constitutionality is not certain.

Ill. Rev. Stat. c. 122, par. 771

Wallace v. Jaffree, 105 S.Ct. 2479, 472 U.S. 38, 86 L.Ed.2d 29 (1985)

School District of Abington Township v. Schempp, 83 S.Ct. 1560, 374 U.S. 203, 10 L.Ed.2d 844 (1963)

Engel v. Vitale, 82 S.Ct. 1261, 370 U.S. 421, 8 L.Ed.2d 601 (1962)

14:60 Is a non-sectarian graduation ceremony benediction, invoking the deity and delivered by a member of the clergy, permissible?

There is some reason for concern that a non-sectarian benediction, invoking the deity and delivered by a member of the clergy, at a public school graduation ceremony violates the First Amendment's "establishment" clause. The use of clergy to provide an inspirational message without reference to a deity at such events raises no Constitutional concerns.

Weisman v. Lee, 728 F.Supp. 68, 908 F.2d 1090 (1st Cir. 1990)

Stein v. Plainwell Community Schools, 610 F.Supp. 43, rev. 822 F.2d 1406 (6th Cir. 1987)

Marsh v. Chambers, 103 S.Ct. 3330, 463 U.S. 783, 77 L.Ed.2d 1019 (1983)

14:70 May a school district erect a Christmas tree or display religious symbols?

Whether any particular religious symbol or display violates the Establishment Clause depends upon the underlying facts. If the court determines the display has the primary effect of advancing or inhibiting religion, it is found unconstitutional.

The same symbol may be found proper or improper depending upon the context in which it is displayed. A display accompanied by a religious message might, for example, make an otherwise permissible display unconstitutional. No recent decisions have addressed religious symbols or displays in schools.

Allegheny County v. American Civil Liberties Union, Greater Pittsburgh Chapter, 109 S.Ct. 3086, __ U.S. __, 106 L.Ed.2d 472 (1989) on remand 887 F.2d 260

Lemon v. Kurtzman, 91 S.Ct. 2105, 403 U.S. 602, 29 L.Ed.2d 745, reh. den. 92 S.Ct. 24, 404 U.S. 876, 30 L.Ed.2d 123, on remand 348 F.Supp. 300, aff'd. 93 S.Ct. 1463, 411 U.S. 192, 36 L.Ed.2d 151 (1971)

PAROCHIAL SCHOOL SERVICES

14:80 Is it constitutionally permissible for a public school district to provide transportation for parochial school students?

A public school district must provide transportation for parochial school students under certain circumstances and subject to certain limitations. If a school district provides a school bus or other conveyance to transport students to and from school, it must transport, without charge, certain parochial school students who live along the public school district's regular bus routes.

Ill. Rev. Stat. c. 122, par. 29-4 et seq.

Illinois ex rel. Board of Education of School District 142, Cook County v. Illinois Board of Education, 62 Ill.2d 517, 344 N.E.2d 5 (1976)

Board of Education School District 142 v. Bakalis, 54 Ill.2d 448, 299 N.E.2d 737 (1973)

Everson v. Board of Education of Ewing Township, 67 S.Ct. 504, 330 U.S. 1, 91 L.Ed. 711, reh. den. 67 S.Ct. 962, 330 U.S. 855, 91 L.Ed. 1297 (1947)

14:90 May a public school board assign public school teachers to perform secular teaching duties in a parochial school?

A public school district may not pay the salaries of public school teachers, guidance counselors, psychologists, and social workers to teach secular subjects in parochial schools.

School District of the City of Grand Rapids v. Ball, 105 S.Ct. 3216, 473 U.S. 373, 87 L.Ed.2d 267 (1985)

Wolman v. Walter, 97 S.Ct. 2593, 433 U.S. 229, 53 L.Ed.2d 714 (1977)

    Roemer v Board of Public Works of Maryland, 96 S.Ct. 2337, 426 U.S. 736, 49 L.Ed.2d 179 (1976)

    Meek v. Pittenger, 95 S.Ct. 1753, 421 U.S. 349, 44 L.Ed.2d 217, reh. den. 95 S.Ct. 2668 (1975)

14:100 May a school board provide free diagnostic services, such as speech, hearing, and psychological services, for nonpublic school students on public school property?

Yes.

Wolman v. Walter, 97 S.Ct. 2593, 433 U.S. 229, 53 L.Ed.2d 714 (1977)

SCHOOL FACILITIES

14:120 May a school board regulate or prohibit the distribution of religious literature on school grounds?

As agents of the State, teachers and other school officials or employees may neither advance nor inhibit religion. Such persons should be prohibited by the school board from the distribution of religious literature on school ground. Students and members of the public are not agents of the State. With respect to these groups, school officials may adopt reasonable rules governing the distribution of literature. Such rules may, for example, limit distribution to specific times and places.

    Equal Access Act, 20 U.S.C. 4071

    Board of Education of Westside Community Schools v. Mergens, 110 S.Ct. 2356, __ U.S. __, 110 L.Ed.2d 191 (1990)

    Garnett v. Benton School District, 865 F.2d 1211 (9th Cir. 1989)

    Widmar v. Vincent, 102 S.Ct. 269, 454 U.S. 263, 70 L.Ed.2d 440 (1981)

**14:130 May a school board deny an adult,
        noncurriculum related religious organization
        the use of school facilities?**

Requests by churches or other adult, noncurriculum related organizations for the after-hours use of school facilities must be handled in a non-dscriminatory manner. An organization may not be denied access purely on the basis of its religious convictions.

Lemon v. Kurtzman, 91 S.Ct. 2105, 403 U.S. 602, 29 L.Ed.2d 745, reh. den. 92 S.Ct. 24, 404 U.S. 876, 30 L.Ed.2d 123, on remand 348 F.Supp. 300, aff'd. 93 S.Ct. 1463, 411 U.S. 192, 36 L.Ed.2d 151 (1971)

15: TEACHER EMPLOYMENT STANDARDS

STATE CERTIFICATION

15:10 Who is a teacher?

A teacher, for most purposes under Illinois law, is any school district employee whose job requires teacher certification. The term "teacher" usually includes superintendents, principals, other certificated administrators, guidance counselors, deans, classroom teachers and may include other job titles.

Ill. Rev. Stat. c. 122, par. 24-11
Ill. Rev. Stat. c. 122, par. 10-23.8
Ill. Rev. Stat. c. 122, par. 10-23.8a
Lester v. Board of Education of School District No. 119, Jo Daviess County, 87 Ill.App.2d 269, 230 N.E.2d 893 (2nd Dist. 1967).

15:20 Must all teachers be certificated?

Most teachers must obtain either regular, substitute or provisional certification. There are a number of special exceptions to regular certification requirements in the areas of vocational education, career education and with respect to joint public school and community college cooperative agreements.

Ill. Rev. Stat. c. 122, par. 10-22.20a
Ill. Rev. Stat. c. 122, par. 21-1 et seq.

15:30 Are there different certification requirements for teachers at different grade levels and for teaching different subject matters?

Yes.

Ill. Rev. Stat. c. 122, par. 21-1 et seq.
23 Ill. Admin. Code 1.1610 et seq.

15:40   Does a teaching certificate indicate the subject areas the teacher may teach?

Teaching certificates issued after June 30, 1986, are endorsed by the State Board of Education for each subject the holder of the certificate is certified to teach. Certificates which were issued prior to July 1, 1986, may have been endorsed on the date of issue (depending on the date of issue) or may, on application to the State Board of Education, be endorsed for each subject the holder is certified to teach.

Ill. Rev. Stat. c. 122, par. 21-1b

Zink v. Board of Education of Chrisman, 146 Ill.App.3d 1016, 497 N.E.2d 835, 100 Ill.Dec. 657 (4th Dist. 1986)

15:50   Must a school board help a teacher secure a teaching certificate?

It is the sole responsibility of a teacher to apply for and secure teaching certification.

Hagopian v. Board of Education of Tampico Community Unit School District No. 4 of Whiteside and Bureau Counties, 56 Ill.App.3d 940, 372 N.E.2d 990, 14 Ill.Dec. 711 appeal after remand 83 Ill.App.3d 1097, 404 N.E.2d 899, 39 Ill.Dec. 308, rev. on other grounds 84 Ill.2d 436, 420 N.E.2d 147, 50 Ill.Dec. 830 (1981)

Relph v. Board of Education of Depue Unit School District No. 103 of Bureau County, 84 Ill.2d 436, 420 N.E.2d 147, 50 Ill.Dec. 830 (1978)

15:60   Under what conditions may a teacher's certificate be suspended or revoked?

A teacher's certificate may be suspended for a period not to exceed one calendar year by either the regional superintendent or State Superintendent of Education upon evidence of immorality, a condition of health detrimental to the welfare of pupils, incompetency, unprofessional conduct, the neglect of any professional duty, willful failure to report an instance of suspected child abuse or neglect as required by the Abused and Neglected Child Reporting Act, or just cause.

Unprofessional conduct includes neglect or unnecessary delay in making of statistical and other reports required by school officers, refusal to attend or participate in institutes, teachers' meetings, professional readings, or to meet other reasonable requirements of the regional superintendent or State Superintendent of Education.

No certificate may be suspended until the teacher has an opportunity for a hearing at the educational service region. Appeal may be had to the State Teacher Certification Board.

Any certificate may be revoked by the State Superintendent of Education for the same reasons which must underlie a suspension. No certificate may be revoked until the teacher has an opportunity for a hearing before the State Teacher Certification Board.

When the holder of any teaching certificate has been convicted of certain sex or narcotics offenses, the regional superintendent or the State Superintendent of Education must suspend the certificate. If the conviction is reversed and the holder is acquitted of the offense in a new trial or the charges against him are dismissed, the suspending authority must terminate the suspension of the certificate. If the conviction becomes final, the State Superintendent of Education must revoke the certificate.

Ill. Rev. Stat. c. 122, par. 2-3.9
Ill. Rev. Stat. c. 122, par. 21-23
Ill. Rev. Stat. c. 122, par. 21-23a

15:70   What recourse is available to a school board if a teacher signs an initial employment contract but refuses to perform?

There is no mechanism whereby a school board can compel a teacher to specifically perform teaching duties pursuant to contract. A school board might sue the teacher for breach of contract, but damages would likely be limited to the cost of finding a suitable replacement.

A school board may petition the regional superintendent of schools to initiate teacher certificate suspension proceedings. Proceedings relative to certification involve a regional hearing, and the decision is appealable to the State Teacher Certification Board.

Ill. Rev. Stat. c. 122, par. 21-23

ADDITIONAL TEACHER QUALIFICATIONS

15:80   Must a school board conduct criminal background checks on applicants for employment?

A school board may not knowingly employ a person for whom a criminal background investigation has not been begun. Applicants for employment with a school district are required as a condition of employment to authorize an investigation to determine if they have been convicted of any of a specified list of criminal and drug offenses. A school board may not knowingly employ a person who has been convicted of any of a list of offenses specified.

Ill. Rev. Stat. c. 122, par. 10-21.9

15:90   May a school board require teachers to show evidence of freedom from communicable diseases?

A school board must require a new employee to present evidence of physical fitness to perform the duties assigned and freedom from communicable disease, including tuberculosis. Evidence must consist of a physical examination and a tuberculin skin test and, if appropriate, an X-ray made by a physician licensed in Illinois or any other state to practice medicine and surgery in all its branches not more than 90 days preceding the time of presentation to the school board. The cost of the examination is paid by the employee.

A school board may from time to time require an examination of any employee by a physician licensed in Illinois to practice medicine and surgery in all of its branches and must pay the expenses of this examination from school funds.

Ill. Rev. Stat. c. 122, par. 24-5

15:100 May a school board require a teacher to undergo a psychiatric examination to determine mental fitness to teach?

Yes. A psychiatric exam may be required in appropriate circumstances.

Ill. Rev. Stat. c. 122, par. 24-5

Dusanek v. Hannon, 677 F.2d 538 (7th Cir. 1982)

Tetmeir v. Board of Education of School District No. 149, Cook County, 5 Ill.App.3d 982, 284 N.E.2d 280 (1st Dist. 1972)

15:110 May a school board require teachers to demonstrate continued professional growth?

A school board may require teachers to demonstrate continued professional growth. A school board may bargain this subject or, in the absence of a recognized bargaining representative or if a bargaining representative fails to make a timely demand to bargain the subject, the board may adopt a policy regulating professional growth.

Ill. Rev. Stat. c. 122, par. 24-5

Heifner v. Board of Education of Morris Community Unit School District No. 101, Grundy County, 32 Ill.App.3d 83, 335 N.E.2d 600 (3rd Dist. 1975)

Last v. Board of Education of Community Unit School District No. 321, Winnebago and Stephenson Counties, 37 Ill.App.2d 159, 185 N.E.2d 282 (2nd Dist. 1962)

Richards v. Board of Education of Township High School District No. 201, 21 Ill.2d 104, 171 N.E.2d 37 (1960)

HIRING PROCEDURES AND CRITERIA

15:130 May a school district use age as a qualification for employment or promotion?

Federal law prohibits age-related discrimination in the hiring, promotion, and other conditions of employment for employees age 40 and over. A school board may attach age requirements to a job if it can show age is a bona fide occupational qualification.

29 U.S.C. 621 et seq.

29 C.F.R. 1625 et seq.

Ill. Rev. Stat. c. 68, par.1-101 et seq.

15:135 May a school district have an anti-nepotism rule which forbids or restricts the employment of spouses?

While anti-nepotism rules are legally permissible generally, those which restrict the employment or assignment of spouses are suspect. Since Illinois has laws preventing marital discrimination, any such proposed rule should be carefully considered before adoption.

Ill. Rev. Stat. c. 122, par. 10-22.4
Ill. Rev. Stat. c. 68, par. 1-103-J et seq.
Kraft, Inc. v. State of Minnesota, 284 N.W.2d 386 (S.Ct. of Minn. 1979)
Yuhas v. Libbey-Owens-Ford Company, 562 F.2d 496 (7th Cir. 1976) cert. den. 98 S.Ct. 1510, 435 U.S. 934, 55 L.Ed.2d 531
Hollister v. North, 50 Ill.App.3d 56, 365 N.E.2d 258, 8 Ill.Dec. 20 (Dist. 1977)

15:140 May a school district give employment preference to veterans?

If all bargaining obligations are met, a school district may give preferential treatment in employment to veterans of any branch of United States military service.

Ill. Rev. Stat. c. 68, par. 2-104(2)

15:150 If a school board elects not to hire a qualified teacher applicant, must it give reasons for the rejection?

Provided there is no policy or contract provision to the contrary and provided there are no constitutional implications to the rejection, a school board may reject the application of any teacher without giving reasons, notwithstanding the applicant is qualified to meet the needs of the school district as specified in the job announcement.

Halfacre v. Board of Education of School District No. 167, 331 Ill.App. 404, 73 N.E.2d 124 (1947)

TEACHING ASSIGNMENTS

15:160 May a school board assign or transfer teachers to and from positions for which they are qualified at will?

In the absence of a constitutional restriction (such as a civil rights implication), or a limitation contained in a collective bargaining agreement, a school board may assign, reassign, or transfer teachers to and from positions they are qualified to fill as the school board sees fit in order to meet the needs of the district. However, a school board may not use transfer to defeat the tenure rights of teachers.

Ill. Rev. Stat. c. 122, par. 24-12

Stamper v. Board of Education of Elementary School District No. 143, 141 Ill.App.3d 884, 491 N.E.2d 36, 96 Ill.Dec. 222 (1st Dist. 1986)

Peters v. Board of Education of Rantoul Township High School District No. 193 of Champaign County, 97 Ill.2d 166, 454 N.E.2d 310, 73 Ill.Dec. 450 (1983)

15:170 Does a teacher's tenured status restrict the authority of a school board to assign the teacher?

Tenure does not limit the power of a school board to transfer or assign a teacher to a position for which the teacher is qualified. The provisions of a collective bargaining agreement or duty to bargain obligations may limit the school board, however.

Stamper v. Board of Education of Elementary School District No. 143, 141 Ill.App.3d 884, 491 N.E.2d 36, 96 Ill.Dec. 222 (1st Dist. 1986)

15:175 May a school district require its employees to administer medication to students?

Neither teachers nor other non-administrative school employees, except certified school nurses, can be required to administer medication to students. This prohibition includes school nurses and uncertified school nurses. Volunteers may be sought, and certified school nurses may be required, to administer medication, but potential bargaining obligations should be considered in each case.

Ill. Rev. Stat. c. 122, par. 10-22.21b

EXTRACURRICULAR ASSIGNMENTS

15:180 May a school board assign its teachers to perform extracurricular duties?

A teacher may be assigned to extracurricular duties which are reasonably related to the educational program and which are not onerous, unreasonably time consuming, demeaning to the professional stature of the teacher or assigned in a discriminatory manner. The performance of extra duties and the salary therefor must be bargained at appropriate times on demand by a recognized bargaining representative.

Where a collective bargaining contract includes an extra duty salary schedule and no limitations on the assignment of extra duties, the union has effectively conceded that the school board has the authority to make extra duty assignments.

Lewis v. North Clay Community Unit School District No. 25, 181 Ill.App.3d 689, 537 N.E.2d 435, 130 Ill.Dec. 368 (5th Dist. 1989)

Board of Education of Berwyn School District No. 100 v. Metskas, 106 Ill.App.3d 943, 436 N.E.2d 587, 62 Ill.Dec. 561 (1st Dist. 1982)

Littrell v. Board of Education of Cave in Rock Community Unit School District No. 2, 45 Ill.App.3d 690, 360 N.E.2d 102, 4 Ill.Dec. 355 (5th Dist. 1977)

District 300 Education Association v. Board of Education of Dundee Community Unit School District No. 300 of Kane et al Counties, 31 Ill.App.3d 550, 334 N.E.2d 165 (2nd Dist. 1975)

Simcox v. Board of Education of Lockport Township High School District No. 205, 443 F.2d 40 (7th Cir. 1970)

PROBATIONARY EMPLOYMENT

15:190 What is the maximum length of time a school board may require a teacher to serve as a probationary employee?

If a teacher has previously had a full term of teaching experience, the maximum probationary period is two years of consecutive full time service. If the teacher has not previously had a full term of full time teaching experience, the school board may extend the maximum probationary period to three years of consecutive full time service. The school board must follow statutory procedures in extending the probationary period to a third year. For purposes of service credit computations for acquisition of tenure determinations, initial employment before November 1 of the first probationary year is treated as a full year of employment, and initial employment after October 31 is not treated as time credited to the acquisition of tenure.

A part time teacher who has never had two consecutive years of full time service may remain a probationary employee indefinitely.

Ill. Rev. Stat. c. 122, par. 24-11

15:200 What is required to extend probationary employment to a third year?

If a teacher has not had one school term of full time teaching experience before the beginning of the probationary period, the employing board may, at its option, extend such probationary period for one additional school term by giving the teacher written notice at least 60 days before the end of the second school term. The notice must be delivered by certified mail, return receipt requested, and must state the reasons for the one year extension and must outline the corrective actions which the teacher should take to satisfactorily complete probation.

Ill. Rev. Stat. c. 122, par. 24-11

Mann v. Board of Education of Red Hill Community Unit School District No. 10, 82 Ill.App.3d 161, 402 N.E.2d 345, 37 Ill.Dec. 455 (5th Dist. 1980)

Jackson v. Board of Education of Trico Community Unit School District No. 176, Jackson County, 63 Ill.App.3d 671, 380 N.E.2d 41, 20 Ill.Dec. 364 (5th Dist. 1978)

Brunstrom v. Board of Education of Riverdale Community Unit School District 100 of Rock Island County, 52 Ill.App.3d 653, 367 N.E.2d 1065, 10 Ill.Dec. 456 (3rd Dist. 1977)

Glover v. Macon Community Unit School District No. 5 of Macon County, 21 Ill.App.3d 1053, 316 N.E.2d 534 (4th Dist. 1974) aff'd. 62 Ill.2d 122, 340 N.E.2d 4

Miller v. School District No. 167 Cook County, 500 F.2d 711 (7th Cir. 1974)

Graham v. Board of Education of Community High School District No. 77 of St. Clair County, 15 Ill.App.3d 1092, 305 N.E.2d 310 (5th Dist. 1973)

15:210 What must be included in a notice to extend probationary employment to a third year?

The reasons given must be truthful and make the teacher aware of means to correct his teaching deficiencies.

Mann v. Board of Education of Red Hill Community Unit School District No. 10, 82 Ill.App.3d 161, 402 N.E.2d 345, 37 Ill.Dec. 455 (5th Dist. 1980)

Jackson v. Board of Education of Trico Community Unit School District No. 176, Jackson County, 63 Ill.App.3d 671, 380 N.E.2d 41, 20 Ill.Dec. 364 (5th Dist. 1978)

Brunstrom v. Board of Education of Riverdale Community Unit School District 100 of Rock Island County, 52 Ill.App.3d 653, 367 N.E.2d 1065, 10 Ill.Dec. 456 (3rd Dist. 1977)

15:220 Is a school board limited to the reasons given at the time of extension of probation to a third probationary year as causes for dismissal when dismissing the teacher after a third year of probation?

A nontenured teacher whose probationary status is extended to a third year may be dismissed at the end of the third year for reasons other than those which caused the school board to extend the probationary period.

Jackson v. Board of Education of Trico Community Unit School District No. 176, Jackson County, 63 Ill.App.3d 671, 380 N.E.2d 41, 20 Ill.Dec. 364 (5th Dist. 1978)

SUBSTITUTE TEACHERS

15:230 Who may be employed as a substitute teacher?

A fully certificated teacher may be employed as a substitute teacher. A teacher not fully certified to teach the subject or grade level for which a substitute is sought may be employed, provided that the teacher holds a substitute teacher's certificate.

A substitute teacher's certificate may be issued upon request of the regional superintendent of schools in any region in which the teacher is to teach. To qualify, an applicant must either hold a valid teaching certificate, or hold a bachelor's degree, or have had two years of teaching experience and meet other State Board of Education rules and regulations.

Ill. Rev. Stat. c. 122, par. 21-9

15:240 How many days a year may an individual be employed as a substitute teacher?

A teacher who is fully certified for the appropriate subject matter or grade level may be employed as a substitute for any number of days per year.

A teacher holding a substitute teacher's certificate may teach in the place of a certified teacher only when no appropriate fully certified teacher is available to teach in a substitute capacity. Such a substitute may teach for no more than 90 paid school days or 450 paid school hours in any one school district in any one school term. When such teaching is partly on a daily and partly on an hourly basis, a school day is considered to be five hours.

Ill. Rev. Stat. c. 122, par. 21-9
Woods v. East St. Louis School District No. 189, 147 Ill.App.3d 776, 498 N.E.2d 801, 101 Ill.Dec. 477 (5th Dist. 1986)

15:250 Do minimum salary laws apply to a substitute teacher?

There is no minimum or maximum salary law which applies to a teacher serving as a day-to-day substitute. However, if a substitute teacher is employed on a continuing basis, his status may be changed from substitute teacher to full-time temporary teacher, in which case minimum salary laws or collectively bargained provisions applicable to full-time certificated employees may apply.

Ill. Rev. Stat. c. 122, par. 24-8
Ill. Rev. Stat. c. 122, par. 21-9
Woods v. East St. Louis School District No. 189, 147 Ill.App.3d 776, 498 N.E.2d 801, 101 Ill.Dec. 477 (5th Dist. 1986)

EVALUATING TEACHERS

15:260 Are schools required to have a formal evaluation plan?

Each school district must establish, in cooperation with its teachers or, when applicable, with the official bargaining representative of its teachers, a plan for evaluating its tenured teachers. In the event any substantive change is made in the evaluation plan, the new plan must be submitted to the State Board of Education for review and comment.

Ill. Rev. Stat. c. 122, par. 24A-4

Board of Education of Leroy Community Unit School District No. 2 v. Illinois Educational Labor Relations Board, 199 Ill.App.3d 347, 556 N.E.2d 857, 145 Ill.Dec. 239 (4th Dist. 1990) petition for leave to appeal granted (October 3, 1990)

15:270 Whom must a school district evaluate?

A school district must evaluate each of its tenured teachers at least once in the course of any two years.

Ill. Rev. Stat. c. 122, par. 24A-5

15:280 What must be included in an evaluation plan?

An evaluation plan must include a description of each teacher's duties and responsibilities and the standards to which that teacher is expected to conform. The plan may provide for evaluation of personnel whose positions require administrative certification by independent evaluators not employed by, or affiliated with the school district. The results of the school district administrators' evaluations shall be reported to the employing school board, together with such recommendations for remediation as the evaluator or evaluators may deem appropriate.

Evaluation of teachers whose positions do not require administrative certification shall be conducted by a qualified administrator and shall include at least the following components:

1) personal observation of the teacher in the classroom by a district administrator qualified pursuant to statute to conduct evaluations unless the teacher has no classroom duties;

2) consideration of the teacher's attendance, planning, and instructional methods, classroom management, where relevant, and competency in the subject matter taught, where relevant;

3) rating of the teacher's performance as "excellent," "satisfactory," or "unsatisfactory";

4) specification as to the teacher's strengths and weaknesses, with supporting reasons for the comments made; and

5) inclusion of a copy of the evaluation in the teacher's personnel file and provision of a copy to the teacher.

Ill. Rev. Stat. c. 122, par. 24A-5

15:290 What procedures are required when a tenured teacher receives an unsatisfactory evaluation rating?

If a tenured teacher receives an unsatisfactory evaluation rating the following procedures are required:

1) Within 30 days after completion of an evaluation rating a teacher as "unsatisfactory," development and commencement by the district of a remediation plan designed to correct deficiencies cited, provided the deficiencies are deemed remediable.

2) Participating in the remediation plan by the teacher rated "unsatisfactory," a qualified district administrator and a consulting teacher selected by the participating administrator or by the principal of the teacher who was rated "unsatisfactory." The consulting teacher must be an educational employee as defined in the Educational Labor Relations Act, have at least five years teaching experience, have a reasonable familiarity with the assignment of the teacher being evaluated, and must have received an "excellent" rating on his or her most recent evaluation. Where no teachers who meet these criteria are available within the district, the district must request and the State Board of Education supply, to participate in the remediation process, an individual who meets these criteria. In a district with an exclusive bargaining agent, the bargaining agent may, if it so chooses, supply a roster of qualified teachers from whom the consulting teacher is to be selected. That roster must, however, contain the names of at least five teachers, each of whom meets the criteria for consulting teacher with regard to the teacher being evaluated, or the names of all teachers so qualified if that number is less than five. In the event of a dispute

as to qualification, the State Board shall determine qualification.

3) Quarterly evaluations and ratings for one year immediately following receipt of an "unsatisfactory" rating of a teacher for whom a remediation plan has been developed. These subsequent evaluations shall be conducted by the participating administrator. The consulting teacher must provide advice to the teacher rated "unsatisfactory" on how to improve teaching skills and to successfully complete the remediation plan. The consulting teacher must participate in developing the remediation plan, but the final decision as to the evaluation shall be done solely by the administrator, unless an applicable collective bargaining agreement provides to the contrary.

4) Reinstatement of a schedule of biennial evaluation for any teacher who completes the one-year remediation plan with a "satisfactory" or better rating, unless the district's plan regularly requires more frequent evaluations.

5) Dismissal in accordance with the School Code of any teacher who fails to complete the one-year remediation plan with a "satisfactory" or better rating.

Ill. Rev. Stat. c. 122, par. 24A-5

TEACHER RESIGNATIONS

15:300 When may a tenured teacher resign without penalty?

A tenured teacher may resign at any time by agreement of the school board or by serving at least 30-days written notice upon the secretary of the board. However, no teacher may resign during the school year to accept another teaching assignment without the concurrence of the school board. A teacher who resigns on terms inconsistent with the above risks suspension of his teaching certificate for a period not to exceed one year.

Ill. Rev. Stat. c. 122, par. 24-14
Ill. Rev. Stat. c. 122, par. 21-23
Braught v. Board of Education of Mount Prospect School District No. 57, 136 Ill.App.3d 486, 483 N.E.2d 623, 91 Ill.Dec. 277 (1st Dist. 1985)

15:310 When is a teacher's resignation effective?

In most circumstances, a teacher resignation is effective on receipt. No acceptance by a school board is required.

Braught v. Board of Education of Mount Prospect School District No. 57, 136 Ill.App.3d 486, 483 N.E.2d 623, 91 Ill.Dec. 277 (1st Dist. 1985)

Arduini v. Board of Education of Pontiac Township High School District 90, Livingston County, 92 Ill.2d 197, 441 N.E.2d 73, 65 Ill.Dec. 281 (1982)

Gras v. Clark, 46 Ill.App.3d 803, 361 N.E.2d 316, 5 Ill.Dec. 177 (2nd Dist. 1977)

16: TEACHER TENURE AND SENIORITY RIGHTS

TEACHER TENURE

16:10 Do all teachers enjoy the same employment rights under Illinois law?

Illinois teachers fall into three broad categories for purposes of statutory employment rights:

First year probationary teachers have the fewest rights. All part time teachers who have not achieved and maintained tenured status have rights similar to first year probationary teachers.

Second and third year probationary teachers comprise the second category, and have slightly greater rights than first year probationary teachers.

The third category is comprised of tenured teachers who have dramatically more rights than either of the other two categories of teachers.

Ill. Rev. Stat. c. 122, sec. 24-11
Ill. Rev. Stat. c. 122, sec. 24-12

16:20 What is tenure?

Tenure is the common name for contractual continued service, which is the status conferred by law upon certificated employees who have satisfactorily completed a term of probationary employment. The employee in contractual continued service is:

1) deemed to be continuously employed from year to year unless given proper notice of honorable dismissal (lay off) or dismissal for cause;

2) entitled to seniority rights granted by law or collective bargaining agreement in the event a school board reduces its staff or discontinues a program; and

3) entitled to substantial rights of due process in the event of dismissal for cause.

Ill. Rev. Stat. c. 122, sec. 24-12

16:30 What is the difference between contractual continued service and tenure?

There is no difference between the terms. Tenure is the common name for contractual continued service.

Ill. Rev. Stat. c. 122, sec. 24-11
Ill. Rev. Stat. c. 122, sec. 24-12

16:40 What is the difference between a probationary teacher and a non-tenured teacher?

The terms have the same meaning, as does the phrase "teacher who has not entered into contractual continued service."

16:50 Must a tenured teacher be issued an annual employment contract?

Tenured teachers have a continuing employment relationship which does not require the issuance of an annual contract. Assuming there is no collectively bargained provision which prevents the issuance of an annual contract and no demand to bargain, a school board may issue individual teacher contracts. The terms of the contract must be consistent with the terms of applicable collectively bargained provisions. A tenured teacher cannot be compelled to sign such a contract, but may voluntarily enter into a contract providing for additional obligations in exchange for additional benefits.

Bond v. Board of Education of Mascoutah Community Unit School District No. 19, 81 Ill.2d 242, 408 N.E.2d 714, 42 Ill.Dec. 136 (1980)

Bagley v. Board of Education of Seneca Community Consolidated School District No. 170, LaSalle County, 83 Ill.App.3d 247, 403 N.E.2d 1285, 38 Ill.Dec. 681 aff'd. 84 Ill.2d 477 (1980)

Littrell v. Board of Education of Cave in Rock Community Unit School District No. 2, 45 Ill.App.3d 690, 360 N.E.2d 102, 4 Ill.Dec. 355 (5th Dist. 1977)

Davis v. Board of Education of Aurora Public School District No. 131 of Kane County, 19 Ill.App.3d 644, 312 N.E.2d 335 (2nd Dist. 1974)

ACQUISITION OF TENURE

16:60 Which employees may acquire tenure?

A teacher may acquire tenure. The term "teacher" in this context includes all school district employees whose jobs require teacher certification. Superintendents, principals, other administrators, deans, department heads, and counselors may acquire teacher tenure if such employees meet statutory requirements.

Tenure does not attach to a particular job, but rather to teaching employment in the school district generally. For example, a principal cannot earn tenure as a principal, but earns tenure as a teaching employee.

Ill. Rev. Stat. c. 122, sec. 10-23.8 et seq.

Ill. Rev. Stat. c. 122, sec. 24-12

Davis v. Board of Education of Farmer City-Mansfield Community Unit School District No. 17, 63 Ill.App.3d 495, 380 N.E.2d 58, 20 Ill.Dec. 381 (4th Dist. 1978)

Lester v. Board of Education of School District No. 119, Jo Daviess County, 87 Ill.App.2d 269, 230 N.E.2d 893 (2nd Dist. 1967)

16:70 When does a teacher acquire tenure?

Any teacher who has been employed in a district as a full-time teacher for a probationary period of two consecutive school terms enters upon contractual continued service unless given written notice of dismissal by the school board. The notice must state the specific reason for the dismissal, and must be delivered by certified mail, return receipt requested, at least 60 days before the end of the school term.

For the purpose of determining contractual continued service, the first probationary year shall be any full-time employment from a date before November 1 through the end of the school year.

A school board may, by following the requisite procedures, extend probation to a third year if the probationary teacher has not previously had one term of full time teaching experience.

Ill. Rev. Stat. c. 122, sec. 24-11

Dunlop v. Colgan, 687 F.Supp. 406 (N.D. Ill. 1988)

Williams v. Board of Education of Hardin County Community Unit School District No. 1, 166 Ill.App.3d 765, 520 N.E.2d 954, 117

Ill.Dec. 603 (5th Dist. 1988) appeal den. 121 Ill.2d 587, 526 N.E.2d 841, 122 Ill.Dec. 448

Bessler v. Board of Education of Charter School District No. 150 of Peoria County, 43 Ill.App.3d 322, 356 N.E.2d 1253, 1 Ill.Dec. 920 (3rd Dist. 1977), aff'd. in part, rev. in part 69 Ill.2d 191, 370 N.E.2d 1050, 13 Ill.Dec. 23

16:80 Does a teacher hired to replace a teacher on an approved leave of absence acquire tenure?

Tenure is not acquired by a person while employed to replace a teacher who is in the military service of the United States, one who is serving in the General Assembly, or one who by agreement of a school board is on leave to teach in a Department of Defense dependents' school.

Ill. Rev. Stat. c. 122, sec. 24-13
Ill. Rev. Stat. c. 122, sec. 24-13.1
Fisher v. Board of Education of West Washington County Community Unit District No. 10, Washington County, 181 Ill. App.3d 653, 537 N.E.2d 354, 130 Ill.Dec. 287 (5th Dist. 1989)

16:90 If a certified teacher is employed in a special education cooperative, in which school district or districts does such a teacher acquire tenure?

A teacher employed full time in a special education cooperative before September 23, 1987 and who achieved tenure in the cooperative acquired tenure in all participating districts in the cooperative. In the event the program is terminated, the teacher must be assigned to any comparable position in a member district for which he is qualified and which is currently held by a non-tenured teacher or one with shorter length of service.

Tenure in all participating school districts is commonly called super-tenure. Teachers employed in a special education cooperative after September 23, 1987 can not acquire super-tenure.

Ill. Rev. Stat. c. 122, sec. 14-9.01
Ill. Rev. Stat. c. 122, sec. 24-11
Seim v. Board of Education of Community Unit School District No. 87 of McLean County, 21 Ill.App.3d 386, 315 N.E.2d 282 (4th Dist. 1974)

16:100 Do teachers employed in a joint agreement vocational area center have super-tenure?

No.

Koppi v. Board of Control of Whiteside Area Vocational Center,
133 Ill.App.3d 591, 479 N.E.2d 36, 88 Ill.Dec. 701 (3rd Dist. 1985)

16:110 Does service as a teacher's aide or a para-professional count toward earning tenure if the person so employed has teacher certification?

No.

Strejcek v. Board of Education of Berwyn School District No. 100,
78 Ill.App.3d 400, 397 N.E.2d 448, 33 Ill.Dec. 942 (1st Dist. 1979)

16:120 Is a teacher employed in a program which is wholly federally funded accruing time toward the acquisition of tenure?

Probably not. Courts have found teachers employed in programs which are wholly federally funded are not "full time teachers" within the meaning of teacher tenure laws.

Kuykendall v. Board of Education of Evanston Township High School District No. 202, 111 Ill.App.3d 809, 444 N.E.2d 766, 67 Ill.Dec. 530 (1st Dist. 1982)

16:130 Can a teacher earn tenure in an extra duty assignment?

No. Tenure is not acquired in-position, but as a generic teaching employee of the school district. A coach cannot acquire tenure as a coach. A collective bargaining agreement may, however, extend contractual rights to such employees.

Smith v. Board of Education of Urbana School District No. 116,
708 F.2d 258 (7th Cir. 1983)

Brunstrom v. Board of Education of Riverdale Community Unit School District 100 of Rock Island County, 52 Ill.App.3d 653, 367 N.E.2d 1065, 10 Ill.Dec. 456 (3rd Dist. 1977)

RIGHTS OF TENURED TEACHERS

16:140 Does tenure protect a teacher's right to a particular job assignment?

The safeguards of tenure do not assure employment in a particular job assignment, grade level, or attendance center, but rather protect the individual's job as a teacher.

Caviness v. Board of Education of Ludlow Community Consolidated School District No. 142 of Champaign County, 59 Ill.App.3d 28, 375 N.E.2d 157, 16 Ill.Dec. 526 (4th Dist. 1978)

Danno v. Peterson, 421 F.Supp. 950 (N.D. Ill. 1976).

Van Dyke v. Board of Education of School District No. 57, Cook County, 115 Ill.App.2d 10, 254 N.E.2d 76 (1st Dist. 1969)

16:150 If two or more school districts combine, do the tenured teachers from the predecessor school districts lose tenure?

No. If by reason of any change in the boundaries of school districts, or by reason of the creation of a new school district, the position held by any teacher having tenured status is transferred from one school board to the control of a new or different board, the tenure of the teacher is not lost. The new or different school board is subject to the tenure laws with respect to the teacher in the same manner as if the teacher were its employee and had been its employee during the time the teacher was actually employed by the board from whose control the position was transferred.

Ill. Rev. Stat. c. 122, sec. 24-12

PART TIME TEACHERS

16:160 Can a part time teacher acquire tenure?

No. To acquire tenure, an employee must complete the statutory two consecutive years of full time service.

Ill. Rev. Stat. c. 122, sec. 24-11

Kuykendall v. Board of Education of Evanston Township High School District No. 202, 111 Ill.App.3d 809, 444 N.E.2d 766, 67 Ill.Dec. 530 (1st Dist. 1982).

Johnson v. Board of Education of Decatur School District No. 61 of Macon County, 87 Ill.App.3d 441, 409 N.E.2d 139, 42 Ill.Dec. 644 (4th Dist. 1980) aff'd. 85 Ill.2d 338, 423 N.E.2d 903, 53 Ill.Dec. 234

16:170 May a school board confer tenure on a part time teacher or on a teacher who has served less than the requisite probationary period?

No. Tenure attaches by operation of law. The requisite probationary period must be served.

Faculty Association of District 205, IEA-NEA v. Illinois Educational Labor Relations Board, 175 Ill.App.3d 880, 530 N.E.2d 548 (4th Dist. 1988) appeal den. 124 Ill.2d 554

    Evans v. Benjamin School District No. 25, 134 Ill.App.3d 875, 480 N.E.2d 1380, 89 Ill.Dec. 637 (2nd Dist. 1985)

    Kuykendall v. Board of Education of Evanston Township High School District No. 202, 111 Ill.App.3d 809, 444 N.E.2d 766, 67 Ill.Dec. 530 (1st Dist. 1982)

SENIORITY AND REDUCTION IN FORCE

16:190 Do probationary or part time teachers accrue seniority rights?

Probationary and part time teachers do not accrue seniority rights as a result of any statutory requirement. Sometimes such employees acquire seniority by reason of a provision in a collective bargaining agreement. In the absence of a demand to bargain or if the affected teachers are not members of a recognized bargaining unit, a school board may unilaterally establish seniority rules for such teachers.

Ill. Rev. Stat. c. 122, sec. 24-12

16:200 What is RIF?

RIF is an acronym for reduction in force, which is the decision of a school board to decrease the number of teachers employed or to discontinue some particular type of teaching service.

Ill. Rev. Stat. c 122, sec. 24-12

16:210 What is the difference between the terms "layoff" and "reduction in force"?

An employee is layed off when an employer conducts a reduction in force.

16:220 What seniority rights may tenured teachers assert against less senior teachers in the event of a reduction in force?

A school board contemplating a reduction in teaching force must first remove or dismiss all non-tenured teachers in a particular position before removing or dismissing any tenured teacher who is legally qualified to hold the position. As between tenured teachers, the teacher or teachers with the shorter length of continuing service to the district must be dismissed first unless an alternate method of determining the sequence of dismissal is established in a collective bargaining agreement. A school board must comply with all procedures required by its collective bargaining agreement in the conduct of a reduction in force.

Ill. Rev. Stat. c. 122, sec. 24-12

Schaefer v. Board of Education of Arlington Heights School District No. 25, 157 Ill.App.3d 884, 510 N.E.2d 1186, 110 Ill.Dec. 155 (1st Dist. 1987) appeal den. 116 Ill.2d 576, 515 N.E.2d 126, 113 Ill.Dec. 317

Catron v. Board of Education of Kansas Community Unit School District No. 3 of Edgar County, 126 Ill.App.3d 693, 467 N.E.2d 621, 81 Ill.Dec. 750 (4th Dist. 1984)

Birk v. Board of Education of Flora Community Unit School District No. 35, Clay County, 104 Ill.2d 252, 472 N.E.2d 407, 84 Ill.Dec. 447 (1984)

Wilson v. Board of Education Limestone Walters School District No. 316, 127 Ill.App.3d 433, 468 N.E.2d 995, 82 Ill.Dec. 341 (3rd Dist. 1984)

Caviness v. Board of Education of Ludlow Community Consolidated School District No. 142 of Champaign County, 59 Ill.App.3d 28, 375 N.E.2d 157, 16 Ill.Dec. 526 (4th Dist. 1978)

16:230 Is the reduction of a tenured teacher from ten month employment to nine month employment a reduction in force?

The reduction of a tenured teacher's employment from a ten month extended contract to a nine month regular contract is a reduction in force. Absent agreement from the teacher, the reduction of a tenured teacher from full time to part time may only be accomplished at the beginning of a new school term following legally sufficient notice to the teacher at least 60 days before the end of the preceding school term.

The notification procedure is the same as that required for notice of dismissal or layoff. The seniority rights of tenured teachers must be respected in any such reduction and all collectively bargained procedures must be followed.

Ill. Rev. Stat. c. 122, sec. 24-12

Duncan v. Board of Education of United Township High School District No. 30, 177 Ill.App.3d 806, 532 N.E.2d 927, 127 Ill.Dec. 98 (3rd Dist. 1988)

Pennell v. Board of Education of Equality Community Unit School District 4, Gallatin County, 137 Ill.App.3d 139, 484 N.E.2d 445, 91 Ill.Dec. 886 (5th Dist. 1986)

Birk v. Board of Education of Flora Community Unit School District No. 35, Clay County, 104 Ill.2d 252, 472 N.E.2d 407, 84 Ill.Dec. 447 (1984)

Wilson v. Board of Education Limestone Walters School District No. 316, 127 Ill.App.3d 433, 468 N.E.2d 995, 82 Ill.Dec. 341 (3rd Dist. 1984)

16:235 Can a tenured teacher who accepts a part time position and later requests return to full time teaching assert bumping rights against a new non-tenured teacher?

Under most circumstances, bumping rights can be asserted only when a reduction in force triggers the bumps. When, however a tenured teacher has retained tenure after a reduction to part time status, the tenured teacher may later return to fulltime status by asserting bumping rights against a new non-tenured teacher who has been hired to teach in a position which the tenured teacher is qualified to fill.

Deem v. Board of Education of Triad Community Unit School District No. 2, Madison County, 200 Ill.App.3d 903, 558 N.E.2d 291, 146 Ill.Dec. 328 (5th Dist. 1990)

16:240 What is required to reduce a tenured teacher from full time to part time employment?

Without the agreement of the teacher, the reduction of a tenured teacher from full time to part time may only be accomplished at the beginning of a new school term following legally sufficient notice to the teacher at least 60 days before the end of the preceding school term. The notification procedure is the same as that required for notice of dismissal or layoff. The seniority rights of tenured teachers must be respected in any such reduction and all collectively bargained procedures must be followed.

Ill. Rev. Stat. c. 122, sec 24-12

Pennell v. Board of Education of Equality Community Unit School District 4, Gallatin County, 137 Ill.App.3d 139, 484 N.E.2d 445, 91 Ill.Dec. 886 (5th Dist. 1986)

Board of Education of Bremen Community High School District No. 228, Cook County v. Bremen District No. 228 Joint Faculty Association, 114 Ill.App.3d 1051, 449 N.E.2d 960, 70 Ill.Dec. 613, aff'd. in part, rev. in part on other grounds 101 Ill.2d 115, 461 N.E.2d 406, 77 Ill.Dec. 783 (1983)

Hagopian v. Board of Education of Tampico Community Unit School District No. 4 of Whiteside and Bureau Counties, 56 Ill.App.3d 940, 372 N.E.2d 990, 14 Ill.Dec. 711 appeal after remand 83 Ill.App.3d 1097, 404 N.E.2d 899, 39 Ill.Dec. 308 rev. on other grounds 84 Ill.2d 436, 420 N.E.2d 147, 50 Ill.Dec. 830 (1981)

16:250 If a teacher has earned tenure and later is reduced to part time without a break in service, does the teacher lose tenure?

No.

Wilson v. Board of Education Limestone Walters School District No. 316, 127 Ill.App.3d 433, 468 N.E.2d 995, 82 Ill.Dec. 341 (3rd Dist. 1984)

Caviness v. Board of Education of Ludlow Community Consolidated School District No. 142 of Champaign County, 59 Ill.App.3d 28, 375 N.E.2d 157, 16 Ill.Dec. 526 (4th Dist. 1978)

Brown v. Board of Education Gallatin Community Unit School District No. 1, 38 Ill.App.3d 403, 347 N.E.2d 791, appeal after remand *Illinois ex rel. Brown v. Board of Education Gallatin Community Unit School District No. 1*, 66 Ill.App.3d 167, 383 N.E.2d 711 (5th Dist. 1976)

16:260 In a reduction in force, must all non-tenured teachers be dismissed before the first tenured teacher is dismissed?

No. A non-tenured teacher must be reduced first only if he holds a position which is to be reduced or if he is bumped by a teacher with greater seniority.

Ill. Rev. Stat. c. 122, 24-12

16:270 In what manner must a school board notify a teacher of honorable dismissal by reason of reduction in teaching force or discontinuance of teaching service?

If a teacher on tenure is removed or dismissed as a result of the decision of the school board to decrease the number of teachers employed by the board or to discontinue some particular type of teaching service, a written notice must be given the teacher by certified mail, return receipt requested, at least 60 days before the end of the school term, together with a statement of honorable dismissal and the reason therefor.

Ill. Rev. Stat. c. 122, sec. 24-12
23 Ill. Admin. Code sec. 51.30
Koerner v. Joppa Community High School District No. 21, 143 Ill.App.3d 162, 492 N.E.2d 1017, 97 Ill.Dec. 358 (5th Dist. 1986)

16:280 When must a school board hold a public hearing before conducting a reduction in force?

Whenever the number of honorable dismissal notices based upon economic necessity exceeds five or 150 percent of the average number of teachers honorably dismissed in the preceding three years, whichever is greater, then the school board must hold a hearing on the question of the dismissals. Following the hearing and board review, the action to approve any such reduction in staff requires a majority vote of the school board.

Ill. Rev. Stat. c. 122, sec. 24-12
23 Ill. Admin. Code sec. 51.20.
Wheatley v. Board of Education of Township High School District No. 205, Cook County, 113 Ill.App.3d 129, 446 N.E.2d 1257, 68 Ill.Dec. 860 (1st Dist. 1983)

SENIORITY AND BUMPING

16:290 At what date are teacher qualifications fixed for purposes of a school board decision to reduce force?

A school board must base its decision to reduce force on the qualifications held by a teacher no later than 60 days before the end of the school term in which the notice of reduction in force is to be sent.

Ill. Rev. Stat. c. 122, sec. 24-12

Hagopian v. Board of Education of Tampico Community Unit School District No. 4 of Whiteside and Bureau Counties, 56 Ill.App.3d 940, 372 N.E.2d 990, 14 Ill.Dec. 711 appeal after remand 83 Ill.App.3d 1097, 404 N.E.2d 899, 39 Ill.Dec. 308 rev. on other grounds 84 Ill.2d 436, 420 N.E.2d 147, 50 Ill.Dec. 830 (1981)

16:300 Are the terms "legally qualified" and "certified" synonymous?

No. Certified refers to State Board of Education teacher certification. Legally qualified has a wider meaning. A teacher may be certified to hold a position, but not legally qualified to hold it.

Zink v. Board of Education of Chrisman, 146 Ill.App.3d 1016, 497 N.E.2d 835, 100 Ill.Dec. 657 (4th Dist. 1986)

Lenard v. Board of Education of Fairfield School District No. 112 of Wayne County, 57 Ill.App.3d 853, 373 N.E.2d 477, 15 Ill.Dec. 131 appeal after remand 74 Ill.2d 260, 384 N.E.2d 1321, 24 Ill.Dec. 163 (1978)

16:310 Must a school board develop a teacher seniority list?

Each year, each school board must, in consultation with any exclusive bargaining representatives, establish a list categorized by positions, showing the length of continuing service of each teacher in the district who is qualified to hold any position. Copies of this list must be distributed to the exclusive bargaining representative on or before February 1 of each year.

Ill. Rev. Stat. c. 122, sec. 24-12

16:315 Is the definition of seniority a mandatory subject of bargaining?

Yes. If questions arise which have not been fully bargained with respect to computation of seniority affecting a recognized bargaining unit, the school board may unilaterally define seniority only after notice to the union and in the absence of a union demand to bargain thereafter.

Ill. Rev. Stat. c. 48, par. 1710

16:320 What are bumping rights?

When a more senior teacher "bumps" a less senior teacher from his job in the event of a reduction in force, he exercises "bumping rights." Bumping rights derive from statutory seniority, and therefore apply only to tenured teachers unless a collective bargaining agreement extends such rights to other classes of teachers.

Ill. Rev. Stat. c. 122, sec. 24-12
Caviness v. Board of Education of Ludlow Community Consolidated School District No. 142 of Champaign County, 59 Ill.App.3d 28, 375 N.E.2d 157, 16 Ill.Dec. 526 (4th Dist. 1978)

16:330 Is a school board required to realign teaching assignments in a reduction in force to protect the jobs of senior tenured teachers?

A school board is not required to combine parts of existing teaching assignments in a reduction in force to protect the jobs of senior tenured teachers. Absent a collectively bargained provision to the contrary, bumping rights may be exercised by tenured teachers to claim "whole positions." A school board may not realign teaching assignments in a reduction in force to defeat the tenure rights of a senior teacher.

Ill. Rev. Stat. c. 122, sec. 24-12
Peters v. Board of Education of Rantoul High School District No. 193 of Champaign County, 97 Ill.2d 166, 454 N.E.2d 310, 73 Ill.Dec. 450 (1983)

16:340 For how long after layoff does a teacher have recall rights?

Unless a collective bargaining agreement provides otherwise, only tenured teachers have recall rights. Recall rights extend for one calendar year from the beginning of the school term following the layoff unless the original layoff exceeded 15 percent of the number of full time equivalent positions filled by certified employees (excluding principals and administrative personnel) during the preceding school year, in which case the recall rights extend for two calendar years from the beginning of the school term following the layoff.

Ill. Rev. Stat. c. 122, sec. 24-12

Walter v. Board of Education of Quincy School District No. 172, 93 2Ill.2d 101, 442 N.E.2d 870, 66 Ill.Dec. 309 (1982)

Huetteman v. Board of Education of Community Unit School District 3A, 56 Ill.App.3d 933, 372, N.E.2d 716, 14 Ill.Dec. 520 (4th Dist. 1978)

16:350 Do probationary employees have recall rights after layoff?

Not unless they are granted recall rights in a collective bargaining agreement. Statutory preferential right of recall applies to tenured teachers and support staff only.

Ill. Rev. Stat. c. 122, sec. 10-23.5

Ill. Rev. Stat. c. 122, sec. 24-11

Ill. Rev. Stat. c. 122, sec. 24-12

17: OTHER TERMS AND CONDITIONS OF TEACHER EMPLOYMENT

TEACHER COMPENSATION

17:10 Is there a statutory minimum teacher salary?

Yes. A school board must pay minimum annual salaries of $10,000 for a teacher holding a bachelor's degree and $11,000 for a teacher holding a master's degree. The following minimum increases must be paid:

• $750 after five years of experience for a teacher with less than a bachelor's degree;

• $1,000 after five years and $1,600 after eight years for a teacher with a bachelor's degree;

• $1,250 after five years and $2,000 after eight years for a teacher with a master's degree.

The minimum salary statute is ambiguous as to what constitutes "years of experience" both for purposes of prior experience credit and for purposes of salary schedule advancement after initial employment.

Ill. Rev. Stat. c. 122, par. 24-8

Winters v. Board of Education of Piasa Community Unit School District No. 9 of Macoupin County, 66 Ill.App.3d 918, 384 N.E.2d 519, 23 Ill. Dec. 725 (4th Dist. 1978)

Hardway v. Board of Education of Lawrenceville Township High School District No. 71, 1 Ill.App.3d 298, 274 N.E.2d 213 (5th Dist. 1971)

17:20 Is there a minimum salary provision which applies to summer school employment?

No. Summer school salaries may be established by a school board subject only to the minimum hourly wage provisions and collective bargaining requirements.

29 U.S.C. 201

17:30 Must a school board recognize all prior teaching experience of a new employee on its salary schedule?

Illinois appellate courts are divided on this issue. Absent the requirements of a collective bargaining agreement, the safer approach is to recognize full prior experience credit.

Ill. Rev. Stat. c. 122, par. 24-8

Winters v. Board of Education of Piasa Community Unit School District No. 9 of Macoupin County, 66 Ill.App.3d 918, 384 N.E.2d 519, 23 Ill.Dec. 725 (4th Dist. 1978)

Hardway v. Board of Education of Lawrenceville Township High School District No. 71, 1 Ill.App.3d 298, 274 N.E.2d 213 (5th Dist. 1971)

17:40 When must a teacher submit evidence of additional education in order to advance on the salary schedule?

Unless a collective bargaining agreement provides otherwise, a teacher who submits a certificate of completion to the school office prior to the first day of the school term must be considered to have the degree stated on the certificate.

Ill. Rev. Stat. c. 122, par. 24-8

Board of Education of Valley View Community Unit School District No. 365U v. Schmidt, 64 Ill.App.3d 513, 381 N.E.2d 400, 21 Ill.Dec. 291 (1st Dist. 1978)

17:50 Is a school board required to pay its teachers "vacation time?"

No statute requires a school board to pay teachers vacation pay.

17:60 Does the Federal Fair Labor Standards Act apply to public schools?

Yes. A public school board is subject to the requirements of the Act, including its minimum wage and overtime provisions. Teachers are not subject to the provisions of the Act; support staff are.

29 U.S.C. 201

Garcia v. San Antonio Metropolitan Transit Authority, 105 S.Ct. 1005 469 U.S. 528, 83 L.Ed.2d 1016 (1985)

17:70   What is the federal Equal Pay Act?

The federal Equal Pay Act is a non-discrimination law. It provides in part:

"No employer . . . shall discriminate, within any establishment in which such employees are employed, between employees on the basis of sex by paying wages to employees in such establishment at a rate less than the rate at which he pays wages to employees of the opposite sex in such establishment for equal work on jobs the performance of which requires equal skill, effort, and responsibility, and which are performed under similar working conditions, except where such payment is made pursuant to (i) a seniority system; (ii) a merit system; (iii) a system which measures earnings by quantity or quality of production; or (iv) a differential based on any other factor other than sex."

29 U.S.C. par. 206(d)(1)

17:80   If a teacher is honorably dismissed as a result of a reduction in force, when must the teacher be paid all accrued earnings?

Any teacher honorably dismissed as a result of a decrease in the total number of teachers or the discontinuance of some educational service must be paid all earned compensation on or before the third business day following the last day of pupil attendance in the regular school term.

Ill. Rev. Stat. c. 122, par. 24-12

17:90   What control may a school board exercise with respect to employee "moonlighting?"

Unless a school board can demonstrate the employee's second job is negatively affecting his performance at school, the school board may not regulate or restrict the employee's outside activities.

Cook County College Teachers Union Local 1600 IFT, AFT, AFL-CIO v. Board of Trustees Community College District No. 505, Cook County, 134 Ill.App.3d 489, 481 N.E.2d 40, 89 Ill.Dec. 688 (1st Dist. 1985)

Kaufmann v. Board of Trustees Community Consolidated District 508, 522 F.Supp. 90 (N.D. Ill. 1981)

Meridith v. Board of Education of Community Unit School District No. 7, 7 Ill.App.2d 477, 130 N.E.2d 5 (3rd Dist. 1955)

17:100 How may teachers be held to account for school property in their possession?

Each teacher has a statutory duty to protect school district property. No teacher may be paid unless the teacher has satisfactorily accounted for books, apparatus, and other property belonging to the school district.

Ill. Rev. Stat. c. 122, par. 24-17

17:110 What options are available to a school district which is financially unable to pay its teachers?

A school district may choose either of two procedures when unable to pay teachers' wages for lack of funds. The school district may establish a voucher system of expenditures, or may require the district treasurer to pay funds of the school district upon an order of the school board signed by the president.

When an order issued for the wages of a teacher is presented to the treasurer and is not paid for want of funds, the treasurer is required to endorse over his signature "not paid for want of funds" with the date of presentation and shall keep a record of that endorsement. The order, thereafter, bears interest at a rate not exceeding the maximum rate authorized by the Bond Authorization Act until the maturity date established by the school board or, in the absence of such maturity date, until the treasurer notifies the clerk or secretary in writing that he has funds to pay the order.

When the treasurer obtains sufficient funds to pay any such order, he must set them aside for such purpose and shall not use them to pay any other order until the order previously presented and not paid is paid or otherwise discharged.

Ill. Rev. Stat. c. 122, par. 8-16
Ill. Rev. Stat. c. 17, par. 6600 et seq.

RETIREMENT SYSTEM CONTRIBUTIONS

17:120 Are teachers covered by Social Security?

No deduction or employer contribution is made from teacher pay for Social Security. Teachers may make Social Security payments by having non-teaching jobs for which such contributions are made. Teachers are required to participate in the Teacher Retirement System. Teachers and other school employees hired after March 31, 1986, are subject to a 1.45 percent Medicare tax.

26 U.S.C. 3121(u)(2)(c)
Ill. Rev. Stat. c. 108 1/2, par. 21-101 et seq.
Ill. Rev. Stat. c. 108 1/2, par. 21-102.12

17:130 What contribution to the Teacher Retirement System on behalf of each teacher is required?

A school board is required to contribute eight percent of each teacher's gross pay to the Teacher Retirement System (TRS). Gross pay includes sums paid the teacher for extra duties and certain fringe benefits provided under a cafeteria plan. TRS has gross income treatments which differ from Internal Revenue Service treatments, and a school board should be wary to examine both effects when considering any new fringe benefit program.

Ill. Rev. Stat. c. 108 1/2, Par. 16-152 et seq.

17:140 What is the significance of the multiplier .086957 for Teacher Retirement System contribution purposes?

If a teacher's gross pay including Teacher Retirement System (TRS) contribution equals X, then the amount of the TRS contribution is calculated by multiplying X(.08). If the amount of X(.08) is subtracted from the teacher's gross pay, the result is the teacher's taxable pay. To get from the teacher's taxable pay to the teacher's gross pay, one must multiply taxable pay by 1.086957. To determine the amount of TRS contribution due knowing only the amount of a teacher's taxable pay, one must multiply taxable pay by .086957. The multiplier .086957 is unnecessary and burdensome if the teacher's gross pay is known.

Ill. Rev. Stat. c. 108 1/2, Par. 16-152 et seq.

SALARY DEDUCTIONS

17:150 Is a school board required to withhold union dues from salary?

A school board must, upon the written request of an employee, withhold from the compensation of that employee any dues, payments, or contributions payable by such employee to any employee labor organization as defined in the Illinois Educational Labor Relations Act. Under such arrangement, an amount must be withheld from each regular payroll period which is equal to the pro rata share of the annual dues plus any payments or contributions. The school board must transmit such withholdings to the specified labor organization within ten working days from the time of the withholding. Dues deduction procedures are usually contained in collective bargaining agreements.

Ill. Rev. Stat. c. 48, par. 1701 et seq.
Ill. Rev. Stat. c. 122, par. 24-21.1

17:160 What is "fair share?"

If included in a collective bargaining agreement, a fair share clause requires a school board to deduct from each teacher's salary a sum equal to the union's cost of representing the teacher in the bargaining process and for grievance representation. Usually the fair share fee is a percentage of union dues in excess of 75 percent and often approaching 100 percent. The specific percentage is established by a union showing of the actual cost of representation. A fair share provision is a common union bargaining demand. A school board may, but need not, agree to fair share.

Ill. Rev. Stat. c. 48, par. 1711

Abood v. Detroit Board of Education, 97 S.Ct. 1782, 431 U.S. 209, 52 L.Ed. 261, reh. den. 97 S.Ct. 2989, 433 U.S. 915, 53 L.Ed.2d 1102 (1977)

Chicago Teachers Union Local 1, AFT, AFL-CIO v. Hudson, 106 S.Ct. 1066, 475 U.S. 292, 89 L.Ed.2d 232 (1986)

17:170 Must a school board withhold delinquent child or family service payments from an employee's salary?

A school district may receive a certified "Order for Withholding" and a "Notice of Delinquency" directing the district to deduct child or family support payments from the salary of an employee. In addition to the required support payment, a school district may deduct a one dollar fee each pay period from the income of the employee in order to meet the requirements of this law.

Ill. Rev. Stat. c. 23, par. 10-16.2

WORKERS' COMPENSATION

17:180 Do the Workers' Compensation Act and the Occupational Disease Act apply to school employees?

The Workers' Compensation Act and the Occupational Disease Act provide benefits, on a no-fault basis, to which school employees may be entitled in the event of job-related injury, illness or death. An employee may qualify for medical expense reimbursement, compensation for lost earnings, and/or permanent disability payments for work-related injury, illness or death.

Ill. Rev. Stat. c. 48, par. 172.36 et seq.
Ill. Rev. Stat. c. 48, par. 138.1(a)1 et seq.

17:190 Are worker compensation benefits available to workers paid by outside organizations, such as the PTA?

A school district may be treated as an employer for worker compensation purposes whether or not the school district pays direct compensation to a worker if the work performed by the worker is primarily for the benefit of the school district and a school district supervisor controls the employee and supervises his work.

Board of Education of the City of Chicago v. Industrial Commission, 57 Ill.2d 330, 312 N.E.2d 244 (1974)

17:200 Are volunteer workers eligible for worker compensation benefits?

No.

Board of Education of the City of Chicago v. Industrial Commission, 53 Ill.2d 167, 290 N.E.2d 247 (1972)

17:205 May an employee recover both sick leave and worker compensation benefits at the same time?

Absent a collectively bargained agreement to the contrary, an employee is entitled to an election of benefits—either sick leave at full pay (to the extent the employee has such benefits available) or worker compensation benefits (to the extent of eligibility).

Chicago Board of Education v. Chicago Teachers Union, 86 Ill.2d 469, 427 N.E.2d 1199, 56 Ill.Dec. 653 (1981)

UNEMPLOYMENT INSURANCE

17:210 Are school employees eligible for unemployment compensation benefits?

School employees may be eligible for unemployment compensation if the conditions of the former employee's severance are qualifying. Employees discharged for cause or who leave work voluntarily are usually ineligible for unemployment compensation. Persons otherwise eligible for unemployment compensation may be disqualified if they are not able, available for, and actively seeking work.

Ill. Rev. Stat. c. 48, par. 300 et seq.

17:220 Is an employee eligible for unemployment compensation benefits after resignation?

An employee may be eligible for unemployment compensation after a voluntary resignation if the resignation was for "good cause."

Davis v. Board of Review of the Department of Labor, 125 Ill.App.3d 67, 465 N.E.2d 576, 80 Ill.Dec. 464 (1st Dist. 1984)

17:230 Are school employees eligible for unemployment compensation between school terms?

A person is ineligible for benefits, on the basis of wages for service in employment in an instructional, research, or principal administrative capacity performed for an educational institution during a period between two successive academic years, or during a period of paid sabbatical leave provided for in the person's contract, if the person performed such service in the first of such academic years [or terms] and if there is a contract or a reasonable assurance the person will perform service in any capacity for any educational institution in the second of such academic years [or terms].

Ill. Rev. Stat. c. 48, par. 442
Doran v. Department of Labor, 116 Ill.App.3d 471, 452 N.E.2d 118, 72 Ill.Dec. 186 (1st Dist. 1983)

17:250 May an employee receiving worker compensation benefits be concurrently eligible for unemployment compensation?

No.

Ill. Rev. Stat. c. 48, par. 436

TEACHER WORKLOAD

17:260 Is there a statutory limit on the work load which may be assigned a school teacher?

There is no statutory provision or State Board of Education rule or regulation governing teacher work load. Work load is to be distinguished from "preparations." Work load is the number of class periods in a specified time period for which any teacher is responsible. Preparations is the number of different lesson plans for different subjects or grade levels which a teacher must prepare in a specified time period. A maximum work load may exist by reason of a provision in a collective bargaining agreement.

17:270 Is there a maximum number of preparations a high school teacher may be assigned?

The State Board of Education has adopted a rule which provides: "No (high school) teacher should have more than five different preparations." Whether this statement absolutely prevents the assignment of a high school teacher to more than five preparations is unclear. There are differences in the meanings of teaching load, preparations and class assignments.

23 Ill. Admin. Code 1.440 c)

17:280 Is a teacher entitled to a duty free lunch?

Every teacher whose duties require attendance at school for four or more clock hours in any school day must be allowed a duty-free lunch period equal to the regular school lunch period but not less than 30 minutes during each school day.

Ill. Rev. Stat. c. 122, par. 24-9

Board of Education of Community Unit School District No. 4, Champaign County v. Champaign Education Association, 15 Ill.App.3d 335, 304 N.E.2d 138 (4th Dist. 1973)

17:290 Do statutes fix the length of a teacher's work day?

The School Code does not fix the length of a teacher's work day. Statutes set forth the minimum number of pupil attendance hours required in order to receive state financial aid. Absent a recognized bargaining unit, a school board may unilaterally establish length of work day. In school districts with recognized bargaining units, work day must be bargained at prescribed times on demand.

17:300 May a school board require a teacher to teach on Saturday?

A school board may not require its teachers to teach on Saturdays or to work on legal school holidays. School boards are also prohibited from making any deduction from the time or compensation of a teacher on account of any legal or special holiday.

Ill. Rev. Stat. c. 122, par. 24-2

*District 300 Education Association v. Board of Education of
Dundee Community Unit School District No. 300 of Kane et al.
Counties, 31 Ill.App.3d 550, 334 N.E.2d 165 (2nd Dist. 1975)*

17:310 Which holidays are school holidays?

A teacher can not be required to teach on Saturdays nor on legal school holidays, which are January 1, New Year's Day; the third Monday in January, the birthday of Dr. Martin Luther King, Jr.; February 12, the birthday of President Abraham Lincoln; the first Monday in March, Casimir Pulaski's birthday; Good Friday; the day designated as Memorial Day by federal law; July 4, Independence Day; the first Monday in September, Labor Day; the second Monday in October, Columbus Day; November 11, Veteran's Day; the Thursday in November commonly called Thanksgiving Day; and December 25, Christmas Day. A school board may grant a special holiday whenever in its judgment it is advisable. No deduction may be made from the time or compensation of a school employee on account of any legal or special holiday.

Other school employees also may not be required to work on legal school holidays, other than those noncertificated school employees whose presence is necessary because of an emergency or for the continued operation of school facilities or property.

Ill. Rev. Stat. c. 122, par. 24-2

LEAVES

17:320 May a school board allow sabbatical leave?

A school board may, by statutory authority, grant a sabbatical leave of absence to a teacher, principal, or superintendent performing contractual continued service, for a period of at least four school months but not in excess of one school term, for resident study, research, travel, or other purposes designed to improve the school system.

The statute which sets forth the conditions under which a sabbatical leave may be granted contains numerous and complicated procedural conditions for the leave. A school board may provide additional leave, provide leave for other classes of employees or add procedural requirements not contained in statute in a collectively bargained agreement or, absent a recognized bargaining representative, by the adoption of a policy.

Ill. Rev. Stat. c. 122, par. 24-6.1

Thrash v. Board of Education School District No. 189, 106 Ill.App.3d 182, 435 N.E.2d 866, 62 Ill.Dec. 68 (5th Dist. 1982)

17:330 Is personal leave or professional leave required by law?

Personal leave is paid leave of absence with or without procedural or use restrictions, and is commonly provided to teachers in amounts ranging from one to three days per year. Professional leave is paid or partially paid leave to attend meetings relating to the improvement of teaching. Neither leave is required by law. A school board may bargain either leave, or in the absence of a timely demand to bargain from a recognized bargaining representative, may regulate such leave by adoption of policy.

17:340 What is sick leave?

Unless the definition is expanded by a collective bargaining agreement or board policy, sick leave is time away from work for personal illness, quarantine at home, or serious illness or death in the immediate family or household. Immediate family is parents, spouse, brothers, sisters, children, grandparents, grandchildren, parents-in-law, brothers-in-law, sisters-in-law, and legal guardians.

Ill. Rev. Stat. c. 122, par. 24-6

17:350 How much sick leave is provided a teacher by law?

Unless a collective bargaining agreement, or board policy in the absence of a recognized bargaining representative, provides more, each full time teacher is entitled by statute to a minimum of 10 sick leave days at full pay in each school year. Unused sick leave must be allowed to accumulate to a minimum available leave of 180 days at full pay, including the leave of the current year.

Ill. Rev. Stat. c. 122, par. 24-6

17:360 Must a school board provide part time teachers sick leave benefits?

There is no statutory requirement that part time teachers be provided with sick leave benefits. Sick leave is a mandatory subject of bargaining. If part time teachers are included in a recognized bargaining unit, their sick leave benefits will be stated in a collective bargaining agreement. If part time teachers are not represented, a school board may unilaterally establish their sick leave benefits.

Ill. Rev. Stat. c. 122, par. 24-6

17:370 When may a school board require a teacher to provide a physician's certificate documenting the teacher's illness?

Unless a collective bargaining agreement or board policy provides otherwise, a school board may require a physician's certificate as a basis for pay during sick leave after an absence of three days for personal illness or as it may deem necessary in other cases. If the treatment is by prayer or spiritual means, a certificate may be required from a spiritual advisor or practitioner of the employee's faith.

If a school board requires a physician's certificate, or a certificate from a spiritual healer, as a basis for pay during leave for sick purposes of less than three days, the school board must pay the expenses incurred by the teacher or other employee in obtaining the physician's certificate.

Ill. Rev. Stat. c. 122, par. 24-5

Deizman v. Board of Education District 201, Cook County, 53 Ill.App.3d 1050, 369 N.E.2d 257 (1st Dist. 1977)

Lippincott v. Board of Education of Community Unit School District No. 5 of Coles County, 342 Ill.App. 642, 97 N.E.2d 566 (3rd Dist. 1951)

17:380 May a teacher be disciplined for excessive use of sick leave?

A teacher may not be disciplined for appropriate use of accumulated sick leave. Once a teacher has exhausted accumulated sick leave, the teacher may not be discharged if the disability giving rise to the use of sick leave is caused by a temporary incapacity.

A school board may collectively bargain a provision in its contract or, in the absence of a recognized bargaining representative or in the absence of demand to bargain by a bargaining representative, adopt a policy defining permanent incapacity and listing it as cause for dismissal.

Ill. Rev. Stat. c. 122, par. 10-22.4
Ill. Rev. Stat. c. 122, par. 24-6
Ill. Rev. Stat. c. 122, par. 24-13
Board of Education, School District No. 151, Cook County v. Illinois State Board of Education, 154 Ill.App.3d 175, 507 N.E.2d 134, 107 Ill.Dec. 470 (1st Dist. 1987)
deOliveira v. State Board of Education, 158 Ill.App.3d 111, 511 N.E.2d 172, 110 Ill.Dec. 337 (2nd Dist. 1987)
Elder v. Board of Education of School District No. 127 1/2, Cook County, 60 Ill.App.2d 56, 508 N.E.2d 423 (1st Dist. 1965)

17:390 Does a teacher lose accumulated sick leave by reason of school district combination?

If by reason of any change in the boundaries of a school district, or by reason of the creation of a new school district, the employment of a teacher is transferred to a new or different school board, the accumulated sick leave of the teacher is not lost, but is transferred to the new or different school district.

Ill. Rev. Stat. c. 122, par. 24-6

17:400 Must a pregnant teacher be permitted to use sick leave for pregnancy?

A school board must allow use of sick leave for employees who are disabled because of pregnancy. However, unless a collective bargaining agreement so provides, a school board need not permit the use of sick leave for pregnancy without disability.

Where no bargaining agreement provides to the contrary, a school board may require a doctor's certificate to establish a pregnant woman's inability to work. When a pregnant employee uses accumulated sick leave for pregnancy based disability, she must return to work when her disabling condition no longer exists.

42 U.S.C. 2000e

Ill. Rev. Stat. c. 122, par. 24-6

Maganuco v. Leyden Community High School District No. 212, 867 F.2d 974 (7th Cir. 1989)

Scherr v. Woodland Consolidated School District No. 50, 867 F.2d 974 (7th Cir. 1989)

Winks v. Board of Education of Normal Community Unit School District No. 5 of McLean County, 78 Ill.2d 128, 398 N.E.2d 823, 34 Ill.Dec. 832 (1979)

17:410 Is a school board required by law to grant maternity leave?

Maternity, paternity and parental leave are permissive under the law, but no such leave is required. However, a school board may not discriminate against pregnant employees with respect to the grant of denial of unpaid leaves of absence. A school board may bargain leaves, or in the absence of a recognized bargaining representative or if a bargaining representative fails to make timely demand to bargain, may regulate leaves by adoption of policy.

42 U.S.C. 2000e

Schafer v. Board of Public Education of School District of Pittsburgh, 732 F.Supp. 565 (W.D. Pa. 1990)

Winks v. Board of Education of Normal Community Unit School District No. 5 of McLean County, 78 Ill.2d 128, 398 N.E.2d 823, 34 Ill.Dec. 832 (1979)

17:420 May a school board require an employee to take a maternity leave?

A school board may not require an employee to take maternity leave if the employee is physically able to work.

42 U.S.C. 2000e

Cleveland Board of Education v. LaFleur, 94 S.Ct. 791, 414 U.S. 632, 39 L.Ed.2d 52 (1974)

17:430 What procedures may an employer use to determine whether a pregnant employee is able to work?

An employer may not single out pregnancy-related conditions for special procedures for determining an employee's ability to work. An employer may use any procedure used to determine the ability of any other employee to work and apply that procedure to pregnancy-related conditions.

If an employer requires employees to submit a doctor's statement before granting leave or paying sick leave benefits, the employer may require employees affected by pregnancy-related conditions to submit such statements.

42 U.S.C. 2000e

Cleveland Board of Education v. LaFleur, 94 S.Ct. 791, 414 U.S. 632, 39 L.Ed.2d 52 (1974)

17:440 Must a school district include maternity coverage in a health insurance program which it provides for its employees?

An employer must include maternity coverage in any health insurance program which the employer provides for its employees.

42 U.S.C. par. 2000e(k)
29 C.F.R. 1604

CONSTITUTIONAL, NONDISCRIMINATION AND RELATED RIGHTS OF TEACHERS

17:450 May a teacher be dismissed for publicly criticizing school board decisions?

The First Amendment right to freedom of speech applies to teachers. Teachers may speak out publicly on issues of public concern without fear of reprisal. Freedom of speech is not absolute, however. There are circumstances under which an employee may be disciplined by reason of something he has said.

Knapp v. Whitaker, 757 F.2d 827 (7th Cir. 1985)

Connick v. Myers, 103 S.Ct. 1684, 461 U.S. 138, 75 L.Ed.2d 708 (1983)

Givhan v. Western Line Consolidated School District, 99 S.Ct. 693, 139 U.S. 410, 58 L.Ed.2d 619 on rem. 592 F.2d 280 (1979)

Mt. Healthy City School District Board of Education v. Doyle, 97 S.Ct. 568, 429 U.S. 274, 50 L.Ed.2d 471, appeal after rem. 670 F.2d 59 (1977)

Brubaker v. Board of Education of School District No. 149, Cook County, 502 F.2d 973 (7th Cir. 1974)

Pickering v. Board of Education of Township High School District No. 205, Will County, Illinois, 88 S.Ct. 1731, 391 U.S. 563 20 L.Ed.2d 811 (1968)

17:460 May teachers engage in political campaigning or other political activities?

Teachers may engage in political campaigning or other political activities. The right to do so extends not only to conventional political causes, but also to political organizations which hold unpopular or controversial views. A school board may regulate the espousal of political views in the classroom by establishment of curriculum.

Ill. Rev. Stat. c. 85, par. 7601 et seq.

McLaughlin v. Tilendis, 398 F.2d 287 (7th Cir. 1968)

17:465 May a school district discriminate against employees on the basis of political preference?

No. A school district may not discriminate as to promotion, recall, transfer or hiring based on party affiliation.

Rutan v. Republican Party of Illinois, 110 S.Ct. 2729, __ U.S.__, 111 L.Ed.2d 52 reh. den. 111 S.Ct. 13, 111 L.Ed.2d 828 (1990)

Branti v. Finkel, 100 S.Ct. 1287, 445 U.S. 507, 63 L.Ed.2d 574 (1980)

Elrod v. Burns, 96 S.Ct. 2673, 427 U.S. 347, 49 L.Ed.2d 547 (1976)

17:470 May a school board require its teachers to be residents of the school district?

Residency may not be used as a factor in deciding whether or not to employ a teacher or in the determination of compensation, retention, promotion, assignment, or transfer.

Ill. Rev. Stat. c. 122, par. 24-4.1

17:480 May a school board adopt a mandatory teacher retirement policy for teachers who reach a specified age?

No. A mandatory retirement policy for any class of employees without demonstration of bona fide occupational qualification violates the federal Age Discrimination Act.

29 U.S.C. 623(f)(2)
29 C.F.R. 1625 et seq.
Ill. Rev. Stat. c. 68, par. 1-101 et seq.

17:490 Can an employer discharge, refuse to hire, or otherwise discriminate against a woman because she has had or is contemplating having an abortion?

No.
42 U.S.C. 2000e et seq.

17:500 What is sexual harassment?

Sexual harassment is any unwelcome sexual advances or requests for sexual favors or any conduct of a sexual nature when (1) submission to such conduct is made either explicitly or implicitly a term or condition of an individual's employment, (2) submission to or rejection of such conduct by an individual is used as the basis for employment decisions affecting such individual, or (3) such conduct has the purpose or effect of substantially interfering with an individual's work performance or creating an intimidating, hostile or offensive working environment.

29 C.F.R. 1604.11
Ill. Rev. Stat. c. 68, par. 1-101 et seq.
Henson v. City of Dundee, 682 F.2d 897 (11th Cir. 1982)
Bundy v. Jackson, 641 F.2d 934 (D.C.Cir 1981)
Tomkins v. Public Service Electric and Gas Company, 568 F.2d 1044 (3rd Cir. 1977)

17:510 Do statutes require report of attacks on school personnel?

Upon receipt of a written complaint from any school personnel, a superintendent must report any incident of battery committed against a teacher, teacher personnel, or administrative personnel to local law enforcement authorities no later than 24 hours after the occurrence of the attack and to the Department of State Police's Illinois Uniform Crime Reporting Program no later than three days after the occurrence of the attack.

Ill. Rev. Stat. c. 122, par. 10-21.7

18: TEACHER DISMISSAL
FOR CAUSE

DISMISSAL OF THE PROBATIONARY TEACHER

**18:10   What steps must be taken when a school district
intends not to renew the contract of a first year
probationary teacher?**

To dismiss a teacher at the end of the first year of probationary employment, the school district must (a) fully comply with
its evaluation plan and collectively bargained evaluation procedure, if applicable, and (b) give written notice of dismissal by
certified mail, return receipt requested. The notice must be
received by the teacher at least 60 days before the end of the
school term. If a school board fails to give such notice, the
teacher is reemployed for the following school term.

Ill. Rev. Stat. c. 122, par. 24-11

**18:20   What steps must be taken when a school district
intends not to renew the contract of a second or
third year probationary teacher?**

To dismiss a second or third year probationary teacher at the
end of a school term, the school district must have fully complied
with its evaluation plan and collectively bargained evaluation
procedure, if applicable.

With respect to a third year probationary teacher, the school
district must have complied with the statutory requirements to
extend probation.

No later than 60 days before the end of the final school term,
the second or third year probationary teacher must receive
written notice of dismissal from the school board. The notice
must state the specific reason for the dismissal, and it must be
delivered by certified mail, return receipt requested. If a school

board fails to give such notice, the teacher is reemployed for the following school term.

Ill. Rev. Stat. c. 122, par. 24-11

Illinois ex rel. Head v. Board of Education of Thornton Fractional South High School District No. 215, 95 Ill.App.3d 78, 419 N.E.2d 505, 50 Ill.Dec. 397 (1st Dist. 1981)

Wade v. Granite City Community Unit School District No. 9, Madison County, 71 Ill.App.2d 34, 218 N.E.2d 19 (5th Dist. 1966)

18:30 Must a notice to remedy deficiencies be issued or a remediation plan be instituted before a probationary employee is dismissed?

The remediation plan requirements of Section 24-A of the School Code apply to tenured employees only. If a school board seeks to dismiss a probationary employee at the end of a school term, no notice to remedy is necessary unless otherwise required by school board policy or as collectively bargained.

A notice to remedy may be necessary under certain circumstances if dismissal is sought during a school term.

Ill. Rev. Stat. c. 122, par. 24-11

Ill. Rev. Stat. c. 122, par. 24-A et seq.

18:40 May a school board dismiss a nontenured (probationary) teacher during a school term?

A school board may dismiss a nontenured teacher during the school year. However, such teachers are contractual employees of the school district and have a "property right" to employment for the term of the contract. To dismiss such an employee the school board has the burden to prove breach of contract and must accord the employee substantive and procedural due process.

Board of Regents of State Colleges v. Roth, 92 S.Ct. 2701, 408 U.S. 564, 33 L.Ed.2d 548 (1972)

18:50 Is a probationary teacher entitled to a hearing on the reasons for his dismissal if his contract is not being renewed for the following year?

The School Code does not require a hearing for a probationary teacher to examine the reasons for dismissal. When a school board has fully complied with statutory and local contract requirements, rules and regulations, no hearing is required.

A probationary teacher may compel a hearing, however, if the school board or its agents fail to comply with collectively bargained provisions relating to dismissal, seek to dismiss the employee while the employee is under contract, or if constitutional issues are raised with respect to the teacher's dismissal.

Howard v. Board of Education of Freeport School District No. 145, 160 Ill.App.3d 309, 513 N.E.2d 545, 112 Ill.Dec. 131 (2nd Dist. 1987)

Newborn v. Morrison, 440 F.Supp. 623 (N.D. Ill. 1977)

Mt. Healthy City School District Board of Education v. Doyle, 97 S.Ct. 568, 429 U.S. 274, 50 L.Ed.2d 471 (1977)

Bishop v. Wood, 96 S.Ct. 2074, 426 U.S. 341, 48 L.Ed.2d 864 (1976)

Board of Regents of State Colleges v. Roth, 92 S.Ct. 2701, 408 U.S. 564, 33 L.Ed.2d 548 (1972)

18:60 Under what circumstances does a school board infringe on a teacher's constitutionally protected liberty interests so as to give rise to due process?

A teacher's constitutionally protected liberty interests may be infringed when (a) the cause for dismissal does serious damage to the person's standing and associations in the community, or (b) the cause for dismissal creates a stigma or inability to take advantage of future employment opportunities.

If a school board infringes on a teacher's constitutionally protected liberty interests in dismissal proceedings, the teacher will be entitled to certain due process guarantees.

Austin v. Board of Education of Georgetown Community Unit School District No. 3 of Vermillion County, Illinois, 562 F.2d 446 (7th Cir. 1977)

Bishop v. Wood, 96 S.Ct. 2074, 426 U.S. 341, 48 L.Ed.2d 864 (1976)

Miller v. School District No. 167, Cook County, Illinois, 354 F.Supp. 922 (N.D. Ill. 1973), aff'd. on other grounds 495 F.2d 658 (7th Cir. 1974)

Hostrop v. Board of Junior College District 515, Cook and Will Counties and State of Illinois, 471 F.2d 488 (7th Cir. 1972), cert. den. 411 U.S. 967 (1973)

Board of Regents of State Colleges v. Roth, 92 S.Ct. 2701, 408 U.S. 564, 33 L.Ed.2d 548 (1972)

Perry v. Sindermann, 92 S.Ct. 2694, 408 U.S. 593, 33 L.Ed.2d 570 (1972)

DISMISSAL OF THE TENURED TEACHER

18:70 May a tenured teacher be fired?

A tenured teacher may be dismissed for commission of a dismissable offense as defined by statute, provided however the school board first must comply with the procedural requirements of its collective bargaining agreement and must provide the requisite statutory substantive and procedural due process.

Ill. Rev. Stat. c. 122, par. 10-22.4
Ill. Rev. Stat. c. 122, par. 24-12
Board of Trustees of Community College District No. 508 v. Cook County College Teachers Union Local 1600, AFT, IFT, AFL-CIO, 167 Ill.App.3d 998, 522 N.E.2d 93, 118 Ill.Dec. 638 (1st Dist. 1987)
Chicago Board of Education v. Payne, 102 Ill.App.3d 741, 430 N.E.2d 310, 58 Ill.Dec. 368 (1st Dist. 1981)
Lowe v. Board of Education of City of Chicago, 76 Ill.App.3d 348, 395 N.E.2d 59, 32 Ill.Dec. 122 (1st Dist. 1979)
Fender v. School District No. 25, Arlington Heights, Cook County, 37 Ill.App.3d 736, 347 N.E.2d 270 (1st Dist. 1976)
Gould v. Board of Education of Ashley Community Consolidated School District No. 15 of Washington County, 32 Ill.App.3d 808, 336 N.E.2d 69 (5th Dist. 1975)

18:80 How many school board votes are required to dismiss a tenured teacher?

A motion to dismiss a tenured teacher for cause requires a majority vote of all the members of the school board to carry.

Ill. Rev. Stat. c. 122, par. 24-12

18:90 To what kind of notice of causes for dismissal is a tenured teacher entitled?

A tenured teacher is entitled to a dismissal notice, or bill of particulars, which states both the cause or causes for the dismissal and the charge or charges supporting the dismissal action. The notice must be sufficiently precise in order that the teacher is fully informed of the causes and charges and is able to prepare a defense.

Ill. Rev. Stat. c. 122, par. 10-22.4
Ill. Rev. Stat. c. 122, par. 24-12

Carrao v. Board of Education, City of Chicago, 46 Ill.App.3d 33, 360 N.E.2d 536, 4 Ill.Dec. 600 (1st Dist. 1977)

Reinhardt v. Board of Education of Alton Community Unit School District No. 11, 61 Ill.2d 101, 329 N.E.2d 218 (1975)

Wade v. Granite City Community Unit School District No. 9, Madison County, 71 Ill.App.2d 34, 218 N.E.2d 19 (5th Dist. 1966)

Donahoo v. Board of Education of School District No. 303 Moultrie County, 346 Ill.App. 241, 105 N.E.2d 833, rev. 413 Ill.App. 422, 109 N.E.2d 787 (1952)

CAUSES FOR DISMISSAL

18:100 What causes will support the dismissal of a tenured teacher?

A school board may dismiss a tenured teacher for incompetency, cruelty, negligence, immorality, or other sufficient cause. A teacher may also be dismissed for failure to complete a one-year remediation plan with a "satisfactory" or better rating, and may be dismissed whenever, in the school board's opinion, he is not qualified to teach or whenever the interests of the schools require it.

Temporary mental or physical incapacity to perform teaching duties, as found by a medical examination, is not a cause for dismissal.

To support a tenured teacher dismissal, a school board must prove a serious infraction or series of infractions; must comply with all of its own internal rules, regulations and policies regarding dismissal, including relevant contract provisions and its evaluation plan; must comply with all relevant statutory requirements; and must provide the teacher with requisite substantive and procedural due process.

Ill. Rev. Stat. c. 122, par. 10-22.4

Ill. Rev. Stat. c. 122, par. 24-12

Wells v. Board of Education of Community Consolidated School District No. 64, Cook County, 85 Ill.App.2d 312, 230 N.E.2d 6 (1st Dist. 1967)

18:110 What is required to dismiss a tenured teacher for incompetency?

Incompetency is a remediable offense. A school board is required to attempt to cure incompetency by evaluation and the adoption of a remediation plan prior to dismissal.

Ill. Rev. Stat. c. 122, par. 10-22.4
Ill. Rev. Stat. c. 122, par. 24-12
Ill. Rev. Stat. c. 122, par. 24A-1 et seq.

18:120 What is cruelty?

Cruelty is the intentional or malicious infliction of physical or mental suffering upon other persons. Cruelty as a cause of tenured teacher dismissal may be either remediable or irremediable depending upon its seriousness.

Lowe v. Board of Education, City of Chicago, 76 Ill.App.3d 148, 395 N.E.2d 59, 32 Ill.Dec. 112 (1st Dist. 1979).

Welch v. Board of Education of Bement Community Unit School District No. 5 of Piatt County, 45 Ill.App.3d 35, 358 N.E.2d 354, 3 Ill.Dec. 679 (4th Dist. 1977)

Rolando v. School Directors of District No. 125, 44 Ill.App.3d 658, 358 N.E.2d 945, 3 Ill.Dec. 402 (3rd Dist. 1976)

18:130 What is negligence?

Negligence is failing to do something a reasonable person would ordinarily do under a particular set of circumstances or doing something that a reasonable and prudent person would ordinarily not do under a given set of circumstances and conditions. Negligence as a cause for dismissal of a tenured teacher may be either remediable or irremediable depending on the circumstances and degree of negligence.

Ill. Rev. Stat. c. 122, par.10-22.4
Ill. Rev. Stat. c. 122, par. 24-12
Board of Education of Niles Township High School District No. 219 Cook County v. Epstein, 72 Ill.App.3d 723, 391 N.E.2d 114, 28 Ill.Dec. 915 (1st Dist. 1979)

18:140 What is immorality?

Immorality is behavior which is inimical to the public welfare according to the standards of society. A dismissal for immorality will not be sustained unless the school board can prove the conduct of the teacher has had some serious negative impact on the teacher's relationship with students, effectiveness in the classroom, relationship with teacher's superiors, or the operation of a school district. Dismissals for immorality often raise constitutional questions.

Ill. Rev. Stat. c. 122, par. 10-22.4

Ill. Rev. Stat. c. 122, par. 24-12

Board of Education of Tonica Community Unit School District No. 360, LaSalle County v. Sickley, 133 Ill.App.3d 921, 479 N.E.2d 1142, 89 Ill.Dec. 136 (3rd Dist. 1985)

Reinhardt v. Board of Education of Alton Community Unit School District No. 11, 61 Ill.2d 101, 329 N.E.2d 218 (1975)

Lombardo v. Board of Education School District No. 27, Cook County, 100 Ill.App.2d 108, 241 N.E.2d 495 (1st Dist. 1968)

18:150 What is insubordination?

Insubordination is willful disregard of implied or specific legitimate directives or an attitude so defiant as to be equivalent. Insubordination is usually a remediable offense and requires legally sufficient warning prior to dismissal.

Christopherson v. Spring Valley Elementary School District, 90 Ill.App.3d 460, 413 N.E.2d 199, 45 Ill.Dec. 866 (3rd Dist. 1980)

Allione v. Board of Education, South Fork Community High School District No. 310, Christian County, 29 Ill.App.2d 261, 173 N.E.2d 13 (3rd Dist. 1961)

Beilan v. Board of Public Education of Philadelphia, 78 S.Ct. 1317, 357 U.S. 399, 2 L.Ed.2d 1414 (1958)

18:160 May a tenured teacher be dismissed for conduct which occurs away from school and during non-school hours?

To dismiss a tenured teacher for behavior which occurs away from school and during non-school hours, the school board must be able to demonstrate that the conduct had a sufficiently serious negative impact on a legitimate school related objective to warrant dismissal of the teacher.

A teacher has constitutional rights which protect the teacher from school board interference in private non-school related conduct. The private deportment of a teacher is properly of concern to a school board only when the behavior of the teacher interferes with the effectiveness of the teacher as a teacher in the school district or with the overall operation of the school district.

Carrao v. Board of Education, City of Chicago, 46 Ill.App.3d 33, 360 N.E.2d 536, 4 Ill.Dec. 600 (1st Dist. 1977)

Reinhardt v. Board of Education of Alton Community Unit School District No. 11, 61 Ill.2d 101, 329 N.E.2d 218 (1975)

18:161 May a school board dismiss a teacher who has been charged with a felony?

Persons charged with crimes are presumed to be innocent until proven guilty. Investigation, arrest, and/or indictment do not establish guilt. In order to dismiss a contractual employee for commission of a crime, the employer must provide the employee with requisite procedural and substantive due process. The employer has the burden of proving the crime was committed and must show that the crime had a connection to the employee's employment sufficient to warrant dismissal.

McBroom v. Board of Education District No. 205, 144 Ill.App.3d 463, 494 N.E.2d 1191, 98 Ill.Dec. 864 (2nd Dist. 1986)

18:162 May a school board dismiss a teacher who has been convicted of a crime?

The employer must demonstrate the crime had a connection to the employee's employment and was sufficiently serious to warrant dismissal. The employer must provide the employee with requisite substantive and procedural due process prior to dismissal.

Reinhardt v. Board of Education of Alton Community Unit School District No. 11, Madison and Jersey Counties, 19 Ill.App.3d 481, 311 N.E.2d 710 (5th Dist. 1974) vacated on other grounds 61 Ill.2d 101, 329 N.E.2d 218

18:170 May a school board dismiss a tenured teacher for conduct which occurred during the teacher's supervision of extracurricular activities?

The teacher may be dismissed if the conduct is sufficiently serious to support dismissal and is either irremediable or repeated after legally sufficient warning. Dismissal requires full procedural compliance with applicable statutes and collectively bargained provisions.

Ill. Rev. Stat. c. 122, par. 10-22.4

REMEDIABILITY

18:180 What is irremediable conduct?

Conduct is irremediable when the damage which has been done to students, faculty, or the school is irreparable. Consideration is also given to whether or not the conduct could have been corrected had the employee been warned.

McCutcheon v. Board of Education, City of Chicago, 94 Ill.App.3d 993, 419 N.E.2d 451, 50 Ill.Dec. 343 (1st Dist. 1981)

Board of Education of School District No. 131 v. Illinois State Board of Education, 82 Ill.App.3d 820, 403 N.E.2d 277, 38 Ill.Dec. 189 (2nd Dist. 1980)

Waller v. Board of Education Century School District No. 100, 13 Ill.App.3d 1056, 302 N.E.2d 190 (5th Dist. 1973)

18:190 Who determines whether a conduct giving rise to discipline is remediable or irremediable?

A school board is empowered to make an initial determination of the remediability or irremediability of conduct. The school board's decision is subject to review by a hearing officer in a dismissal case and in some cases reviewable in other tribunals with respect to other forms of discipline.

The determination of the remediability of any particular conduct is important in deciding whether the employee requires legally sufficient warning before dismissal. If conduct is determined to be irremediable, no such warning is necessary before dismissal.

Ill. Rev. Stat. c. 122, par. 24-12
Ill. Rev. Stat. c. 122, par. 24A-1 et seq.

Gilliland v. Board of Education of Pleasant View Consolidated School District No. 622 of Tazewell County, 67 Ill.2d 143, 365 N.E.2d 322, 8 Ill.Dec. 84 (1977)

Welch v. Board of Education of Bement Community Unit School District No. 5 of Piatt County, 45 Ill.App.3d 35, 358 N.E.2d 354, 3 Ill.Dec. 679 (4th Dist. 1977)

Fender v. School District No. 25, Arlington Heights, 37 Ill.App.3d 736 (1st Dist. 1976)

Everett v. Board of Education of District 201, Cook County, 22 Ill.App.3d 594, 317 N.E.2d 753 (1st Dist. 1974)

Waller v. Board of Education Century School District No. 100, 13 Ill.App.3d 1056, 302 N.E.2d 190 (5th Dist. 1973)

Miller v. Board of Education, School District No. 132, Cook County, 51 Ill.App.2d 20, 240 N.E.2d 471 (1st Dist. 1964)

18:200 Which party has the burden of proving irremediability?

The school board has the burden of proving that conduct leading to dismissal is not remediable.

Gilliland v. Board of Education of Pleasant View Consolidated School District No. 622 of Tazewell County, 67 Ill.2d 143, 365 N.E.2d 322, 8 Ill.Dec. 84 (1977)

18:210 If a tenured teacher's conduct is properly determined to be irremediable, must a school board issue a warning (notice to remedy) before dismissal?

No. A notice to remedy is essential only where the teacher's conduct is determined to be remediable.

Lowe v. Board of Education, City of Chicago, 76 Ill.App.3d 348, 395 N.E.2d 59, 32 Ill.Dec. 112 (1st Dist. 1979)

Welch v. Board of Education of Bement Community Unit School District No. 5 of Piatt County, 45 Ill.App.3d 35, 358 N.E.2d 354, 3 Ill.Dec. 679 (4th Dist. 1977)

Wells v. Board of Education of Community Consolidated School District No. 64, Cook County, 85 Ill.App.2d 312, 230 N.E.2d 6 (1st Dist. 1967)

18:220 If a school board determines a teacher's behavior is improper and remediable but not related to classroom competence, what warning is required prior to dismissal?

If a school board has determined a tenured teacher's improper but remediable behavior is related to classroom competence, the remediation requirements of section 24A of the School Code apply. If the behavior is not related to classroom competence, or is related to the classroom competence of a non-tenured teacher whom the school board is seeking to dismiss before the end of the school term, the school board must invoke the following procedures prior to dismissal:

1) The teacher must be provided with a notice to remedy the behavior in question;

2) The notice must specifically identify the objectionable behavior and state that if not remedied the teacher may be subject to dismissal;

3) The notice must provide the teacher with reasonably specific corrective action the school board requires the teacher to undertake if appropriate; and

4) The notice must identify a reasonable period of time in which the school board expects the corrective action to be successfully completed if appropriate.

Ill. Rev. Stat. c. 122, par. 24-12

Grissom v. Board of Education of Buckley Loda Community School District No. 8, 75 Ill.App.2d 314, 388 N.E.2d 398, 26 Ill.Dec. 683 (4th Dist. 1979)

Gilliland v. Board of Education of Pleasant View Consolidated School District No. 622 of Tazewell County, 67 Ill.2d 143, 365 N.E.2d 322, 8 Ill.Dec. 84 (1977)

Paprocki v. Board of Education of McHenry Community High School District No. 156, 31 Ill.App.3d 112, 334 N.E.2d 841 (2nd Dist. 1975)

Everett v. Board of Education of District 201, Cook County, 22 Ill.App.3d 594, 317 N.E.2d 753 (1st Dist. 1974)

Waller v. Board of Education Century School District No. 100, 13 Ill.App.3d 1056, 302 N.E.2d 190 (5th Dist., 1973)

Wells v. Board of Education of Community Consolidated School District No. 64, Cook County, 85 Ill.App.2d 312, 230 N.E.2d 6 (1st Dist. 1967)

Werner v. Community Unit School District No. 4, Marshall County, 40 Ill.App. 491, 190 N.E.2d 184 (2nd Dist. 1963)

18:230 What is a notice to remedy?

A notice to remedy is a legally sufficient written warning issued by a school board and properly delivered to an employee which warns the employee of improper conduct and the consequences thereof.

Ill. Rev. Stat. c. 122, par. 24-12

Paprocki v. Board of Education of McHenry Community High School District No. 156, 31 Ill.App.3d 112, 334 N.E.2d 841 (2nd Dist. 1975)

18:240 How much time must teachers be given to correct remediable deficiencies?

A school board must give a teacher a reasonable amount of time to remedy. The amount of time which is necessary depends upon the deficiencies to be remedied.

Ill. Rev. Stat. c. 122, par. 24-12

Board of Education of School District No. 131 v. Illinois State Board of Education, 82 Ill.App.3d 820, 403 N.E.2d 277, 38 Ill.Dec. 189 (2nd Dist. 1980)

Litin v. Board of Education of City of Chicago, 72 Ill.App.3d 889, 391 N.E.2d 62, 28 Ill.Dec. 863 (1st Dist. 1979)

Aulwurm v. Board of Education of Murphysboro Community Unit School District of Jackson County, 67 Ill.2d 434, 317 N.E.2d 1337 (1977)

DUE PROCESS AND TEACHER DISMISSAL

18:250 What pre-hearing procedures apply to the dismissal of a tenured teacher?

A "Loudermill-type" pretermination hearing may be required before the school board votes on the dismissal of a teacher. The school board must approve a motion containing specific charges by a majority vote of all its members. Written notice of the charges must be served on the teacher within five days of the adoption of the motion. The notice must contain a bill of particulars. No hearing on the charges is required unless the teacher, within ten days of receiving the notice, requests in writing of the school board a hearing be scheduled, in which case the school board must schedule a hearing on the charges before a disinterested hearing officer pursuant to statutory requirements.

Ill. Rev. Stat. c. 122, par. 24-12

Massie v. East St. Louis School District No. 189, 203 Ill.App.3d 965, 561 N.E.2d 246, 148 Ill.Dec. 940 (5th Dist. 1990)

Cleveland Board of Education v. Loudermill, 105 S.Ct. 1487, 470 U.S. 532, 84 L.Ed.2d 494 (1985) on remand 763 F.2d 202

Morelli v. Board of Education of District 303, Tazewell County, 42 Ill.App.3d 722, 356 N.E.2d 438, 1 Ill.Dec. 312 (3rd Dist. 1976)

18:260 Is prehearing discovery permitted in a tenured teacher dismissal?

A party to a tenured teacher dismissal is entitled to:

1) discovery of the names and addresses of persons who may be called as expert witnesses at the hearing (failure to reveal the name and address of a witness precludes that person from testifying at the hearing in the absence of a showing of good cause and the express permission of the hearing officer);

2) a list of persons and their addresses who may have knowledge of facts related to the charges or the defenses thereto. This is not to be construed as a list of witnesses, but no person whose name is not so disclosed may testify except upon good cause shown and by permission of the hearing officer;

3) bills of particulars upon order of the hearing officer for good cause shown;

4) written interrogatories upon order of the hearing officer for good cause shown;

5) production of relevant documents upon order of the hearing officer for good cause shown.

Ill. Rev. Stat. c. 122, par. 24-12

23 Ill. Admin. Code, sec. 51.55

18:270 How is a tenured teacher dismissal hearing conducted?

The order of proceedings is as follows:

1) The hearing is opened by the recording of the place, time, and date of the hearing, the presence of the hearing officer and

the parties and counsel, if any, and any stipulations as to facts. Pre-hearing motions are heard at this time.

2) Upon the opening of the hearing, the hearing officer allows the parties to make opening statements.

3) The school board proceeds first to present its evidence sustaining the dismissal.

4) Either party may confront the witnesses, offer evidence, and present a defense.

5) All testimony is taken under oath administered by the hearing officer.

6) The hearing officer may issue subpoenas requiring the attendance of witnesses or production of documents and, at the request of either of the parties, shall issue such subpoenas but may limit the number of witnesses to be subpoenaed in behalf of either party to not more than ten.

7) The hearing officer causes a record of the proceedings to be kept and must employ a competent reporter to take stenotype notes of all the testimony. The State Board of Education pays for the attendance and services of the court reporter.

8) Exhibits, when offered by either party, may be received in evidence by the hearing officer. The names and addresses of all witnesses and exhibits in order received shall be made a part of this record. The hearing officer makes rulings on the admissibility of exhibits.

9) The hearing officer for good cause shown may continue the hearing upon the request of the teacher or the board or upon his own initiative, and adjourns when the teacher and the board agree thereto.

10) The hearing may proceed in the absence of either party, who, after due notice, fails to be present or fails to obtain a continuance.

11) The hearing officer is required to consider and give weight to all the teacher's evaluations.

12) The hearing officer may, in his discretion, vary the normal procedure under which the board first presents its claim, but in any case shall afford full and equal opportunity to all parties for presentation of relevant proofs.

13) Upon the close of the hearing, each party may make a closing statement (orally and/or written at the discretion of the hearing officer) incorporating arguments of fact and law.

14) The hearing is not considered closed until all evidence has been submitted and briefs, if allowed, have been received by the hearing officer.

Ill. Rev. Stat. c. 122, par. 24-12
23 Ill. Admin. Code 51.60(c).

18:280 Who may serve as a hearing officer for a tenured teacher dismissal?

The hearing officer in a tenured teacher dismissal case must be selected through a statutory procedure from a list supplied by the State Board of Education. Hearing officers must possess the following minimum qualifications:

1) accreditation by a national arbitration association;
2) not a resident of the school district seeking the dismissal;
3) disinterested and impartial; and
4) no financial or personal interest in the result of the hearing.

Ill. Rev. Stat. c. 122, par. 24-12
23 Ill. Admin. Code 51.20

18:290 Is a tenured teacher dismissal hearing open to the public?

The hearing in a tenured teacher dismissal case may be made open to the public at the request of either the school board or the teacher.

Ill. Rev. Stat. c. 122, par. 24-12
23 Ill. Admin. Code 51.40(a)

18:300 Who pays the hearing officer in a tenured teacher dismissal case?

The per diem allowance for the hearing officer is paid by the State Board of Education.

Ill. Rev. Stat. c. 122, par. 24-12

18:310 What procedures are followed in appointing a hearing officer to a tenured teacher dismissal case?

Notice of the appointment of the hearing officer is mailed to the hearing officer by the State Board of Education, and the signed acceptance of the hearing officer must be filed with the State Board within five days of receipt of notice of appointment.

Upon notice of appointment as a hearing officer, the prospective hearing officer must disclose any circumstances which he believes might disqualify him. Upon receipt of such information, the State Board must immediately disclose it to the parties. The parties may waive the presumptive disqualification. But if either party declines to waive the presumptive disqualification, the State Board must declare a vacancy.

If a hearing officer resigns, dies, withdraws, refuses, is unable or disqualified to perform his duties, the State Board must, on proof satisfactory to it, declare the position vacant. Vacancies are filled in the same manner as the making of the original appointment. If a vacancy occurs during the course of a hearing, the entire matter must be reheard by the new hearing officer.

All communication from the parties to the hearing officer must be in writing and copies must be sent at the same time to the opposing party and the State Board of Education.

Ill. Rev. Stat. c. 122, par. 24-12
23 Ill. Admin. Code 51.40

18:320 How does a hearing officer render a decision in a tenured teacher dismissal case?

A hearing officer in a tenured teacher dismissal case must abide by the following procedures:

1) The hearing officer must, with reasonable dispatch, make a decision in writing as to whether or not the teacher is to be dismissed. The decision must include findings of fact.

2) The decision should be rendered no later than 30 days from the date of closing the hearing.

3) A copy of the decision must be given to the State Board of Education to be forwarded to both the teacher and the school board.

4) The decision of the hearing officer is final unless reviewed under the Administrative Review Act.

5) If neither party appeals the decision, then either party desiring a transcript of the hearing must pay for the cost thereof.

6) In the event review is instituted, any costs of preparing and filing the record of proceedings is paid by the State Board of Education.

7) The record of the hearing must include all pleadings and exhibits; a statement of matters officially noticed; a transcript of the hearing; and the decision of the hearing officer.

Ill. Rev. Stat. c. 122, par. 24-12
23 Ill. Admin. Code 51.60 et seq.

18:330 What rules of evidence apply to tenured teacher dismissal hearings?

Formal rules of evidence do not apply to tenured teacher dismissal hearings, but the following guidelines apply:

1) The parties may offer such evidence as they desire and shall produce such additional evidence as the hearing officer may deem necessary to an understanding and determination of the dispute.

2) The hearing officer is the judge of the relevancy and materiality of the evidence offered and strict conformity to legal rules of evidence is not necessary.

3) Objections to evidentiary offers may be made and are noted in the record. The hearing officer has the power to make rulings and the power to exclude evidence. Offers of proof are permitted.

4) Any hostile witness may be examined as if under cross examination.

5) All documents not filed with the hearing officer at the hearing but which are arranged at the hearing or subsequently by agreement of the parties to be submitted, must be filed with the State Board of Education for transmission to the hearing officer and other parties.

Ill. Rev. Stat. c. 122, par. 24-12
23 Ill. Admin. Code 51.60(d)

18:340 What burden of proof does a school board have in a teacher dismissal case?

A school board must prove its case by a preponderance of the evidence.

Board of Education of Minooka Community Consolidated School District No. 201 v. Ingels, 75 Ill.App.3d 334, 394 N.E.2d 69, 31 Ill.Dec. 153 (3rd Dist. 1979)

18:350 May a school board raise charges not included in the bill of particulars for the first time at a dismissal hearing?

New charges or proofs unrelated to the bill of particulars are not permitted.

Ill. Rev. Stat. c. 122, par. 24-12
Aulwurm v. Board of Education of Murphysboro Community Unit School District of Jackson County, 67 Ill.2d 434, 317 N.E.2d 1337 (1977)

18:360 What is the time limit for appealing a hearing officer's decision in a teacher dismissal case?

Appeal must be perfected within 35 days of the date the hearing officer's decision was mailed.

Ill. Rev. Stat. c. 110, par. 3-103
Board of Education of St. Charles Community Unit School District No. 303 v. Adelman, 137 Ill.App.3d 965, 485 N.E.2d 584, 92 Ill.Dec. 773 (2nd Dist. 1985)

TEACHER SUSPENSION

18:370 May a school board suspend a tenured teacher without pay pending the outcome of a dismissal hearing?

If, in the opinion of a school board, the interests of the school require it, the board may suspend a teacher without pay pending a dismissal hearing. However, if reinstated, the teacher shall have lost salary restored.

Ill. Rev. Stat. c. 122, par. 24-12

Spinelli v. Immanuael Lutheran Evangelical Congregation, Inc., 118 Ill.2d 389, 515 N.E.2d 1222, 113 Ill.Dec. 915 (1987)

Yuen v. Board of Education of Community Unit School District No. 46, Kane County, 77 Ill.App.2d 353, 222 N.E.2d 570 (3rd Dist. 1966)

Pearson v. Board of Education of Community Unit School District No. 5 of Macoupin County, 27 Ill.App.2d 12, 169 N.E.2d 7 (3rd Dist. 1960)

18:380 Must a school board provide a teacher a hearing on a suspension without pay pending dismissal?

It is likely that no hearing beyond that required to review the dismissal need be provided because the relevant statute specifies all necessary procedures. However, there is some case law which suggests a separate hearing must be held before the suspension without pay is invoked.

Ill. Rev. Stat. c. 122, par. 24-12

Massie v. East St. Louis School District No. 189, 203 Ill.App.3d 965, 561 N.E.2d 246, 148 Ill.Dec. 940 (5th Dist. 1990)

Spinelli v. Immanuael Lutheran Evangelical Congregation, Inc., 118 Ill.2d 389, 515 N.E.2d 1222, 113 Ill.Dec. 915 (1987)

Cleveland Board of Education v. Loudermill, 105 S.Ct. 1487, 470 U.S. 532, 84 L.Ed.2d 494 (1985) on remand 763 F.2d 202

Barszcz v. Board of Trustees of Community College District No. 504, Cook County, 400 F.Supp. 675 (N.D. Ill. 1975)

18:390 May a school board suspend a teacher without pay for disciplinary reasons without a dismissal pending?

A school board may invoke a disciplinary suspension without pay provided it has an underlying collectively bargained contract provision allowing such a suspension or, in the absence of a demand to bargain it by a recognized bargaining unit, a policy allowing such a suspension.

Spinelli v. Immanuael Lutheran Evangelical Congregation, Inc., 118 Ill.2d 389, 515 N.E.2d 1222, 113 Ill.Dec. 915 (1987)

19: SCHOOL ADMINISTRATORS

DUTIES OF ADMINISTRATORS

19:10 What are the duties of a superintendent?

A superintendent has charge of the administration of the schools under the direction of the school board. In addition to his administrative duties, a superintendent is required to make recommendations to the board concerning the budget, building plans, the locations of sites, the selection, retention, and dismissal of teachers and all other employees, the selection of textbooks, instructional material, and courses of study. The superintendent has reporting responsibilities under the Abused and Neglected Child Reporting Act. The superintendent must keep or cause to be kept the records and accounts as directed and required by the board, aid in making reports required by the board, and perform such other duties as the board may delegate to him.

Ill. Rev. Stat. c. 122, par. 10-21.4

19:20 What are the duties of a principal?

A principal must hold a valid supervisory or administrative certificate. He supervises the operation of one or more attendance centers. The principal administers his duties under the supervision of the superintendent and in accordance with reasonable rules and regulations of the school board, for the planning, operation, and evaluation of the educational program of the attendance area to which he is assigned.

A principal's job description must specify his primary responsibility is the improvement of instruction. A majority of the principal's time must be spent on curriculum and staff development through both formal and informal activities, establishing clear lines of communication regarding school goals, accomplishments, practices, and policies with parents and teachers.

A principal is required to submit recommendations to the superintendent concerning the appointment, retention, promotion, and assignment of all personnel assigned to the attendance center.

Ill. Rev. Stat. c. 122, par. 10-21.4a

19:30 May a school district employ one administrator as both superintendent and principal?

Yes, provided the full-time equivalency of the combination results in a maximum of one full-time position.

23 Ill. Admin. Code 1.310 f) 1)

19:40 May a school board assign one principal to supervise more than one attendance center?

Yes.

23 Ill. Admin. Code 1.310
Kenney v. Interim General Superintendent of Schools, 112 Ill.App.3d 342, 445 N.E.2d 356, 67 Ill.Dec. 876 (1983)
Dolnick v. General Superintendent of Schools of Chicago, 67 Ill.App.3d 8, 384 N.E.2d 408, 23 Ill.Dec. 614 (1st Dist. 1978)

19:50 Who may serve as principal in the absence of the principal?

If a principal is absent due to extended illness or leave of absence, an assistant principal may be assigned as acting principal for a period not to exceed 60 school days.

Ill. Rev. Stat. c. 122, par. 10-21.4a
23 Ill. Admin. Code 1.310 b)

19:60 Are department chairpersons required to have administrative or supervisory teaching certificates?

Department chairpersons are required to have administrative or supervisory endorsements if first assigned to their jobs after September 1, 1978 and if their jobs require supervision or evaluation of teachers.

Ill. Rev. Stat. c. 122, par. 21-7.1
23 Ill. Admin. Code 1.310 e)

19:70 Are there continuing education requirements for administrators who evaluate certified personnel?

Administrators who evaluate certified personnel must participate in a State Board of Education training program on evaluation of certified personnel at least once every two years.

Ill. Rev. Stat. c. 122, par. 24A-3

19:80 May an administrator issue a teacher a notice to remedy?

A notice to remedy is an official warning to a teacher that the teacher's behavior, if not remedied, may lead to dismissal. Only a school board may issue a notice to remedy.

Ill. Rev. Stat. c. 122, par. 24-12
Board of Education of School District No. 131 v. Illinois State Board of Education, 82 Ill App.3d 820, 404 N.E.2d 277, 38 Ill.Dec. 189 (2nd Dist. 1980)

EMPLOYMENT CONTRACTS

19:90 May a school board issue multi-year employment contracts to its administrators?

Superintendents or principals may be given multi-year contracts. If the individual serving as a superintendent or principal is serving for the first time as a superintendent or principal in Illinois, any multi-year contract offered the administrator must be for a two year term. If the individual has prior experience as a superintendent or principal in Illinois, any multi-year contract offered the administrator must be for a three year term. A multi-year contract may be extended for an additional three years at the end of any year.

Ill. Rev. Stat. c. 122, par. 10-23.8
Ill. Rev. Stat. c. 122, par. 10-23.8a

19:100 What is a rollover provision in an administrator's employment contract?

The School Code permits the extension of principal or superintendent multi-year contracts for an additional three years at the end of any year. Some principal and superintendent contracts are written so they automatically extend for an additional three years at the end of each year if the school board does not give notice of non-renewal. The contract clause which provides for the automatic contract extension is commonly called "a rollover" clause.

Ill. Rev. Stat. c. 122, par. 10-23.8
Ill. Rev. Stat. c. 122, par. 10-23.8a

19:105 Does an administrator's multi-year contract survive the dissolution or consolidation of the school district which employs him?

The liabilities of dissolved school districts, including the remaining obligations under any multi-year administrator contracts, become the responsibility of the annexing or newly-consolidated district.

Ill. Rev. Stat. c. 122, par. 7-12
Ill. Rev. Stat. c. 122, par. 7A-11
Ill. Rev. Stat. c. 122, par. 11C-1 et seq.

TENURE

19:110 May an administrator acquire tenure?

Any administrator who has teacher certification acquires tenure after employment for two full time consecutive school terms unless the administrator is employed under the terms of a multi-year contract.

However, the tenured administrator is not necessarily entitled to any particular position. Rather, tenure entitles the administrator to continued employment in the district so long as there is a position available for which he is qualified.

Ill. Rev. Stat. c. 122, par. 10-23.8
Ill. Rev. Stat. c. 122, par. 10-23.8a
Ill. Rev. Stat. c. 122, par. 24-11 et seq.
Davis v. Board of Education of Farmer City-Mansfield Community Unit School District, 63 Ill.App.3d 495, 380 N.E.2d 58, 20 Ill.Dec. 381 (4th Dist. 1978)
Lane v. Board of Education of Fairbury Cropsey Community Unit School District No. 3, 38 Ill.App.3d 742, 348 N.E.2d 470 (4th Dist. 1976)
Danno v. Peterson, 421 F.Supp. 950 (N.D.Ill. 1976)

*Lester v. Board of Education of School District No. 119 of Jo
Daviess County,* 87 Ill.App.2d 269, 230 N.E.2d 893 (2nd Dist. 1967)
   *McNely v. Board of Education of Community Unit School District
No. 7,* 9 Ill.2d 143, 137 N.E.2d 63 (1956)

19:120 If an administrator has acquired tenure and is subsequently removed from his administrative position, does he have "bumping rights?"

Yes.

Ill. Rev. Stat. c. 122, par. 24-12
*Brubaker v. Community Unit School District No. 16, Sangamon
and Morgan Counties,* 46 Ill.App.3d 588, 360 N.E.2d 1228, 4 Ill.Dec.
853 (4th Dist. 1977).

19:130 Does an administrative employee waive any rights by accepting a multi-year employment contract?

By accepting the terms of a multi-year contract, a superintendent or principal waives all rights otherwise granted him
under sections 24-11 through 24-16 of the School Code, which
includes tenure rights, for the duration of his employment as a
superintendent or principal in the district. The relevant statute
is unclear as to whether acceptance of a multi-year contract
prevents an administrator from ever again having tenure in the
school district or whether tenure can be regained or is reac-
quired if a one year contract or series of one year contracts is
issued and served after a multi-year contract has been issued
and served.

Ill. Rev. Stat. c. 122, par. 10-23.8
Ill. Rev. Stat. c. 122, par. 10-23.8a

RECLASSIFICATION OF PRINCIPALS

19:140 What rights are due principals on demotion or reclassification to a lower paying position?

No principal who has completed two or more years of administrative service in a school district may be reclassified by
demotion or reduction in rank from one position in a school
district to another for which a lower salary is paid without

written notice from the board of the proposed reclassification by April 1 of the year in which the principal's contract expires. Within 10 days of the principal's receipt of this notice, the school board must provide the principal with a written statement of facts regarding the reclassification, and the principal must be granted, upon request, a private hearing with the board to discuss the reclassification.

If the principal is not satisfied with the results of the private hearing, he may within five days thereafter request a public hearing on the reclassification. The principal may be represented by counsel at either hearing.

If the school board decides to proceed with the reclassification, it shall give the principal written notice of its decision within 15 days of the private hearing, or 15 days of the public hearing, whichever is later. The decision of the school board thereupon becomes final. Nothing in the law prohibits a school board from ordering lateral transfers of principals to positions of similar rank and equal salary.

Ill. Rev. Stat. c. 122, par. 10-23.8b

Meadows v. School District U-46, 141 Ill.App.3d 335, 490 N.E.2d 140, 95 Ill.Dec. 667 (2nd Dist. 1986)

Swanson v. Board of Education of Foreman Community Unit School District No. 124, Mason County, 135 Ill.App.3d 466, 481 N.E.2d 1248, 90 Ill.Dec. 337 (4th Dist. 1985)

Lyznicki v. Board of Education, School District No. 167, Cook County, 707 F.2d 949 (7th Cir. 1983)

19:150 Is a principal entitled to hearing officer review of a school board decision to reclassify?

No.

Ill. Rev. Stat. c. 122, par. 10-23.8b

DISMISSAL RIGHTS

19:160 May a school board dismiss an administrator during the term of his contract?

A school board may not dismiss an administrator during the term of his contract without providing both substantive and procedural due process. The type of due process necessary varies according to the kind of contract the administrator has. Under certain circumstances the due process protections of the teacher tenure laws apply. A school board seeking to dismiss an administrator during the term of his contract must be able to prove substantial breach of contract by the administrator.

Ill. Rev. Stat. c. 122, par. 24-12

19:170 What rights are due a superintendent on dismissal?

A school board seeking to dismiss a superintendent at the end of his contract must:

1) Give the superintendent written notice of intent not to renew his contract, stating the specific reasons for non-renewal, by April 1 of the contract year unless the contract specifically provides otherwise. Failure to provide such notice automatically extends the superintendent's contract for one additional year.

2) Within 10 days of receipt of such notice the superintendent may request a closed session hearing concerning the dismissal.

3) At the hearing, the superintendent may present evidence, witnesses, and defenses respecting the dismissal.

A superintendent who serves a school district full time without a break in service under the terms of three successive one year contracts, or without written contract, acquires teaching tenure in the school district. A school board may not dismiss such a superintendent from employment in the school district without respecting the dismissal causes and procedures set forth in the School Code. Such a superintendent may be relieved of his superintendency pursuant to the procedures set forth above, but is entitled to bump into a teaching job for which he is qualified.

The law is unclear as to the tenure rights of a superintendent who has once been employed by the school district under the terms of a multi-year contract.

Ill. Rev. Stat. c. 122, par. 10-21.4
Ill. Rev. Stat. c. 122, par. 10-23.8
Ill. Rev. Stat. c. 122, par. 24-12

19:180 What notice is due a principal on non-renewal of his contract?

A school board seeking to dismiss a principal at the end of his contract must give notice of intent not to renew the contract at least 90 days before the contract expires. Failure to do so automatically extends the principal's contract for one additional year. A principal who has acquired teaching tenure may have bumping rights.

Ill. Rev. Stat. c. 122, par. 10-23.8a

20: NONCERTIFICATED EMPLOYEES

DUTIES OF NONCERTIFICATED EMPLOYEES

20:10 Who are the noncertificated employees of a school district?

Noncertificated employees, referred to in the School Code as "educational support personnel," include all employees whose positions do not require state teacher certification. Both terms encompass secretarial and clerical employees, maintenance and janitorial staff, bookkeepers, bus drivers, security staff, and food service employees, among others.

20:20 May a school board employ educational support personnel (noncertificated) to assist in academically-related activities?

A school board may employ noncertificated personnel or use volunteer personnel for non-teaching duties that do not require instructional judgment or evaluation of pupils. A school board also may use such employees or volunteers to assist in the instruction of pupils under the immediate supervision of a certificated teacher. The teacher must be continuously aware of the noncertificated person's activities and must be able to control or modify them.

Teacher aides require an approval form issued by the State Teacher Certification Board. Approval requires completion of 30 semester hours of college training or completion of an approved teacher aide program.

Ill. Rev. Stat. c. 122, par. 10-22.34 et seq.
23 Ill. Admin. Code 1.630
23 Ill. Admin. Code 25

20:30 What certification requirements apply to playground supervisors, cafeteria supervisors, or study hall monitors?

Playground and cafeteria supervisors do not require certification. Neither position involves instruction or instructional judgment. Whether a study hall supervisor must meet certification standards, and if so which standards must be met, is not clear. The answer depends in part on the facts of any particular situation. The safest approach is to employ certificated teachers as study hall supervisors. A school district should be aware there are bargaining implications involved in assigning such duties to either certificated or noncertificated staff.

Ill. Rev. Stat. c. 122, par. 10-22.34 et seq.
23 Ill. Admin. Code 1.630

20:40 May a school board assign a teacher aide to substitute teach when the aide's supervising teacher is absent?

A teacher aide cannot legally substitute teach unless he holds certification as a teacher or substitute teacher.

Ill. Rev. Stat. c. 122, par. 10-22.34
Ill. Rev. Stat. c. 122, par. 21-1 et seq.
23 Ill. Admin. Code 1.630

20:50 May a school board hire extra-duty supervisors or chaperones?

A school board may designate noncertificated persons of good character to serve as supervisors, chaperones, or sponsors, either on a voluntary or on a compensated basis for school activities not connected with the academic programs of the schools.

Ill. Rev. Stat. c. 122, par. 10-22.34a

20:60 Do noncertificated employees enjoy the same defenses against tort liability that are accorded teachers under the principles of "in loco parentis?"

No. Illinois law accords certificated employees special protections against liability for student injuries. Whereas the negligence standard which applies to teachers in the supervision of students is "willful and wanton misconduct," the standard for a noncertificated employee is ordinary negligence.

In the area of liability for student injuries, the protections of "in loco parentis" represent an important distinction between certificated and noncertificated staff.

Illinois v. Davis, 88 Ill.App.3d 728, 410 N.E.2d 673, 43 Ill.Dec. 473 (2nd Dist. 1980)

Edmunson v. Chicago Board of Education, 62 Ill.App.3d 211, 379 N.E.2d 27, 19 Ill.Dec. 512 (1st Dist. 1978)

Possekel v. O'Donnell, 51 Ill.App.3d 313, 366 N.E.2d 589, 9 Ill.Dec. 332 (1st Dist. 1977)

WAGES AND HOURS

20:70   What are the maximum hour limits of the Fair Labor Standards Act?

A school board is required to abide by the provisions of the federal Fair Labor Standards Act (FLSA). The FLSA requires that employees be paid overtime at the rate of not less than 1.5 times the regular hourly rate for time worked over 40 hours in any work week.

School administrators and teachers are usually exempt from the provisions of the FLSA. The FLSA wage and hour limits almost always apply to noncertificated personnel. The FLSA contains many technical provisions which define inclusions and exclusions.

29 U.S.C. 200 et seq.
29 U.S.C. 207
29 U.S.C. 213

20:80   Can the overtime provisions of the Fair Labor Standards Act be avoided by providing employees with compensatory time off?

In most cases, the obligation to pay overtime cannot be satisfied by giving the employee compensatory time off unless the compensatory time off is given in the week in which the overtime occurred. There are very limited exceptions to this rule.

29 U.S.C. 200 et seq.

20:90 Can an employer avoid the hour and overtime provisions of the Fair Labor Standards Act by employing the same employee in two different jobs?

The overtime pay provisions of the Fair Labor Standards Act apply to employees who are employed by a single employer in two different jobs. In most cases, a school district must pay overtime to an employee who exceeds 40 hours in a work week even if the excess results from the employee working more than one job for the same employer.

29 U.S.C. 207 f)

20:100 Is an employer obligated to pay overtime to an employee who voluntarily works overtime?

The employer may be required to pay overtime for such work if the work is known to, and tacitly approved by, the employee's supervisors.

29 U.S.C. 207

20:110 Can the wage and hour provisions of the Fair Labor Standards Act be avoided by bargaining a contrary result?

Compliance with the Fair Labor Standards Act cannot normally be avoided by collectively bargaining a contrary result. There are very limited exceptions which involve guaranteed hour agreements.

29 U.S.C. 200 et seq.

20:120 What state retirement program serves noncertificated school employees and how are employee contributions to the program treated?

Noncertificated employees of the school district are covered by the Illinois Municipal Retirement Fund. Each school district must pay employee contributions to the IMRF for all compensation earned. Such contributions are treated as employer contributions in determining tax treatment under the Internal Revenue Code and are thereby treated as non-taxable income for IRS purposes.

Ill. Rev. Stat. c. 108 1/2, par. 7-132
Ill. Rev. Stat. c. 108 1/2, par. 7-171

20:130 Are noncertificated employees entitled to minimum sick leave by law?

If a noncertificated employee is eligible to participate in the Illinois Municipal Retirement Fund under the 600 hour standard or under any other eligibility participation standard allowed by Section 7-198 of the Illinois Pension Code, the employee is entitled to a minimum statutory grant of 10 sick leave days per year cumulative to a minimum of 180 days. The minimums set forth above may be increased by contract when a bargaining unit is involved or by school board policy in other instances.

Ill. Rev. Stat. c. 122, par. 24-6

HIRING NONCERTIFICATED EMPLOYEES

20:140 Are criminal background checks required of employees of an independent contractor doing business with a school district?

If the employees of the independent contractor have direct, daily contact with students, a criminal background check is required.

Ill. Rev. Stat. c. 122, par. 10-21.9

20:144 Must a school district complete a criminal background check before hiring a non-certificated employee?

A school board may not employ any person for whom a criminal background investigation has not been initiated.

Ill. Rev. Stat. c. 122, par. 10-21.9 (d)

20:150 May a school board make residency in the school district a condition of employment for educational support personnel?

No.

Ill. Rev. Stat. c. 122, par. 10-23.5

DISMISSAL

20:160 Is a noncertificated educational support employee entitled to due process prior to dismissal for cause?

Assuming a collective bargaining agreement does not provide additional contractual rights, or the employer has not taken steps to assure employment at will, educational support personnel have implicit one year employment contracts. These contractual rights create a property right in continued employment. The employee cannot be deprived of this property right without due process.

To dismiss a noncertificated employee for cause requires a pretermination hearing which allows the employee a fair opportunity to refute the alleged causes for dismissal.

Ill. Rev. Stat. c. 122, par. 10-23.5

Cleveland Board of Education v. Loudermill, 105 S.Ct. 1487, 470 U.S. 532, 84 L.Ed.2d 494 on remand 763 F.2d 202 (1985)

20:161 May a school board dismiss a contractual employee who has been charged with a felony?

Persons charged with crimes are presumed to be innocent until proven guilty. Investigation, arrest, and/or indictment do not establish guilt. In order to dismiss a contractual employee for commission of a crime, the employer must provide the employee with requisite procedural and substantive due process. The employer has the burden of proving the crime was committed and must show that the crime had a connection to the employee's employment sufficient to warrant dismissal.

McBroom v. Board of Education District No. 205, 144 Ill.App.3d 463, 494 N.E.2d 1191, 98 Ill.Dec. 864 (2nd Dist. 1986)

20:162 May a school board dismiss a contractual employee who has been convicted of a crime?

The employer must demonstrate the crime had a connection to the employee's employment and was sufficiently serious to warrant dismissal. The employer must provide the employee with requisite substantive and procedural due process prior to dismissal.

Reinhardt v. Board of Education of Alton Community Unit School District No. 11, Madison and Jersey Counties, 19 Ill.App.3d 481, 311 N.E.2d 710 (5th Dist. 1974) vacated on other grounds 61 Ill.2d 101, 329 N.E.2d 218

20:170 Do educational support personnel have seniority rights?

Unless a collective bargaining agreement provides otherwise, educational support personnel acquire seniority within the respective category of position in which they are employed from the first day of continuous service to the school district.

Ill. Rev. Stat. c. 122, par. 10-23.5

20:174 Are part time educational support personnel entitled to seniority rights?

Yes. Unlike teachers, both full and part time educational support personnel are entitled to seniority by law.

Ill. Rev. Stat. c. 122, par. 10-23.5

20:176 Do educational support personnel serve a probationary period before earning seniority rights?

No. Again unlike teachers, seniority accrues to educational support personnel employees from their first day of employment, rather than after a probationary period.

Ill. Rev. Stat. c. 122, par. 10-23.5

20:180 What is the procedure for reducing the number of educational support staff employed by the district?

When the school board decides to decrease the number of educational support staff employed or to discontinue some particular type of educational support service, written notice must be given to the employee(s) by certified mail, return receipt requested, at least 60 days before the end of the school term, together with a statement of honorable dismissal and the reason therefor. The employee(s) with the shorter length of continuing service with the district, within the respective category of position, must be dismissed first unless an alternative method of determining the sequence of dismissal is lawfully established in a collective bargaining agreement.

A collectively bargained alternative provision for determining the sequence of dismissal must not impair the operation of any affirmative action program in the district, regardless of whether it exists by operation of law or is conducted on a voluntary basis by the board.

Ill. Rev. Stat. c. 122, par. 10-23.5

20:190 Do educational support personnel have recall rights after layoff?

Yes. After a layoff, any vacancies occurring for the following school term or within one year from the beginning of that school term must be tendered to the employees removed from that specific category of position if they are qualified to hold such positions.

Ill. Rev. Stat. c. 122, par. 10-23.5

20:200 Must a school board recall educational support personnel from a layoff pool in seniority order?

Employees need not be recalled from the recall pool in seniority order unless a collective bargaining agreement requires it.

Ill. Rev. Stat. c. 122, par. 10-23.5

SCHOOL BUS DRIVERS

20:210 What are the qualifications for employment as a school bus driver?

A school bus driver must hold a valid school bus driver permit. To obtain a permit, an applicant must submit the results of a medical examination showing physical fitness to operate a school bus, have a safe driving record pursuant to statutory definition, demonstrate he has never been convicted of any of a list of specified criminal offenses, be at least 21 years of age, and hold a valid and properly classified driver's license. There are numerous other requirements contained in the relevant statute.

Ill. Rev. Stat. c. 95 1 / 2, par. 6-106.1

20:220 May a school board suspend or revoke an employee's school bus driver permit?

No. A regional superintendent of schools may suspend or revoke a school bus driver permit for specific causes provided in Illinois motor vehicle laws. A school board does not have this authority.

Ill. Rev. Stat. c. 95 1 / 2, par. 6-106.1(d)

20:230 What happens if a school bus driver fails the drug and alcohol test required by statute?

If an applicant fails the mandatory drug and alcohol test necessary to obtain a school bus driver permit, the regional superintendent of schools may refuse the applicant a permit.

Ill. Rev. Stat. c. 95 1 / 2, par. 6-106.1

20:240 May a school bus driver who has an accident while driving a school bus refuse a drug or alcohol test?

No. The driver is subject to the implied consent requirements for commercial motor vehicle drivers.

Ill. Rev. Stat. c. 95 1 / 2, par. 6-516(c)
Ill. Rev. Stat. c. 95 1 / 2, par. 11-501.2

21: COLLECTIVE BARGAINING

ILLINOIS EDUCATIONAL LABOR RELATIONS ACT

21:10 What is the Illinois Educational Labor Relations Act?

The Illinois Educational Labor Relations Act is a state law which regulates the recognition of exclusive bargaining representatives and the collective bargaining relationships and procedures for all public school employers and all public school employees in the state.

Under terms of the Act, covered employees may organize, form, join, or assist in employee organizations, or engage in lawful concerted activities for the purpose of collective bargaining or other mutual aid and protection, or bargain collectively through representatives of their own free choice. Except as limited by the Act, employees also have the right to refrain from any or all such activities.

Ill. Rev. Stat. c. 48, par. 1701 et seq.
Ill. Rev. Stat. c. 48, par. 1703

21:20 Does the National Labor Relations Board have any jurisdiction with respect to Illinois educational labor relations?

No.

21:30 How is the Illinois Educational Labor Relations Act implemented and enforced?

The Illinois Educational Labor Relations Board (IELRB) promulgates and enforces rules necessary to carry out the purposes of the Act.

Ill. Rev. Stat. c. 48, par. 1701 et seq.

21:40 What is the Illinois Educational Labor Relations Board?

The Illinois Educational Labor Relations Board (IELRB) is a three-member board appointed by the Governor with the advice and consent of the Senate. No more than two IELRB members may be from the same political party. Members must have a minimum of five years experience directly related to labor and employment relations in representing educational employers or educational employees in collective bargaining matters. Members serve six year terms of office and may be removed only by the Governor upon notice and only for neglect of duty or malfeasance in office and for no other cause.

Ill. Rev. Stat. c. 48, par. 1705
Board of Education of Mundelein Elementary School District No. 75 v Illinois Educational Labor Relations Board, 179 Ill.App.3d 696, 534 N.E.2d 1022, 128 Ill.Dec. 577 (4th Dist. 1989)

21:50 Do rulings of the Illinois Educational Labor Relations Board have the effect of law?

Yes. But any party aggrieved by a final order of the Illinois Educational Labor Relations Board may appeal to either the First or Fourth District Appellate Courts at the option of the appellant.

Ill. Rev. Stat. c. 48, par. 1716

21:60 Does the Open Meetings Act apply to collective bargaining negotiations and grievance arbitrations?

No. Bargaining meetings and arbitration hearings are not subject to the Open Meetings Act. The notice requirements and the closed meeting exceptions of the Open Meetings Act are not applicable.

Ill. Rev. Stat. c. 48, par. 1718
Gosnell v. Hogan, 179 Ill.App.3d 161, 534 N.E.2d 434, 128 Ill.Dec. 252 (5th Dist. 1989)

COVERED EMPLOYERS AND EMPLOYEES

21:70 What employers are covered by the Illinois Educational Labor Relations Act?

Employers covered by the Act are the governing bodies of any public school district, combination of public school districts (including the governing bodies of joint agreements of any type formed by two or more school districts), and any State agency whose major function is providing educational services.

Ill. Rev. Stat. c. 48, par. 1702

21:80 Which school employees are covered by the Illinois Educational Labor Relations Act?

The Act covers any school district employee except supervisory, managerial, confidential, short-term, or student employees.

Ill. Rev. Stat. c. 48, par. 1702(b)

21:90 What is a supervisory employee?

A supervisor is any individual having authority in the interests of the employer to hire, transfer, suspend, lay off, recall, promote, discharge, reward, or discipline other employees within the appropriate bargaining unit and adjust their grievances, or to effectively recommend such action if the exercise of such authority is not of a merely routine or clerical nature, but requires the use of independent judgment. The term supervisor includes only those individuals who devote a preponderance of their employment time to exercising such authority.

Ill. Rev. Stat. c. 48, par. 1702(g)
Illinois Department of Management Services, 5 PERI 2012
(IELRB Decision and Order, April 28, 1989)
Virden Community Unit School District No. 4, 4 PERI 1060
(IELRB Hearing Officer, March 31, 1988)

21:100 What is a managerial employee?

A managerial employee is an individual who is engaged predominantly in executive and management functions and is charged with the responsibility of directing the effectuation of management policies and practices.

Ill. Rev. Stat. c. 48, par. 1702(o)
Lincoln Way Community High School District No. 210, 5 PERI 1025
(Executive Director's Recommended Decision and Order, January 11, 1989)

21:110 What is a confidential employee?

A confidential employee is an employee who (1) in the regular course of his duties, assists and acts in a confidential capacity to persons who formulate, determine, and effectuate management policies with regard to labor relations, or (2) in the regular course of his duties has access to information relating to the effectuation or review of the employer's collective bargaining policies.

Ill. Rev. Stat. c. 48, par. 1702(n)
Danville Community Consolidated School District No. 118, 5 PERI 1084 (IELRB Opinion and Order, April 12, 1989)
Board of Education of Plainfield Community Consolidated School District No. 202, Will and Kendall Counties v. Illinois Educational Labor Relations Board, et al., 143 Ill.App.3d 898, 493 N.E.2d 1130, 98 Ill.Dec. 109 (4th Dist. 1986)

21:115 What is a short-term employee?

A short-term employee is one who is employed for less than two consecutive calendar quarters during a calendar year and who does not have reasonable assurance that he or she will be rehired by the same employer for the same service in a subsequent calendar year.

Ill.Rev Stat. c. 48, par. 1702 (q)

21:120 May noncertificated employees seek union recognition and bargaining rights under the Educational Labor Relations Act?

Noncertificated school employees may seek recognition and bargaining rights under the Act provided they are school board employees and not the employees of an independent contractor. The employees of independent contractors (such as independent bus companies or janitorial service companies) are not covered under the Act.

Ill. Rev. Stat. c. 48, par. 1702(b)

Decatur School District No. 61, 3 PERI 1022 (IELRB Opinion and Order, February 10, 1987)

Alpha School Bus Company, 2 PERI 1008 (Executive Director's Recommended Decision and Order, November 7, 1985)

STATUTORY OBLIGATIONS OF EMPLOYERS

21:130 Does the Illinois Educational Labor Relations Act require school boards and their employees to bargain collectively?

The Act requires educational employers to collectively bargain with representatives of duly recognized employee bargaining units. If an appropriate bargaining unit gains voluntary recognition or recognition by election, the employer must bargain with it.

Ill. Rev. Stat. c. 48, par. 1710

21:140 What matters are educational employers obligated to bargain with their employees?

Covered employers are required to bargain collectively with regard to policy matters directly affecting wages, hours, and terms and conditions of employment, as well as the impact thereon, upon request by an employee representative. However, employers are not required to bargain over matters of inherent managerial policy.

Ill. Rev. Stat. c. 48, par. 1703

Ill. Rev. Stat. c. 48, par. 1704

Central City Education Association, IEA-NEA v. Illinois Educational Labor Relations Board and Central City Community Consolidated School District No. 133, 199 Ill.App.3d 559, 557 N.E.2d 418, 145 Ill.Dec. 648 (1st Dist. 1990) leave to appeal allowed

Board of Education Decatur District No. 61 v. Illinois Educational Labor Relations Board, 180 Ill.App.3d 770, 536 N.E.2d 743, 129 Ill.Dec. 693 (4th Dist. 1989)

21:150 What are the inherent managerial policies which employers are not required to bargain?

Matters of inherent managerial policy include such areas of discretion or policy as the functions of the employer, standards

of services, the overall budget, the organizational structure, and
selection of new employees and direction of employees.

A balancing test is used to determine whether a particular
subject is more nearly a "wage, hour or term and condition of
employment" which must be bargained, or a management right
which need not be bargained.

Ill. Rev. Stat. c. 48, par. 1704

*Central City Education Association, IEA-NEA v. Illinois
Educational Labor Relations Board and Central City Community
Consolidated School District No. 133,* 199 Ill.App.3d 559, 557 N.E.2d
418, 145 Ill.Dec. 648 (1st Dist. 1990) leave to appeal allowed

*Board of Education, Leroy Community Unit School District No. 2 v.
Illinois Educational Labor Relations Board,* 199 Ill.App.3d 347, 556
N.E.2d 857, 145 Ill.Dec. 239 (4th Dist. 1990) leave to appeal allowed

*Board of Education Decatur District No. 61 v. Illinois Educational
Labor Relations Board,* 180 Ill.App.3d 770, 536 N.E.2d 743, 129
Ill.Dec. 693 (4th Dist. 1989)

21:160 Is the school board free to make unilateral decisions on matters of inherent managerial policy?

Yes, a school board may make decisions on matters of inherent managerial policy. However, when any such decision
affects the wages, hours, and terms and conditions of employment of any employee, the school board may be required to
bargain the decision and or the impact of any decision upon
timely request of a recognized bargaining agent. Whether or not
the employer has an obligation to bargain in any given cir-
cumstance may be governed by a subjective balancing test. This
obligation regarding the impact of managerial policy decisions
is called "impact bargaining."

*Central City Education Association, IEA-NEA v. Illinois
Educational Labor Relations Board and Central City Community
Consolidated School District No. 133,* 199 Ill.App.3d 559, 557 N.E.2d
418, 145 Ill.Dec. 648 (1st Dist. 1990) leave to appeal allowed

21:170 How does bargaining the impact of a decision differ from bargaining the decision itself?

Decisional bargaining requires the employer to bargain with
the exclusive bargaining agent over a decision to do something

before the decision is made or implemented. Impact bargaining means that the employer is free to make an unfettered decision but is obligated to bargain, on demand, the effects of the decision on wages, hours and terms or conditions of employment.

Central City Education Association, IEA-NEA v. Illinois Educational Labor Relations Board and Central City Community Consolidated School District No. 133, 199 Ill.App.3d 559, 557 N.E.2d 418, 145 Ill.Dec. 648 (1st Dist. 1990) leave to appeal allowed

Berkeley School District No. 87, 2 PERI 1066 (IELRB Opinion and Order, May 30, 1986)

21:180 May an employer subcontract work performed by bargaining unit members to outside persons or firms?

Bargaining unit work may not be subcontracted until the employer has first met its obligation to bargain.

Buckellew v. Board of Education of Georgetown-Ridge Farm Community Unit School District No. 4, 214 Ill.App.3d 506, 575 N.E.2d 556, 159 Ill.Dec. 58 (4th Dist. 1991)

Service Employees International Local Union No. 316 v. Illinois Educational Labor Relations Board and Carbondale Community High School District No. 165, 153 Ill.App.3d 744, 505 N.E.2d 418, 106 Ill.Dec. 112 (4th Dist. 1987)

21:190 In addition to bargaining a union contract, may a school board be required to bargain during the term of that contract?

During the term of a collective bargaining agreement — absent a zipper clause — the school board must bargain over wages, hours and terms and conditions of employment which were not fully bargained during the bargaining of the collective bargaining agreement. This is called "interim bargaining" or "midterm bargaining."

A school board may be required to bargain the impact of managerial policy decisions during the term of the bargaining agreement.

Waverly Community Unit School District No. 6, 5 PERI 1002 (IELRB Opinion and Order, November 23, 1988)

21:200 What is a zipper clause?

A zipper clause is a negotiated contract clause under which a union waives its right to engage in mid-term bargaining over mandatory subjects of bargaining. A zipper clause is a form of waiver of a union right to bargain.

Board of Regents of the Regency University System (Northern Illinois University) 7 PERI 1113 (IELRB Opinion and Order, October 24, 1991)

East Richland Education Association v. IELRB, 173 Ill.App.3d 878, 528 N.E.2d 751, 124 Ill.Dec. 63 (4th Dist. 1988)

Rock Falls Elementary School District No. 13, 2 PERI 1150 (IELRB Opinion and Order, May 14, 1987) aff'd. sub nom.

21:202 Is a waiver or zipper clause a mandatory subject of bargaining?

An employer proposal that a union waive a right the union has under the bargaining act is a permissive subject of bargaining. The employer may not insist to impasse on the waiver without committing an unfair labor practice. A union may voluntarily agree to a waiver, but the employer should be cautious because the waiver may be withdrawn unilaterally by the union during an appropriate bargaining period. If the waiver was bargained to neutralize some otherwise consequential language in the collective bargaining agreement, the effect of the removal of the waiver would be to leave the offending language in the contract but without the neutralizing waiver. Waivers frequently take the form of attempts to exclude contract language from the grievance procedure, side agreements, zipper clauses and other attempts to avoid bargaining obligations.

Board of Regents of the Regency University System (Northern Illinois University) 7 PERI 1113 (IELRB Opinion and Order, October 24, 1991)

BARGAINING UNITS

21:210 What is a bargaining unit?

A bargaining unit is a group of employees who have gained recognition, determined an exclusive representative and have bargaining rights under the terms of the Educational Labor Relations Act.

Ill. Rev. Stat. c. 48, par. 1702(m)

21:220 What is a wall-to-wall bargaining unit?

A wall-to-wall bargaining unit is a bargaining unit composed of both professional and noncertificated employees. To form a wall-to-wall bargaining unit, both the professional and the non-certificated employees must vote to approve the combined bargaining unit.

Ill. Rev. Stat. c. 48, par. 1707

Riverside-Brookfield Township District No. 208, 5 PERI 1136 (IELRB Decision and Order, July 25, 1989)

21:230 On what basis is a bargaining unit determined to be appropriate?

In determining the appropriateness of a unit, the Educational Labor Relations Board must decide in each case, in order to ensure employees the fullest freedom in exercising the rights guaranteed by the Illinois Educational Labor Relations Act, the unit appropriate for the purpose of collective bargaining based upon, but not limited to, such factors as historical pattern of recognition; community of interest, including employee skills and functions; degree of functional integration; interchangeability and contact among employees; common supervision, wages, hours and other working conditions of the employees involved; and the desires of the employees.

Ill. Rev. Stat. c. 48, par. 1707(a)

EXCLUSIVE BARGAINING REPRESENTATIVE

21:240 What is an exclusive representative?

An exclusive representative is the labor organization which has been designated by the Illinois Educational Labor Relations Board as the representative of the majority of educational employees in an appropriate unit, or one that has historically been recognized as the representative of an appropriate unit, or one that is voluntarily recognized by an employer upon evidence that the organization has been designated as the exclusive representative by a majority of the employees in an appropriate unit.

Ill. Rev. Stat. c. 48, par. 1702(d)

21:250 How may an exclusive representative gain recognition by election?

A labor organization may gain recognition as the exclusive representative of an employee unit by an election of the employees in the unit. Petitions requesting an election are filed with the Illinois Educational Labor Relations Board (IELRB). The IELRB investigates the petition and if it has reasonable cause to suspect a question of representation exists, it gives notice and conducts a hearing. If it finds upon the record of the hearing a question of representation exists, it must direct that an election be held no later than 90 days after the date the petition was filed. In many cases the parties waive hearing, enter into a consent agreement, and an election is held pursuant to the consent agreement.

Ill. Rev. Stat. c. 48, par. 1707
80 Ill. Admin. Code 1110.50 et seq.

21:260 What ballot choices are required in the election of an exclusive bargaining representative?

An incumbent bargaining representative is automatically placed on any ballot. An intervening labor organization may be placed on the ballot if the intervenor can demonstrate a 15 percent showing of interest. Any other bargaining representative seeking recognition requires a 30 percent showing of interest. In any election the voters must be given the choice of "no representative".

Ill. Rev. Stat. c. 48, par. 1707
Ill. Rev. Stat. c. 48, par. 1708

21:270 How are representation elections conducted?

Representation elections are conducted by secret ballot in accordance with rules and regulations established by the Illinois Educational Labor Relations Board (IELRB). Usually, notice of election announcing the election, noticing election dates, times and places and describing the proposition to be voted on is posted in prominent places in the school district for thirty days before the election. Absentee ballots are permitted when an individual would otherwise be unable to cast a ballot.

If none of the choices on the ballot receives a majority, a run-off is conducted between the two choices receiving the largest number of valid votes cast in the election. The IELRB must certify the results of the election within five working days after the final tally of votes unless a charge is filed by a party alleging improper conduct occurred which affected the outcome of the election.

Ill. Rev. Stat. c. 48, par. 1708
80 Ill. Admin. Code 1110.10 et seq.

21:280 What is decertification?

A decertification results when an incumbent representative no longer represents the majority of the employees in the bargaining unit. A decertification petition requires an allegation and showing of interest by at least 30 percent of the employees in the appropriate bargaining unit. An employer cannot instigate or lend support to a decertification petition.

Ill. Rev. Stat. c. 48, par. 1707 (c)
80 Ill. Admin. Code 1100.60 et seq.

21:290 When may employee representation be challenged?

A petition seeking a representation election may only be filed during certain specified time periods. There is a waiting period after a previous election in a particular bargaining unit before another petition may be filed, and petitions may only be filed during a specified window period during the life of a collective bargaining agreement.

Ill. Rev. Stat. c. 48, par. 1707
80 Ill. Admin. Code 1110.70

21:300 How are election objections filed?

A charge alleging improper election conduct which affected the outcome of an election may be filed with the Illinois Educational Labor Relations Board (IELRB) within five days of the final tally of votes. The IELRB must investigate the allegations, and if it finds probable cause that improper conduct occurred and could have affected the outcome of the election, it must set a hearing on the matter on a date falling within two weeks of when it received the charge.

If the Board determines, after the hearing, the outcome of the election was affected by improper conduct, it must order a new election and must order corrective action which it considers necessary to ensure the fairness of the new election. If it determines upon investigation or after hearing the alleged improper conduct did not take place or it did not affect the results of the election, it must immediately certify the election results.

Ill. Rev. Stat. c. 48, par. 1708

80 Ill. Admin. Code 1110.150

Decatur Federation of Teachers IFT-AFT, AFL-CIO v. Educational Labor Relations Board, 199 Ill.App.3d 190, 556 N.E.2d 780, 145 Ill.Dec. 162 (4th Dist. 1990)

Champaign Community Unit School District No. 4, 5 PERI 1124 (Executive Director's Recommended Decision and Order, June 15, 1989)

Centralia School District No. 135, 4 PERI 1044 (IELRB Opinion and Order, February 25, 1988)

NONUNION EMPLOYEES

21:310 May a contract provision require employees to join a union as a condition of employment?

No. A school board may enter into a collectively bargained agreement which requires all employees covered by the agreement to pay a "fair share" fee, but may not make union membership a condition of employment.

Ill. Rev. Stat. c. 48, par. 1711

Abood v. Detroit Board of Education, 97 S.Ct. 1782, 431 U.S. 209 52 L.Ed. 261, reh. den. 97 S.Ct. 2989, 433 U.S. 915, 53 L.Ed.2d 1102 (1977)

Chicago Teachers Union Local 1, AFT, AFL-CIO v. Hudson, 106 S.Ct. 1066, 475 U.S. 292, 89 L.Ed.2d 232 (1986)

21:320 Must an exclusive bargaining representative represent non-union employees?

An exclusive bargaining representative has "a duty of fair representation" which extends to all members of the bargaining unit, whether the bargaining unit member is a union member or not. If the exclusive bargaining representative fails to provide fair representation for any bargaining unit member, the member has a cause of action against the union.

Ill. Rev. Stat. c. 48, par. 1703

NEA, IEA Classroom Teachers Council of District 15 (Kostka), 5 PERI 1067 (Executive Director's Recommended Decision and Order, March 13, 1989)

21:330 What is the difference between fair share, agency shop and union shop?

Fair share and agency shop are synonymous terms and are permissible under the Educational Labor Relations Act. They are contract provisions which require non-union teachers to pay a representation fee to the union as a condition of employment.

The fair share agreement between a school board and a teachers union may require the non-union member to pay an amount to defray the cost of collective bargaining, contract administration, and union grievance representation. A union may not collect money from non-union members to be used in support of ideological causes which are not germane to its duties as collective bargaining agent. Thus, political action assessments may not be included in fair share fees. Union shop is a contract provision which makes union membership a condition of employment. A union shop provision is illegal.

Ill. Rev. Stat. c. 48, par. 1711

80 Ill. Admin. Code 1125.10 et seq.

Lehnert v. Ferris Faculty Association, 111 S.Ct. 1950, __U.S. __, __ L.Ed.2d __ (1991)

Abood v. Detroit Board of Education, 97 S.Ct. 1782, 431 U.S. 209 52 L.Ed. 261, reh. den. 97 S.Ct. 2989, 433 U.S. 915, 53 L.Ed.2d 1102 (1977)

Chicago Teachers Union Local 1, AFT, AFL-CIO v. Hudson, 106 S.Ct. 1066, 475 U.S. 292, 89 L.Ed.2d 232 (1986)

21:340 May an employer exclude a union representative from a grievance adjustment meeting if the grievant is a non-union teacher and so requests?

No. Any individual employee or group of employees may at any time present grievances to the employer and have them adjusted without the intervention of the bargaining representative, provided that the adjustment is not inconsistent with the terms of a collective bargaining agreement then in effect. However, the bargaining representative must be given an opportunity to be present at such adjustment.

Ill. Rev. Stat. c. 48, par. 1703

UNFAIR LABOR PRACTICES

21:350 What is "bargaining in good faith?"

Parties subject to bargaining obligations must meet at reasonable times and confer in good faith with respect to wages, hours, and other terms and conditions of employment, and execute a written contract incorporating any agreements reached. Bargaining in good faith does not require a party to agree to a proposal or to make a concession. The totality of bargaining conduct is examined to determine whether or not any particular bargaining was conducted in good faith.

Ill. Rev. Stat. c. 48, par. 1710
Kewanee Community Unit School District No. 229, 4 PERI 1136 (IELRB Opinion and Order, September 15, 1988)

21:360 What is the remedy for failure to bargain in good faith?

Either the employee representative or the employer may file an unfair labor practice charge with the Illinois Educational Labor Relations Board alleging failure to bargain in good faith.

Ill. Rev. Stat. c. 48, par. 1710
Ill. Rev. Stat. c. 48, par. 1714
Thornton Township High School District No. 205, 5 PERI 1134 (Executive Director's Recommended Decision and Order, July 10, 1989)

21:370 What is an unfair labor practice charge?

An unfair labor practice charge is an allegation of conduct which is prohibited in Ill. Rev. Stat. c. 48, par. 1714.

Ill. Rev. Stat. c. 48, par. 1714
80 Ill. Admin. Code 1120.10 et seq.

21:380 Who may file an unfair labor practice charge?

An unfair labor practice charge may be filed by an employer, an individual or a labor organization.

Ill. Rev. Stat. c. 48, par. 1714
80 Ill. Admin. Code 1120.20 a)

21:390 What are union unfair labor practices?

Employee organizations, their agents or representatives, or educational employees are prohibited from:

1) Restraining or coercing employees in the exercise of the rights guaranteed under the Educational Labor Relations Act.

2) Restraining or coercing an educational employer in the selection of his representative for the purposes of collective bargaining or the adjustment of grievances.

3) Refusal of the exclusive bargaining representative to bargain collectively in good faith with an educational employer.

4) Violating any of the rules and regulations promulgated by the Educational Labor Relations Board regulating the conduct of representation elections.

5) Refusing to reduce a collective bargaining agreement to writing and signing such agreement.

6) Refusing to comply with the provisions of a binding arbitration award.

Ill. Rev. Stat. c. 48, par. 1714 a)

21:400 What are employer unfair labor practices?

Educational employers, their agents or representatives are prohibited from:

1) Interfering, restraining, or coercing employees in the exercise of the rights guaranteed under the Illinois Educational Labor Relations Act.

2) Dominating or interfering with the formation, existence, or administration of any employee organization.

3) Discriminating in regard to hiring or tenure of employment or any term or condition of employment to encourage or discourage membership in any employee organization.

4) Discharging or otherwise discriminating against an employee because he or she has signed or filed an affidavit, authorization card, petition or complaint, or given any information or testimony under the Educational Labor Relations Act.

5) Refusing to bargain collectively in good faith with an employee representative which is the exclusive representative of employees in an appropriate unit, including, but not limited to, the discussing of grievances with the exclusive representative; provided, however, that if an alleged unfair labor practice involves interpretation or application of the terms of a collective bargaining agreement, and said agreement contains a grievance and arbitration procedure, the Educational Labor Relations Board may defer the resolution of such dispute to the grievance and arbitration procedure contained in said agreement.

6) Refusing to reduce a collective bargaining agreement to writing and signing such agreement.

7) Violating any of the rules and regulations promulgated by the Educational Labor Relations Board regulating the conduct of representation elections.

8) Refusing to comply with the provisions of a binding arbitration award.

Ill. Rev. Stat. c. 48, par. 1714 b)

21:410 How is an unfair labor practice charge filed?

An unfair labor practice charge may be filed with the Educational Labor Relations Board (IELRB) on forms provided by the IELRB. A charge must be signed and must contain the name address and affiliation of both the charging party and respon-

dent. It also must contain a complete statement of facts supporting the alleged unfair labor practice, including dates, times and
places of occurrence of each act alleged and the sections of the
Act alleged to have been violated. It must also include a statement of relief sought.

Upon receipt of a charge, the IELRB investigates. If the
IELRB determines the charge states an issue of law or fact
sufficient to warrant a hearing, it issues a complaint. Thereafter, a hearing is held on the charges and a decision rendered.
The parties have the right to various appeals.

Ill. Rev. Stat. c. 48, par. 1715
23 Ill. Admin. Code 1120.20 et seq.
Lake Zurich School District No. 45, 1 PERI 1031 (IELRB Opinion
and Order, November 30, 1984)

21:420 Is there a limitations period for unfair labor practice charges?

No order may be issued on an unfair labor practice occurring
more than six months before the filing of the charge alleging the
unfair labor practice.

Ill. Rev. Stat. c. 48, par. 1715
80 Ill. Admin. Code 1100.30
80 Ill. Admin. Code 1120.20 d)
*Charleston Community Unit School District No. 1 v. Illinois
Educational Labor Relations Board and Charleston Education
Association, IEA-NEA*, 203 Ill.App.3d 619, 561 N.E.2d 331, 149
Ill.Dec. 53 (4th Dist. 1990)
*Wapella Education Association, IEA-NEA v. Illinois Educational
Labor Relations Board*, 177 Ill.App.3d 153, 531 N.E.2d 1371, 126
Ill.Dec. 532 (4th Dist. 1988)

21:430 Must a school board permit union representatives to enter the schools during the school day to meet with school employees?

The agents of an exclusive bargaining representative must
be allowed to meet with school employees in school buildings
during employee duty-free times.

Ill. Rev. Stat. c. 122, par. 24-25

IMPASSES AND STRIKES

21:440 What is impasse?

Impasse exists if, in view of all the circumstances of bargaining, further discussions would be futile. Impasse does not exist if there is a ray of hope with a real potentiality for agreement if explored in good faith bargaining sessions. In examining whether or not impasse has been reached the following factors are examined:

1) bargaining history;

2) the good faith of the parties in negotiations;

3) the length of the negotiations;

4) the importance of the issue(s) as to which there is disagreement; and

5) the contemporaneous understanding of the parties as to the state of negotiations.

Ill. Rev. Stat. c. 48, par. 1712

80 Ill. Admin. Code 1130.10 et seq.

Kewanee Community School District No. 229, 4 PERI 1136 (IELRB Opinion and Order, September 15, 1988)

21:450 What is the difference between a mediator, a fact-finder and an arbitrator?

All three terms refer to third parties brought into a dispute in an effort to assist in its resolution. A mediator can suggest a resolution to the parties, usually does not make his recommendation public, and has no authority to enforce any recommended solution.

A factfinder also suggests resolutions but usually makes his recommendations public. Like a mediator, a factfinder has no power of enforcement.

An arbitrator makes a formal ruling, makes the ruling public, and has power to enforce the ruling.

Mediation of contract formation disputes is mandatory at the request of either party under the Educational Labor Relations Act; factfinding and interest arbitration are permissive under the Act.

Ill. Rev. Stat. c. 48, par. 1712

80 Ill. Admin. Code 1130.30 et seq.

80 Ill. Admin. Code 1130.50

21:460 Must a contract bargaining dispute be submitted to binding arbitration?

No. Interest arbitration — the process whereby an arbitrator is employed to resolve differences which arise between the parties in reaching contract agreement — is permissible under the Illinois Educational Labor Relations Act (the parties may agree to it). But it is not required.

Grievance arbitration is a process whereby an arbitrator is employed to resolve differences which arise between the parties in interpreting the meaning of contract language. Grievance arbitration is mandatory under the Illinois Educational Labor Relations Act.

Ill. Rev. Stat. c. 48, par. 1712

21:470 What options are there in the selection of a mediator?

Unless an applicable collective bargaining agreement provides otherwise, the parties to a bargaining dispute have several options in the selection of a mediator. The parties may mutually agree to engage:

1) any qualified, impartial individual who is mutually acceptable to the parties under terms established by the parties.

2) an individual assigned or selected under the auspices of a private service, such as the American Arbitration Association. Filing fees are often charged, and the mediators selected or assigned charge the parties a per diem fee.

3) a federal mediator assigned by the Federal Mediation and Conciliation Service (FMCS). FMCS does not charge for its services. If either party requests the use of mediation services from the FMCS, the other party must either join in the request or bear the additional cost of mediation services from another source.

The IELRB may invoke mediation at the request of either party or on its own motion after a reasonable period of negotiation and absent agreement by the parties on a mediator. Mediators provided by the IELRB charge the parties a per diem fee.

Ill. Rev. Stat. c. 48, par. 1712
8u Ill. Admin. Code 1130.30
80 Ill. Admin.Code 1130.80

21:480 What is a no-strike clause?

A no-strike clause is a contract provision which prohibits strikes during the term of a contract agreement. A no-strike clause does not prohibit a strike after an agreement expires. The Educational Labor Relations Act requires each collective bargaining agreement to contain a no-strike clause. A no-strike clause may explicitly define the meaning of the term "strike" to prohibit work slow-downs and other job actions during the term of a contract.

Ill. Rev. Stat. c. 48, par. 1710(c)
80 Ill. Admin. Code 1130.70 a)

21:490 When are strikes permitted?

Educational employees shall not engage in a strike except under the following conditions:

1) they are represented by an exclusive bargaining representative;

2) mediation has been used without success;

3) at least five days have elapsed after a notice of intent to strike has been given by the exclusive bargaining representative to the educational employer, the regional superintendent, and the Illinois Educational Labor Relations Board;

4) the collective bargaining agreement between the educational employer and educational employees, if any, has expired; and

5) the employer and the exclusive bargaining representative have not mutually submitted the unresolved issues to arbitration.

Ill. Rev. Stat. c. 48, par. 1713
80 Ill. Admin. Code 1130.40

21:500 May striking school board employees picket the home of a school board member or administrator?

It is unlawful to picket before or about the residence or dwelling of any person, except when the residence or dwelling is used as a place of business. Peaceful picketing is not prohibited if it is at a place of a meeting or assembly or is on premises commonly used to discuss subjects of general public interest.

Ill. Rev. Stat. c. 38, par. 21.1-2

GRIEVANCE RESOLUTION

21:510 What is a grievance?

What constitutes a grievance is usually defined in a collective bargaining agreement. Commonly, the definition provides that a grievance is an allegation by an employee, group of employees or exclusive bargaining representative that there has been a violation of a specific provision of the contract.

Staunton Community Unit School District No. 6 v. Illinois Educational Labor Relations Board, 200 Ill.App.3d 370, 158 N.E.2d 751, 146 Ill.Dec. 788 (4th Dist. 1990)

Moraine Valley Community College, 5 PERI 1102 (IELRB Opinion and Order, May 12, 1989)

21:520 Must a collective bargaining agreement allow grievance arbitration?

The collective bargaining agreement negotiated between representatives of the educational employees and the educational employer must contain a grievance resolution procedure which must apply to all employees in the unit and must provide for binding arbitration of disputes concerning the administration or interpretation of the agreement.

Ill. Rev. Stat. c. 48, par. 1710(c)

80 Ill. Admin. Code 1130.70 a)

River Grove School District No. 85 1/2, 3 PERI 1019 (IELRB Opinion and Order, January 30, 1987)

21:530 What is the difference between interest arbitration and grievance arbitration?

Interest arbitration is a process whereby an arbitrator is employed to resolve differences which arise between the parties in reaching contract agreement. Under the Illinois Educational

Labor Relations Act, interest arbitration is permissible (the parties may agree to it).

Grievance arbitration is a process whereby an arbitrator is employed to resolve differences which arise between the parties in interpreting the meaning of contract language. Grievance arbitration is mandatory under the Illinois Educational Labor Relations Act.

Ill. Rev. Stat. c. 48, par. 1710(c)
Ill. Rev. Stat. c. 48, par. 1712

21:540 Which body has jurisdiction to vacate or modify an arbitration award?

The Illinois Educational Labor Relations Board has sole and exclusive jurisdiction to vacate or modify arbitration awards. A school board seeking to appeal a decision of an arbitrator must refuse to comply with the provisions of the arbitrator's award and await an unfair labor practice. Circuit courts lack jurisdiction to vacate or modify arbitration awards.

Ill. Rev. Stat. c. 48, par. 1714
Ill. Rev. Stat. c. 48, par. 1716
Board of Education Warren Township High School District No. 121 v. Warren Township High School Federation of Teachers Local 504, IFT/AFL-CIO, 128 Ill.2d 155, 538 N.E.2d 524, 131 Ill.Dec. 149 (1989)
Board of Education of Community Unit School District No. 1 v. Compton, 123 Ill.2d 216, 526 N.E.2d 149, 122 Ill.Dec. 9 (1988)

CONTRACTUAL PROVISIONS

21:550 What is the maximum term of a collective bargaining agreement?

A collective bargaining agreement may be negotiated for a period not exceeding three years. A collective bargaining agreement of less than three years may be extended up to three years if the extension is agreed to in writing before the filing of an election petition.

Ill. Rev. Stat. c. 48, par. 1707

21:560 May a collective bargaining agreement give teachers or other employees more rights than are provided by law?

The parties to the collective bargaining process may implement a provision in a collective bargaining agreement if that provision has the effect of supplementing any provision in any state statute pertaining to wages, hours, or other conditions of employment.

However, the parties may not implement any contract provision that contradicts any such state statute. Whether a contract provision granting employees more rights than are provided by law is legal, therefore, depends upon whether it is construed as supplementary or contradictory to state statutes.

Ill. Rev. Stat. c. 48, par. 1710(b)

21:570 May an employee group agree in a collective bargaining agreement to give up some statutory rights in exchange for other rights or money? For example, could a teacher bargaining unit trade tenure for a large salary increase?

No. The parties to a collective bargaining agreement may not effect or implement a provision in a collective bargaining agreement if the implementation of that provision would be inconsistent or in conflict with any statute enacted by the General Assembly.

No provision in a collective bargaining agreement may be effected or implemented if such provision has the effect of negating, abrogating, replacing, reducing, diminishing, or limiting in any way any employee rights, guarantees, or privileges pertaining to wages, hours, or other conditions of employment provided in statute. Any such provision in a collective bargaining agreement is void and unenforceable, but does not affect the validity, enforceability, and implementation of other permissible provisions of the collective bargaining agreement.

Ill. Rev. Stat. c. 48, par. 1710(b)

21:580 May a collective bargaining agreement include a cost of living adjustment (COLA) clause or any other clause which ties salary increases to outside factors?

Yes.

Libertyville Education Association IEA-NEA v. Board of Education, 56 Ill.App.3d 503, 371 N.E.2d 676, 13 Ill.Dec. 741 (2nd Dist. 1977)

21:590 What benefits must be provided employees after expiration of a collective bargaining agreement and before a successor agreement is reached?

The school board must maintain the status quo. An employer's unilateral alteration of prevailing terms and conditions of employment under negotiation during the course of bargaining is an unfair labor practice.

Vienna School District No. 55 v. Illinois Educational Labor Relations Board, 162 Ill.App.3d 503, 515 N.E.2d 476, 113 Ill.Dec. 667 (4th Dist. 1987)

22: SCHOOL DISTRICTS AND LIABILITY FOR INJURIES

TORT IMMUNITY

22:10 What is a tort?

A tort is a private or civil wrong or injury, other than a breach of contract, for which the law provides a remedy in an action for damages. The elements of every tort require a duty flowing from the defendant to the plaintiff, a breach of that duty and damages which proximately result.

22:20 Are there tort liability immunities which apply to school boards?

Neither a school board nor its employees or agents may be held liable for injuries caused under certain conditions specified in the tort immunity section of the statutes.

Ill. Rev. Stat. c. 85, par. 1-101 et seq.

22:30 May a school district be held liable for civil rights violations?

A school district may be held liable for civil rights violations. An employee or agent of a school district has available a qualified good faith immunity defense. This defense is not available to a school district.

Owen v. City of Independence, 100 S.Ct. 1398, 445 U.S. 622, 63 L.Ed.2d 673 on rem. 623 F.2d 550, reh. den.100 S.Ct. 2979, 446 U.S. 993, 64 L.Ed.2d 850 (1980)

22:35 Is a school district liable for civil rights violations committed by school district employees?

A school district is potentially liable when it sanctions or orders the action which results in the violation. Violations may be explicitly or implicitly sanctioned by the policy or past practice of a school district.

Spann for Spann v. Tyler Independent School District, 876 F.2d 437 (5th Cir. 1989)

Pembaur v. Cincinnati, 106 S.Ct. 1292, 475 U.S. 469, 89 L.Ed.2d 452 (1986)

PUNITIVE DAMAGES

22:40   What are punitive damages?

Punitive damages are those given in addition to compensation for a loss sustained in order to punish and make an example of the wrongdoer.

25 C.J.S. Damages 2

22:50   May a school district be liable for punitive damages?

No.

Ill. Rev. Stat. c. 85, par. 2-102

Collins v. School District No. 189, St. Clair County, 115 Ill.App.3d 100, 450 N.E.2d 387, 70 Ill.Dec. 914 (5th Dist. 1983)

LIABILITY OF INDIVIDUALS

22:60   Can a school employee, volunteer, or school board member be held personally liable for an act or failure to act which was done or not done for the benefit of the school?

The school district must indemnify and protect school board members, employees, volunteers and student teachers against civil rights damage claims and suits, constitutional rights damage claims and suits and death and bodily injury and property damage claims and suits, including the costs of defense, when damages are sought for negligent or wrongful acts alleged to have been committed in the scope of employment or under the direction of the school board.

Ill. Rev. Stat. c. 85, par. 1-101 et seq.

Ill. Rev. Stat. c. 122, par. 10-20.20

Bridewell v. Board of Education of Shawnee Community Unit School District No. 84 of Union, et al. Counties, 2 Ill.App.3d 684, 276 N.E.2d 745 (5th Dist. 1971)

22:70 May a school employee, volunteer or school board member be personally liable for punitive damages?

Punitive damages are intended to punish the party on whom they are assessed. Indemnity and immunity protections insulate public officials from liability for punitive damages in any action arising out of an act or omission made by the public official while serving in an official executive, legislative, quasi legislative or quasi judicial capacity.

In all other circumstances, school-connected individuals may be liable for punitive damages. Punitive damage awards are rare, however, and are imposed only in instances of extraordinary wrongdoing.

Ill. Rev. Stat. c. 85, par. 2-102

Ill. Rev. Stat. c. 122, par. 10-20.20

22:75 What are the risks when a school board member exceeds his authority?

A school board member who acts outside the scope of his authority may be personally liable for his wrongdoing.

INJURIES TO EMPLOYEES

22:80 May a school employee sue the school district for a work-related injury?

Unless a collective bargaining agreement provides a basis for a grievance, school employees are subject to worker compensation statutes and may recover only under the provisions of those laws.

Ill. Rev. Stat. c. 48, par. 138.1 et seq.

22:90   Does the Occupational Safety and Health Act (OSHA) apply to public school districts?

No. The federal Occupational Safety and Health Act excludes school districts.

29 U.S.C.A. par. 652 (5)

INJURIES TO STUDENTS

22:100 Under what circumstances may a school employee be held liable for injuries to students while in school?

If an in loco parentis relationship is found to exist between an injured student and a defendant school employee, neither the employee nor the school district can be liable for ordinary negligence. The student can recover only if he can prove willful and wanton misconduct.

If an in loco parentis relationship does not exist, the employee would be liable for injuries arising out of ordinary negligence, and the school board would be liable for the employee's negligent or wrongful acts if they were committed within the scope of employment or under the direction of the school board.

Ill. Rev. Stat. c. 122, par. 10-20.20

Ill. Rev. Stat. c. 122, par. 24-24

Plesnicar v. Kovach, 102 Ill.App.3d 867, 430 N.E.2d 648, 58 Ill.Dec. 616 (1st Dist. 1981)

O'Brien v. Township High School District No. 214, 83 Ill.2d 462, 415 N.E.2d 1015, 47 Ill.Dec. 702 (1980)

Thomas v. Chicago Board of Education, 60 Ill.App.3d 729, 377 N.E.2d 55, 17 Ill.Dec. 865, rev. on other grounds 77 Ill.App.2d 165, 395 N.E.2d 538, 32 Ill.Dec. 308 (1st Dist. 1978)

Kobylanski v. Chicago Board of Education, 63 Ill.2d 165, 347 N.E.2d 705 (1976)

Clay v. Chicago Board of Education, 22 Ill.App.3d 437, 318 N.E.2d 153 (1st Dist. 1974)

22:110 Which employees enjoy the protections of in loco parentis?

Teachers and other certificated employees stand in place of parents for students under their supervision and, therefore, cannot be held liable for ordinary negligence. Noncertificated employees do not enjoy this defense against ordinary negligence claims.

Ill. Rev. Stat. c 122, par. 24-24

22:120 What is willful and wanton misconduct?

Willful and wanton misconduct is an intentional act or an act committed under circumstances exhibiting a reckless disregard for the safety of others, such as a failure, after knowledge of impending danger, to exercise ordinary care to prevent it or a failure to discover the danger through recklessness, or careless-ness when it could have been discovered by ordinary care.

Braun v. Board of Education of Red Bud Community Unit School District No. 132, 151 Ill.App.3d 787, 502 N.E.2d 1076, 104 Ill.Dec. 416 appeal den. 115 Ill.2d 538, 511 N.E.2d 426, 110 Ill.Dec. 454 (5th Dist. 1986)

Gammon v. Edwardsville Community Unit School District No. 7, 82 Ill.App.3d 586, 403 N.E.2d 43, 38 Ill.Dec. 28 (5th Dist. 1980)

22:130 What is the difference between negligence and willful and wanton misconduct?

Ordinary negligence is a failure to exercise that degree of care which the ordinary prudent person would exercise under similar conditions. Willful and wanton misconduct requires an inten-tional act or an act committed under circumstances exhibiting a reckless disregard for the safety of others.

Ramos v. Waukegan Community Unit School District No. 60, 188 Ill.App.3d 1031, 544 N.E.2d 1302, 136 Ill.Dec. 527 (2nd Dist. 1989)

Lynch v. Board of Education of Collinsville Community Unit School District No. 10, 82 Ill.2d 415, 412 N.E.2d 447, 45 Ill.Dec. 96 (1980)

Thomas v. Chicago Board of Education, 77 Ill.2d 165, 395 N.E.2d 538, 32 Ill.Dec. 308 (1979)

Gerrity v. Beatty, 71 Ill.2d 47, 373 N.E.2d 1323, 15 Ill.Dec. 639 (1978)

McCauley v. Chicago Board of Education, 66 Ill.App.3d 676, 384 N.E.2d 100, 23 Ill.Dec. 464 (1st Dist. 1978)

Kobylanski v. Chicago Board of Education, 63 Ill.2d 165, 347 N.E.2d 705 (1976)

Clay v. Chicago Board of Education, 22 Ill.App.3d 437, 318 N.E.2d 153 (1st Dist. 1974)

Mancha v. Field Museum of Natural History, 5 Ill.App.3d 699, 283 N.E.2d 899 (1st Dist. 1972)

Woodman v. Litchfield Community Unit School District No. 12, Montgomery County, 102 Ill.App.2d 330, 242 N.E.2d 780 (5th Dist. 1968)

Fustin v. Board of Education of Community Unit School District No. 2, 101 Ill.App.2d 113, 242 N.E.2d 308 (5th Dist. 1968)

22:140 Does the in loco parentis status of teachers extend to activities outside school?

The in loco parentis status of teachers is restricted to those activities which are connected to the total school program. It extends to extracurricular activities, but may not extend to other activities which have a more tenuous connection to the total school program.

Montag v. Board of Education of School District No. 40, Rock Island County, 112 Ill.App.3d 1039, 446 N.E.2d 299, 68 Ill.Dec. 565 (3rd Dist. 1983)

Weiss v. Collinsville Community Unit School District No. 10, Madison County, 119 Ill.App.3d 68, 456 N.E.2d 614, 74 Ill.Dec. 893 (5th Dist. 1983)

Plesnicar v. Kovach, 102 Ill.App.3d 867, 430 N.E.2d 648, 58 Ill.Dec. 616 (1st Dist. 1981)

Lynch v. Board of Education of Collinsville Community Unit School District No. 10, 82 Ill.2d 415, 412 N.E.2d 447, 45 Ill.Dec. 96 (1980)

Woodman v. Litchfield Community Unit School District No. 12, Montgomery County, 102 Ill.App.2d 330, 242 N.E.2d 780 (5th Dist. 1968)

Fustin v. Board of Education of Community Unit School District No. 2, 101 Ill.App.2d 113, 242 N.E.2d 308 (1968)

22:145 What duty does a school district have to a student riding or leaving a school bus?

A school district has a very high duty of care to students while they are riding a school bus. The duty becomes a duty of reasonable care with respect to the students once they have left the bus and are on their way home. This latter duty means the school district cannot expose the students to unreasonable risks by reason of the school district's selection of bus routes, drop off points or procedures.

Garrett v. Grant School District No. 124, 139 Ill.App.3d 569, 487 N.E.2d 699, 93 Ill.Dec. 879 (2nd Dist. 1985)

Posteher v. Pana Community Unit School District, 96 Ill.App.3d 709, 421 N.E.2d 1049, 52 Ill.Dec. 198 (4th Dist. 1981)

Katamay v. Chicago Transit Authority, 53 Ill.2d 27, 289 N.E.2d 623 (1972)

Sims v. Chicago Transit Authority, 351 Ill.App. 314, 115 N.E.2d 96, rev. on other grounds 4 Ill.2d 60, 122 N.E.2d 221 (1954)

22:150 What responsibilities and liabilities do school districts incur when providing medical treatment to students?

When a medical emergency occurs and trained medical personnel are unavailable, teachers standing in loco parentis may render necessary emergency treatment to pupils. Teachers are not expected to possess expert medical knowledge but rather, to act reasonably and prudently.

Ill. Rev. Stat. c. 85, par. 6-104 et seq.

22:160 If an Illinois public school student is injured on an out-of-state field trip, which state's immunity laws control?

Immunity defenses to tort claims are governed by the laws of the state in which the lawsuit is properly brought.

Nevada v. Hall, 99 S.Ct. 1182, 440 U.S. 410, 59 L.Ed.2d 416 reh. den. 99 S.Ct. 2018, 441 U.S. 917, 60 L.Ed.2d 389 (1979)

22:170 Is there a cause of action for educational malpractice?

Educational malpractice lawsuits have, for the most part, been unsuccessful. There is no recognized duty to educate, the breach of which would create a cause of action.

Donohue v. Copiague Union Free School District, 418 N.Y.S.2d 375, 47 N.Y.2d 440 (1979)

SAFETY REQUIREMENTS

22:180 What safety requirements are contained in the School Code to protect persons on school property from injury?

Every student, teacher, and visitor must wear an industrial quality eye protective device when participating in or observing any of the following courses in public schools:

1) vocational or industrial arts shops or laboratories involving experience with the following: hot molten metals; milling, sawing, turning, shaping, cutting, grinding, or stamping of any solid materials; heat treatment, tempering, or kiln firing of any metal or other materials; gas or electric arc welding; repair or servicing of any vehicle; caustic or explosive materials;

2) chemical or combined chemical-physical laboratories involving caustic or explosive chemicals or hot liquids or solids.

Ill. Rev. Stat. c. 122, par. 698.11

22:190 What other statutory safety requirements are imposed on school boards to protect persons from injury while on school property?

School building construction and maintenance are subject to stringent State Board of Education regulations in the Illinois Life-Safety Code. Schools also are subject to the occupational safety standards contained in the Illinois Health and Safety Act and enforced by the Illinois Department of Labor. Other safety standards applicable to schools include various environmental requirements, such as asbestos abatement and safe drinking water, traffic safety, and the common law "duty of care" owed to students while on school premises.

Ill. Rev. Stat. c. 48, par. 137.1 et seq.
Ill. Rev. Stat. c. 122, par. 2-3.12
23 Ill. Admin. Code 175
23 Ill. Admin. Code 185
Jastram v. Lake Villa School District No. 41, 192 Ill.App.3d 599, 549 N.E.2d 9, 139 Ill.Dec. 29 (2nd Dist. 1989)

22:200 What immunities and/or defenses against tort liability would be available to a school board for injuries arising out of violations of statutory safety requirements?

School boards owe a "duty of care" to students, employees and visitors where the safety of buildings, grounds and equipment are concerned. The protections of in loco parentis are available only where an injury arises from the supervisory duties of a certificated employee, and would not protect the school district where the injury arises, for example, from faulty equipment or unsafe building conditions.

Whether any of the immunities specified in the tort immunity statute would apply to unsafe building conditions would depend upon the facts in each situation.

Ill. Rev. Stat. c. 85, par. 1-101 et seq.

VISITORS ON SCHOOL PROPERTY

22:210 What standard of care does a school district owe invitees on school property?

A school district must exercise reasonable care with respect to invitees on school property. Invitees include spectators at athletic contests and parents attending a conference day.

Borushek v. Kincaid, 78 Ill.App.3d 295, 397 N.E.2d 172, 33 Ill.Dec. 839 (1st Dist. 1979)

Tanari v. School Directors of District No. 502, County of Bureau, 69 Ill.2d 63, 373 N.E.2d 5, 14 Ill.Dec. 874 (1977)

JUDGMENTS

22:220 What amounts may a school district levy in order to pay a tort settlement or judgment or its cost of defense?

A school board may levy, or have levied on its behalf, annual taxes against all taxable property within the school district at a rate that will produce a sum which will be sufficient to pay the total costs of specified settlements and judgments, to pay the cost of protecting itself or its employees against liability, property damage or loss, including all costs and reserves of being a member of an insurance pool, to pay the costs of principal and interest on certain specified bonds, to pay the cost of risk care management programs and for other purposes specified in the statute.

Ill. Rev. Stat. c. 85, par. 9-107

22:230 What manner of payment may a school board elect in paying a settlement or judgment?

If a school board does not pay a tort judgment during the fiscal year in which it becomes final, and, if in the opinion of the school board, the payment of the judgment creates an unreasonable financial hardship for the school district, it shall pay the balance of the judgment with interest in installments subject to conditions set forth in statute.

Ill. Rev. Stat. c. 85, par. 9-104
Evans v. City of Chicago, 689 F.2d 1286 (7th Cir. 1982)

22:240 Is a school district which loses a civil rights suit responsible to pay the attorney fees and expert witness fees of the plaintiff?

The school district defendant would be liable to pay the attorney fees of the plaintiff, but not the plaintiff's expert witness fees.

West Virginia University Hospital v. Casey, 111 S.Ct. 1138, __ U.S. __ , __ L.Ed. __ (1991)

23: PROPERTY TAX INCOME

AUTHORITY TO LEVY TAXES

23:10   On what property may a school board levy taxes?

A school district may levy on all taxable property within school district boundaries, including property which at the time of the levy was part of the school district but which at a later date in the same tax year was detached.

Illinois ex rel. Nordstom v. Barry, 11 Ill.2d 259, 142 N.E.2d 26 (1957)

    Illinois ex rel. Davis v. Spence, 3 Ill.2d 244, 120 N.E.2d 565 (1954)

23:20   May vocational education or special education cooperatives levy taxes?

No.

Ill. Rev. Stat. c. 122, par. 10-22.31

23:30   May a school district levy a personal property tax?

No.

Ill. Const. art. IX, sec. 5(c)

Cherry Bowl, Inc. v. Property Tax Appeal Board, 100 Ill.App.3d 326, 426 N.E.2d 618, 55 Ill.Dec. 472 (2nd Dist. 1981)

    Central Illinois Light Co. v. Johnson, 84 Ill.2d 275, 418 N.E.2d 275, 49 Ill.Dec. 676 (1981)

PROPERTY ASSESSMENTS

23:40   How is property assessed?

The county assessor appraises all real property. railroad property used for transportation, private car lines, pollution control equipment, and capital stock are assessed by the State

Department of Revenue, which certifies these valuations to the county clerk.

The county assessor's appraisals are subject to appeal by the taxpayer to the county board of appeals. The assessor's appraisals are equalized by the Illinois Department of Revenue. The purpose of equalization is to develop a common level of assessments among counties. (Equalization of assessments is essential to provide an equitable basis for distributing state aid to schools.) The Department equalizes assessments by means of multipliers assigned to each county.

The multiplier is applied to all assessments in a county to adjust assessments by a given percentage in order to bring the county level to a specified percentage of fair market value. In all Illinois counties except Cook, the statutory standard for equalization of property assessments is 33 1/3 percent of fair market value. In Cook County, property assessment standards vary with the classification or type of property, ranging from 16 percent of fair market value for residential property up to 38 percent for some commercial property.

Ill. Rev. Stat. c. 120, par. 499.1 et seq.
Ill. Rev. Stat. c. 120, par. 501.20 et seq.

23:50 How does a school district secure information on the taxable property located within its boundaries?

The county clerk must furnish the school board of any school district, upon request, a certificate showing the last ascertained full, fair cash value of the taxable property of the district. When a school district lies partly in two or more counties, the county clerk of each county in which any part of the district lies must furnish the school board, upon request, a certificate showing the last ascertained full, fair cash value of the taxable property in that part of the district lying in each county.

Ill. Rev. Stat. c. 122, par. 17-10
Board of Education of Beach Park Community Consolidated School District No. 3, Lake County v. Hess, 140 Ill.App.3d 653, 488 N.E.2d 1358, 95 Ill.Dec. 15 (2nd Dist. 1986)

23:60 What happens to the value of taxable property in an area that is included in a tax increment financing district?

The equalized assessed valuation of property within a tax increment financing district is frozen at its current valuation insofar as its impact on school district property tax revenue is concerned. Revenue generated by the school district tax levy on any future increase in assessed valuation is paid over to a special tax increment district re-development fund controlled by the municipality that created it.

Under provisions of the Real Property Tax Increment Allocation Development Act, revenue derived from future increases in assessed value may be lost to the school district for up to 23 years, depending upon provisions of the municipal ordinance creating the tax increment financing district.

Ill. Rev. Stat. c. 24, par. 11-74.4-1 et seq.

Ill. Rev. Stat. c. 122, par. 18-8

Illinois ex rel. City of Canton v. Crouch, 79 Ill.2d 356, 403 N.E.2d 242 (1980)

23:70 May a school board intervene if it believes that certain taxable property is under-assessed?

Yes, a school board may challenge any property assessment by filing a complaint with the county board of review within 20 calendar days after assessment books are delivered to the board of review. Decisions of the county board of review may be appealed to the State Tax Appeals Board and then to the courts on Administrative Review.

Ill. Rev. Stat. c. 120, par. 589.2, 108b

Ill. Rev. Stat. c. 120, par. 590.1, 109a

Ill. Rev. Stat. c. 120, par. 592.4, 111.4

TAX LEVIES

23:80 What is a certificate of tax levy?

A certificate of tax levy is a document authorized by formal action of the school board, signed by the president and clerk or secretary of the board, and issued to the county clerk. The document certifies the amount of money necessary in each fund to be levied against the equalized assessed valuation of the taxable property of the school district for a given fiscal year.

Ill. Rev. Stat. c. 122, par. 17-11

23:90 When is a certificate of tax levy filed?

The certificate of tax levy must be filed with each county clerk on or before the last Tuesday in December annually.

Ill. Rev. Stat. c. 122, par. 17-11
Board of Education of Community Unit School District No. 16 v. Barrett, 67 Ill.2d 11, 364 N.E.2d 89, 7 Ill.Dec. 102 (1977)

23:100 When are property taxes levied and when are they collected?

Taxes which are levied on the current year's budget and filed in December with the county clerk are extended in the spring and usually received by a school treasurer in June and September, after the current school year has ended.

Ill. Rev. Stat. c. 120, par. 681 et seq.

23:110 May a county clerk refuse to levy a school district's taxes if the district does not file its levy within the required time?

The governing authority of each county, taxing district and school district must file with the county clerk within 30 days of their adoption a certified copy of its appropriation and budget resolutions, as well as an estimate, certified by its chief fiscal officer, of revenues, by source, anticipated to be received by the school district in the following fiscal year. Failure to file the required documents (after timely notice) authorizes the county clerk to refuse to extend the tax levy imposed by the governing authority until the documents are filed.

Ill. Rev. Stat. c. 120, par. 681 et seq.

23:120 If a school district is located in two or more counties, must the school district file a certificate of levy with the county clerk in each county?

When a school district lies partly in two or more counties, the school board, after ascertaining as nearly as practical the amount to be raised by special taxes through levy, is required to prepare a certificate of tax levy for each county in which the district lies and deliver one such certificate to each of the county clerks of the counties which are a part of the district.

Ill. Rev. Stat. c. 122, par. 17-12

23:130 May a school district amend its tax levy?

A school board may amend its certificate of tax levy to the amount necessary to qualify for the maximum amount of state aid under the following circumstances:

1) the school board has authority to levy taxes at an operating tax rate which would qualify the school district for the maximum amount of state aid under School Code section 18-8; and

2) after a certificate of tax levy has been filed, a change in the assessed valuation resulting from the application of the equalization multiplier by the Department of Revenue causes the school district's operating tax rate to be less than that required to qualify for the maximum amount of state aid.

Within 20 days of such change in assessed valuation, the school board may amend its certificate of tax levy to provide for the amount required to qualify for the maximum amount of state aid.

Ill. Rev. Stat. c. 122, par. 17-3.2
Ill. Rev. Stat. c. 122, par. 17-11.1
Ill. Rev. Stat. c. 122, par. 18-8
In re County Collector of McHenry County, 181 Ill.App.3d 345, 536 N.E.2d 1288 (2nd Dist. 1989)

23:134 May a school board file an additional tax levy following voter approval of a tax rate increase?

The school board may make an additional tax levy whenever the voters approve a tax rate increase in the educational and/or operations and maintenance fund after the levy has been filed. To do so, the board must approve an additional or supplemental budget by a majority vote of its full membership and file an additional levy for that fiscal year. Because the tax rate is increased with voter approval, adoption of the additional budget and levy probably complies with the Truth in Taxation Act.

Ill. Rev. Stat. c. 120, par. 861 et seq.
Ill. Rev. Stat. c. 122, par. 17-3.2
In re County Collector of McHenry County, 181 Ill.App.3d 345, 536 N.E.2d 1288 (2nd Dist. 1989)

23:136 What is the latest date by which a school board may file an amended or additional tax levy?

Assuming that a school board has received voter approval for an increased tax rate or otherwise meets the criteria necessary for an amended levy, the amended certificate of levy must be filed with the county clerk in time to be incorporated in the tax bills without materially impeding the county's ability to extend and collect taxes.

Ill. Rev. Stat. c. 122, par. 17-3.2
Ill. Rev. Stat. c. 122, par. 17-11.1
In re County Collector of McHenry County, 181 Ill.App.3d 345, 536 N.E.2d 1288 (2nd Dist. 1989)

LEVY HEARINGS

23:140 When must a school board hold a public hearing on a proposed tax levy?

A school district proposing to increase its aggregate levy more than 105 percent of its prior year's extension, exclusive of the cost of an election, must publish notice of hearing and thereafter hold a hearing as required by law.

Ill. Rev. Stat. c. 120, par. 861 et seq.

23:150 When must a school board estimate its annual aggregate tax levy?

Not less than 20 days prior to adoption of its aggregate tax levy, a school board must determine the amount of money, exclusive of any portion of that levy attributable to election costs, estimated to be necessary to be raised by taxation for that year on the taxable property within its district.

Ill. Rev. Stat. c. 120, par. 864

23:160 What is included in a school board's aggregate levy?

The "aggregate levy" includes the entirety of a board's annual levy except any portion of a tax levy attributable to paying the cost of conducting an election which is required under the general election laws and taxes levied to pay the principal and interest on bonds, notes, and other obligations which were secured by property tax levies and amounts due under a public building commission lease.

Ill. Rev. Stat. c. 120, par. 864

Board of Education of Township High School District 211, Cook County, v. Kusper, 92 Ill.2d 333, 422 N.E.2d 179, 65 Ill.Dec. 868 (1982)

PROPERTY TAX RATES

23:170 What amounts may a school board levy in the educational fund, operations and maintenance fund and transportation fund?

A school district may levy amounts for these funds within the tax rate limits established by law. Tax rate limits for each of these funds, which differ according to type of district, may be increased by referendum.

Further, a cap on property taxes may limit school district levies in these funds in the counties of DuPage, Kane, Lake, McHenry and Will. The county clerk in these counties may not extend taxes in the aggregate for any taxing district in excess of 105 percent of the previous year's extension or the percentage increase in the consumer price index for the prior levy year (whichever is less). Although some portions of the tax levy are exempted from the cap, the cap can limit the amount of the extension to less than what the authorized tax rate would otherwise produce.

Ill. Rev. Stat. c. 120, par. 2501-1 et seq.
Ill. Rev. Stat. c. 122, par. 17-2 et seq.
Ill. Rev. Stat. c. 122, par. 17-4
Ill. Rev. Stat. c. 122, par. 17-5 et seq.

23:175 What is a tax rate and how is it calculated?

A tax rate in Illinois reflects the dollars levied per $100 of equalized assessed valuation of real property. A tax rate is calculated by dividing the dollar amount of the tax levy by the total equalized assessed valuation (EAV) of the taxing district and multiplying the product by 100. Thus, a levy of $200,000 divided by a tax base of $20 million EAV would produce a tax rate of $1.00 per $100 EAV.

23:180 What are the school district types that distinguish among different tax rates authorized by law?

A "unit school district" provides education in grades kindergarten through twelve. "Dual district" is a term describing either an elementary school district or a high school district. An elementary school district provides education in grades kindergarten through eight and a high school district provides education in grades nine through 12. Each is called a dual district because both are required in a given geographical area to provide the same range of education as is provided by a unit district.

23:190 What are the maximum allowable tax rates without referendum?

A school board may annually levy a tax not to exceed the maximum rates and for the specified purposes upon all the taxable property of the district at the value, as equalized or assessed by the Department of Revenue, as follows:

1) Districts maintaining only grades 1 through 8 may levy up to .92 percent for educational purposes and .25 percent for operations and maintenance purposes.

2) Districts maintaining only grades 9 through 12 may levy up to .92 percent for educational purposes and .25 percent for operations and maintenance purposes.

3) Districts maintaining grades 1 through 12 may levy up to 1.84 percent for educational purposes and .375 for operations and maintenance purposes. (The school board may raise the permissive rate for operations and maintenance, subject to back door referendum, to .465 percent for the 1991-92 school year and .50 percent thereafter.)

4) All districts may levy up to .06 percent for a capital improvements fund if approved by the voters.

5) Districts maintaining only grades 1 through 8 may levy up to .12 percent for transportation purposes, except that under certain specified conditions a rate of up to .20 percent is permissible; districts maintaining only grades 9 through 12 may levy up to .12 percent for transportation purposes; and districts maintaining grades 1 through 12 may levy up to .20 percent for transportation purposes.

6) Districts providing summer classes may levy up to .15 percent for educational purposes if approved by the voters.

In addition, most school districts located in DuPage, Kane, Lake, McHenry and Will counties are subject to the Property Tax Extension Limitation Act. The Act effectively imposes a limit on the aggregate tax rate when the current year's tax extension reaches 105 percent of the prior year's extension or the percentage increase in the Consumer Price Index, whichever is less.

Ill. Rev. Stat. c. 120, par. 2501-1 et seq.

Ill. Rev. Stat. c. 122, par. 17-2

23:200 May a school district levy a tax for special education?

A school board may, by proper resolution, levy an annual tax in support of special education programs, including construction and maintenance of special education facilities. The maximum rate is .02 percent in dual districts and .04 percent in unit districts without referendum. With voter approval, rates may be increased to .125 percent and .25 percent, respectively.

Ill. Rev. Stat. c. 122, par. 17-2.2a

23:205 May a school district levy property taxes for gifted or talented education?

No. A school district may receive state aid as reimbursement for these programs, but may not levy a tax in support of them. Ill. Rev. Stat. c. 122, par. 14A-1 et seq.

23:210 How may a school board levy to support summer school?

A school board may, by proper resolution, cause a proposition to authorize an annual tax for summer school education purposes to be submitted to the voters of the district at a regularly scheduled election. If a majority of the votes cast on this proposition is in favor, the board may thereafter levy the tax as authorized in the referendum to a maximum of .15 percent. Ill. Rev. Stat. c. 122, par. 17-2.1

23:220 What is the fire prevention, safety, environmental, and energy fund?

Under certain conditions specified in statute, a school district may levy for fire prevention, safety or environmental or energy purposes. Ill. Rev. Stat. c. 122, par. 17-2.11 et seq.

REFERENDUM TO INCREASE TAX RATES

23:230 May a school board levy taxes at rates exceeding the maximums authorized by statute?

A school board may levy taxes at rates exceeding statutory maximums only where (a) the statute permits increases by referendum and (b) voters approve such an increase at a referendum. Statutes permit school boards to seek voter approval to increase maximum tax rates in the education fund, operations and maintenance fund, and transportation fund.

In addition, unit districts may, by school board resolution, raise their authorized rates in the operations and maintenance fund, subject to back door referendum.

Ill. Rev. Stat. c. 122, par. 17-3 et seq.
Ill. Rev. Stat. c. 122, par. 17-4
Ill. Rev. Stat. c. 122, par. 17-5 et seq.

23:235 May property tax limitations be raised by referendum?

Yes. In a school district subject to the Property Tax Extension Limitation Act, a voter-approved tax rate increase raises the aggregate extension base on which the district's property tax limitation is calculated. Also, voters may approve a cap on property tax extensions that is higher than the cap specified by law—105 percent of the prior year's extension or the percentage increase in the Consumer Price Index, whichever is less. The voter-approved cap is not permanent, however; it allows the extension to rise for that year only.

Ill. Rev. Stat. c. 120, par. 2501-1 et seq.

23:240 What is a back door referendum?

A back door referendum is the submission of a public question to the voters of a political subdivision, initiated by a petition of voters or residents of the political subdivision, to determine whether an action by the governing body of the subdivision should be adopted or rejected.

Ill. Rev. Stat. c. 46, par. 28-2
Ill. Rev. Stat. c. 122, par. 17-2
Ill. Rev. Stat. c. 122, par. 17-2.2
Ill. Rev. Stat. c. 122, par. 20-7

23:250 Which school district tax levies are subject to back door referendum?

School district tax levies which are subject to back door referenda are the educational fund; operations and main-

tenance fund; funding bonds to pay orders for teachers' wages
or other claims; non-high school tuition; and working cash fund
bonds.

Ill. Rev. Stat. c. 122, par. 12-13
Ill. Rev. Stat. c. 122, par. 17-2
Ill. Rev. Stat. c. 122, par. 17-5
Ill. Rev. Stat. c. 122, par. 19-9
Ill. Rev. Stat. c. 122, par. 20-7

TAX ABATEMENTS

23:270 May a school district participate in a tax abatement program?

Yes. School districts are among the local governments
authorized by law to abate property taxes to help spur commercial or industrial growth. A school board may agree to forgive
all or a portion of the taxes on the assessed valuation of new or
expanded commercial / industrial property for up to 10 years.

Ill. Rev. Stat. c. 120, par. 643

24: STATE AID AND OTHER SCHOOL INCOME

SOURCES OF INCOME

24:10 In addition to property taxes, what other sources of income are used to support public schools in Illinois?

An Illinois school district derives income from any or all of the following:

- state aid, both general and special-purpose categorical aid;
- corporate personal property replacement tax;
- federal aid in various forms;
- investment income;
- fees and charges;
- insurance proceeds;
- gifts.

24:20 Where lies the primary responsibility for financing Illinois public schools?

The state constitution imposes upon the state the primary responsibility for financing the public schools. To carry out this responsibility, the state provides various forms of direct financial support and authorizes school boards to levy taxes on property, borrow money, invest idle funds, accept gifts, charge certain fees, and purchase insurance to protect school district assets.

State law also imposes upon school boards the duty "to provide for the revenue necessary to maintain schools in their districts."

Ill. Const. art. X, sec. 1
Ill. Rev. Stat. c. 122, par. 10-20.3

24:30 What determines school district income?

A school district's income is affected by each of the following factors:

1) State Guarantees — Each year, the state establishes a per pupil revenue guarantee. The guarantee is the state's resource distribution target. Part of guarantee monies come from the state and part come from local property taxes. Most school districts can obtain more than the guarantee amount only by increasing tax rates, usually requiring voter approval. Some districts receive less than the guarantee because they cannot or do not obtain enough income from property taxes. The guarantee places a ceiling on the school district budget unless voters decide to tax themselves at a higher rate.

2) Pupil Enrollment — School district revenue from state aid increases and decreases in response to changes in student enrollment, because state aid is based in part on student enrollment.

3) Property Values — The total property value in a school district determines how much revenue the district is capable of raising from property taxes. Property values are set by the marketplace and the assessor.

4) Tax Rates — Tax rates reflect the dollars levied per $100 of equalized assessed valuation of real property. The rate at which a community taxes itself also reflects its level of effort to support its schools. State law establishes maximum tax rates that may be levied by various types of school districts. Some rates may be raised with voter approval at a referendum. The state of Illinois requires a minimum effort, expressed as an operating tax rate, for a school district to qualify for general state aid. The Property Tax Extension Limitation Act places an effective limit on the aggregate tax rates of some school districts in DuPage, Kane, Lake, McHenry and Will counties.

Ill. Rev. Stat. c. 120, par. 2501-1 et seq.

Ill. Rev. Stat. c. 122, par. 18-9

Ill. Rev. Stat. c. 122, par. 18-10

STATE MANDATES

24:40 What is a state mandate?

A state mandate is any state-initiated statutory or executive action which requires a local government to establish, expand or modify its activities in such a way so as to necessitate additional expenditures from local revenues. As a result of the Mandates Act, the state is required to fully or partially fund certain program requirements which are statutorily imposed on units of local government.

Ill. Rev. Stat. c. 85, par. 2201 et seq.

24:50 Are there funding exemptions to the State Mandates Act?

The state is not obligated to pay for a mandate if it:

1) is imposed to accommodate a request from local government;

2) imposes additional duties of a nature which can be carried out by existing staff and procedures at no appreciable net cost increase;

3) creates additional costs but also provides offsetting savings resulting in no aggregate increase in net costs;

4) imposes a cost that is wholly or largely recovered from federal, state, or other external financial aid;

5) imposes additional annual net costs of less than $1,000 for each of the several local governments affected or less than $50,000 in the aggregate for all local governments affected; or

6) results from legislation enacted by the General Assembly to comply with a federal mandate.

Failure on the part of the General Assembly to make necessary appropriations relieves the local government of the obligation to implement a mandate unless an exemption is explicitly stated in the act establishing the mandate.

Ill. Rev. Stat. c. 85, par. 2201 et seq.

Ill. Rev. Stat. c. 85, par. 2208

Board of Education of Maine Township High School District No. 207 v. State Board of Education, 139 Ill.App.3d 460, 487 N.E.2d 1053, 94 Ill.Dec. 176 (1st Dist. 1985)

24:60   Is the state obligated to pay a percentage of school operating costs?

While the state has the primary responsibility to finance free public schools, the General Assembly is not obligated to fund schools at any particular level.

San Antonio Independent School District v. Rodriguez, 93 S.Ct. 1278, 411 U.S. 1, 36 L.Ed.2d 16, reh. den. 93 S.Ct. 1919, 411 U.S. 959, 36 L.Ed.2d 418 (1973)

Blase v. Illinois, 55 Ill.2d 94, 302 N.E.2d 46 (1973)

McInnis v. Shapiro, 293 F.Supp. 327 (D.C. Ill. 1968), aff'd. 394 U.S. 322

STATE AID

24:70   What is state aid?

State aid is money provided by the General Assembly to assist in supporting public education. State aid may be categorical or general.

Ill. Rev. Stat. c. 122, par. 18-1 et seq.

24:80   What are the differences between general state aid and categorical state aid?

Categorical state aid is earmarked for a particular purpose and may be used for that purpose only. Categorical aid is provided for special education, adult education, vocational education, bilingual education, and gifted education. General state aid may be used at the discretion of the school district for any legal school purpose. The computation bases for aid distribution differ for categorical and general state aid.

Ill. Rev. Stat. c. 122, par. 10-22.20
Ill. Rev. Stat. c. 122, par. 14A-5
Ill. Rev. Stat. c. 122, par. 14B-8
Ill. Rev. Stat. c. 122, par. 14C-12
Ill. Rev. Stat. c. 122, par. 18-1 et seq.
Ill. Rev. Stat. c. 122, par. 203-1

24:90   What is the source of state aid funds?

State aid comes from the Common School Fund. This fund consists of moneys appropriated by the General Assembly for the support of common schools. It includes moneys set aside for education from drivers' license fees, the Retailers' Occupation and Use Tax (sales tax), the Illinois State Lottery, and other sources. It also includes federal monies which are transferred through the state to support federal programs in the schools.

Ill. Rev. Stat. c. 120, par. 440 et seq.
Ill. Rev. Stat. c. 120, par. 1152

STATE AID COMPUTATIONS

24:100 What factors are used in computing a school district's general state aid?

The factors used in computing a school district's general state aid are:

1) the grade level of the students in the district;

2) the district's equalized assessed valuation;

3) the district's weighted average daily attendance;

4) the operating tax rate levied by the district;

5) the combined authorized tax rate of the district;

6) any applicable reductions in a district's equalized assessed valuation (i.e., resulting from the Farmland Assessment Act);

7) the number of special needs students in a district;

8) whether or not the district participates in a tax abatement or tax increment allocation program under the Real Property Tax Increment Allocation Redevelopment Act;

9) the amount of money a district receives as a replacement for taxes previously received from the corporate personal property tax;

10) the number of days the schools of the district are operating with students in attendance;

11) whether or not kindergarten students attend school for full day or one-half day sessions; and

12) whether the schools in the district are recognized by the State Board of Education as meeting state-required standards for recognition.

Ill. Rev. Stat. c. 122, par. 18-8
Ill. Rev. Stat. c. 122, par. 18-9

24:110 What is the state aid grade level weighting formula?

Pupils in grades pre-kindergarten through grade six are weighted 1.00; pupils in grades seven and eight are weighted 1.05; and pupils in grades 9-12 are weighted 1.25. A school district's pupil count includes weightings for federally defined low-income pupils.

Ill. Rev. Stat. c. 122, par. 18-8

24:120 What school district state aid is provided for children in first grade and below who attend school for less than a full day?

State aid for children in the first grade and below may be claimed as follows:

1) A session of at least four clock hours may be counted as a day of attendance for first-grade pupils and pupils in full-day kindergartens, and a session of two or more hours may be counted as one-half day of attendance by pupils in half-day kindergartens.

2) For handicapped children below the age of six years who cannot attend two or more clock hours because of handicap or immaturity, a session of not less than one clock-hour may be counted as one-half day of attendance; however, for such children whose educational needs so require, a session of four or more clock hours may be counted as a full day of attendance.

Ill. Rev. Stat. c. 122, par. 18-8 (i) et seq.

24:130 How is a school district's equalized assessed valuation determined for state aid purposes?

The total value of the real property in a district is determined by assessment and the application of multipliers which are calculated and assigned by the county board of review and the Department of Revenue. Theoretically, this system equalizes property assessments throughout the state at 33 1 / 3 percent of the fair market value of property, although there are exceptions with respect to farm land property and in Cook County, where different classifications of real property are assessed at differing percentages of fair market value.

In determining a school district's wealth for state aid purposes, a district's corporate personal property replacement funds are divided by a total tax rate to generate a corporate personal property replacement equalized assessed valuation. This amount is combined with the district's real property equalized assessed valuation to determine its wealth for computing state aid.

Ill. Rev. Stat. c. 122, par. 18-8

STATE AID PENALTIES

24:140 What is the penalty for failure to have school the minimum number of pupil attendance days?

If any school district fails to provide the minimum number of pupil attendance days, the school district's state aid is proportionally reduced. The school district may also suffer recognition penalties.

Ill. Rev. Stat. c. 122, par. 18-12
Cronin v. Lindberg, 66 Ill.2d 47, 360 N.E.2d 360, 4 Ill.Dec. 424 (1976)

24:150 What is an "act of God" day?

Under certain circumstances, a school district may receive full state aid even though it has not provided the minimum school term. The State Superintendent of Education may determine that a failure to provide the minimum school term was occasioned by an act of God— or by conditions beyond the control of the school district—which posed a hazardous threat to the health and safety of pupils.

Ill. Rev. Stat. c. 122, par. 18-12

STATE AID DISTRIBUTION SYSTEM

24:160 How are funds from the Common School Fund delivered to school districts?

Appropriations earmarked for the Common School Fund are sent to the State Board of Education. The State Board of Education apportions moneys for each region in the state and sends the funds to the regional superintendents. The regional superintendents pay the distributive share of any township and fractional township or district to the respective school treasurer or other authorized person. Payments are made on a monthly basis.

Ill. Rev. Stat. c. 122, par. 3-9

24:170 How is state aid distributed when the Common School Fund is not fully funded by the General Assembly?

If the money available in the Common School Fund is less than the money required to fully fund the state aid claims of all the school districts in the state, the amount of money which is placed in the Common School Fund is apportioned to each county so that each school district in that county has its state aid claim proportionately reduced.

Ill. Rev. Stat. c. 122, par. 18-8
Illinois ex rel. Carruthers v. Cooper, 404 Ill. 395, 89 N.E.2d 40 (1950)

24:175 What is a "delayed state aid payment?"

The term describes legislation enacted in 1991 to shift a general state aid payment from the last month of one fiscal year (June) to the first month of the following fiscal year (July). Unless affected school districts receive an extra state aid payment in some future month, the effect of the legislation is a reduction in general state aid for the 1991-92 fiscal year.

Ill. Rev. Stat. c. 122, par. 18-11

INVESTMENT INCOME

24:180 How is a depositary for school funds selected?

Trustees of schools in Class II county (Cook) school units or school boards in Class I county (all other counties) school units shall designate one or more banks or savings and loan associations, situated in the State of Illinois, in which school funds and moneys in the custody of the township treasurer or school treasurer shall be kept.

Ill. Rev. Stat. c 122, par. 8-7

24:184 What kinds of investments are lawful for school moneys?

The investment of all public funds is regulated by law. Financial institutions must meet specified standards and obligations. Certificates of deposit, government securities, the commercial paper of private corporations, and interest bearing bank deposits are among the investment vehicles that are permissible for school funds if they meet specified standards.

In addition, school districts may combine their funds for investment purposes. Township and school treasurers are authorized to enter into agreements of any defined or undefined term regarding the deposit, investment, reinvestment or withdrawal of school funds, including, without limitation, agreements with other township and school treasurers and agreements with community college districts authorized by the Community College Act.

Ill. Rev. Stat. c 85, par. 901 et seq.
Ill. Rev. Stat. c 122, par. 8-7

24:186 How may earnings from invested school funds be used?

Although moneys from various fund accounts may be combined for investment purposes, the amount of money belonging to each account must be reflected in the records of the treasurer. Interest earned on invested school funds must be credited to the same fund account as the principal and may be used for any lawful purpose for which the principal may be used.

Ill. Rev. Stat. c 122, par. 8-7

24:188 May school boards invest borrowed funds, such as the proceeds of a bond issue or sale of tax anticipation warrants?

Yes. However, such investments are subject to federal restrictions on arbitrage. The interest earned by an investor on school district debt instruments is treated as tax exempt under federal and state tax codes, which often enables school districts to borrow at lower rates of interest than the rates they earn when they reinvest those funds. In order to retain tax exempt status, the proceeds of district borrowing must meet certain requirements of the Internal Revenue Code that limit investment earnings for the district.

26 U.S.C. 1233

GIFTS

24:190 May a school district accept a gift, grant or bequest?

A school district or attendance center may accept a gift, grant or bequest. If the donor expresses an intention that the property be used for a particular purpose, the school board must effectuate the donor's intention until the school board in its discretion determines it is no longer practical to do so.

Ill. Rev. Stat. c. 122, par. 16-1

Wauconda Community Unit School District No. 118, Lake County v. LaSalle National Bank, 143 Ill.App.3d 52, 492 N.E.2d 995, 97 Ill.Dec. 336 (2nd Dist 1986)

Community Unit School District No. 4 v. Booth, 1 Ill.2d 545, 116 N.E.2d 161 (1954)

24:200 May a tax exempt foundation be created to help raise funds for school purposes?

Yes. Although a school district is an eligible recipient of tax deductible charitable gifts, school officials and/or interested citizens also may make a school or school district the beneficiary of support from a tax exempt foundation qualified to accept gifts, donations, bequests and other contributions.

Ill. Rev. Stat. c. 122, par. 2-3.74

24:210 What laws govern the creation and operation of a tax exempt educational foundation?

In order to acquire tax exempt status eligible to accept tax deductible contributions, an educational foundation must be organized as a not-for-profit corporation or as a charitable trust and make application to the federal Internal Revenue Service. In addition, any charitable corporation that solicits contributions in Illinois must register with the Attorney General and file informational returns with the Internal Revenue Service and the Attorney General. A foundation organized as a not-for-profit corporation also must file an annual report with the Illinois Secretary of State.

26 U.S.C. 501(c)3
Ill. Rev. Stat. c. 14, par. 57
Ill. Rev. Stat. c. 32, par. 101.01 et seq.

25: BUDGETING AND MANAGING SCHOOL FUNDS

THE BUDGET

25:10 What is a school district budget?

Each school board must budget its income and expenses each year and make the budget available for public inspection. A public hearing must be held prior to the adoption of the budget. The budget is the school district's plan for receipt and expenditure of moneys. It is the basis for a school district's tax levy.

Ill. Rev. Stat. c. 122, par. 2-3.27 et seq.

Ill. Rev. Stat. c. 122, par. 17-1

Illinois ex rel. Stanfield v. Pennsylvania Railroad, 3 Ill.2d 524, 121 N.E.2d 548 (1954)

Illinois ex rel. Schlaeger v. Belmont Radio Corporation, 388 Ill. 11, 57 N.E.2d 479 (1944)

Illinois ex rel. Toman v. Siebel, 388 Ill. 98, 57 N.E.2d 378 (1944)

25:20 What must be included in a budget?

Within or before the first quarter of each fiscal year, a school board must adopt an annual budget which it deems necessary to defray all necessary expenses and liabilities of the district, and which must specify the objects and purposes of each item and amount needed for each object or purpose. The budget is entered on a form provided by the State Board of Education and contains a statement of the cash on hand at the beginning of the fiscal year, an estimate of the cash expected to be received during such fiscal year from all sources, an estimate of the expenditures contemplated for the year, and a statement of the estimated cash expected to be on hand at the end of the year.

The estimate of taxes to be received may be based upon the amount of actual cash receipts which may reasonably be expected by the district during the fiscal year, estimated from the experience of the district in prior years and with due regard for other circumstances which may substantially affect receipts.

Ill. Rev. Stat. c. 122, par. 17-1

25:30 May a school board amend its budget?

A school board may from time to time amend its budget by the same procedure utilized to establish the original budget.

Ill. Rev. Stat. c. 122, par. 17-1

25:40 How does a school board amend its budget after a tax rate increase has been approved at a referendum for the educational fund or operations and maintenance fund?

Whenever the voters of a school district have voted in favor of an increase in the annual tax rate for educational or operations and maintenance purposes or both at an election held after the adoption of the annual school budget for any fiscal year, a school board may adopt or pass during that fiscal year an additional or supplemental budget under the sole authority of section 17-3.2 of the School Code by a vote of a majority of the full membership of the board, any other provision of the School Code notwithstanding, in and by which such additional or supplemental budget the board shall appropriate such additional sums of money as it may find necessary to defray expenses and liabilities of the district to be incurred for educational or operations, building and maintenance purposes or both of the district during that fiscal year, but not in excess of the additional funds estimated to be available by virtue of such voted increase in the annual tax rate for educational or operations, building and maintenance purposes or both.

Ill. Rev. Stat. c. 122, par. 17-3.2

In re County Collector of McHenry County, 181 Ill.App.3d 345, 536 N.E.2d 1288 (2nd Dist. 1989)

ACCOUNTING PROCEDURES

25:50   What accounting system can a school district use?

A school district may use either a cash basis or accrual system of accounting; however, any board electing to use the accrual system may not change to a cash basis without the permission of the State Board of Education.

Ill. Rev. Stat. c. 122, par. 2-3.27
Ill. Rev. Stat. c. 122, par. 10-17

25:60   What is a school district fund?

A fund is an independent fiscal accounting entity requiring its own set of books. A fund is governed by statutes, regulations, and restrictions that limit its use to a specific activity or certain objective. Each fund must be accounted for so the identity of its resources and obligations and its revenue and expenditure is continually maintained.

23 Ill. Admin. Code 110.110 et seq.

25:70   May a school board deposit general state aid in any fund it chooses?

A school district may deposit general state aid in any fund except the working cash fund.

Ill. Rev. Stat. c. 122, par. 18-8 A 5(h)

FUND ACCOUNTS

25:80   What is the educational fund?

The educational fund is used for all transactions not designated to another fund. The educational fund must be used to pay the direct costs of instruction, health, attendance and lunch programs and all costs of administration. Certain revenues must be credited to this fund, including educational tax levies, textbook rentals, athletics and lunch programs. The salaries of janitors, and maintenance employees and the costs of fuel, lights, gas, water, telephone service, and custodial supplies and equipment must be charged to this fund unless a school board by resolution, determines to pay such costs from the operations and maintenance fund.

Ill. Rev. Stat. c. 122, par. 17-2
23 Ill. Admin. Code 110.Tab.A

25:90 What is the operations and maintenance fund?

The costs of maintaining, improving or repairing school building and property, renting buildings and property for school purposes, and the payment of insurance premiums on school buildings are charged to the operations and maintenance fund. Certain costs which otherwise would be charged to the educational fund may be paid out of the operations and maintenance fund if the school board passes a resolution authorizing the charge.

Ill. Rev. Stat. c. 122, par. 17-2
23 Ill. Admin. Code 110.Tab.A

25:100 What options does a school board have in paying costs out of the district's operations and maintenance fund?

Any sum expended or obligations incurred for the improvement, maintenance, repair, or benefit of school buildings and property, including the cost of interior decorating and the installation, improvement, repair, replacement, and maintenance of building fixtures, for the rental of buildings and property for school purposes, or for the payment of all premiums for insurance upon school buildings and school building fixtures or for the purchase of equipment to be used in the school lunch program must be paid from the tax levied for operations and maintenance purposes and the purchase of school grounds.

The board may provide by resolution the payment of all salaries of janitors, engineers, or other custodial employees and all costs of fuel, lights, gas, water, telephone service, and custodial supplies and equipment or the cost of a professional survey of the conditions of school buildings, or any one or more of the preceding items shall be paid from the tax levied for operations and maintenance purposes and the purchase of school grounds in which event such salaries or specified costs, or both, must be so paid until the next fiscal year after the repeal of such resolution. Expenditures for all similar purposes not specified for this fund are made from the educational fund.

Ill. Rev. Stat. c. 122, par. 17-7
23 Ill. Admin. Code 110.Tab.A

25:110 What is the transportation fund?

Any transportation operating costs incurred for transporting pupils to and from school and school-sponsored activities and the costs of acquiring equipment must be paid from a transportation fund. The transportation fund consists of moneys received from any tax levy for such purpose, state reimbursement for transportation, all funds received from other districts for transporting pupils, and any charges for transportation services rendered to individuals or auxiliary enterprises of the school. For the purpose of this fund, "transportation operating cost" includes all costs of transportation except interest and rental of building facilities.

Ill. Rev. Stat. c. 122, par. 17-8
23 Ill. Admin. Code 110.Tab.A

25:115 May a school district enter into a multi-year transportation contract with a private carrier?

A school district may enter into a contract for up to three years for transportation of pupils to and from school. The contract may be extended for up to two more years by mutual agreement of the parties and, after that, may be extended on a year-to-year basis. No contract may be extended on a year-to-year basis if the school board receives a timely request from another interested contractor that a contract be let for bid.

Ill. Rev. Stat. c. 95 1/2, par. 6-106.11
Ill. Rev. Stat. c. 122, par. 29-6.1

25:120 What is the bond and interest fund?

The bond and interest fund is used to account for bond revenues and expenditures. A separate bond and interest fund must be established for each bond issue.

23 Ill. Admin. Code 110.Tab.A

25:130 What is the municipal retirement fund?

A municipal retirement fund is created when a school district levies a tax to pay social security or retirement contributions for non-certificated employees. If a separate tax is not levied, costs are charged to the fund from which salaries are paid.

Ill. Rev. Stat. c. 108 1/2, par. 7-171
Ill. Rev. Stat. c. 108 1/2, par. 21-1
Ill. Rev. Stat. c. 108 1/2, par. 22- 403
23 Ill. Admin. Code 110.Tab.A

25:140 What is the site and construction fund?

New buildings and additions are generally constructed after an election authorizing special financing. The proceeds of each bond issue are placed in a site and construction fund to separate these moneys from operating moneys. The special moneys may be spent for purposes specified in the bond issue and on the ballot. Often the cost of furniture and other equipment needed to open a new building is included in the amount of the bond issue.

Expenditures which would ordinarily be charged to the educational fund, but which may be charged to the site and construction fund (unless paid before the site and construction fund is created) include election expenses, fidelity insurance, architect fees, legal fees for title searches, bond legal opinions and other administrative costs directly related to the construction project.

Expenditures which would ordinarily be charged to the operations and maintenance fund, but which may be charged to the site and construction fund (unless paid before the site and construction fund is created) include actual construction costs, builder's risk insurance, land purchase and other site costs, landscaping, parking lots, sidewalks, utility connections and other times directly related to the construction project.

23 Ill. Admin. Code 110.Tab.A

25:150 What is a rent fund?

When a tax is levied to provide revenue for paying rent to the Capital Development Board for a state-owned school building, the receipt of taxes and the payment of rent are recorded in the rent fund.

Ill. Rev. Stat. c. 122, par. 35-23
23 Ill. Admin. Code 110.Tab.A

25:160 What is a capital improvement fund?

With voter approval at a referendum, a school board may create a capital improvement fund, levy an annual tax of up to .06 percent, and accumulate moneys in the fund to be spent only in accordance with purposes set forth in the resolution calling for the referendum and on the referendum ballot.

Ill. Rev. Stat. c. 122, par. 17-2(4)
Ill. Rev. Stat. c. 122, par. 17-2.3
23 Ill. Admin. Code 110.Tab.A

OTHER FUNDS

25:170 May a school board create revolving funds?

A school board may, by resolution, establish revolving funds for school cafeterias, lunch rooms, athletics, petty cash or similar purposes, provided such funds are in the custody of a bonded employee who shall be responsible to the board and to the treasurer, subject to regular annual audit by licensed public accountants and other such examinations as the school board shall deem advisable and kept in accordance with regulations prescribed by the State Board of Education.

A monthly report and an annual summary of all receipts and expenditures of the fund shall be submitted to the school board and the treasurer. All funds advanced by the treasurer to operate such revolving funds must be carried on the treasurer's books as cash obligations due to the district and all receipts of such revolving funds shall be deposited daily in a bank or savings and loan association to be approved by the treasurer unless there is no bank or savings and loan association in the community, in which event receipts shall be deposited intact not less than once each week in the bank or savings and loan association approved by the treasurer.

All reimbursements to any such revolving funds from the district funds shall be completely itemized as to whom paid, for what purpose, and against what budgetary item the expenditure is chargeable.

Ill. Rev. Stat. c. 122, par. 10-20.19(2)

25:180 What control must a school board exercise over funds raised by student organizations?

A school board must establish rules and regulations governing conditions under which school classes, clubs, and associations may collect or acquire funds in the name of any school; and, under such regulations as the State Board of Education may prescribe, provide for the safeguarding of such funds for the educational, recreational, or cultural purposes they are designed to serve.

Ill. Rev. Stat. c. 122, par. 10-20.19(2)

FINANCIAL REPORTS AND AUDITS

25:190 What financial reports are required of Illinois school districts?

Prior to December 1 of each year, each school district is required to compile and publish in a newspaper of general circulation published in the school district a statement of financial affairs showing the district's revenue, expenditures and financial condition in a form prescribed by the State Board of Education. The report also must be filed with the regional superintendent of schools by December 15. Any resident of the district may obtain a copy of the report by paying a reasonable fee to defray the cost of copying.

Ill. Rev. Stat. c. 122, par. 10-17

25:200 When are school district accounts audited?

Each school district is required to cause an annual audit of its accounts to be made by a person who is lawfully qualified to practice public accounting in Illinois. A copy of the audit must be provided the regional superintendent on or before October 15 of each year, or by a time extended by the regional superintendent not to exceed 60 days.

Ill. Rev. Stat. c. 122, par. 3-7

25:205 What is a school district's fiscal year?

A school district may establish its fiscal year. July 1 to June 30 is commonly selected.

Ill. Rev. Stat. c. 122, par. 17-1

PURCHASING AND BIDDING REQUIREMENTS

25:210 What steps are required to release payment for school district purchases?

When the school board provides the treasurer with evidence that it has formally approved payment, the treasurer releases funds. The school board may provide the treasurer with a certified copy of the minutes of its meeting, reflecting the approval of specific bills approved and the budget item to be debited, or the board may adopt a voucher system or other procedure that meets standards of the State Board of Education.

Ill. Rev. Stat. c. 122, par. 8-16
Ill. Rev. Stat. c. 122, par. 10-20.19(1)

25:220 When do bidding requirements apply?

A school board is required to let all contracts for supplies, materials, or work or contracts with private carriers for transportation of pupils involving an expenditure in excess of $10,000 to the lowest responsible bidder considering conformity with specifications, terms of delivery, quality and serviceability after due advertisement.

However, certain contracts are exempted from competitive bidding requirements, including:

1) contracts for the services of individuals possessing a high degree of professional skill where the ability or fitness of the individual plays an important part;

2) contracts for the printing of finance committee reports and departmental reports

3) contracts for the printing or engraving of bonds, tax warrants, and other evidences of indebtedness;

4) contracts for the purchase of perishable food and perishable beverages;

5) contracts for materials and work which have been awarded to the lowest responsible bidder after due advertisement, but due to unforeseen revisions not the fault of the contractor for materials and work must be revised, causing expenditures not in excess of 10 percent of the contract price;

6) contracts for the maintenance or servicing of, or provision of repair parts for, equipment which are amde with the manufacturer or authorized service agent of that equipment where the provision of parts, maintenance, or servicing can best be performed by the manufacturer or authorized service agent;

7) purchases and contracts for the use, purchase, delivery, movemenrt, or installation of data processing equipment, software, or services and telecommunications and interconnect equipment, software, and services;

8) contracts for duplicating machines and supplies;

9) contracts for the purchade of natural gas when the cost is less than that offered by a public utility;

10) purchases of equipment previously owned by some entity other than the district itself;

11) contracts for repair, maintenance, remodeling, renovation, or construction, or a single project involving an expenditure not to exceed $20,000 and not involving a change or increase in the size, type, or extent of an existing facility;

12) contracts for goods or services procured from another governmental agency;

13) contracts for goods or services which are economically procurable from only one source, such as for the purchase of magazines, books, periodicals, pamphlets, and reports and for utility services such as water, light, heat, telelphone or telegraph;

14) where funds are expended in an emergency and such emergency expenditure is approved by three-fourths of the members of the board.

All competitive bids for contracts involving an expenditure in excess of $10,000 must be sealed by the bidder and must be opened by a member or employee of the school board at a public bid opening at which the contents of the bids must be announced. Each bidder must receive at least three days' notice of the time and place of bid opening. At least one public notice must be given in a newspaper published in the district at least ten days before the bid date.

Ill. Rev. Stat. c. 122, par. 10-20.21

25:225 Must a school board award contracts for architectural or engineering services to the lowest bidder?

No. Professional services are exempted from bidding requirements. When a school board needs architectural, engineering or land surveying services, the contract must be awarded on the basis of demonstrated competence and qualifications. Unless it already has a satisfactory relationship with one or more firms, the school board must advertise for (a) statements of interest in a particular projects and (b) statements of qualifications and performance data. The school board must evaluate firms submitting these statements and select the top three based on qualifications, ability of professional personnel, past record and experience, performance data on file, willingness to meet time and budget requirements, location, workload and other applicable factors. The top three firms must be ranked in order of preference.

The school board must attempt to negotiate a satisfactory contract first with the top ranked firm and, if that fails, with the second and third firms, in the order ranked. Another list of three firms may developed if the board is unable to negotiate a satisfactory contract with one of the first three firms.

Ill. Rev. Stat. c. 85, par. 6401 et seq.
Ill. Rev. Stat. c. 122, par. 10-20.21

25:230 What may a school board consider to determine whether a bidder is responsible?

A school board may consider any of the following factors to determine if a bidder is responsible:

1) the quality of the work performed on other similar jobs;

2) the financial status of the bidder to assure a financial solvency sufficient to complete the contract;

3) the bidder's quantity and quality of experience on similar jobs;

4) the bidder's reputation;

5) the ability of the bidder to provide a satisfactory performance bond;

6) the bidder's reliability in completing similar contracts under the terms and conditions of those contracts; and

7) the board's past experience with the bidder.

Ill. Rev. Stat. c. 122, par. 10-20.21

Carlson v. Moline Board of Education School District No. 40, 124 Ill.3d 967, 464 N.E.2d 1269, 80 Ill.Dec. 256 (3rd Dist. 1984)

Cardinal Glass v. Board of Education of Mendota Community Consolidated School District 289, 113 Ill.App.3d 442, 447 N.E.2d 546, 69 Ill.Dec. 329 (3rd Dist. 1983)

Beaver Glass and Mirror Company, Inc. v. Board of Education of Rockford School District No. 205, Winnebago County, 59 Ill.App.3d 880, 376 N.E.2d 377, 17 Ill.Dec. 378 (2nd Dist. 1978)

25:240 What recourse is available to an unsuccessful low bidder?

A low bidder who is not awarded the contract may bring suit challenging the award of the contract.

L.E. Zannini & Co. v. Board of Education, Hawthorn School District 73, 138 Ill.App.3d 467 486 N.E.2d 426, 93 Ill.Dec. 323 (2nd Dist. 1985)

Cardinal Glass v. Board of Education of Mendota Community Consolidated School District 289, 113 Ill.App.3d 442, 447 N.E.2d 546, 69 Ill.Dec. 329 (3rd Dist. 1983)

25:250 May a school board reject all bids?

Yes.

Premier Electric Construction Co. v. Board of Education of City of Chicago, 70 Ill.App.3d 866, 388 N.E.2d 1088, 27 Ill.Dec. 125 (1st Dist. 1979)

25:260 May a school district give preference to local bidders when letting contracts?

If the contract requires competitive bidding, the school board may not give preference to a local bidder.

Cardinal Glass v. Board of Education of Mendota Community Consolidated School District 289, 113 Ill.App.3d 442, 447 N.E.2d 546, 69 Ill.Dec. 329 (3rd Dist. 1983)

25:270 Are there any penalties for improperly influencing the outcome of school district bidding or purchasing procedures in order to favor a local bidder or other favored bidder?

Yes, any action by a governmental body or employee to knowingly favor or assist any bidder over other bidders may be in violation of laws prohibiting the rigging or rotating of contracts or otherwise interfering with the letting of public contracts. Prohibited actions include the providing of information or criteria to one bidder that is not available to all bidders and the specification of particular subcontractors.

Most violations of the public contracts law are Class 3 or Class 4 felonies carrying fines up to $10,000 and imprisonment ranging from three to ten years.

Ill. Rev. Stat. c. 38, par. 33E-1 et seq.

26: SCHOOL BOARD BORROWING AND DEBT

INTERFUND TRANSFERS AND LOANS

26:10 May a school board loan or transfer money among the various funds established by law (e.g. educational fund, operations and maintenance fund)?

In the absence of statutory authority to make a particular interfund transfer or loan, a school board may not transfer or loan funds from one fund to another fund.

Ill. Rev. Stat. c. 122, par. 10-22.44

Illinois ex rel. Redfern v. Pennsylvania Central Company, 47 Ill.2d 412, 266 N.E.2d 334 (1971)

26:20 May a school board transfer money among line items within a fund?

A school board may make transfers between the various items in any fund not exceeding in the aggregate 10 percent of the total of the fund as set forth in the budget.

Ill. Rev. Stat. c. 122, par. 17-1

26:30 May a school board transfer money from the educational fund to the operations and maintenance fund?

A school board of any school district having a population of less than 500,000 inhabitants may, by proper resolution and without prior approval of the electors, transfer from the educational fund to the operations and maintenance fund of the school district an amount of money not to exceed 30 percent of the tax actually received in the operations and maintenance fund for the year previous to the transfer. Such a transfer may, however, only be made in any year that the total assessed value of the taxable property in the district is less than the total assessed value of taxable property in the district for the assessment year of 1969.

Ill. Rev. Stat. c. 122, par. 17-2A

26:40   Which interfund loans are permissible?

The following interfund loans are permissible:

1) Operations and maintenance fund moneys may be loaned to the educational fund or transportation fund;

2) Educational fund moneys may be loaned to the operations and maintenance fund or transportation fund;

3) Transportation fund moneys may be loaned to the educational fund or operations and maintenance fund;

4) Working cash fund moneys may be loaned to the educational fund, transportation fund, or operations and maintenance fund.

Moneys must be repaid to the loaning fund within one year, except working cash fund loans which must be repaid upon the collection of anticipated taxes. Exceptions to the payment of working cash fund loans exist when tax anticipation notes are outstanding.

Ill. Rev. Stat. c. 122, par. 10-22.33

WORKING CASH FUND

26:50   What is a working cash fund?

A school district may create a working cash fund by levying up to five cents per one hundred dollars of equalized assessed valuation. No working cash fund levy is permitted if bonds in the amount of 85 percent of the prior tax extensions for educational purposes have been issued for the working cash fund or if the amount of taxes to be extended will increase the working fund to an amount exceeding 85 percent of the taxes last extended for educational purposes.

Ill. Rev. Stat., c. 122, par. 20-1 et seq.

Application of Walgenbach, 166 Ill.App.3d 629, 520 N.E.2d 78, 117 Ill.Dec. 88 (2nd Dist. 1988)

Application of Walgenbach, 104 Ill.2d 121, 470 N.E.2d 1015, 117 Ill.Dec. 88 (2nd Dist. 1984)

26:60 What is the purpose of the working cash fund?

The purpose of the working cash fund is to enable the school district "to have in its treasury at all times sufficient money to meet demands for ordinary and necessary expenses." Because school revenue is not always received according to schedule, the working cash fund provides school board with a source of internal borrowing to meet short-term needs and reduce the need to borrow from outside sources that bear interest costs.

Ill. Rev. Stat. c. 122, par. 20-1

26:70 May a school board abolish a working cash fund after such a fund has been created?

Any school district may abolish its working cash fund, upon the adoption of a resolution so providing, and direct the transfer of any balance in such fund to the educational fund at the close of the then current school year. Any outstanding loans to the transportation or operations and maintenance fund must be paid to the educational fund at the close of the then current school year. Thereafter, all outstanding working cash taxes of such school district must be collected and paid into the educational fund.

Ill. Rev. Stat. c. 122, par. 20-8 et seq.
Bell v. School District No. 84, 47 Ill. 406, 95 N.E.2d 496 (1950)

26:80 May a school board that has abolished its working cash fund re-create the fund?

Yes.

Ill. Rev. Stat. c. 122, par. 20-9

AUTHORITY TO BORROW

26:90 Are school boards authorized to borrow money?

School boards may borrow money and issue bonds for various purposes and in various ways specified by law.

Ill. Rev. Stat. c. 122, par. 10-22.14

26:100 Is there any limit to the amount of money that a school board may borrow?

The maximum debt limitation for a unit district is 13.8 percent of the value of the taxable property located in the school district as determined by the last assessment before the indebtedness is be incurred. The maximum debt limitation for an elementary district or high school district is 6.9 percent of the value of the taxable property located in the school district.

These debt limits, which apply to the aggregate of all forms of debt, may be increased by referendum or in certain emergency situations.

In addition to these limits on aggregate debt, there are limits to the amounts that may be borrowed against anticipated taxes and state aid.

Ill. Rev. Stat. c. 122, par. 19-1
Illinois ex rel. Lindheimer v. Hamilton, 373 Ill. 124, 25 N.E. 2d 517 (1940)

SHORT TERM BORROWING

26:110 What forms of short term debt may a school board incur in order to meet current operating expenses?

School boards are authorized to issue warrants or notes against anticipated property tax income; issue notes against anticipated state aid and corporate personal property replacement taxes; and to issue general obligation orders in the payment of teachers salaries.

Ill. Rev. Stat. c. 17, par. 6602
Ill. Rev. Stat. c. 122, par. 8-16
Ill. Rev. Stat. c. 122, par. 17-16
Ill. Rev. Stat. c. 122, par. 18-18
Ill. Rev. Stat. c. 122, par. 32-4.14

26:120 What are tax anticipation warrants?

Tax anticipation warrants are issued in anticipation of the collection of taxes and may be issued to the extent of 85 percent of the total amount of the tax levied. The warrants must be repaid upon receipt of tax moneys by the district and bear interest at a statutory rate.

Ill. Rev. Stat. c. 17, par. 6602
Ill. Rev. Stat. c. 122, par. 17-16
Ill. Rev. Stat. c. 122, par. 18-8

26:130 When may a school board issue tax anticipation warrants?

When there is no money in the treasury of the school district to pay necessary expenses of the district, including amounts necessary to pay maturing principal and interest of bonds, a school board may issue warrants or may provide a fund to meet the expenses by issuing and disposing of warrants, drawn against and in anticipation of any taxes levied for the payment of the necessary expenses of the district, either for transportation, educational or for all operations and maintenance purposes, or for payments to the Illinois Municipal Retirement Fund, or for the payment of maturing principal and interest of bonds, as the case may be, to the extent of 85 percent of the total amount of the tax so levied. The warrants must show upon their face they are payable in the numerical order of their issuance solely from such taxes when collected and such taxes are to be set aside and held for their payment.

Ill. Rev. Stat. c. 122, par. 17-16
Ill. Rev. Stat. c. 122, par. 18-18
Hamer v. Board of Education of School District No. 113, Lake County, 132 Ill.App.2d 46, 267 N.E.2d 1 (2nd Dist. 1971)

26:140 How are tax anticipation warrants retired?

Tax anticipation warrants are payable solely from the taxes collected from the levy against which the warrants were issued.

Schreiner v. City of Chicago, 406 Ill. 75, 92 N.E.2d 133 (1950)
Leviton v. Board of Education of the City of Chicago, 374 Ill. 594, 30 N.E.2d 497 (1943)
Berman v. Board of Education of the City of Chicago, 360 Ill. 535, 196 N.E. 464 (1935)
Illinois ex rel. Mathews v. Board of Education of the City of Chicago, 349 Ill. 390, 182 N.E. 455 (1932)

26:150 When may a school board issue tax anticipation notes?

A school board is authorized to issue full faith and credit tax anticipation notes as a means of securing operating funds. The issuance of such notes provides an alternative to the issuance of tax anticipation warrants.

Tax anticipation notes are direct general obligations of the school district and the full faith and credit of the school district is pledged for the punctual payment of the principal and interest on the notes. Such notes may be issued in excess of any statutory debt limitation and do not reduce the debt incurring power of the district. The notes have a fixed maturity date, within two years from their date of issue, and the resolution authorizing their issuance must be filed with the county clerk of each county in which the district is located before the end of the calendar year during which the taxes being anticipated were levied.

No notes can be issued during any fiscal year in which there are tax anticipation warrants outstanding against the tax levied for such fiscal year. Tax anticipation notes may not be issued in an amount exceeding 85 percent of the taxes levied for a specific purpose for the year during which the notes are issued.

Ill. Rev. Stat. c. 17, par. 6602 et seq.
Ill. Rev. Stat. c. 85, par. 821 et seq.

26:160 For what purposes may monies received from tax anticipation be used?

Monies from tax anticipation warrants are in place of the taxes in anticipation of which the warrants were issued. The money may be used only for the purpose for which the taxes were levied.

Illinois ex rel. Mathews v. Board of Education of the City of Chicago, 349 Ill. 390, 182 N.E. 455 (1932)

26:170 What are corporate personal property replacement tax notes?

Corporate personal property replacement tax notes provide a means for a school district to finance anticipated cash flow deficits by issuing notes to anticipate replacement tax revenues. The replacement tax was intended to offset the revenue lost as a result of the abolition of the ad valorem personal property taxes which were abolished by the 1970 Constitution.

Personal property replacement tax notes may not be issued in an amount exceeding 75 percent of the entitlement of replacement taxes for the years anticipated. The entitlement amount must be certified by the director of the Department of Revenue. Personal property replacement tax notes may be issued for the current and next two succeeding calendar years from the time of the issuance of the notes. Notes must have a specific due date not more than 24 months after the date of issuance.

Ill. Rev. Stat. c. 85, par. 824 et seq.

26:175 What are state aid anticipation certificates?

The school board of any district, by resolution, may borrow against its general state aid entitlement by issuing state aid anticipation certificates. The board may borrow up to 75 percent of its state aid allocation as certified by the State Superintendent of Education, less any funds available for transfer from the district's working cash fund. However, the total amount of state aid anticipation certificates, general obligation notes and tax anticipation warrants outstanding for any fiscal year may not exceed 85 percent of the taxes levied by the district for that year. State aid anticipation certificates may be outstanding for no more than 13 months and must be repaid by assigning state aid payments directly to the lender or to a trustee from the regional superintendent.

Proceeds from state aid anticipation certificates may be used only for the purposes set forth in the school board resolution authorizing their issuance.

To deal with the lost June state aid payment, any district that has reached its maximum short term indebtedness may borrow up to 100 percent of the state aid payment to be received in July. The certificates must be redeemed no later than August 1 from July state aid payments.

Ill. Rev. Stat. c. 122, par. 18-18

26:180 What are teachers' orders?

Teachers' orders are teachers' payroll warrants issued by a school district which may be cashed at a bank. By agreement between the school district and the bank, the district will redeem the orders at a future date when tax receipts are received and pay the bank a stipulated rate of interest.

Ill. Rev. Stat. c. 122, par. 8-16

BOND ISSUES

26:190 What forms of long term debt is a school board authorized to incur through the issuance of bonds?

A school board may issue bonds as follows:

1) Building and School Site Bonds, with voter approval, for the purchase of a school site, construction of new facilities, equipping the facility, and repairing, remodeling or adding to an existing facility. School districts participating in vocational education or special education joint agreements may also issue such bonds.

2) Fire Prevention, Life Safety, Environmental and Energy Conservation Bonds, without voter approval, for the purpose of meeting fire prevention, life safety, environmental reasons, and/or to reduce the consumption of energy.

3) Funding Bonds, with voter approval if voters petition for an election (back door referendum), to pay for the salaries of teachers or claims against the district when they cannot be paid out of current revenues.

4) Refunding Bonds which are used to pay off outstanding bonds and interest due when funds are not available for payment, or when restructuring of such outstanding bond issues is advantageous to the district.

5) Working Cash Bonds, with voter approval if voters petition for an election (back door referendum), for the purpose of creating or increasing the Working Cash Fund. A district may not issue working cash bonds totaling more than 85 percent of the educational levy, plus 85 percent of the last known Corporate Personal Property Replacement Tax entitlement.

The amount of a public school district's debt is limited by statute.

Ill. Rev. Stat. c. 17, par. 6652
Ill. Rev. Stat. c. 122, par. 17-2.11
Ill. Rev. Stat. c. 122, par. 17-2.11a
Ill. Rev. Stat. c. 122, par. 19-1 et seq.
Ill. Rev. Stat. c. 122, par. 20-1 et seq.

26:200 What is a bond?

A bond is a written certificate or evidence of a debt signed by the president and clerk of the school board to pay a specific sum of money, frequently called the face value, at a fixed time in the future, frequently called the date of maturity, and at a fixed rate of interest.

Ill. Rev. Stat. c. 17, par. 6601 et seq.
Ill. Rev. Stat. c. 85, par. 841 et seq.
Ill. Rev. Stat. c. 122, par. 19-2 et seq.

26:210 What powers do school boards have to borrow money by issuing bonds to pay for real property or improvements?

The powers of school directors and boards of education differ with respect to borrowing money by the issuance of bonds. For the purpose of building or repairing schoolhouses or purchasing or improving school sites, the directors of any school district, when authorized by a majority of the votes cast on such proposition conducted in accordance with the general election law, may borrow money and, as evidence of such indebtedness, may issue bonds, signed by the president and clerk of the board, in denominations of not less than $100 and bearing interest at a rate set by statutory formula.

Any school district governed by a board of education having less than 500,000 inhabitants and not governed by a special Act may borrow money for the purpose of building, equipping, altering, or repairing school buildings or purchasing or improving school sites, acquiring and equipping playgrounds, recreation grounds, athletic fields, and other buildings or land used or useful for school purposes, or for the purpose of purchasing a site, with or without a building or buildings thereon, or for the building of a house or houses on such site, or for the building of a house or houses on the school site of the school district, for residential purposes of the superintendent, principal, or teachers of the school district, and issue its negotiable coupon bonds therefor signed by the president and secretary of the board, in denominations of not less than $100 nor more than $5,000, payable at such place and at such time or times, not exceeding 20 years from the date of issuance, as the board of education may prescribe, and bearing interest at a rate set by statutory formula, payable annually, semiannually, or quarterly, but no such bonds shall be issued unless the proposition to issue them is submitted to the voters of the district at a referendum held at a regularly scheduled election after the board has certified the proposition to the proper election authorities in accordance with the general election law.

Ill. Rev. Stat. c. 17, par. 6602
Ill. Rev. Stat. c. 122, par. 19-2
Ill. Rev. Stat. c. 122, par. 19-3
Wilcoxen v. Board of Education of Canton Union School District No. 66, 116 Ill.App.3d 380, 452 N.E.2d 132, 72 Ill.Dec. 200 (3rd Dist. 1980)
Carstens v. East Alton-Wood River Community Unit School District, 27 Ill.2d 88, 187 N.E.2d 682 (1963)

26:220 What is the maximum bond interest rate a school board may pay?

The maximum bond interest rate allowable may not exceed the greater of 9 percent per annum or 125 percent of the rate specified in a statutorily designated bond index rate.

Ill. Rev. Stat. c. 17, par. 6602
Bates v. Board of Education, Allendale Community Consolidated School District No. 17, 136 Ill.2d 260, 555 N.E.2d 1 (1990)

26:230 What is the maximum maturity for a school bond issue?

A school bond issue must have a maturity date not exceeding 20 years from date of issue.

Ill. Rev. Stat. c. 122, par. 17-2.11a
Ill. Rev. Stat. c. 122, par. 19-3
Ill. Rev. Stat. c. 122, par. 20-2

26:240 Must a school district abolish its working cash fund to issue working cash fund bonds?

No. A school district may issue working cash fund bonds pursuant to statute in an amount not exceeding in the aggregate 85 percent of the taxes permitted to be levied for educational purposes for the current year plus 85 percent of the school district's personal property replacement tax entitlement. Working cash fund bonds are subject to back door referendum.

Ill. Rev. Stat. 20-2 et seq.
In re Walgenbach, 104 Ill.2d 121, 470 N.E.2d 1015, 83 Ill.Dec. 595 (1984)

26:250 What are tort judgment bonds?

Tort judgment bonds may be used by all types of school districts and the taxes which may be levied for these bonds are not subject to any minimum or maximum rate requirements. Tort judgment bond revenues are used by school districts for the payment of liabilities created by a settlement or a tort judgment, defense costs, to pay liabilities under the Unemployment Insurance Act, Workers' Compensation Act, Occupational Diseases Act, or a risk care management program.

Ill. Rev. Stat. c. 85, par. 9-105

26:260 May a school board issue bonds to pay teachers' orders when the bond issue would exceed the debt limitations established by law?

Bonds issued to pay teachers' orders may, when added to other indebtedness of the school district, exceed any statutory debt limit.

Ill. Rev. Stat. c. 122, par. 19-8

DEBT AND FINANCIAL DIFFICULTY

26:270 What happens when a school board reaches its debt limit?

A school board that has reached its debt limit may continue to incur new debt by issuing orders to pay teachers salaries. Those orders will have first claim on any revenue that becomes available. If funds are not available to cover other types of expenditures, a school board can only take steps to curtail expenditures or increase revenue. The school district cannot close its doors.

Long before a school board's financial situation reaches this point, however, the State Board of Education will intervene and require the local board to adopt a spending plan that is fiscally sound and designed to rid the district of its indebtedness.

Ill. Rev. Stat. c 122, par. 1A-8

26:280 When does the State Board of Education determine a school district has financial difficulties?

The State Board of Education, after proper investigation of a school district's financial condition, may certify a district is in financial difficulty when any of the following conditions occur:

1) The salaries of any teachers or other employees have remained unpaid for a period of 90 days;

2) The tuition due another school district remains unpaid on and after January first of the year following the school year it was due and there is no dispute regarding the validity or amount of the claim;

3) Any amount due any joint agreement or cooperative educational program under a joint agreement remains unpaid for a period of 120 calendar days beyond the date specified in the joint board's articles of agreement;

4) The school district has defaulted in payment of any of its debt instruments: notes, warrants, or bonds or interest on such instruments or in payment of rentals due any authority for a period of 90 calendar days and no action has been initiated within that period of time to make payment;

5) The district has contracted any loan not authorized by law;

6) The district has issued school orders for wages;

7) The district has issued tax anticipation warrants in anticipation of a second year's taxes when warrants in anticipation of current year taxes are still outstanding;

8) The district has for two consecutive years adopted a budget in which budgeted expenditures exceed budgeted revenues and reserves.

No school district is deemed to be in financial difficulty by reason of any of the above circumstances arising as a result of the failure of the county to make any distribution of property tax money due the district at the time such distribution is due; or if the district clearly demonstrates to the satisfaction of the State Board of Education at the time of its determination that such condition no longer exists. The State Board of Education is empowered to require school districts in financial difficulty to develop, adopt and submit a financial plan within 45 days after certification of financial difficulty. The financial plan must be developed according to guidelines presented to the district by the State Board of Education within 14 days of certification. The guidelines address the specific nature of each district's financial difficulties.

Any proposed budget of the district must be consistent with the financial plan approved by the State Board.

A district certified to be in financial difficulty must report to the State Board of Education at such times and in such manner as the State Board may direct concerning the district's compliance with each financial plan. The State Board may review the district's operations, obtain budgetary data and financial statements, require the district to produce reports, and have access to any other information in the possession of the district that it deems relevant. The State Board may issue recommendations or directives within its powers to the district to assure compliance with the financial plan. The district must produce such budgetary data, financial statements, reports, and other information and comply with such directives.

Ill. Rev. Stat. c. 122, par. 1A-8

TABLE OF CASES

Listed here are all of the court decisions cited in the text of *Illinois School Law Survey*. Cases are arranged in alphabetical order by name of plaintiff.

Each case listed carries a full legal citation followed by the question number(s) in **bold face** where the case may be found cited in the text.

Board of Education of Hendrick Hudson Central School District, Board of Education Westchester County v. Rowley, 102 S.Ct. 3034, 458 U.S. 176, 73 L.Ed.2d 690 (1982) **13:160**

Board of Education of Jonesboro Community Consolidated School District v. Regional Board of School Trustees of Union County, 86 Ill.App.3d 230, 407 N.E.2d 1084, 41 Ill.Dec. 586 (5th Dist. 1980) **8:220**

Board of Education of Maine Township High School District No. 207 v. State Board of Education, 139 Ill.App.3d 460, 487 N.E.2d 1053, 94 Ill.Dec. 176 (1st Dist. 1985) **24:50**

Board of Education of Metropolis Community High School District No. 20, Massac County v. County Board of School Trustees, Massac County, 34 Ill.App.3d 901, 341 N.E.2d 10 (5th Dist. 1976) **8:170**

Board of Education of Minooka Community Consolidated School District No. 201 v. Ingels, 75 Ill.App.3d 334, 394 N.E.2d 69, 31 Ill.Dec. 153 (3rd Dist. 1979) **18:340**

Board of Education of Minooka Community High School District No. 111 Grundy, Kendall and Will Counties v. Carter, 119 Ill.App.3d 857, 458 N.E.2d 50, 75 Ill.Dec. 882, (3rd Dist. 1983) **1:260, 9:360**

Board of Education of Mundelein Elementary School District No. 75 v. Illinois Educational Labor Relations Board, 179 Ill.App.3d 696, 534 N.E.2d 1022, 128 Ill.Dec. 577 (4th Dist. 1989) **21:40**

Board of Education of Niles Township High School District 219, Cook County v. Regional Board of School Trustees of Cook County, 127 Ill.App.3d 210, 468 N.E.2d 1247, 82 Ill.Dec. 467 (1st Dist. 1984) **8:200**

Board of Education of Niles Township High School District No. 219 Cook County v. Epstein, 72 Ill.App.3d 723, 391 N.E.2d 114, 28 Ill.Dec. 915 (1st Dist. 1979) **18:130**

Board of Education of Pearl City Community Unit School District No. 200 v. Regional Board of School Trustees of Stephenson County, 98 Ill.App.3d 599, 424 N.E.2d 808, 54 Ill.Dec. 58 (2nd Dist. 1981) **8:220**

Board of Education of Plainfield Community Considated School District No. 202, Will and Kendall Counties v. Illinois Educational Labor Relations Board, et al., 143 Ill.App.3d 898, 493 N.E.2d 1130, 98 Ill.Dec. 109 (4th Dist. 1986) **21:110**

Board of Education of Rockford School District No. 205 Winnebago and Boone Counties v Hearing Board of Counties of Boone and Winnebago, 152 Ill.App.3d 936, 505 N.E.2d 32, 105 Ill.Dec. 906, (2nd Dist. 1987) appeal den. 115 Ill.2d 535, 511 N.E.2d 425, 110 Ill.Dec 453 **8:200**

Board of Education of Rogers, Arkansas v. McCluskey, 102 S.Ct. 3469, on remand 688 F.2d 596, reh. den. 103 S.Ct. 16 (1982) **12:30**

Board of Education of School District 33 v. City of West Chicago, 55 Ill.App.2d 401, 205 N.E.2d 63 (2nd Dist. 1965) **1:260**

Board of Education of School District No. 108, Tazewell Co. for Use of A.Y. McDonald Manufacturing Company v. Collum, 77 Ill.App.2d 479, 222 N.E.2d 804 (3rd Dist. 1966) **9:310**

Board of Education of School District No. 131 v. Illinois State Board of Education, 82 Ill.App.3d 820, 403 N.E.2d 277, 38 Ill.Dec. 189 (2nd Dist. 1980) **18:180, 18:240, 19:80**

Board of Education of School District No. 150 v. City of Peoria, 76 Ill.2d 469, 394 N.E.2d 399, 31 Ill.Dec. 197 (1979) **1:260**

Board of Education of School District No. 33, DuPage County v. City of West Chicago, 55 Ill.App.2d 401, 205 N.E.2d 63 (2nd Dist 1965) **9:330**

Board of Education of Springfield School District No. 186 v. Scott, 105 Ill.App.2d 192, 244 N.E.2d 821 (4th Dist. 1969) **8:270**

Brandt v. Board of Co-op Educational Services, Third Supervisory District, Suffolk County, New York, 820 F.2d 41, appeal after remand 845 F.2d 416 (2nd Cir. 1988) **6:226**

Branti v. Finkel, 100 S.Ct. 1287, 445 U.S. 507, 63 L.Ed.2d 574 (1980) **17:465**

Braught v. Board of Education of Mount Prospect School District No. 57, 136 Ill.App.3d 486, 483 N.E.2d 623, 91 Ill.Dec. 277 (1st Dist. 1985) **15:300, 15:310**

Braun v. Board of Education of Red Bud Community Unit School District No. 132, 151 Ill.App.3d 787, 502 N.E.2d 1076, 104 Ill.Dec. 416 appeal den. 115 Ill.2d 538, 511 N.E.2d 426, 110 Ill.Dec. 454 (5th Dist. 1986) **22:120**

Breen v. Kahl, 419 F.2d 1034 (7th Cir. 1969) **12:50**

Bridewell v. Board of Education of Shawnee Community Unit School District No. 84 of Union, et al. Counties, 2 Ill.App.3d 684, 276 N.E.2d 745 (5th Dist. 1971) **22:60**

Bromberek School District No. 65 v. Sanders, 174 Ill.App.3d 301, 508 N.E.2d 1336, 124 Ill.Dec. 228 (1st Dist. 1988) appeal den. 124 Ill.2d 553, 535 N.E.2d 912, 124 Ill.Dec. 147 **6:60**

Brown v. Board of Education Gallatin Community Unit School District No. 1, 38 Ill.App.3d 403, 347 N.E.2d 791, appeal after remand Illinois ex rel. *Brown v. Board of Education Gallatin Community Unit School District No. 1,* 66 Ill.App.3d 167, 383 N.E.2d 711 (5th Dist. 1976) **16:250**

Brown v. Board of Education of Topeka, Shawnee County, Kansas, 74 S.Ct. 686, 347 U.S. 483, 98 L.Ed. 873, 38 ALR2d 1180, supp. 75 S.Ct. 753, 349 U.S. 294, 99 L.Ed. 1083 (1954) **11:130**

Brown v. Kirk, 33 Ill.App.3d 477, 342 N.E.2d 137, rev. on other grounds 64 Ill.2d 144, 355 N.E.2d 12 (1975) **3:130**

Brubaker v. Board of Education of School District No. 149, Cook County, 502 F.2d 973 (7th Cir. 1974) **17:450**

Brubaker v. Community Unit School District No. 16, Sangamon and Morgan Counties, 46 Ill.App.3d 588, 360 N.E.2d 1228, 4 Ill.Dec. 853 (4th Dist. 1977) **19:120**

Brunstrom v. Board of Education of Riverdale Community Unit School District 100 of Rock Island County, 52 Ill.App.3d 653, 367 N.E.2d 1065, 10 Ill.Dec. 456 (3rd Dist. 1977) **15:200, 15:210, 16:130**

Buckellew v. Board of Education of Georgetown-Ridge Farm Community Unit School District No. 4, 214 Ill.App.3d 506, 575 N.E.2d 556, 159 Ill.Dec. 58 (4th Dist. 1991) **21:180**

Bundy v. Jackson, 641 F.2d 934 (D.C.Cir 1981) **17:500**

Bunsen v. County Board of School Trustees of Lake County, 48 Ill.App.2d 291, 198 N.E.2d 735 (2nd Dist. 1964) **2:140**

Burgner v. County Board of School Trustees of Peoria County, 60 Ill.App.2d 267, 208 N.E.2d 54 (3rd Dist. 1965) **8:260**

Burlington School Committee of the Town of Burlington, Massachusetts v. Department of Education of Massachusetts, 105 S.Ct 1996, 471 U.S. 359, 85 L.Ed.2d 385 (1985) **13:340**

Burnidge v. County Board of School Trustees of Kane County, 25 Ill.App.2d 503, 167 N.E.2d 21 (3rd Dist. 1960) **8:240, 8:250**

Burris v. Board of Education, 221 Ill.App. 397 (4th Dist. 1920) **11:110**

Camara v. Municipal Court of City and County of San Francisco, 87 S.Ct. 1727, 387 U.S. 523, 18 L.Ed.2d 930 (1967) **12:260**

Cardinal Glass v. Board of Education of Mendota Community Consolidated School District 289, 113 Ill.App.3d 442, 447 N.E.2d 546, 69 Ill.Dec. 329 (3rd Dist. 1983) **25:230, 25:240, 25:260**

Carey v. Piphus, 97 S.Ct. 1642, 435 U.S. 247, 52 L.Ed.2d 355 (1978) **12:330, 12:380**

McInnis v. Shapiro, 293 F.Supp. 327 (D.C. Ill. 1968), aff'd. 394 U.S. 322 **24:60**

McLaughlin v. Tilendis, 398 F.2d 287 (7th Cir. 1968) **17:460**

McNaughton v. Circleville Board of Education, 46 Ohio Misc. 12, 345 N.E.2d 649 (1974) **12:30**

McNely v. Board of Education of Community Unit School District No. 7, 9 Ill.2d 143, 137 N.E.2d 63 (1956) **19:110**

McSomebodies v. Burlingame Elementary School, 897 F.2d 974 (9th Cir. 1989) **13:400**

Meadows v. School District U-46, 141 Ill.App.3d 335, 490 N.E.2d 140, 95 Ill.Dec. 667 (2nd Dist. 1986) **19:140**

Meek v. Pittenger, 95 S.Ct. 1753, 421 U.S. 349, 44 L.Ed.2d 217, reh. den. 95 S.Ct. 2668 (1975) **14:90**

Menssen v. Eureka Unit District No. 140, 70 Ill.App.3d 9, 388 N.E.2d 273, 26 Ill.Dec. 649 (4th Dist. 1979) **4:420, 6:310**

Meridith v. Board of Education of Community Unit School District No. 7, 7 Ill.App.2d 477, 130 N.E.2d 5 (3rd Dist. 1955) **17:90**

Metzger by and through Metzger v. Osbeck, 841 F.2d 518 (3rd Cir. 1988) **12:200**

Meyer v. State of Nebraska, 43 S.Ct. 625, 262 U.S. 390, 67 L.Ed. 1042 (1923) **14:30**

Miceli v. Lavelle, 114 Ill. App.3d 311, 448 N.E.2d 989 (1st. Dist. 1983) **3:100, 3:110**

Miller v. Board of Education, School District No. 132, Cook County, 51 Ill.App.2d 20, 240 N.E.2d 471 (1st Dist. 1964) **18:190**

Miller v. School District No. 167, Cook County, Illinois, 354 F.Supp. 922 (N.D. Ill. 1973), aff'd. on other grounds 495 F.2d 658 (7th Cir. 1974) **15:200, 18:60**

Miller v. School District No. 189 East St. Louis, 26 Ill.App.3d 172, 325 N.E.2d 43 (5th Dist. 1975) **10:230, 10:240**

Miner v. Yantis, 410 Ill. 401, 102 N.E.2d 524 (1952) **9:160**

Mitten by and through Mitten v. Muscogee County School District, 877 F.2d 932 (11th Cir. 1989) cert. den. 110 S.Ct. 1117, __ U.S. __, __ L.Ed.2d ___ **13:400**

Montag v. Board of Education of School District No. 40, Rock Island County, 112 Ill.App.3d 1039, 446 N.E.2d 299, 68 Ill.Dec. 565 (3rd Dist. 1983) **12:20, 22:140**

Moore v. District of Columbia, 886 F.2d 335 (D.C. Cir. 1989) **13:400**

Moraine Valley Community College, 5 PERI 1102 (IELRB Opinion and Order, May 12, 1989) **21:510**

Morelli v. Board of Education of District 303, Tazewell County, 42 Ill.App.3d 722, 356 N.E.2d 438, 1 Ill.Dec. 312 (3rd Dist. 1976) **18:250**

Morgan v. Board of Education of Trico Community Unit School District No. 176, 22 Ill.App.3d 241, 317 N.E.2d 393 (5th Dist. 1974) **10:160, 10:320, 11:20, 11:30**

Morrison by Morrison v. Chicago Board of Education, 188 Ill.App.3d 588, 544 N.E.2d 1099, 136 Ill.Dec. 324 (1st Dist. 1989) **11:20**

Morton v. Board of Education of City of Chicago, 69 Ill.App.2d 38, 216 N.E.2d 305 (1st Dist. 1966) **11:40**

Mt. Healthy City School District Board of Education v. Doyle, 97 S.Ct. 568, 429 U.S. 274, 50 L.Ed.2d 471, appeal after rem. 670 F.2d 59 (1977) **17:450, 18:50**

Muth v. Central Bucks School District, 839 F.2d 113 (3rd Cir. 1988), cert. denied 109 S.Ct. 103, cert. granted 109 S.Ct. 52, rev. sub nom. on other grounds *Dellmuth v. Muth*, 109 S.Ct. 2397, 491 U.S. 223, 105 L.Ed2d 181 (1989) on remand *Muth v. Central Bucks School District*, 884 F.2d 1384 **13:280**

Nabhani v. Coglianese, 552 F.Supp. 657 (N.D. Ill. 1983) **6:10**

Pontiac Township High School District No. 90 v. Regional Board of School Trustees for Livingston County, 183 Ill.App.3d 885, 539 N.E.2d 885, 132 Ill.Dec. 322 (4th Dist. 1989) **8:270**

Pope v. Parkinson, 48 Ill.App.3d 797, 363 N.E.2d 438, 6 Ill.Dec. 756 (4th Dist. 1977) **2:220**

Possekel v. O'Donnell, 51 Ill.App.3d 313, 366 N.E.2d 589, 9 Ill.Dec. 332 (1st Dist. 1977) **20:60**

Posteher v. Pana Community Unit School District, 96 Ill.App.3d 709, 421 N.E.2d 1049, 52 Ill.Dec. 198 (4th Dist. 1981) **20:205**

Premier Electric Construction Co. v. Board of Education of City of Chicago, 70 Ill.App.3d 866, 388 N.E.2d 1088 27 Ill.Dec. 125 (1st Dist. 1979) **25:250**

Prest by Prest v. Sparta Community Unit School District No. 140, 157 Ill.App.3d 569, 510 N.E.2d 595, 109 Ill.Dec. 727 (5th Dist. 1987) **12:10**

Prosser v. Village of Fox Lake, 91 Ill.2d 389, 438 N.E.2d 134, 63 Ill.Dec. 396 (1982) **6:290**

Ramos v. Waukegan Community Unit School District No. 60, 188 Ill.App.3d 1031, 544 N.E.2d 1302, 136 Ill.Dec. 527 (2nd Dist. 1989) **22:130**

Reinhardt v. Board of Education of Alton Community Unit School District No. 11, 61 Ill.2d 101, 329 N.E.2d 218 (1975) **18:90 18:140, 18:160,**

Reinhardt v. Board of Education of Alton Community Unit School District No. 11, Madison and Jersey Counties, 19 Ill.App.3d 481, 311 N.E.2d 710 (5th Dist. 1974)vacated on other grounds 61 Ill.2d 101, 329 N.E.2d 218, **18:162, 20:162**

Relph v. Board of Education of Depue Unit School District No. 103 of Bureau County, 84 Ill.2d 436, 420 N.E.2d 147, 50 Ill.Dec. 830 (1978) **15:50**

Resnick v. East Brunswick Township Board of Education, 77 N.J. 88, 389 A.2d 944 (1978) **9:430**

Rhinehart v. Board of Education of Bloomington School District No. 87, McLean County, 132 Ill.App.2d 1078, 271 N.E.2d 104 (4th Dist. 1971) **8:210, 8:270**

Richards v. Board of Education of Township High School District No. 201, 21 Ill.2d 104, 171 N.E.2d 37 (1960) **15:110**

Richmond v. County Board of School Trustees of Whiteside County, 93 Ill.App.2d 142, 235 N.E.2d 657 (3rd Dist. 1968) **8:220**

River Grove School District No. 85 1/2, 3 PERI 1019 (IELRB Opinion and Order, January 30, 1987) **21:520**

Riverside-Brookfield Township District No. 208, 5 PERI 1136 (IELRB Decision and Order, July 25, 1989) **21:220**

Robertson by Robertson v. Granite City Community Unit School District No. 9, 684 F.Supp. 1002 (S.D. Ill. 1988) **13:100**

Robinson v. Oak Park and River Forest High School, Board of Education District 200, 213 Ill.App.3d 77, 571 N.E.2d 931, 156 Ill.Dec. 951 (1st Dist. 1991) **12:340, 12:370**

Rock Falls Elementary School District No. 13, 2 PERI 1150 (IELRB Opinion and Order, May 14, 1987) aff'd. sub nom. **21:200**

Rockford Newspapers, Inc. v. Northern Illinois Council on Alcoholism and Drug Dependence, 64 Ill.App.3d 94, 380 N.E.2d 1192, 21 Ill.Dec. 16 (2nd Dist. 1978) **2:220**

Roemer v Board of Public Works of Maryland, 96 S.Ct. 2337, 426 U.S. 736, 49 L.Ed.2d 179 (1976) **14:90**

Rolando v. School Directors of District No. 125, 44 Ill.App.3d 658, 358 N.E.2d 945, 3 Ill.Dec. 402 (3rd Dist. 1976) **18:120**

Rutan v. Republican Party of Illinois, 110 S.Ct. 2729, __ U.S.__, 111 L.Ed.2d 52 reh. den. 111 S.Ct. 13, 111 L.Ed.2d 828 (1990) **17:465**

Staunton Community Unit School District No. 6 v. Illinois Educational Labor Relations Board, 200 Ill.App.3d 370, 158 N.E.2d 751, 146 Ill.Dec. 788 (4th Dist. 1990) **21:510**

Stein v. County Board of School Trustees of DuPage County, 40 Ill.2d 477, 240 N.E.2d 668 (1968) **3:20**

Stein v. Howlett, 52 Ill.2d 570, 289 N.E.2d 409 (1972) **7:470**

Stein v. Plainwell Community Schools, 610 F.Supp. 43, rev. 822 F.2d 1406 (6th Cir. 1987) **14:60**

Streator Township High School District No. 40 v. County Board of School Trustees of Livingston County, 14 Ill.App.2d 251, 144 N.E.2d 531 (2nd Dist. 1957) **8:110**

Strejcek v. Board of Education of Berwyn School District No. 100, 78 Ill.App.3d 400, 397 N.E.2d 448, 33 Ill.Dec. 942 (1st Dist. 1979) **16:110**

Swanson v. Board of Education of Foreman Community Unit School District No. 124, Mason County, 135 Ill.App.3d 466, 481 N.E.2d 1248, 90 Ill.Dec. 337 (4th Dist. 1985) **19:140**

T.G. on Behalf of D.G. v. Board of Education of Piscataway, New Jersey, 576 F.Supp. 420 (D.C. N.J. 1983), aff'd., 738 F.2d 420, cert. denied 105 S.Ct. 592, 469 U.S. 1086, 83 L.Ed.2d 701 **13:150**

Tanari v. School Directors of District No. 502, County of Bureau, 69 Ill.2d 63, 373 N.E.2d 5, 14 Ill.Dec. 874 (1977) **22:210**

Teresa P. v. Berkeley Unified School District, 724 F. Supp. 698 (N.D. Cal. 1989) **10:140**

Tetmeir v. Board of Education of School District No. 149, Cook County, 5 Ill.App.3d 982, 284 N.E.2d 280 (1st Dist. 1972) **15:100**

Thomas v. Board of Education of Community Unit School District of Pope County, 117 Ill.App.3d 374, 453 N.E.2d 150, 721 Ill.Dec. 845 (5th Dist. 1983) **2:210**

Thomas v. Chicago Board of Education, 60 Ill.App.3d 729, 377 N.E.2d 55, 17 Ill.Dec. 865, rev. on other grounds 77 Ill.App.2d 165, 395 N.E.2d 538, 32 Ill.Dec. 308 (1st Dist. 1978) **12:20, 22:100, 22:130**

Thornton Township High School District No. 205, 5 PERI 1134 (Executive Director's Recommended Decision and Order, July 10, 1989) **21:360**

Thrash v. Board of Education School District No. 189, 106 Ill.App.3d 182, 435 N.E.2d 866, 62 Ill.Dec. 68 (5th Dist. 1982) **17:320**

Thrasher v. General Casualty Co. of Wisconsin, 732 F.Supp. 966 (W.D. Wisc. 1990) **12:200**

Tinker v. Des Moines Independent School District, 89 S.Ct. 733, 393 U.S. 503, 21 L.Ed.2d 731 (1969) **12:120**

Tometz v. Board of Education Waukegan City School District No. 61, 39 Ill.2d 593, 237 N.E.2d 498 (1968) **11:120**

Tomkins v. Public Service Electric and Gas Company, 568 F.2d 1044 (3rd Cir. 1977) **17:500**

Treasury Employees' Union v. Van Raab, 109 S.Ct. 1384, __ U.S. __, 103 L.Ed.2d 685 (1989) **12:250**

Trico Community Unit School District No. 176 v. County. Board of School Trustees, 8 Ill.App.2d 494, 131 N.E.2d 829 (5th Dist. 1956) **8:230, 8:260**

Turner v. Board of Education North Chicago Community High School District 123, 54 Ill.2d 68, 294 N.E.2d 264 (1973) **11:180, 11:210**

Van Dyke v. Board of Education of School District No. 57, Cook County, 115 Ill.App.2d 10, 254 N.E.2d 76 (1st Dist. 1969) **16:140**

Vander Malle v. Ambach, 667 F.Supp. 1015 (S.D. N.Y. 1987) **13:220**

Vienna School District No. 55 v. Illinois Educational Labor Relations Board, 162 Ill.App.3d 503, 515 N.E.2d 476, 113 Ill.Dec. 667 (4th Dist. 1987) **21:590**

Winters v. Board of Education of Piasa Community Unit School District No. 9 of Macoupin County, 66 Ill.App.3d 918, 384 N.E.2d 519, 23 Ill. Dec. 725 (4th Dist. 1978) **17:10, 17:30**

Wisconsin v. Pea Ridge School District, 855 F.2d 560 (8th Cir. 1988) **12:200**

Wisconsin v. Yoder, 92 S.Ct. 1526, 406 U.S. 205, 32 L.Ed.2d 15 (1972) **14:30**

Wolman v. Walter, 97 S.Ct. 2593, 433 U.S. 229, 53 L.Ed.2d 714 (1977) **14:90, 14:100**

Wood v. Strickland, 95 S.Ct. 992, 420 U.S. 308, 43 L.Ed.2d 214, reh. den. 95 S.Ct. 1589, 42 U.S. 921, 43 L.Ed.2d 790 (1975) **12:70, 12:80, 12:380**

Woodman v. Litchfield Community Unit School District No. 12, Montgomery County, 102 Ill.App.2d 330, 242 N.E.2d 780 (5th Dist. 1968) **22:130, 22:140**

Woods v. East St. Louis School District No. 189, 147 Ill.App.3d 776, 498 N.E.2d 801, 101 Ill.Dec. 477 (5th Dist. 1986) **15:240**

Wort v. Vierling, 778 F.2d 1233 (7th Cir. 1985) **11:170**

Yuen v. Board of Education of Community Unit School District No. 46, Kane County, 77 Ill.App.2d 353, 222 N.E.2d 570 (3rd Dist. 1966) **18:370**

Zamora v. Pomeroy, 639 F.2d 662 (10th Cir. 1981) **12:260, 12:270**

Zink v. Board of Education of Chrisman, 146 Ill.App.3d 1016, 497 N.E.2d 835, 100 Ill.Dec. 657 (4th Dist. 1986) **15:40, 16:300**

Zorach v. Clauson, 92 S.Ct. 679, 343 U.S. 306, 96 L.Ed. 954 (1952) **14:40**

QUICK REFERENCE INDEX

This Quick Reference Index refers to question numbers rather than to page numbers. The reader is cautioned that, where a topic is discussed in a series of questions, only the first question is listed here. The reader often will find additional information under questions immediately following those listed.

The authors have tried to make the entries in this Quick Reference Index reasonably narrow and detailed. The user who is trying to locate a narrow question of law, therefore, is advised to first look for that specific topic. If that proves unfruitful, look for a broader topic that may lead to a productive area of the text.

-D-

-F-

-N-

-O-

-U-V-W-X-Y-Z-

For laws pertaining to Chicago
Public School District 299, see

Chicago
School
Law
Survey

First Edition published May, 1992 by

Illinois Association of School Boards
1209 South Fifth Street
Springfield, Illinois 62703